Instructor's Resource Manual with Tests

Denise Robichaud   Andreana Grimaldo
Quinsigamond Community College

Maria Anderson

John Tobey   Jeffrey Slater

Basic College Mathematics

Fifth Edition

PEARSON

Prentice
Hall

Upper Saddle River, NJ 07458

Editor-in-Chief: Chris Hoag
Senior Acquisitions Editor: Paul Murphy
Supplement Editor: Christina Simoneau
Executive Managing Editor: Kathleen Schiaparelli
Assistant Managing Editor: Becca Richter
Production Editor: Donna Crilly
Supplement Cover Manager: Paul Gourhan
Supplement Cover Designer: Joanne Alexandris
Manufacturing Buyer: Michael Bell

© 2005 Pearson Education, Inc.
Pearson Prentice Hall
Pearson Education, Inc.
Upper Saddle River, NJ 07458

Printed in the United States of America

10 9 8 7 6 5 4 3

ISBN 0-13-149059-1

Pearson Education Ltd., *London*
Pearson Education Australia Pty. Ltd., *Sydney*
Pearson Education Singapore, Pte. Ltd.
Pearson Education North Asia Ltd., *Hong Kong*
Pearson Education Canada, Inc., *Toronto*
Pearson Educación de Mexico, S.A. de C.V.
Pearson Education—Japan, *Tokyo*
Pearson Education Malaysia, Pte. Ltd.

Instructor's Resource Manual with Tests

Basic College Mathematics, Fifth Edition
John Tobey   Jeffrey Slater

TABLE OF CONTENTS

Instructor's Resource Manual with Tests

Basic College Mathematics, Fifth Edition
John Tobey   Jeffrey Slater

TEST FORMS

Instructor's Resource Manual with Tests

Basic College Mathematics, Fifth Edition
John Tobey   Jeffrey Slater

Mini-Lecture 1.1
Understanding Whole Numbers

Learning Objectives:

1. Write numbers in expanded form and in standard notation.
2. Give the place value of a digit.
3. Write a word name for a number and a number for a word name.
4. Application problems.

Examples:

1. Write each number in expanded notation.

   a) 8516　　　　　b) 244,306　　　　　c) 77,079,101　　　　　d) 845,333,129

   Write each number in standard notation.

   e) 400 + 30 + 2　　　f) 60,000 + 4,000 + 300 + 20 + 9　　　g) 500,000 + 40 + 1

2. Identify the place value of each digit in the numbers.

   a) 3,654　　　　　b) 265,812　　　　　c) 56,203,411

3. Write a word name for each number.

   a) 325　　　　　b) 60,448　　　　　c) 9,542,006

   Write a number for each word name.

   d) two hundred fifty-three
   e) seven thousand, ninety-eight
   f) three hundred forty million, one hundred thirty-two

Teaching Notes:

- Students who do not have English as their first language might need extra help learning the number period vocabulary such as ones, thousands, millions, billions, etc. Refer them to the *Place-value Chart* in the textbook.
- Some students who do not have English as their first language are accustomed to using periods instead of commas as above.

Answers: 1a) 8000+500+10+6, b) 200,000+40,000+4000+300+6, c) 70,000,000+7,000,000+70,000+9000+ 100+1, d) 800,000,000+40,000,000+5,000,000+300,000+30,000+3000+100+20+9, e) 432, f) 64,329, g) 500,041; 2a) 3-thousands, 6-hundreds, 5-tens, 4-ones, b) 2-hundred thousands, 6-ten thousands, 5-thousands, 8-hundreds, 1- ten, 2-ones, c) 5-ten millions, 6-millions, 2-hundred thousands, 3-thousands, 4-hundreds, -1-tens, 1-ones; 3a) three hundred twenty-five, b) sixty thousand, four hundred forty-eight, c) nine million, five hundred forty-two thousand, six, d) 253, e) 7,098, f) 340,000,132

Mini-Lecture 1.2
Adding Whole Numbers

Learning Objectives:

1. Master basic addition facts.
2. Add several single digit numbers.
3. Add numbers of several digits, without carrying.
4. Add numbers of several digits, with carrying.
5. Application problems.

Examples:

1. Add quickly.

    a) $5 + 3$ b) $4 + 7$ c) $8 + 9$ d) $6 + 2$ e) $3 + 3$

2. Add.

    a) $6 + 4 + 3 + 7$ b) $8 + 8 + 0 + 5$

3. Add with no carrying required.

    a) $\begin{array}{r} 53 \\ + 12 \\ \hline \end{array}$
    b) $\begin{array}{r} 1123 \\ + 345 \\ \hline \end{array}$
    c) $\begin{array}{r} 40{,}001 \\ 32{,}442 \\ + 15{,}333 \\ \hline \end{array}$

4. Add with carrying required.

    a) $\begin{array}{r} 96 \\ + 47 \\ \hline \end{array}$
    b) $\begin{array}{r} 5678 \\ + 3574 \\ \hline \end{array}$
    c) $\begin{array}{r} 6505 \\ 173 \\ 7044 \\ + 168 \\ \hline \end{array}$

5. A plane is flying at an altitude of 5932 ft. It then increases its altitude by 7384 ft. Find its new altitude.

Teaching Notes:

- Some students need to practice basic addition facts at home in order to master them.
- Some students need to write the carry digit in order to get the right answer for addition with carrying.
- Most students find this section easy.

Answers: *1a) 8, b) 11, c) 17, d) 8, e) 6; 2a) 20, b) 21; 3a) 65, b) 1468, c) 87,776; 4a) 143, b) 9252, c) 13,890; 5) 13,316*

Mini-Lecture 1.3
Subtracting Whole Numbers

Learning Objectives:

1. Master basic subtraction facts.
2. Subtract, without borrowing.
3. Subtract, with borrowing.
4. Find a missing number using subtraction.
5. Application problems.

Examples:

1. Subtract quickly.

   a) $9 - 3$ b) $6 - 2$ c) $8 - 7$ d) $7 - 4$ e) $5 - 5$

2. Subtract with no borrowing.

   a) $98 - 51$ b) $54 - 22$ c) $\begin{array}{r} 664 \\ -51 \\ \hline \end{array}$

3. Subtract with borrowing.

   a) $\begin{array}{r} 51 \\ -\,12 \\ \hline \end{array}$ b) $\begin{array}{r} 1123 \\ -345 \\ \hline \end{array}$ c) $\begin{array}{r} 40{,}001 \\ -\,15{,}333 \\ \hline \end{array}$

4. Solve for the missing number.

   a) $x + 5 = 9$ b) $54 = x + 20$ c) $100 + x = 233$

5. Earl has $729 in his checking account. After he writes a check to the bookstore for $249, how much is remaining in his account?

Teaching Notes:

- Some students need to practice basic subtraction facts at home in order to master them.
- Most students find subtraction without borrowing easy.
- Many students need to write the borrowing step in order to get the right answer for subtraction with borrowing.
- Some students have a lot of trouble using borrowing when zeros are involved.

Answers: 1a) 6, b) 4, c) 1, d) 3, e) 0; 2a) 47, b) 32, c) 613; 3a) 39, b) 778, c) 24,668; 4a) 4, b) 34, c) 133; 5) $480

Mini-Lecture 1.4
Multiplying Whole Numbers

Learning Objectives:

1. Master basic multiplication facts.
2. Multiply by a single-digit number.
3. Multiply by powers of 10.
4. Multiply by a several-digit number.
5. Application problems.

Examples:

1. Multiply quickly.

   a) 3×2 b) $(4)(5)$ c) $9 \bullet 0$ d) $8(9)$ e) $2 \times 4 \times 10$

2. Multiply.

   a) $\begin{array}{r} 51 \\ \times\ 2 \\ \hline \end{array}$ b) $\begin{array}{r} 1123 \\ \times\ \ \ 5 \\ \hline \end{array}$ c) $\begin{array}{r} 40,001 \\ \times\ \ \ \ \ 3 \\ \hline \end{array}$

3. Multiply by powers of 10.

   a) 2×10 b) 2×100 c) 2×1000
   d) From the pattern you've observed, what would $754 \times 10,000$ equal?

4. Multiply.

   a) $\begin{array}{r} 18 \\ \times\ 22 \\ \hline \end{array}$ b) $\begin{array}{r} 534 \\ \times\ 54 \\ \hline \end{array}$ c) $\begin{array}{r} 4,302 \\ \times\ \ 107 \\ \hline \end{array}$ d) $\begin{array}{r} 160 \\ \times\ 200 \\ \hline \end{array}$

5. a) Jenny pays $275 per month for her car payment. How much does she pay per year?

   b) Frank bought 8 CDs at $15 each. How much did he pay total?

Teaching Notes:

- Some students need to practice basic multiplication facts at home in order to master them.
- Some students do not know the different types of symbols that mean multiply.
- Some students are not sure what multiplying by zero gives.
- Some students are not sure how to line up the products when the multiplier contains zero.

Answers: *1a) 6, b) 20, c) 0, d) 72, e) 80; 2a) 102, b) 5615, c) 120,003; 3a) 20, b) 200, c) 2000, d) 7,540,000; 4a) 396, b) 28,836, c) 460,314, d) 32,000; 5a) $3300, b) $120*

Mini-Lecture 1.5
Dividing Whole Numbers

Learning Objectives:

1. Master basic division facts.
2. Divide by a single-digit number.
3. Divide by a two- or three-digit number.
4. Application problems.

Examples:

1. Divide quickly.

   a) $6 \div 2$ b) $7\overline{)49}$ c) $9 \div 0$ d) $4\overline{)0}$ e) $56 \div 8$ f) $3 \div 1$

2. Divide. If needed, show remainder with R next to quotient.

   a) $9\overline{)189}$ b) $6\overline{)324}$ c) $5\overline{)4255}$

   d) $6\overline{)51}$ e) $4\overline{)1290}$ f) $8\overline{)32222}$

3. Divide. If needed, show remainder with R next to quotient.

   a) $61\overline{)488}$ b) $23\overline{)2272}$ c) $13\overline{)9360}$

4. Solve the application problem.

   A telethon raises $4,903,800 over 20 hours. What was the average amount of money raised per hour?

Teaching Notes:

- Some students need to practice division facts at home in order to master them.
- Many students do not know that division by zero is "undefined" and that zero divided by any non-zero number results in zero.
- Some students do not know how to check a division answer if there is a remainder and must be shown several examples.

Answers: 1a) 3, b) 7, c) undefined, d) 0, e) 7, f) 3; 2a) 21, b) 54, c) 851, d) 8R3, e) 322R2, f) 4027R6; 3a) 8, b) 98R18, c) 720; 4) $245,190

Mini-Lecture 1.6
Exponents and the Order of Operations

Learning Objectives:

1. Write a number in exponent form.
2. Evaluate expressions with whole number exponents.
3. Evaluate expressions using the correct order of operations.

Examples:

1. Write each number in exponent form.

   a) $4 \times 4 \times 4$ b) $2 \times 2 \times 2 \times 2$ c) $1 \times 1 \times 1 \times 1 \times 1$ d) 8

2. Evaluate the expressions.

   a) 3^2 b) 2^3 c) 4^4 d) 10^3

   e) 7^1 f) 9^0 g) $11^0 + 4^3$ h) $7^3 + 2^3$

3. Evaluate using the correct order of operations.

   a) $5 \times 7 - 6$ b) $8 \times 3^2 - 6 \div 2$

   c) $5 \times (4 - 3) + 5^2$ d) $15 \div 3 \times 8 \times 9 \div (12 - 2^3)$

   e) $2^2 + 3^3 + 1^2$ f) $112 - 4 \times 8 \times 2 \times 0$

   g) $50 \div 25 \times 5 - 8 + 3 \times (17 - 11)$

Teaching Notes:

- Students who have never seen exponents before often write the exponent right next to the base, and same-sized, instead of right and smaller.
- Many students have trouble with order of operations.
- Try to avoid referring to PEMDAS or else many students will think you must always multiply before dividing, and add before subtracting.
- Refer students to the **Order of Operations** charts in the textbook.

Answers: *1a) 4^3, b) 2^4, c) 1^5, d) 8^1; 2a) 9, b) 8, c) 256, d) 1000, e) 7, f) 1, g) 65, h) 351; 3a) 29, b) 69, c) 30, d) 90, e) 32, f) 112, g) 20*

Mini-Lecture 1.7
Rounding and Estimating

Learning Objectives:

1. Round whole numbers.
2. Estimate an answer using rounding.
3. Application problems.

Examples:

1. Round to the nearest ten.

   a) 212   b) 3,487   c) 14   d) 15,861

   Round to the nearest hundred.

   e) 312   f) 1,267   g) 83   h) 14,961

   Round to the nearest thousand.

   i) 3,549   j) 677   k) 27,217   l) 1,171

2. Use the principle of estimation (round to one non-zero digit) to find an estimate for each calculation.

   a) $57 + 24 + 88 + 71$ b) $975,922 - 493,438$ c) 867×72

   d) $384,119 \times 193$ e) $52 \div 11$ f) $4,357 \div 213$

3. a) A local pizzeria makes 277 pizzas on an average day. Estimate how many pizzas are made in one year.

   b) The price of a Super Bowl ticket increased from $34 in 1982 to $280 in 2000. Estimate the increase. Determine the exact increase.

Teaching Notes:

- Some students are unfamiliar with rounding and will need to be repeatedly reminded to look at the digit to the right of the rounding position.
- A common mistake students make is to leave the digits to the right of the rounding position intact instead of changing them to zeros after rounding.
- Refer students to the *Principle of Estimation* chart in the textbook.

Answers: 1a) 210, b) 3490, c) 10, d) 15,860, e) 300, f) 1300, g) 100, h) 15,000, i) 4000, j) 1000, k) 27,000, l) 1000; 2a) 240, b) 500,000, c) 63,000, d) 80,000,000, e) 5, f) 20; 3a) about 120,000, b) est. $270, exact $246

Mini-Lecture 1.8
Solving Applied Problems Involving Whole Numbers

Learning Objectives:

1. Use the Mathematics Blueprint to solve problems involving one type of operation.
2. Use the Mathematics Blueprint to solve problems involving more than one type of operation.

Examples:

1. Solve problems involving one type of operation.

   a) Students at a party ordered 8 large pizzas. Each pizza is cut into 6 slices. How many slices are there in all?

   b) If a new amusement park covers 54 acres and there are 44,010 square feet in 1 acre, how many square feet of land does the amusement park cover?

   c) The town of Chelmsford, Massachusetts, has a population of 45,322. The town of Bedford, Massachusetts, has a population of 31,004. What is the difference in population between these two towns?

2. Solve problems involving more than one type of operation.

   a) Lisette bought six beach towels for $15 each, eight bottles of sunscreen for $5 each, and 2 pairs of sunglasses for $23 each. How much did she spend in all?

   b) Justin had a balance of $15 in his checking account. He made deposits of $784, $556, $413, and $50. He wrote out checks for $551, $347, $12, and $81. When all the deposits are recorded and all the checks clear, what balance will he have in his checking account?

   c) Egbichi wants to determine the miles-per-gallon rating of her Ford Mustang. She filled the tank when the odometer read 38,861 miles. After ten days, the odometer read 39,437 miles and the tank required 18 gallons to be filled. How many miles per gallon did Egbichi's car achieve?

Teaching Notes:

- Many students struggle with application problems.
- Refer students to the *Mathematics Blueprint For Problem Solving* in the textbook.
- Encourage students to use estimation to check whether their application problem answers are reasonable.

Answers: *1a) 48 slices, b) 2,376,540 sqft, c) 14,318 people; 2a) $176, b) $827, c) 32 mi/gal*

Mini-Lecture 2.1
Understanding Fractions

Learning Objectives:

1. Identify the numerator and denominator.
2. Use a fraction to represent part of a whole.
3. Draw a sketch to illustrate a fraction.
4. Application problems.

Examples:

1. Name the numerator and denominator in each fraction.

   a) $\dfrac{1}{5}$ b) $\dfrac{2}{3}$ c) $\dfrac{15}{17}$ d) $\dfrac{1}{9}$

2. Use a fraction to represent the shaded part of the object or objects.

   a)   b)

3. Draw a sketch to illustrate the fractional part.

   a) $\dfrac{4}{7}$ of an object   b) $\dfrac{3}{4}$ of an object

4. Charlie drove 43 minutes to go to a Celtics game. 17 minutes of his trip were spent in bumper-to-bumper traffic. What fractional part of his time was spent in bumper-to-bumper traffic?

Teaching Notes:

- Most students find this section easy.
- Some students forget which part of the fraction is the numerator and which is the denominator. An easy way for them to remember which is which is that the *d*enominator is *d*own at the bottom.

Answers: *1a) num=1,den=5, b) num=2,den=3, c) num=15,den=17, d) num=1,den=9; 2a) 7/15, b) 5/6; 3a) answers vary, b) answers vary; 4) 17/43*

Mini-Lecture 2.2
Simplifying Fractions

Learning Objectives:

1. Write a number as a product of prime factors.
2. Identify composite and prime numbers.
3. Reduce a fraction using common factors.
4. Reduce a fraction using prime factors.
5. Determine whether two fractions are equal.

Examples:

1. Write each number as a product of prime factors.

   a) 6   b) 20   c) 30   d) 84

2. Determine whether each number is prime or composite. If it is composite, write it as the product of prime factors.

   a) 62   b) 13   c) 89   d) 95

3. Reduce each fraction using common factors.

   a) $\dfrac{5}{10}$ b) $\dfrac{16}{64}$ c) $\dfrac{42}{77}$ d) $\dfrac{88}{90}$

4. Reduce each fraction by the method of prime factors.

   a) $\dfrac{4}{16}$ b) $\dfrac{15}{35}$ c) $\dfrac{27}{72}$ d) $\dfrac{66}{77}$

5. Determine whether the fractions are equal.

   a) $\dfrac{1}{3}$ and $\dfrac{2}{6}$ b) $\dfrac{21}{33}$ and $\dfrac{7}{13}$ c) $\dfrac{4}{10}$ and $\dfrac{24}{60}$

Teaching Notes:

- A common mistake in prime factorization is to not factor completely. For example: $60 = 4 \times 3 \times 5$ or $2^2 \times 15$, instead of $2^2 \times 3 \times 5$
- Prime factorization is an important skill for finding least common denominators later in this chapter.
- Many students prefer the common factor method for reducing fractions.
- Refer students to the ***Divisibility Tests*** chart in the textbook.

Answers: *1a) 2x3, b) 2^2x5, c) 2x3x5, d) 2^2x3x7; 2a) 2x31, b) prime, c) prime, d) 5x19; 3a) ½, b) ¼, c) 6/11, d) 44/45; 4a) ¼, b) 3/7, c) 3/8, d) 6/7; 5a) yes, b) no, c) yes*

Mini-Lecture 2.3
Converting between Improper Fractions and Mixed Numbers

Learning Objectives:

1. Change a mixed number to an improper fraction.
2. Change an improper fraction to a mixed number.
3. Reduce a mixed number or an improper fraction.
4. Change an improper fraction to a mixed number and reduce.

Examples:

1. Change each mixed number to an improper fraction.

   a) $2\dfrac{3}{4}$
   b) $6\dfrac{2}{9}$
   c) $1\dfrac{43}{58}$
   e) $103\dfrac{4}{5}$

2. Change each improper fraction to a mixed number or a whole number.

   a) $\dfrac{8}{5}$
   b) $\dfrac{81}{9}$
   c) $\dfrac{48}{11}$
   d) $\dfrac{196}{9}$

3. Reduce each mixed number or improper fraction.

   a) $3\dfrac{10}{15}$
   b) $5\dfrac{32}{64}$
   c) $\dfrac{27}{15}$
   d) $\dfrac{143}{22}$

4. Change each improper fraction to a mixed number, then reduce.

   a) $\dfrac{370}{144}$
   b) $\dfrac{567}{105}$

Teaching Notes:

- Most students find it easy to convert back and forth between mixed numbers and improper fractions.
- Some students find the reducing part difficult.
- Some students periodically forget how to convert between improper fractions and mixed numbers, and vice-versa, and will need to be reminded in future sections.

Answers: _1a) 11/4, b) 56/9, c) 101/58, e) 519/5; 2a) 1 3/5, b) 9, c) 4 4/11, d) 21 7/9; 3a) 3 2/3, b) 5 ½, c) 9/5, d) 13/2; 4a) 2 41/72, b) 5 2/5_

Mini-Lecture 2.4
Multiplying Fractions and Mixed Numbers

Learning Objectives:

1. Multiply two fractions that are proper or improper.
2. Multiply a whole number and a fraction.
3. Multiply mixed numbers.
4. Solve for the unknown number.
5. Application problems.

Examples:

1. Multiply the fractions. Make sure all final answers are simplified.

   a) $\dfrac{1}{2} \times \dfrac{3}{4}$
   b) $\dfrac{5}{9} \times \dfrac{3}{15}$
   c) $\dfrac{5}{6} \times \dfrac{9}{2}$
   d) $\dfrac{5}{24} \times \dfrac{36}{25}$

2. Multiply the fractions and whole numbers. Make sure all final answers are simplified.

   a) $7 \times \dfrac{3}{5}$
   b) $\dfrac{4}{9} \times 18$
   c) $1 \times \dfrac{18}{36}$
   d) $\dfrac{4}{5} \times 25 \times \dfrac{35}{16}$

3. Multiply. Change mixed numbers to improper fractions before multiplying.

   a) $3\dfrac{1}{2} \times 1\dfrac{1}{4}$
   b) $2\dfrac{3}{4} \times \dfrac{8}{9}$
   c) $\dfrac{6}{6} \times 8\dfrac{3}{4}$
   d) $7\dfrac{1}{2} \times 10\dfrac{2}{15}$

4. Solve for x.

   a) $\dfrac{3}{4} \cdot x = \dfrac{21}{32}$
   b) $x \cdot \dfrac{5}{6} = \dfrac{15}{54}$

5. Jodi bought a car for $25,500. After one year the car was worth 4/5 of the original price. What was the car worth after one year?

Teaching Notes:

- Most students need to be shown how to turn a whole number into a fraction.
- Most students do better if they cancel before multiplying.
- Most students do not know that mixed numbers must be changed to improper fractions before multiplying. Some try to multiply the whole number parts together, and then multiply the fraction parts together.

Answers: 1a) 3/8, b) 1/9, c) 3 ¾, d) 3/10; 2a) 4 1/5, b) 8, c) ½, d) 43 ¾; 3a) 4 3/8, b) 2 4/9, c) 8 ¾, d) 76; 4a) 7/8, b) 3/9; 5) $20,400

Mini-Lecture 2.5
Dividing Fractions and Mixed Numbers

Learning Objectives:

1. Divide two proper or improper fractions.
2. Divide a whole number and a fraction.
3. Divide or multiply mixed numbers.
4. Solve for the unknown number.
5. Application problems.

Examples:

1. Divide the fractions. Make sure all final answers are simplified.

    a) $\dfrac{1}{2} \div \dfrac{3}{4}$
    b) $\dfrac{5}{9} \div \dfrac{3}{15}$
    c) $\dfrac{5}{6} \div \dfrac{9}{2}$
    d) $\dfrac{5}{24} \div \dfrac{36}{24}$

2. Divide the fractions and whole numbers. Make sure all final answers are simplified.

    a) $7 \div \dfrac{3}{5}$
    b) $\dfrac{4}{9} \div 0$
    c) $\dfrac{2}{\frac{18}{36}}$
    d) $\dfrac{\frac{4}{5}}{28}$

3. Divide or Multiply.

    a) $3\dfrac{1}{2} \div 1\dfrac{1}{6}$
    b) $2\dfrac{3}{4} \times \dfrac{8}{9}$
    c) $\dfrac{5}{3} \div 8\dfrac{3}{4}$
    d) $\dfrac{7\frac{1}{2}}{1\frac{3}{4}}$

4. Solve for x.

    a) $x \div \dfrac{2}{3} = \dfrac{9}{4}$
    b) $x \div \dfrac{6}{5} = \dfrac{15}{54}$

5. Irving drove his car to Worcester, a distance of 200 miles, in $4\dfrac{1}{6}$ hours. What was his average speed (in miles per hour)?

Teaching Notes:

- Some students cancel before taking the reciprocal of the second fraction.
- Many students have trouble deciding which number does the dividing in word problems.
- Remind students that mixed numbers must be changed to improper fractions before multiplying or dividing.

Answers: _1a) 2/3, b) 2 7/9, c) 5/27, d) 5/36; 2a) 11 2/3, b) undefined, c) 4, d) 1/35; 3a) 3, b) 2 4/9, c) 4/21, d) 4 2/7;_
4a) 3/2 or 1 ½, b) 3/9 or 1/3; 5) 48 mph

Mini-Lecture 2.6
The Least Common Denominator and Creating Equivalent Fractions

Learning Objectives:

1. Find the least common multiple (LCM) of two numbers.
2. Find the least common denominator (LCD) given two or three fractions.
3. Build a fraction to an equivalent fraction with a given LCD.
4. Find the LCD of two or three fractions and build equivalent fractions.

Examples:

1. Find the LCM for each pair of numbers.

   a) 4 and 3   b) 6 and 15   c) 8 and 48   d) 24 and 36

2. Find the LCD for each group of fractions.

   a) $\dfrac{7}{9}$, $\dfrac{5}{6}$ b) $\dfrac{3}{15}$, $\dfrac{13}{20}$ c) $\dfrac{7}{12}$, $\dfrac{5}{18}$

   d) $\dfrac{1}{9}$, $\dfrac{5}{7}$, $\dfrac{14}{63}$ e) $\dfrac{7}{8}$, $\dfrac{9}{14}$, $\dfrac{11}{16}$ f) $\dfrac{1}{20}$, $\dfrac{13}{16}$, $\dfrac{3}{4}$

3. Build each fraction to an equivalent fraction with the specified LCD.

   a) $\dfrac{1}{4} = \dfrac{?}{12}$ b) $\dfrac{5}{7} = \dfrac{?}{49}$ c) $\dfrac{3}{8} = \dfrac{?}{32}$

4. Find the LCD. Build up the fractions to equivalent fractions having the LCD as the denominator.

   a) $\dfrac{3}{8}$, $\dfrac{5}{16}$ b) $\dfrac{1}{24}$, $\dfrac{7}{40}$ c) $\dfrac{5}{6}$, $\dfrac{11}{15}$, $\dfrac{3}{20}$

Teaching Notes:

- Most students prefer to find LCDs by listing the multiples until a common one appears.
- It is important for students to also use the prime factor method because they will use this method for algebraic fractions in future courses.
- Many students forget to multiply the missing factor into the numerator in example 4.
- Refer students to the *Three-Step Procedure for Finding the Least Common Denominator* and the *Building Fraction Property* in the textbook.

Answers: 1a) 12, b) 30, c) 48, d) 72; 2a) 36, b) 60, c) 36, d) 63, e) 112; f) 80; 3a) 3, b) 35, c) 12; 4a) 16, 6/16, 5/16, b) 120, 5/120, 21/120, c) 60, 50/60, 44/60, 9/60

M-14

Mini-Lecture 2.7
Adding and Subtracting Fractions

Learning Objectives:

1. Add and subtract fractions with a common denominator.
2. Add and subtract fractions without a common denominator.
3. Solve for the unknown number.
4. Application problems.

Examples:

1. Add or subtract. Simplify all answers.

   a) $\dfrac{3}{8} + \dfrac{2}{8}$

   b) $\dfrac{3}{14} + \dfrac{4}{14}$

   c) $\dfrac{2}{3} - \dfrac{1}{3}$

   d) $\dfrac{9}{15} - \dfrac{3}{15}$

2. Add or subtract. Simplify all answers.

   a) $\dfrac{2}{4} + \dfrac{1}{8}$

   b) $\dfrac{5}{6} + \dfrac{7}{8}$

   c) $\dfrac{7}{12} + \dfrac{9}{30}$

   d) $\dfrac{2}{3} + \dfrac{2}{24} + \dfrac{1}{6}$

   e) $\dfrac{3}{4} - \dfrac{5}{8}$

   f) $\dfrac{2}{3} - \dfrac{3}{16}$

   g) $\dfrac{5}{6} - \dfrac{8}{12}$

   h) $\dfrac{4}{5} - \dfrac{8}{10}$

3. Solve for the unknown number. Simplify all answers.

   a) $x + \dfrac{1}{9} = \dfrac{5}{18}$

   b) $x - \dfrac{3}{8} = \dfrac{3}{16}$

   c) $x + \dfrac{4}{5} = \dfrac{9}{11}$

4. Amanda started running on Monday. She ran $\dfrac{1}{3}$ mile. On Wednesday she ran $\dfrac{3}{4}$ mile. How many miles has she ran so far this week?

Teaching Notes:

- Most students find example 1 easy.
- Some students try to cross-cancel instead of finding the LCD in example 2.
- Some students add (or subtract) the denominators instead of finding the LCD.
- Some students forget to multiply the numerator when building equivalent fractions.
- Some students find example 3 very difficult.

Answers: _1a) 5/8, b) ½, c) 1/3, d) 2/5; 2a) 5/8, b) 1 17/24, c) 53/60, d) 11/12, e) 1/8, f) 29/48, g) 1/6, h) 0; 3a) 3/18 or 1/6, b) 9/16, c) 1/55; 4) 1 1/12 mi_

Mini-Lecture 2.8
Adding and Subtracting Mixed Numbers and the Order of Operations

Learning Objectives:

1. Add or subtract mixed numbers, without carrying or borrowing.
2. Add or subtract mixed numbers, with carrying or borrowing.
3. Evaluate expressions using the correct order of operations.

Examples:

1. Add or subtract. Express the answer as a mixed or whole number. Simplify all answers.

   a) $8\dfrac{3}{10}+1\dfrac{1}{10}$
   b) $8\dfrac{7}{15}+3\dfrac{3}{10}$
   c) $12\dfrac{3}{8}-10\dfrac{1}{4}$
   d) $5\dfrac{2}{5}-3\dfrac{1}{10}$

2. Add or subtract. Express the answer as a mixed or whole number. Simplify all answers.

   a) $14\dfrac{6}{7}+15\dfrac{1}{2}$
   b) $11\dfrac{13}{20}+4\dfrac{3}{5}$
   c) $12-4\dfrac{3}{8}$
   d) $16\dfrac{3}{8}-10\dfrac{1}{2}$

3. Evaluate using the correct order of operations.

   a) $\left(\dfrac{2}{3}\right)^2$
   b) $\left(\dfrac{1}{2}\right)^2$
   c) $\dfrac{4}{5}-\dfrac{1}{2}\times\dfrac{6}{5}$
   d) $\dfrac{1}{4}\times\dfrac{3}{4}+\dfrac{3}{8}\div\dfrac{3}{4}$

   e) $\left(\dfrac{5}{6}-\dfrac{7}{12}\right)\times\dfrac{7}{9}$
   f) $\dfrac{4}{3}\div\left(\dfrac{3}{5}-\dfrac{3}{10}\right)$
   g) $\left(\dfrac{1}{3}\right)^2\times\dfrac{27}{30}$
   h) $\left(\dfrac{2}{3}\right)^2\div\dfrac{5}{9}$

4. Jan walked $49\dfrac{1}{5}$ yards and Mark walked $21\dfrac{3}{10}$ yards. How much farther did Jan walk?

Teaching Notes:

- Many students have difficulty with this section.
- Some students like to see the following approach for borrowing:

  $11\dfrac{9}{20}$ $\rightarrow$ $^{10}1\!\!\!\backslash$ $1\dfrac{9}{20}$ $\rightarrow$ $10\dfrac{29}{20}$

- Some students make the following mistake: $(1/2)^2 = 2/4$
- Some students confuse the multiplying and adding/subtracting processes, and make common denominators for multiply and/or cross cancel for adding/subtracting.

Answers: _1a) 9 2/5, b) 11 23/30, c) 2 1/8, d) 2 3/10; 2a) 30 5/14, b) 16 ¼, c) 7 5/8, d) 5 7/8; 3a) 4/9, b) ¼, c) 1/5, d) 11/16, e) 7/36, f) 4 4/9, g) 1/10, h) 4/5; 4) 27 9/10 yd_

Mini-Lecture 2.9
Solving Applied Problems Involving Fractions

Learning Objectives:

1. Solve real-life problems with fractions.

Examples:

a) Find the perimeter of the square.

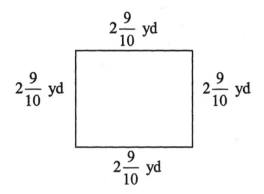

$2\frac{9}{10}$ yd

$2\frac{9}{10}$ yd $2\frac{9}{10}$ yd

$2\frac{9}{10}$ yd

b) Jody is using a recipe that calls for $\frac{1}{4}$ cup of milk per batch. If she has $5\frac{3}{4}$ cups of milk available, how many batches can she make?

c) Robert and Paul each took some chips from a bag of potato chips which contained $9\frac{1}{2}$ ounces of chips. Robert took $2\frac{1}{3}$ ounces of chips and Paul took $3\frac{5}{6}$ ounces of chips. How many ounces of chips were left in the bag?

d) What is the area in square yards of a rectangular garden that is $11\frac{1}{2}$ yards long and $12\frac{1}{6}$ yards wide?

Teaching Notes:

*   Many students have difficulty with application problems.
*   Refer students to the ***Mathematics Blueprint for Problem Solving*** chart in the textbook.
*   Encourage students to estimate their answers as a way of checking the exact answers.

Answers: 1a) 11 3/5 yd, b) 23 batches, c) 3 1/3 oz, d) 139 11/12 square yards

Mini-Lecture 3.1
Using Decimal Notation

Learning Objectives:

1. Write a word name for a decimal.
2. Write a decimal for a word name.
3. Change from fractional notation to decimal notation.
4. Change from decimal notation to fractional notation.

Examples:

1. Write a word name for each decimal.

   a) 0.35   b) 0.007   c) 4.12   d) 32.1

   e) $144.25   f) $34,256.09

2. Write in decimal notation.

   a) five tenths
   b) thirty three hundredths
   c) seven hundred sixty four thousandths
   d) six and eleven ten-thousandths

3. Change each fraction into a decimal.

   a) $\dfrac{6}{10}$ b) $\dfrac{73}{100}$ c) $\dfrac{105}{1000}$ d) $\dfrac{3333}{10,000}$ e) $3\dfrac{9}{10}$

4. Change each decimal into a fraction. Reduce whenever possible.

   a) 0.3   b) 0.8   c) 3.25   d) 122.004

Teaching Notes:

- Most students find examples 1 and 2 easy.
- Some students have trouble with examples 3 and 4, especially when a whole number part is involved.
- Refer students to the *Decimal Place Values* chart in text.

Answers: *1a) thirty-five hundredths, b) seven thousandths, c) four and twelve hundredths, d) thirty-two and one tenth, e) one hundred forty-four and 25/100 dollars, f) thirty-four thousand two hundred fifty-six and 9/100 dollars; 2a) 0.5, b) 0.33, c) 0.764, d) 6.0011; 3a) 0.6, b) 0.73, c) 0.105, d) 0.3333, e) 3.9; 4a) 3/10, b) 4/5, c) 3 ¼, d) 122 1/250*

Mini-Lecture 3.2
Comparing, Ordering, and Rounding Decimals

Learning Objectives:

1. Compare decimals.
2. Place decimals in order from smallest to largest.
3. Round decimals to a specified decimal place.

Examples:

1. Fill in the blank with one of the symbols <, =, or >.

   a) 0.3 ___ 0.5   b) 0.33 ___ 0.31   c) 1.56 ___ 1.560

   d) 22.001 ___ 21.001   e) $\frac{7}{10}$ ___ 0.7   f) 0.006 ___ $\frac{6}{100}$

2. Arrange each set of decimals from smallest to largest.

   a) 0.415, 0.42, 0.409, 0.4102   b) 23.082, 23.02, 23.088, 23.079

3. Round each number to the place indicated.

   a) 5.38 to the nearest tenth.   f) $5.247 to the nearest cent.
   b) 0.753 to the nearest tenth.   g) $819.983 to the nearest cent.
   c) 103.843 to the nearest hundredth.   h) $5.247 to the nearest dollar.
   d) 7.385 to the nearest one.   i) $819.983 to the nearest dollar.
   e) 19.1299 to the nearest thousandth.

Teaching Notes:

- Some students find a number line useful for example 1.
- Some students think that the number with more decimal places is larger when comparing decimals.
- Most students find examples 3a)-e) easy.
- Some students are confused by rounding money values to the nearest cent because the cent position is in the hundredths spot, but they think of the cent as being in the ones position (1 cent position) instead of in the one-hundredths-of-a-dollar position.

Answers: *1a) <, b) >, c) =, d) >, e) =, f) <; 2a) 0.409, 0.4102, 0.415, 0.42, b) 23.02, 23.079, 23.082, 23.088; 3a) 5.4, b) 0.8, c) 103.84, d) 7, e) 19.130, f)$5.25, g) $819.98, h) $5, i) $820*

Mini-Lecture 3.3
Adding and Subtracting Decimals

Learning Objectives:

1. Add decimals.
2. Subtract decimals.
3. Application problems.

Examples:

1. Add the following numbers.

   a) $56.3 + 12.2$ b) $56.3 + 19.8$ c) $1.665 + 9.888$

   d) $1.84 + 20.749$ e) $10 + 1.24$ f) $1.2 + 0.337 + 6$

2. Subtract the following numbers.

   a) $48.7 - 42.3$ b) $48.7 - 2.9$ c) $30.44 - 16.3$

   d) $7 - 4.1$ e) $5.00725 - 1.06921$

3. Add or subtract as needed to solve the following application problems.

   a) Jasmine drove on a summer trip. When she began, the odometer read 32,046.22 miles. When she was done, the odometer read 32,731.19 miles. How many miles did she travel during her trip?

   b) Keith purchased some clothing at the mall. He bought a shirt for $28.99, a pair of jeans for $39.99, and a watch for $24.50. How much did he spend?

Teaching Notes:

- Most students find this section easy.
- Some students need to be shown how to add the extra zeros to the ends of the decimal parts of numbers, and where to place the decimal for whole numbers.
- Some students need to write in the borrowing steps in order to subtract without errors.
- Some students must be reminded of how to borrow across zeros when subtracting.

Answers: _1a) 68.5, b) 76.1, c) 11.553, d) 22.589, e) 11.24, f) 7.537; 2a) 6.4, b) 45.8, c) 14.14, d) 2.9, e) 3.93804; 3a) 684.97 mi, b) $93.48_

Mini-Lecture 3.4
Multiplying Decimals

Learning Objectives:

1. Multiply a decimal by a decimal or a whole number.
2. Multiply a decimal by a power of 10.
3. Application problems.

Examples:

1. Multiply the following numbers.

   a) 2.2 x 6

   b) 0.22 x 0.6

   c) 22 x 0.6

   d) 0.581
   x 2.9

   e) 73.12
   x 22.34

   f) 0.6288
   x 5003

2. Do the following multiplications, and notice the emerging pattern.

   a) 5.4 x 10

   b) 0.33 x 10

   c) 5.4 x 100

   d) 0.33×10^2

   e) 5.4 x 1000

   f) 0.33×10^3

   g) From the pattern you've observed, what would 765.52×10^5 equal?

3. a) A retail store purchases 100 sweaters at $35.65 each. How much did the store pay for the order?

   b) A college is purchasing carpeting for a new student lounge. What is the price of a carpet that is 21.3 yards wide and 180.4 yards long if the cost is $11.25 per square yard?

Teaching Notes:

- Most students find example 1 easy.
- Many students do not see the multiplying by powers of 10 pattern in example 2 on their own, and must be shown.
- Some students are confused by the shortcut for multiplying by powers of 10 and prefer doing out the multiplication the long way.

Answers: 1a) 13.2, b) 0.132, c) 13.2, d) 1.6849, e) 1633.5008, f) 3145.8864; 2a) 54, b) 3.3, c) 540, d) 33, e) 5400, f) 330, g) 76,552,000; 3a) $3565, b) $43,228.35

Mini-Lecture 3.5
Dividing Decimals

Learning Objectives:

1. Divide a decimal by a whole number.
2. Divide a decimal by a decimal.
3. Divide and round the answer as indicated.
4. Application problems.

Examples:

1. Divide until there is a remainder of zero.

    a) $8\overline{)50.4}$ b) $32\overline{)20.16}$ c) $\dfrac{1.62}{6}$

2. Divide until there is a remainder of zero.

    a) $2.6\overline{)54.6}$ b) $0.8112 \div 0.06$ c) $168.3 \div 2.2$

3. Divide and round to the nearest hundredth.

    a) $20.9 \div 15$ b) $0.6\overline{)0.557}$ c) $4.399 \div 0.13$

    Divide and round to the nearest thousandth.

    d) $8.45 \div 71$ e) $0.3\overline{)79.46}$ f) $444.22 \div 0.13$

4. Mark owns a Ford Escort that travels 360 miles on 15.5 gallons of gas. How many miles per gallon does it achieve? (Round your answer to the nearest tenth.)

Teaching Notes:

- Most students find example 1 easy.
- Most students do not know, or have forgotten, how to do the division in example 2. But once they are shown how to move the decimals, most students find this type of division easy.
- Most students are unaware that the division in example 3 must be carried to one place beyond the rounding position.

Answers: 1a) 6.3, b) 0.63, c) 0.27; 2a) 21, b) 13.52, c) 76.5; 3a) 1.39, b) 0.93, c) 33.84, d) 0.119, e) 264.867, f) 3417.077; 4) 23.2 mpg

Mini-Lecture 3.6
Converting Fractions to Decimals and the Order of Operations

<u>Learning Objectives</u>:

1. Convert a fraction to a decimal, without rounding.
2. Convert a fraction to a decimal, rounding when necessary.
3. Use the correct order of operations with decimals.

<u>Examples</u>:

1. Write as an equivalent decimal. Divide until there is a remainder of zero or a repeating decimal.

   a) $\dfrac{1}{4}$ b) $\dfrac{2}{5}$ c) $\dfrac{2}{3}$ d) $4\dfrac{5}{6}$

2. Write as an equivalent decimal or decimal approximation. Round your answer to the nearest thousandth if needed.

   a) $\dfrac{2}{7}$ b) $5\dfrac{13}{27}$ c) $\dfrac{39}{23}$ d) $\dfrac{11}{19}$

3. Evaluate using the correct order of operations.

   a) $6.2 + (4.3)^2 - 9.72$ b) $2.25 + 1.06 \times 4.85$

   c) $2.25 - 1.06 \times (4.85 - 3.95)$ d) $25.1 + 11.4 \div 7.5 \times 3.75$

   e) $(0.2)^3 + (7 - 2.4) \times 5.5$ f) $4.9 \times 3.6 \times 2.1 - 0.1 \times 0.2 \times 0.3$

<u>Teaching Notes</u>:

- Most students find examples 1 and 2 easy once they are shown how to do it.
- Many students need to be reminded of the order of operations.
- Some students perform $(4.3)^2$ as 4^2 point 3^2 the first time they see a problem such as 3a).
- Many students need to be reminded to work in a neat and organized manner in order to arrive at the correct answer.

<u>Answers</u>: 1a) 0.25, b) 0.4, c) $0.\overline{6}$, d) 4.8$\overline{3}$; 2a) 0.286, b) 5.481, c) 1.696, d) 0.579; 3a) 14.97, b) 7.391, c) 1.296, d) 30.8, e) 25.308, f) 37.038

Mini-Lecture 3.7
Estimating and Solving Applied Problems Involving Decimals

Learning Objectives:

1. Estimate sums, differences, products, and quotients of decimals.
2. Solve applied problems using operations with decimals.

Examples:

1. Round to one non-zero digit. Then estimate the result of the calculation.

   a) $2.3 + 6.7$

   b) $434.23 - 201.6$

   c) $457,223,102.44 + 113,244,541$

   d) 2.3×6.7

   e) 434.23×201.6

   f) $56,200 \div 3,000.23$

2. Solve the following application problems. Round to the nearest hundredth if needed.

   a) At McDonald's, Amanda bought a soda for $0.95, a medium French fry for $1.39, and a fish sandwich for $2.69. How much did Amanda pay for her meal?

   b) Carmine has $20 to spend on groceries. He spends $1.29 on lettuce, $0.89 on tomatoes, $1.00 on cucumbers, $3.29 on soda, $10.95 on meat, and $2.99 on ice cream. Did Carmine have enough money for this purchase?

   c) Juan and Anita are having their roof reshingled and need to determine its area in square feet. The dimensions of the roof are 38.5 feet by 61.8 feet. What is the area of the roof in square feet?

   d) Three employees of Prime Real Estate are sharing a commission of $8,241.33. How much does each employee receive?

Teaching Notes:

- Most students find estimation easy once they are shown a method.
- Some students struggle with application problems.
- Refer students to the *Mathematics Blueprint for Problem Solving* in the text.
- Encourage students to use estimation to check whether their application problem answers are reasonable.

Answers: *1a) 9, b) 200, c) 600,000,000, d) 14, e) 80,000, f) 20; 2a) $5.03, b) no, c) 2379.3 sq ft, d) $2747.11*

Mini-Lecture 4.1
Ratios and Rates

Learning Objectives:

1. Use a ratio to compare two quantities with the same units.
2. Use a rate to compare two quantities with different units.
3. Write as a unit rate.
4. Application problems.

Examples:

1. Write the ratio in lowest terms. Express your answer as a fraction.

   a) 9:17
   b) 72 to 76
   c) $12 to $38
   d) $9\frac{1}{3}$ to $9\frac{1}{2}$

2. Write as a rate in simplest form.

   a) 5 cars for 20 people
   b) 186 miles in 8 hours
   c) 82 hours for 18 projects

3. Write as a unit rate.

   a) 132 miles on 3 gallons of gas
   b) 1200 cars in 400 households

   c) 243 miles in 9 hours
   d) $950 earned in 5 weeks

4. Solve the following problems using ratios and unit rates.

   a) A couple went out for the evening and spent $38 on dinner and $24 at the movies. What is the ratio of dollars spent on dinner to the total amount spent for the evening?

   b) One jar of jelly costs $2.32 for 16 ounces. Another jar costs $2.03 for 13 ounces. Find which is the better buy (lower cost per ounce) for the following items. Round unit prices to two decimal places.

Teaching Notes:

- Some students will forget to reduce the fractions here.
- Some students will wonder why improper fractions do not need to be changed to mixed numbers when working with ratios and rates.
- Many students need to be reminded of the division rule for fractions.
- Many students find application problems such as example 4b) difficult.

Answers: 1a) 9/17, b) 18/19, c) 6/19, d) 56/57; 2a) 1car/4people, b) 93/4 mph, c) 41hours/project; 3a) 44 mpg, b) 3 cars/household, c) 27 mph, d) $190/wk; 4a) 19/31, b) $2.32 for 16 oz

Mini-Lecture 4.2
The Concept of Proportions

Learning Objectives:

1. Write a proportion.
2. Determine whether a statement is a proportion.
3. Application problems.

Examples:

1. Write a proportion.

   a) 3 is to 5 as 6 is to 10   b) 6.5 is to 5 as 52 is to 40   c) $3\frac{1}{3}$ is to 4 as $4\frac{1}{6}$ is to 5

2. Determine whether the equation is a proportion.

   a) $\frac{1}{2} \overset{?}{=} \frac{3}{6}$ b) $\frac{4}{10} \overset{?}{=} \frac{16}{39}$ c) $\frac{1}{2} \overset{?}{=} \frac{4.8}{9.6}$ d) $\frac{40}{39.2} \overset{?}{=} \frac{5}{5.3}$

   e) $\frac{2\frac{5}{9}}{5} \overset{?}{=} \frac{5\frac{1}{9}}{10}$ f) $\frac{8}{17} \overset{?}{=} \frac{4}{8\frac{1}{2}}$ g) $\frac{318 \text{ feet}}{4 \text{ rolls}} \overset{?}{=} \frac{954 \text{ feet}}{12 \text{ rolls}}$

3. Solve the following application problems. Answer yes or no, and provide a reason for your answer.

   a) A car traveled 578 miles in 8.5 hours. A truck traveled 272 miles in 4 hours. Did they travel at the same speed?

   b) Sharon earned gross pay of $793.80 working 42 hours each week in a web design agency. Jesse's gross weekly pay was $737.10 for a 39-hour work week with a different agency. Was Sharon's pay per hour the same as Jesse's?

Teaching Notes:

- It is important to start with an easy proportion such as 1a) so that students see that proportions are equivalent fractions.
- Many students have trouble with proportions involving complex fractions.
- Refer students to the *Equality Test for Fractions* chart in the textbook.

Answers: 1a) 3/5 = 6/10, b) 6.5/5 = 52/40, c) (3 1/3)/4 = (4 1/6)/5; 2a) yes, b) no, c) yes, d) no, e) yes, f) yes, g) yes; 3a) yes, reasons vary, b) yes, reasons vary

Mini-Lecture 4.3
Solving Proportions

Learning Objectives:

1. Solve for the variable in an equation of the form $a \times n = b$.
2. Find the missing number in a proportion.
3. Application problems.

Examples:

1. Solve for n.

   a) $5 \times n = 30$

   b) $45 = n \times 5$

   c) $n \times 7 = 34.3$

   d) $23.6 = 4 \times n$

   e) $n \times \dfrac{1}{2} = 3$

   f) $12 = \dfrac{4}{3} \times n$

2. Find the missing number in a proportion. Round to the nearest tenth if needed.

   a) $\dfrac{x}{10} = \dfrac{8}{20}$

   b) $\dfrac{3}{x} = \dfrac{9}{15}$

   c) $\dfrac{1}{2} = \dfrac{x}{17}$

   d) $\dfrac{2}{7} = \dfrac{3}{x}$

   e) $\dfrac{2}{x} = \dfrac{0.6}{1.2}$

   f) $\dfrac{x}{6.8} = \dfrac{0.08}{5}$

   g) $\dfrac{5}{\frac{2}{9}} = \dfrac{45}{x}$

   h) $\dfrac{1}{5\frac{1}{2}} = \dfrac{x}{11}$

3. Find the value of n. Round to the nearest hundredth when necessary.

   a) $\dfrac{\text{n ounces}}{23 \text{ quarts}} = \dfrac{39.6 \text{ ounces}}{9 \text{ quarts}}$

   b) $\dfrac{27 \text{ liters}}{\text{n grams}} = \dfrac{4 \text{ liters}}{18.8 \text{ grams}}$

   c) $\dfrac{3 \text{ kilometers}}{1.86 \text{ miles}} = \dfrac{\text{n kilometers}}{5 \text{ miles}}$

   d) $\dfrac{2\frac{1}{5} \text{ feet}}{6 \text{ pounds}} = \dfrac{\text{n feet}}{10 \text{ pounds}}$

Teaching Notes:

- Some students prefer to solve examples such as 2a) and 2b) by inspection using the concept of equivalent fractions.
- Refer students to the ***To Solve for a Missing Number in a Proportion*** chart in the textbook.

Answers: *1a) 6, b) 9, c) 4.9, d) 5.9, e) 6, f) 9; 2a) 4, b) 5, c) 8.5, d) 10.5, e) 3.7, f) 0.1, g) 2, h) 2; 3a) 101.2, b) 126.9, c) 8.06, d) 3.67*

Mini-Lecture 4.4
Solving Applied Problems Involving Proportions

Learning Objectives:

1. Solve applied problems using proportions.

Examples:

a) It takes Kim 22 minutes to type and spell check 14 pages of a manuscript. Find how long it takes her to type and spell check 77 pages. Round answer to the nearest whole number if needed.

b) On an architect's blueprint, 1 inch corresponds to 12 feet. If an exterior wall is 44 feet long, find how long the blueprint measurement should be. Write answer as a mixed number if needed.

c) It is recommended that there be at least 11.2 square feet of ground space in a garden for every newly planted shrub. A garden is 25.6 feet by 21 feet. Find the maximum number of shrubs the garden can accommodate.

d) In a random sampling from a survey concerning music listening habits, 140 out of 200 at-home mothers preferred salsa to punk rock. Taking all the data from the survey, 392 at-home mothers expressed a preference for salsa over punk rock. How many at-home mothers would you estimate took part in the survey?

e) At a college in eastern Minnesota, 7 out of every 10 students worked either a full-time or part-time job in addition to their studies. If 4900 students were enrolled at the college, how many did not have a full-time or part-time job?

f) Traveling in France, Donny exchanged 12 U.S. dollars for 85.2 francs. A few days later, he exchanged 24 U.S. dollars for francs and got the same exchange rate. How many francs did Donny receive? Round to the nearest tenth.

Teaching Notes:

- Many students have trouble setting up the proportion at first, and need to be shown how to line up the units and put in "x" for the unknown value.
- Remind students to use estimation to see if their answers are reasonable.
- Refer students to the *Mathematics Blueprint For Problem Solving* chart in the textbook.

Answers: *1a) 121 min, b) 3 2/3 in., c) 48 shrubs, d) 560 mothers, e) 3430 students, f) 170 francs*

Mini-Lecture 5.1
Understanding Percent

Learning Objectives:

1. Express a fraction whose denominator is 100 as a percent.
2. Write a percent as a decimal.
3. Write a decimal as a percent.
4. Application problems.

Examples:

1. Write as a percent.

   a) $\dfrac{4}{100}$ b) $\dfrac{70}{100}$ c) $\dfrac{357}{100}$ d) $\dfrac{0.3}{100}$ e) $\dfrac{6.2}{100}$ f) $\dfrac{0.039}{100}$

2. Write as a decimal.

   a) 30%   b) 0.22%   c) 9.5%   d) 623%

   e) 0.4%   f) 97.61%   g) 0.022%   j) 100%

3. Write as a percent.

   a) 0.25   b) 0.8   c) 0.616   d) 0.031

   e) 1.0   f) 3.33   g) 1.89   h) 0.00037

4. In a survey of 100 people, 41 preferred onions on their hot dogs. What percent preferred onions?

Teaching Notes:

- Many students do not understand why the decimal moves 2 places right or left when changing between % and decimal.
- Some students find it easier to remember which way to move the decimal if they are shown an alphabetical approach:

  D to P move right

  Decimal ————————————————→ Percent
         ←————————————————
  P to D move left

- Refer students to the *Changing a Percent to a Decimal* and *Changing a Decimal to a Percent* charts in the textbook.

Answers: 1a) 4%, b) 70%, c) 357%, d) 0.3%, e) 6.2%, f) 0.039%; 2a) 0.3, b) 0.02, c) 0.095, d) 6.23, e) 0.004, f) 0.9761, g) 0.00022, j) 1; 3a) 25%, b) 80%, c) 61.6%, d) 3.1%, e) 100%, f) 333%, g) 189%, h) 0.037%; 4) 41%

Mini-Lecture 5.2
Changing Between Percents, Decimals, and Fractions

Learning Objectives:

1. Change a percent to a fraction.
2. Change a fraction to a decimal percent.
3. Change a fraction to a fractional percent.
4. Change a percent, a decimal, or a fraction to equivalent forms.

Examples:

1. Write the percent as a fraction or as a mixed number.

   a) 92%   b) 7%   c) 15.5%   d) 9.76%

   e) 320%   f) $\frac{1}{2}$%   g) $2\frac{5}{6}$%   h) $44\frac{4}{9}$%

2. Write as a percent. Round to the nearest hundredth of a percent when necessary.

   a) $\frac{1}{2}$ b) $\frac{3}{4}$ c) $\frac{6}{10}$ d) $\frac{9}{20}$

   e) $\frac{7}{12}$ f) $\frac{4}{9}$ g) $2\frac{1}{5}$ h) $4\frac{5}{8}$

3. Write as a percent containing a fraction.

   a) $\frac{3}{7}$ b) $\frac{9}{14}$ c) $\frac{13}{90}$ d) $\frac{7}{40}$

4. Fill in the chart. Round decimals to ten-thousandths and percents to hundredths.

	Fraction	Decimal	Percent
a)	$\frac{2}{7}$		
b)		0.05	
c)			5.75%

Teaching Notes:

- Many students have trouble dealing with mixed numbers in this section.
- Some students forget to reduce fraction answers and must be reminded.

Answers: *1a) 23/25, b) 7/100, c) 31/200, d) 61/625, e) 3 1/5, f) 1/200, g) 17/600, h) 4/9; 2a) 50%, b) 75%, c) 60%, d) 45%, e) 58.33%, f) 44.445, g) 220%, h) 462.5%; 3a) 42 6/7 %, b) 64 2/7 %, c) 14 4/9 %, d) 17 ½ %; 4a) 0.2857, 28.57%, b) 1/20, 5%, c) 23/400, 0.0575*

M-30

Mini-Lecture 5.3A
Solving Percent Problems Using Equations

Learning Objectives:

1. Translate a percent problem into an equation.
2. Solve a percent problem by solving an equation (missing amount).
3. Solve a percent problem by solving an equation (missing base).
4. Solve a percent problem by solving an equation (missing %).
5. Application problems.

Examples:

1. Translate into a mathematical equation.

   a) What is 50% of 80?   b) 70% of what number is 32?   c) What % of 30 is 24?

2. Solve. Find the missing amount.

   a) What is 10% of 70?   b) What is 32% of 224?   c) Find 190% of 375.

3. Solve. Find the missing base.

   a) 50% of what number is 30?   b) 65% of what is 91?   c) 6.6 is 33% of what?

4. Solve. Find the missing %.

   a) 25 is what % of 125?   b) What percent of 80 is 0.8?   c) 126 is what % of 28?

5. a) The Smith family paid 22% of the purchase price of a $231,000 home as a down payment. Determine the amount of the down payment.

   b) One day 144 office workers were sick with colds. If this were 72% of the total number of office workers, how many office workers were there altogether?

   c) Lisa bought a share of stock for $48.24. She was paid a dividend of $12.06. Determine what percent of the stock price is the dividend.

Teaching Notes:

- Encourage students not to skip the step of translating the percent problem into an equation. Most students find this step very useful once they practice it.
- Remind students that *amount = percent × base*.

Answers: *1a) n=50% x 80, b) 70% x n=32, c) n x 30=24; 2a) 7, b) 71.68, c) 712.5; 3a) 60, b) 140, c) 20; 4a) 20%, b) 1%, c) 450%; 5a) $50,820, b) 200 workers, c) 25%*

Mini-Lecture 5.3B
Solving Percent Problems Using Proportions

Learning Objectives:

1. Identify the parts of the percent proportion.
2. Solve a percent problem using the percent proportion (missing amount).
3. Solve a percent problem using the percent proportion (missing base).
4. Solve a percent problem using the percent proportion (missing %).
5. Application problems.

Examples:

1. Identify the amount, base, and percent. Do not solve for any unknowns.

   a) 75% of 720 is 434.   b) What is 66% of 39?   c) 56% of what is 2443?

2. Solve using the percent proportion. Find the missing amount.

   a) What is 25% of 80?   b) What is 10% of 440?   c) Find 8.1% of 300.

3. Solve using the percent proportion. Find the missing base.

   a) 50% of what number is 90?   b) 4% of what is 15?   c) 64 is 80% of what?

4. Solve using the percent proportion. Find the missing %.

   a) 30 is what % of 150?   b) What percent of 20 is 0.4?   c) 0.8 is what % of 32?

5. a) 25% of doctors in a hospital are female. If there are 840 doctors altogether, how many doctors are female?

   b) An inspector found 60 defective watches during an inspection. If this is 0.005% of the total number of watches inspected, how many watches were inspected?

   c) In a recent survey of 180 people, 36 said that their favorite color of car was white. What percent of the people surveyed liked white cars?

Teaching Notes:

- Remind students that $\dfrac{amount}{base} = \dfrac{percent}{100}$.
- Many students find it difficult at first to identify the parts of the percent proportion.

Answers: 1a) amt=434, base=720, %=75, b) amt=1, base=39, %=66, c) amt=2443, base=6, %=56; 2a) 20, b) 44, c) 24.3; 3a) 180, b) 375, c) 80; 4a) 20%, b) 2%, c) 2.5%; 5a) 210 female, b) 1,200,000 watches, c) 20%

Mini-Lecture 5.4
Solving Applied Percent Problems

Learning Objectives:

1. Solve general applied percent problems.
2. Solve problems when percents are added.
3. Solve discount problems.

Examples:

1. a) Rita now earns $10.50 per hour. This is 20% more than what she earned last year. What did she earn per hour last year?

   b) Jeff puts aside $72.50 per week for his monthly car payment. He earns $362.50 per week. What percent of his income is set aside for car payments?

   c) Every day Elise orders either cappuccino or espresso from the coffee bar. She had 73 espressos and 292 cappuccinos this year. What percent of the coffees were espressos?

2. a) Lisa has $36.00 to spend on dinner. She wants to tip the waitress 20% of the cost of her meal. How much money can she spend on the meal itself?

   b) Nolan is building a new house. When the house is finished it will cost $322,400. The price of building the house this year is 4% higher than it would have been last year. What would the price of the house have been last year?

   c) In total a medical research facility spent $21,000,000 to develop a drug. 40% of this cost was for staff and 35% was for equipment. How much was spent to cover both the staff and the equipment?

3. a) Find the amount of discount. The original price is $121.40, the discount rate is 60%.

   b) Find the sale price. The original price is $17,700.00, the discount rate is 22%.

   c) A $2500 table is on sale at 5% off. Find the discount.

Teaching Notes:

- Most students find this section difficult.
- Some students become _extremely_ frustrated with these problems and must master each different type of problem one at a time.
- Refer students to the **_Mathematics Blueprint For Problem Solving_** in the textbook.

Answers: _1a) $8.75/hr, b) 205, c) 20%; 2a) $30, b) $310,000, c) $15,750,000; 3a) $72.84, b) $13,806, c) $125_

Mini-Lecture 5.5
Solving Commission, Percent of Increase or Decrease, and Interest Problems

Learning Objectives:

1. Solve commission problems.
2. Solve percent-of-increase or percent-of-decrease problems.
3. Solve simple interest problems.

Examples:

1. a) A sales representative is paid a commission rate of 3.3%. Find her commission if she sold $52,020 worth of goods last month.

   b) A salesperson earned a commission of $5316 for selling $44,300 worth of batteries to various stores. Find the commission rate.

   c) A sales representative for a medical supply company was paid $175,500 in commissions last year. If his commission rate was 5%, what was the sales total for the medical supplies he sold last year?

2. a) Find the percent of increase when the original amount is 20 and the new amount is 28.

   b) Find the percent of decrease when the original amount is 170 and the new amount is 136.

   c) One share of stock which originally sold for $120 now sells for $108. What is the percent of decrease?

3. a) Koral placed $2000 in a one year-CD paying simple interest of 7.5% for one year. How much interest will Koral earn in one year?

   b) Tony borrowed $4000 to finish college at an interest rate of 4.0% per year. How much interest will Tony need to pay next year?

Teaching Notes:

- Many students find this section difficult.
- Refer students to the following formulas in the textbook:

  Commission = commission rate × value of sales

  Percent of increase (decrease) = <u>*amount of increase (decrease)*</u>
  original amount

  Interest = principal × rate × time

Answers: *1a) $1716.66, b) 12%, c) $3,510,000; 2a) 40%, b) 20%, c) 10%; 3a) $150, b) $160*

Mini-Lecture 6.1
American Units

Learning Objectives:

1. Identify the basic unit equivalencies in the American system.
2. Convert from one unit of measure to another.
3. Application problems.

Examples:

1. From memory, write the equivalent value.

   a) 1 mile = ____ feet

   b) ____ hours = 1 day

   c) 1 hour = ____ minutes

   d) 1 foot = ____ inches

   e) ____ ounces = 1 pound

   f) 1 ton = ____ pounds

   g) ____ quarts = 1 gallon

   h) ____ feet = 1 yards

   i) 1 pint = ____ cups

2. Convert units. When necessary, express your answer as a decimal.

   a) 72 inches = __ feet

   b) 7.6 miles = __ feet

   c) 69 yards = __ feet

   d) 4800 seconds = __ minutes

   e) 7.2 weeks = __ days

   f) 4 days = __ hours

   g) 16.2 gallons = __ quarts

   h) 36 pints = __ quarts

   i) 20 cups = __ pints

   j) 18,000 pounds = __ tons

   k) 0.75 pounds = __ ounces

   l) 2560 ounces = __ tons

3. Solve the following application problems using American unit conversions.

   a) A container holds 5 ¾ pints of liquid. How many fluid ounces is this?
   b) A street sign prohibits vehicles over 2.5 tons from entering a certain street. How many pounds is that?
   c) Rope sells for 11¢ per inch at the local hardware store. If Sylvia needs 13 ½ feet of this rope, how much money will she spend?
   d) Keith billed a total of 24,480 minutes to one of his company's clients. How many days was this?

Teaching Notes:

- Remind students to always put the unit they are converting to in the numerator, and the unit they are converting from in the denominator so it cancels.
- Many students are confused by conversions requiring more than one unit fraction.

Answers: 1a) 5280, b) 24, c) 60, d) 12, e) 16, f) 2000, g) 4, h) 3, i) 2; 2a) 6, b) 40,128, c) 207, d) 80, e) 50.4, f) 96, g) 64.8, h) 18, I) 10, j) 9, k) 12, l) 1.28; 3a) 92, b) 5000, c) $17.82, d) 17

Mini-Lecture 6.2
Metric Measurements: Length

Learning Objectives:

1. Understand prefixes in metric units.
2. Convert between common metric units of length.
3. Convert between uncommon metric units of length.
4. Add metric measurements of length.
5. Application problems.

Examples:

1. Write the prefix and prefix abbreviation for each of the following.

   a) tenth   b) hundredth   c) thousandth   d) ten   e) hundred   f) thousand

2. Convert between these common metric units.

   a) 6 km = __m   b) 2.98 m = __cm   c) 36.63 m = __mm

   d) 330 mm = __cm   e) 148 cm = __m   f) 2,200,000 cm = __km

3. Convert between these uncommon metric units.

   a) 22.21 dekameters = __meters   b) 3.11 meters = __hectometer

   c) 52.8 hectometer = __decimeters   d) 1.96 decimeters = __millimeters

4. Change to a convenient unit of measure and add.

   a) 479 m + 5.5 km + 646 m   b) 161 mm + 973 cm + 13.7 cm

5. a) Sam went jogging yesterday. Which would be the most likely measurement for the
      distance he jogged - *km, cm, mm, or m?*
   b) A bacteria culture measures 118 millimeters at its widest point. How many
      centimeters wide is the culture?

Teaching Notes:

- Encourage students to work towards using no notes when converting common units.
- Remind students that kilometer, meter, and centimeter are the most common units.
- Refer students to the *Changing from Larger Metric Units to Smaller Ones* and the
  Changing from Smaller Metric Units to Larger Ones decimal charts in the textbook.

Answers: *1a) deci, d, b) centi, c, c) milli, m, d) deka, da, e) hector, h, f) kilo, k; 2a) 6000, b) 298, c) 36,630, d) 33, e)*
1.48, f) 22; 3a) 222.1, b) 0.0311, c) 52,800, d) 196; 4a) 6.625 km, b) 1003.3 cm; 5a) km, b) 11.8 cm

Mini-Lecture 6.3
Metric Measurements: Volume and Weight

Learning Objectives:

1. Write metric units of volume and weight.
2. Convert between metric units of volume.
3. Convert between metric units of weight.
4. Add metric measurements of volume or weight.
5. Application problems.

Examples:

1. Write the abbreviated metric unit that represents each measurement.

   a) one liter

   b) one thousand liters

   c) one thousandth of a liter

   d) one gram

   e) one thousand grams

   f) one thousandth of a gram

2. Convert between units of volume.

   a) $2.7 \text{ L} = \underline{} \text{ mL}$ b) $476 \text{ mL} = \underline{} \text{ L}$ c) $414.2 \text{ mL} = \underline{} \text{ cm}^3$ d) $97 \text{ L} = \underline{} \text{ cm}^3$

3. Convert between units of weight.

   a) $2 \text{ kg} = \underline{} \text{ mg}$ b) $42 \text{ kg} = \underline{} \text{ g}$ c) $148 \text{ mg} = \underline{} \text{ g}$ d) $78 \text{ t} = \underline{} \text{ kg}$

4. Change to a convenient unit of measure and add.

   a) $735 \text{ mL} + 41.6 \text{ L} + 87 \text{ L}$ b) $826 \text{ mg} + 6.6 \text{ kg} + 73 \text{ g}$

5. a) A doctor might prescribe 13 kiloliters of a very strong medicine. True or False?
   b) What is the most reasonable estimate for the weight of a pebble – *g, kg, mg* ?
   c) In a lab experiment, 500 mL of salt water was added to 1.78 L of water. Later 340 mL of the solution was drained off. How much of the solution still remains?
   d) The manager of a university cafeteria needs to purchase 55 kg of mayonnaise. If his wholesaler sells mayonnaise in 5000-g jugs for $3.95 each, how much will the manager have to spend?

Teaching Notes:

- Remind students that metric ton, kilogram, gram, and milligram are common metric weight units, and that kiloliter, liter, and milliliter are common metric volume units.
- Some students become confused with all the unit abbreviations. Refer them ahead to the *Unit Abbreviation* chart at the beginning of section 6.4.

Answers: 1a) L, b) kL, c) mL, d) g, e) kg, f) mg; 2a) 2700, b) 0.476, c) 414.2, d) 97,000; 3a) 2,000,000, b) 42,000, c) 0.148, d) 78,000; 4a) 129.335 L, b) 6673.826 g; 5a) false, b) g, c) 1.94 L, d) $4345

Mini-Lecture 6.4
Converting Units

Learning Objectives:

1. Convert between metric and American length units.
2. Convert between metric and American volume units.
3. Convert between metric and American weight units.
4. Convert between metric and American speed units.
5. Convert between Fahrenheit and Celsius degrees.
6. Application problems.

Examples:

1. Perform each length conversion. Round to the nearest hundredth when necessary.

   a) 7 km to mi   b) 5.7 m to in.   c) 19.7 in. to cm   d) 85.7 m to yd

2. Perform each volume conversion. Round to the nearest hundredth when necessary.

   a) 40 L to gal   b) 42 qt to L   c) 11 L to qt   d) 6.2 gal to L

3. Perform each weight conversion. Round to the nearest hundredth when necessary.

   a) 59 kg to lb   b) 6 oz to g   c) 75.5 lb to kg   d) 26.1 g to oz

4. Perform each speed conversion. Round to the nearest hundredth when necessary.

   a) 22 mi/hr to km/hr   b) 23.4 km/hr to mi/hr   c) 54.9 mi/hr to ft/sec

5. Perform each temperature conversion. Round to the nearest hundredth when necessary.

   a) 860°F to Celsius   b) 125°C to Fahrenheit

6. a) A weather forecaster has predicted a high temperature of 27°C for tomorrow. Find
      this temperature in degrees Fahrenheit.
   b) Jackie and Mike drove 440 miles through the United States and 146 kilometers
      through Canada. How many kilometers did they travel in total?
   c) Roy weighs 186 pounds. How much does he weigh in kilograms?

Teaching Notes:

- Remind students to use "multiply by a unit fraction" whenever possible.
- Some students become confused with all the unit abbreviations. Refer them to the unit
  abbreviation chart at the beginning of this section.

*Answers: 1a) 4.34, b) 224.35, c) 50.04, d) 93.41; 2a) 10.56, b) 39.73, c) 11.66, d) 23.50; 3a) 129.8, b) 170.1,
c) 34.28, d) 0.92; 4a) 35.42, b) 14.51, c) 80.52; 5a) 460°C, b) 257°F; 6a) 80.6°F, b) 854.4 km, c) 84.444kg*

Mini-Lecture 6.5
Solving Applied Measurement Problems

Learning Objectives:

1. Solve applied problems involving metric and American units.

Examples:

a) A rectangular oil painting measures 79 cm by 142 cm. The painting is framed in material that costs $4 per meter. What will it cost to frame the painting?

b) A beverage company received an order from the local college's cafeteria. It filled 100 bottles with 75 liters of soda. How many milliliters of soda were in each bottle?

c) A ship arrived from Columbia carrying 4.6 tons of coffee beans. If the port tax on coffee beans is $0.016 per pound, what is the tax on the entire shipment of coffee beans? (Round to the nearest cent if necessary.)

d) A recipe from a French cookbook said to preheat the oven to 160°C. Joe set his American oven to 327.2°F. What was the discrepancy in degrees Fahrenheit between the two temperatures?

e) Brian and Heather drove 469 miles in 7 hours. What was their average speed in kilometers per hour? (Round to the nearest whole number if necessary.)

f) Jennifer bought 19 quarts of milk for the preschool where she works. Her French co-worker says that the center will only need 11 liters of milk. How many extra quarts of milk did Jennifer buy?

g) A box of cereal contains 15 ounces of cereal. Of this, 11 ounces are sugar-coated puffs and the remaining ounces are miniature marshmallows. How many grams of marshmallows are in the box?

h) Karen and Ivan traveled at 120 kilometers/hour for 3.2 hours. Their total trip will be 650 miles long. How many miles do they still need to travel? (Round to the nearest whole mile if necessary.)

Teaching Notes:

- Refer students to:
  - section 6.1 for conversions within American system
  - section 6.2 for conversions within metric length units
  - section 6.3 for conversions within metric volume and weight units
  - section 6.4 for conversions between metric and American systems

Answers: 1a) $17.68, b) 750 ml, c) $147.20, d) 7.2 °F, e) 108 km/hr, f) 7.34 qt, g) 113.4 g, h) 412 mi

Mini-Lecture 7.1
Angles

Learning Objectives:

1. Understand angle types.
2. Identify types of angles.
3. Find the measure of angles.
4. Application problems.

Examples:

1. Draw an example of each term.

   a) adjacent angles   b) vertical angles   c) supplementary angles
   d) complementary angles   e) acute angle   f) obtuse angle
   g) transversal   h) alternate interior angles

2. Identify which angles, if any, are the type listed.

   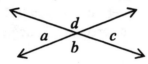

   a) obtuse   b) acute   c) supplementary

   d) complementary   e) same measure   f) adjacent

3. Find the measure of the angle(s).

   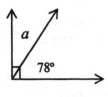   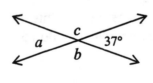   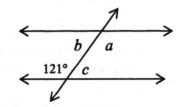

   a) $\angle a$ b) $\angle a$, $\angle b$, and $\angle c$ c) $\angle a$, $\angle b$, and $\angle c$

4. A cruise ship is leaving Hawaii and is heading 65° north of west. It then turns left 13°. Describe the new course in terms of how many degrees north of west the ship is heading.

Teaching Notes:

- Some students are unfamiliar with the vocabulary in this section and need repetition.
- Refer students to the *Parallel Lines Cut by a Transversal* description in the textbook.

Answers: *1a-h) answers vary; 2a) b,d, b) a,c, c) a and d, a and b, b and c, c and d, d) none, e) a and c, b and d,*
f) a and b, b and c, c and d, a and d; 3a) 12°, b) a=37°, b=143°, c=143°, c) a=121°, b=59°, c=59°; 4) 52°N of W

Mini-Lecture 7.2
Rectangles and Squares

Learning Objectives:

1. Find the perimeters and areas of rectangles and squares.
2. Find the perimeters and areas of shapes made up of rectangles and squares.
3. Application problems.

Examples:

1. Find the perimeters and areas of the rectangle and square.

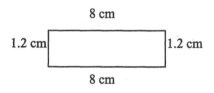 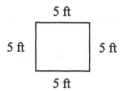

   a) perimeter = ____   b) perimeter = ____
       area = ____   area = ____

2. Find the perimeters and areas of the shapes.

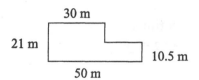

   a) perimeter = ____
   b) area = ____

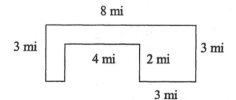

   a) perimeter = ____
   b) area = ____

3. A badminton area will feature four badminton courts, taking up a total area of 400 ft by 80 ft. If sand costs $0.37 per square foot, how much will it cost to sand the court area?

Teaching Notes:

- Some students are unfamiliar with the concept of perpendicular sides.
- Some students have trouble visualizing how the shapes in example 2 are made up of squares and rectangles. They need to see a sketch of the underlying shapes.
- Some students have trouble remembering the perimeter formula. Remind them that they just need to remember that the perimeter is the sum of all the sides.

Answers: *1a) per=18.4 cm, area=9.6 cm², b) per=20 ft, area=25 sqft; 2a) per=111.5 m, area=840 m², b) per=26 mi, area=16 mi²; 3) $11,840*

Mini-Lecture 7.3
Parallelograms, Trapezoids, and Rhombuses

Learning Objectives:

1. Understand the meaning of parallelogram, trapezoid, and rhombus.
2. Find the perimeters and areas of parallelograms, trapezoids, and rhombuses
3. Find the perimeters and areas of shapes made up of parallelograms and trapezoids.

Examples:

1. Draw an example of the shape.

   a) parallelogram   b) rhombus   c) trapezoid

2. Find the perimeter and area of each shape.

   a)

   13.4 in.

   8.2 in.   8.2 in.   6.5 in.   perimeter = _____
                                                 area = _____
   13.4 in.

   b)

   4 m

   4 m   4 m   3 m   perimeter = _____
                                      area = _____
   4 m

   c)

   25 ft

   23 ft   23 ft   20 ft   perimeter = _____
                                           area = _____
   18 ft

3. Find the perimeter and area of the shape made up of a parallelogram and trapezoid.

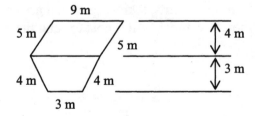

   9 m

   5 m   5 m   4 m

   4 m   4 m   3 m

   3 m

Teaching Notes:

- Students must be clear on the meaning of parallel lines.
- Encourage students to see the logic behind the area formulas.

Answers: 1a-c) answers vary; 2a) per=43.2 in., area=87.1 in.^{2}, b) per=16 m, area=12 m^2, c) per=89 ft, area=430 ft^2; 3) per=30 m, area=54 m^2

M-42

Mini-Lecture 7.4
Triangles

Learning Objectives:

1. Understand basic triangle facts.
2. Find the missing angle in a triangle.
3. Find the perimeter and area of a triangle.

Examples:

1. Fill in the missing information and draw an example of each.

   a) A triangle is a three-sided figure with _____ angles.
   b) The sum of the measures of the angles in a triangle is _____.
   c) A triangle with two equal sides is called an _____.
   d) A triangle with three equal sides is called an _____.
   e) A triangle with one 90° angle is called a _____.

2. Find the missing angle in the triangle.

   a) Two angles are 28° and 72°.   b) Two angles are 139° and 20°.

3. Find the perimeter and area of the triangle.

   a)

   5 m
   3 m
   4 m

   perimeter = _____
   area = _____

   b)

   25 ft
   15 ft   10 ft
   33 ft

   perimeter = _____
   area = _____

   c) An equilateral triangle with sides of 6.8 yd and height of 5.4 yd.

Teaching Notes:

- Students must be clear on the meanings of isosceles, equilateral, and right triangle.
- Students have trouble visualizing the height of a triangle if the height lies outside of the triangle.

Answers: 1a) 3, b) 180°, c) isosceles triangle, d) equilateral triangle, e) right triangle; 2a) 80°, b) 21°; 3a) per=12 m, area=6 m², b) per=73 ft, area=165 sqft, c) per=20.4 yd, area=18.36 yd²

Mini-Lecture 7.5
Square Roots

Learning Objectives:

1. Evaluate the square root of a number that is a perfect square.
2. Approximate the square root of a number that is not a perfect square.
3. Evaluate the sums of square roots of perfect squares.
4. Application problems.

Examples:

1. Evaluate the square root.

    a) $\sqrt{4}$ b) $\sqrt{25}$ c) $\sqrt{16}$ d) $\sqrt{121}$ e) $\sqrt{169}$

2. Approximate the square root to the nearest thousandth.

    a) $\sqrt{8}$ b) $\sqrt{33}$ c) $\sqrt{105}$ d) $\sqrt{136}$ e) $\sqrt{50}$

3. Evaluate the square roots first, then perform the operations. Round square roots to the nearest thousandth if necessary.

    a) $\sqrt{121} + \sqrt{25}$ b) $\sqrt{169} - \sqrt{16} - \sqrt{4}$ c) $\sqrt{25} \times \sqrt{121}$

    d) $\sqrt{33} + \sqrt{25}$ e) $\sqrt{136} - \sqrt{50}$ f) $\sqrt{105} \times \sqrt{8}$

4. Solve the following application problems. Round to the nearest thousandth when needed.

    a) Find the length of the side of a square with area 289 m^2.

    b) Find the length of the side of a square with area 311 cm^2.

    c) The diagonal of an indoor volleyball court in some gyms measures $\sqrt{1300}$ ft. Find the length of this diagonal to the nearest tenth of a foot.

Teaching Notes:

- Encourage students to evaluate the square roots of perfect squares up to $\sqrt{144}$ without using a calculator or table.
- For example 2 refer students to the table of square root approximations in this section of the textbook.

Answers: _1a) 2, b) 5, c) 4, d) 11, e) 13; 2a) 2.828, b) 5.745, c) 10.247, d) 11.662, e) 7.071; 3a) 16, b) 7, c) 55, d) 10.745, e) 4.591, f) 17.233; 4a) 17 m, b) 17.635 cm, c) 36.1 ft_

Mini-Lecture 7.6
The Pythagorean Theorem

Learning Objectives:

1. Understand the terminology of right triangles and the Pythagorean Theorem.
2. Find the missing length of a right triangle when two of the lengths are given.
3. Solve for the missing sides of special right triangles.
4. Application problems.

Examples:

1. Draw a right triangle and label the sides as "leg", "leg", and "hypotenuse". Then write the Pythagorean Theorem.

2. Find the missing length in the right triangle. Round to the nearest thousandth.

   a)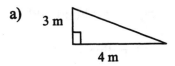
   3 m
   4 m

   b) 6 ft
   18 ft

   c) leg = 12 m, leg = 4 m

   d) hypotenuse = 22 yd, leg = 14 yd

   e) leg = 6 ft, leg = 6 ft

   f) leg = 53 cm, hypotenuse = 75 cm

3. Using your knowledge of special right triangles, find the missing information. Round to the nearest tenth.

   a) A 30°- 60°- 90° triangle has a hypotenuse of 10 in. Find the length of each leg.

   b) A 45°- 45°- 90° triangle has a leg of 8 m. Find the length of the other leg and of the hypotenuse.

4. a) A 30-ft ladder is placed against a college classroom building at a point 22 ft above the ground. What is the distance from the base of the ladder to the building?
   b) Betty's kite is flying 45 yd directly above a rock. The rock is 23 yd from where she is standing. Find the length of the string holding the kite.

Teaching Notes:

- Students must be clear on the meaning of hypotenuse.
- Some students have difficulty solving the Pythagorean Theorem for a missing leg.
- Many students must be reminded of special right triangle properties.

*Answers: 1a) answers vary, (hypotenuse)² = (leg)² + (leg)²; 2a) 5m, b)16.971ft, c) 12.649m, d) 16.971yd, e) 8.485ft,
f) 53.066cm; 3a) 5in, 8.7in, b) leg=8m, hyp=11.3m; 4a) about 20ft, b) about 51yd*

Mini-Lecture 7.7
Circles

Learning Objectives:

1. Convert diameter to radius, and convert radius to diameter.
2. Find the circumference and area of a circle.
3. Application problems.

Examples:

1. Find the diameter or radius of each circle. Round to the nearest hundredth.

   a) radius r = 10 ft

   b) radius r = 6.2 cm

   c) radius r = 34.9 m

   d) diameter d = 49 yd

   e) diameter d = 0.02 cm

   f) diameter d = 13.4 in.

2. Find the circumference and area of each circle. Round to the nearest hundredth.

   a) radius = 12 cm

   b) radius = 24.06 ft

   c) radius = 0.3 in.

   d) diameter = 44.4 m

   e) diameter = 1.004 yd

   f) diameter = 2300 mi

3. Solve the following application problems. Round to the nearest hundredth.

   a) A bicycle wheel makes six revolutions. Determine how far the bicycle travels in feet if the diameter of the wheel is 24 in.

   b) A radio station sends out radio waves in all directions from a tower at the center of the circle of broadcast range. Determine how large an area is reached if the diameter of the broadcast range is 135 mi.

   c) Find the area of the shaded region.

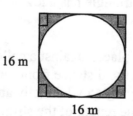

16 m

16 m

Teaching Notes:

- Some students need to be reminded to square the radius before multiplying by π.
- Many students have difficulty solving problems such as 3a) and 3c) and need to see several examples of each type.
- Encourage students to start by drawing and labeling the circle whenever they are unsure where to begin with a problem.

Answers: 1a) 20ft, b) 12.4cm, c) 69.8m, d) 24.5yd, e) 0.01cm, f) 6.7in; 2a) circ=75.4cm, area=452.4cm², b) circ=151.2ft, area=1818.6ft², c) cir=1.88in, area=0.28in², d) circ=139.49m, area=1548.30m², e) circ=3.15yd, area=0.79yd², f) circ=7225.66mi, area=4,154,756.28mi²; 3a) 37.70ft, b) 14,313.88mi², c) 54.94m²

Mini-Lecture 7.8
Volume

Learning Objectives:

1. Find the volume of a rectangular solid.
2. Find the volume of a cylinder.
3. Find the volume of a sphere.
4. Find the volume of a cone.
5. Find the volume of a pyramid.

Examples:

1. Find the volume of each rectangular solid. Round to the nearest tenth.

   a) width = 16 mm, length = 22 mm, height = 21 mm
   b) width = 1.3 ft, length = 4.5 ft, height = 3.1 ft

2. Find the volume of each cylinder. Round to the nearest tenth.

   a) diameter = 12 cm, height = 34 cm   b) diameter = 55.4 mm, height = 3.3 mm

3. Find the volume of each sphere. Round to the nearest tenth.

   a) radius = 4 in.   b) radius = 240 mi   c) hemisphere, radius = 4 cm

4. Find the volume of each cone. Round to the nearest tenth.

   a) height = 14 in., radius = 6 in.   b) height = 22 cm, radius = 13 cm

5. Find the volume of each pyramid. Round to the nearest thousandth.

   a) height 12 m, rectangular base 6 m by 10 m
   b) height 0.5 cm, rectangular base 0.2 cm by 0.2 cm

Teaching Notes:

- Some students find it helpful to visualize the volume of a solid as the product of a base area and the height.
- Encourage students to start by drawing and labeling the solid whenever they are unsure where to begin with a problem.
- Refer students to the volume formulas and drawings in the textbook.

Answers: *1a) 7392mm³, b) 18.1ft³; 2a) 3845.3cm2, b) 7954.7mm³; 3a) 268.1in³, b) 57,905,835.8mi³, c) 134.0cm³; 4a) 527.8in³, b) 3893.5cm³; 5a) 240m³, b) 0.007cm³*

Mini-Lecture 7.9
Similar Geometric Figures

Learning Objectives:

1. Find the corresponding sides of similar triangles.
2. Find the missing side of similar triangles.
3. Find the missing side of similar geometric figures.
4. Application problems.

Examples:

1. Find the corresponding sides of similar triangles.

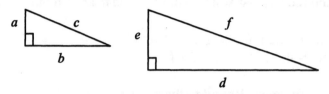

2. Find the missing side *n* of similar triangles. Round to the nearest tenth.

   a)   b)

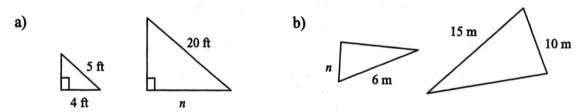

3. Find the missing side of similar geometric figures. Round to the nearest tenth.

   a)   b)

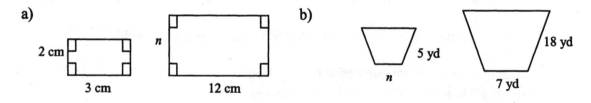

4. Jerry is rock climbing in Colorado. He is 6 feet tall and his shadow measures 9 feet long. The rock he wants to climb casts a shadow of 580 feet. How tall is the rock?

Teaching Notes:

- Some students find it helpful to briefly review proportion problems before doing the examples above.
- Encourage students to draw and label a diagram before solving an application problem.

Answers: 1) c and f, a and e, b and d; 2a) 16ft, b) 4m; 3a) 8cm, b) 1.9yd; 4) 386.7ft

Mini-Lecture 7.10
Solving Applied Problems Involving Geometry

Learning Objectives:

1. Solve applied problems involving geometric shapes.

Examples:

a) The Parker family started a vegetable garden. The rectangular garden measures 17 ft long and 12 ft wide. To keep out animals, they had to surround it with fencing, which costs $0.70 per foot. How much did the fencing cost, to the nearest cent?

b) The McCabes want to put siding on the front of their home in Boston. The house dimensions are 26 ft by 35 ft. There is one door that measueres 6 ft by 3 ft. There are also 7 windows measuring 3 ft by 3 ft. Excluding windows and doors, how many square feet of siding will be needed?

c) A conical pile of grain is 20 ft in diameter and 17 ft high. How many bushels of grain are in a pile if 1 cubic foot = 0.8 bushel? Round to the nearest tenth.

d) A satellite orbits the Earth in a circular pattern. Assume that the radius of orbit is 6800 km. If the satellite goes through one orbit around the Earth in 3 hours, what is its speed in kilometers per hour? Round to the nearest whole number.

e) A candy company makes decorative cylinder-shaped canisters and fills them with red hot candies. They want to make 600 canisters and need to determine how much candy to buy. If the canisters are 6 inches in diameter and 5 inches tall, what is the total number of cubic inches that will be filled with candy?

f) A commercial painter can paint 172 square feet in 24 minutes. She will be painting four planks of wood. They measure 3 ft by 11 ft, 6 ft by 18 ft, 2 ft by 17 ft, and 3 ft by 18 ft. How many minutes will it take her to paint all the planks? Round to the nearest whole minute.

Teaching Notes:

- Many students find these application problems difficult.
- Refer students to the *Mathematics Blueprint for Problem Solving* in the textbook.
- Some students enjoy sharing real-life examples of how they used similar problem solving to solve a home- or work-related problem.

Answers: 1a) $40.60, b) 829 ft^2, c) 1424.2 bushels, d) 14,241 km/hr, e) 84,823 in^3, f) 32 min

Mini-Lecture 8.1
Circle Graphs

Learning Objectives:

1. Read a circle graph with numerical values.
2. Read a circle graph with percentage values.

Examples:

1. An Olympic softball pitcher has thrown 680 pitches during the first part of the softball season. The following circle graph shows the results of her pitches. Use the circle graph to answer the accompanying questions.

Results of 680 Pitches

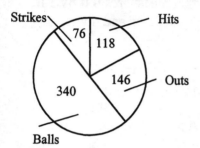

a) What category had the fewest pitches?
b) How many pitches were balls?
c) How many pitches were either hits or balls?
d) What is the ratio of the number of strikes to the total number of pitches?
e) What is the ratio of the number of balls to the number of strikes?

2. The following circle graph indicates the percent of the total game points that were scored in each quarter of a Celtics game. Use the circle graph to answer the accompanying questions.

Celtics Scoring per Quarter

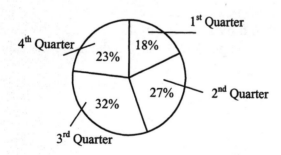

a) In which quarter did the Celtics score the most points?
b) What percent of the points were scored during the first two quarters?
c) If the total number of points scored during the game was 90, how many points were score during the fourth quarter?
d) How many points were scored in the last two quarters?

Teaching Notes:

- Remind students that the order of a ratio is important.
- Some students are confused about when it is all right to add percents. Tell students that it is all right to add percents in example 2b) because both percents are of the same value – they are percents of the total points scored in the basketball game.

Answers: *1a) strikes, b) 340, c) 458, d) 19/170, e) 85/19; 2a) 3rd, b) 45%, c) about 21, d) about 50*

Mini-Lecture 8.2
Bar Graphs and Line Graphs

Learning Objectives:

1. Read and interpret a bar graph.
2. Read and interpret a double bar graph.
3. Read and interpret line graphs.

Examples:

1. The following bar graph shows the population of Concord, MA, from 1940 to 2000.

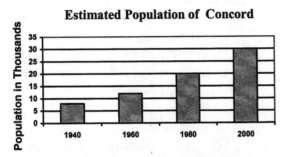

a) What was the population in 1980?
b) What was the population in 1940?
c) Between what years did the population of Concord increase the smallest amount? What is the amount?

2. The following double bar graph shows the points scored per quarter in a basketball game.

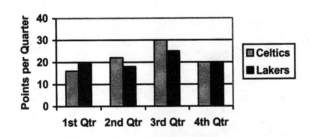

a) How many points did the Celtics score in the 3rd quarter?
b) How many points did the Lakers score in the 4th quarter?
c) In what quarter was there the biggest difference in scoring? What was the difference?

3. The following line graph shows the average monthly rent in Worcester, MA.

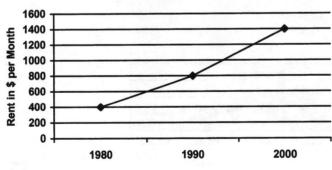

a) What was the rent in 1990?
b) Between which years did the rent increase the most?
c) What was the increase in rent between 1980 and 2000?

Teaching Notes:

- Ask students for local rent values and make a comparison line graph on top of example 3.

Answers: 1a) 20,000, b) 8,000, c) 1940 to 1960, about 4000; 2a) 30, b) 20, c) 3rd, about 5; 3a) $800/month, b) 1990 to 2000, c) $1000/month

Mini-Lecture 8.3
Histograms

Learning Objectives:

1. Understand and interpret a histogram.
2. Construct a histogram from raw data.

Examples:

1. The following histogram shows the number of students by test score range.

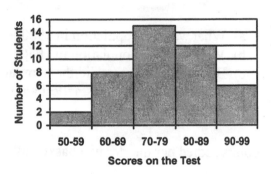

a) How many students scored a C on the test if the Professor considers a test score of 70-79 a C?
b) How many students scored less than 70 on the test?
c) How many students scored between 80 and 99 on the test?

2. Each italicized/bold number below is the number of miles the Briskie family has driven in a week.

a) Determine the frequency of the class intervals.

				Miles Driven (Class Interval)	Tally	Frequency
152	*236*	*563*	*363*	100 – 199	___	___
162	*333*	*257*	*380*	200 – 299	___	___
415	*498*	*140*	*299*	300 – 399	___	___
385	*213*	*545*	*367*	400 – 499	___	___
315	*293*	*415*	*312*	500 – 599	___	___

b) Construct a histogram using the frequency data.

(Answer)

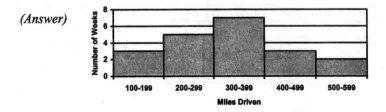

Teaching Notes:

• Many students will need to see another example for constructing a histogram from data.

Answers: 1a) 15, b) 10, c) 18; 2a) frequencies=3,5,7,3,2

Mini-Lecture 8.4
Mean, Median, and Mode

Learning Objectives:

1. Find the mean of a set of numbers.
2. Find the median of a set of numbers.
3. Find the mode of a set of numbers.

Examples:

1. Find the mean of each list of numbers. Round to the nearest thousandth when necessary.

   a) The numbers of points Joe scored playing basketball over the last four games were as follows: 18, 7, 25, 18

   b) The numbers of miles Jackie ran over the last four days were as follows: 5, 9, 10, 7

   c) The captain of the college baseball team achieved the following results:

	Hits	Times at Bat
Game 1	1	4
Game 2	3	6
Game 3	2	5

   Find his batting average by dividing his total number of hits by the total times at bat.

2. Find the median of each list of numbers. Round to the nearest tenth if necessary.

   a) Number of hits in 5 softball games: 5, 11, 15, 7, 2
   b) Number of pages in 4 books: 320, 250, 350, 311
   c) Annual salaries of local cable television employees: $15,500, $21,340, $17,885, $32,429, $20,479

3. Find the mode(s) of each list of numbers. Round to the nearest tenth if necessary.

   a) 20, 33, 33, 49   b) 394, 348, 332, 348, 329, 394   c) 82, 44, 13, 90

Teaching Notes:

- Some students need to see another example similar to 1c).
- Most students need to be told to rearrange the numbers from smallest to largest when determining the median, and to average the two middle values if there is an even number of values.

Answers: 1a) 17 pts, b) 7.75 mi, c) 0.400; 2a) 7 hits, b) 315.5 pgs, c) $20,479; 3a) 33, b) 394, 348, c) no mode

Mini-Lecture 9.1
Adding Signed Numbers

Learning Objectives:

1. Add two numbers with the same sign.
2. Add two signed numbers with different signs.
3. Add three or more signed numbers.
4. Application problems.

Examples:

1. Add each pair of signed numbers that have the same sign.

   a) $-5 + (-3)$

   b) $5 + 4$

   c) $-2.1 + (-7.3)$

   d) $-10 + (-10)$

   e) $4.9 + 8.1$

   f) $-\dfrac{3}{4} + \left(-\dfrac{5}{8}\right)$

2. Add each pair of signed numbers that have different signs.

   a) $5 + (-3)$

   b) $-5 + 3$

   c) $-23 + 17$

   d) $4 + (-50)$

   e) $6.2 + (-3.3)$

   f) $-\dfrac{2}{12} + \dfrac{3}{24}$

3. Add.

   a) $13 + (-5) + 2$

   b) $(-15) + 3 + (-10) + 22$

   c) $(-7.2) + (-3.5) + 2.4$

   d) $\left(\dfrac{8}{9}\right) + \left(-\dfrac{2}{3}\right) + \left(-\dfrac{3}{18}\right)$

4. Last night the temperature was -5°F. The temperature dropped 12°F this afternoon. What was the new temperature?

Teaching Notes:

- Some students understand signed numbers better if they think of depositing and withdrawing money from a bank account.
- Some students need to see the problems done on a number line at first.
- Refer students to the ***Addition Rule for Two Numbers with the Same/Different Sign*** charts in the textbook.

Answers: *1a) –8, b) 9, c) –9.4, d) –20, e) 13, f) –1 3/8; 2a) 2, b) –2, c) –6, d) –46, e) 2.9, f) –1/24; 3a) 10, b) 0, c) –8.3, d) 1/18; 4) -17°F*

Mini-Lecture 9.2
Subtracting Signed Numbers

Learning Objectives:

1. Subtract one signed number from another.
2. Solve problems involving both addition and subtraction of signed numbers.
3. Solve simple applied problems that involve the subtraction of signed numbers.

Examples:

1. Subtract the signed numbers by adding the opposite of the second number to the first number.

   a) 3 - 5

   b) 3 – (-5)

   c) -3 - 5

   d) -3 – (-5)

   e) -20 – 6

   f) 13 – (-2)

   g) $-\dfrac{3}{4} - \left(\dfrac{5}{8}\right)$

   h) 5.4 – 9.2

   i) -6.6 – (-2.9)

2. Perform each set of operations, working from left to right.

   a) 3 – (-9) + 6

   b) -5 – 7 – (-12)

   c) 12 + (-4) – 13

   d) -2 + 8 – (-15) + 9

   e) 44 + (-3) + (-2)

   f) -2 – 4 + (-5)

3. a) Find the difference in altitude between a mountain 5436 feet high and a gorge 213 feet below sea level.

   b) Find the difference in temperature in Conway, New Hampshire, between -3°F during the day and -12°F during the night.

   c) In January the value of one share of a certain stock was $45. During the next three days, the value rose $5 ¼, fell $2 ½ , and fell $1 ¼. What was the value of one share at the end of those three days?

Teaching Notes:

- Many students find subtracting signed numbers difficult at first.
- Some students forget to change the sign of the second number after changing subtraction to addition. Encourage students to show the step: 3 – 5 = 3 + (-5)
- Refer students to the **Subtraction of Signed Numbers** charts in the textbook.

Answers: 1a) –2, b) 8, c) –8, d) 2, e) –26, f) 15, g) –1 3/8, h) –3.8, i) –3.7; 2a) 18, b) 0, c) –5, d) 30, e) 39, f) –11; 3a) 5649 ft, b) 9 °F, c) $46 1/5

Mini-Lecture 9.3
Multiplying and Dividing Signed Numbers

Learning Objectives:

1. Multiply two signed numbers.
2. Divide two signed numbers.
3. Multiply three or more signed numbers.
4. Application problems.

Examples:

1. Multiply.

   a) $(3)(5)$

   b) $(3)(-5)$

   c) $(-3)(-5)$

   d) $(-24)(3)$

   e) $(2.2)(-3.3)$

   f) $\left(-\dfrac{3}{4}\right)\left(-\dfrac{8}{9}\right)$

2. Divide.

   a) $-16 \div 8$

   b) $24 \div 2$

   c) $-9 \div -3$

   d) $45.6 \div -3.8$

   e) $-6.4 \div -17.6$

   f) $-\dfrac{3}{5} \div \dfrac{15}{20}$

   g) $\dfrac{\dfrac{4}{7}}{-\dfrac{3}{14}}$

   h) $\dfrac{-33.3}{-12}$

3. Multiply each set of signed numbers.

   a) $(-4)(-3)(2)$

   b) $5(-7)(3)(-6)(-1)$

   c) $9(-3)(5)(0)$

   d) $(-6)(5)(5)\left(\dfrac{3}{4}\right)$

   e) $8(-2.2)(-4.7)(9)$

4. The temperatures in Boston for the first three days of January were -2°F, 10°F, and 4°F. What was the average temperature for those three days?

Teaching Notes:

- Most students find the multiply and divide rules for signed numbers easy to remember.
- Remind students that multiplication is commutative. So in example 3d), they can choose to move the ¾ next to the –6 and cancel before multiplying.

Answers: *1a) 15, b) –15, c) 15, d) –72, e) –7.26, f) 2/3; 2a) –2, b) 12, c) 3, d) –12, e) 0.3̄6̄, f) –4/5, g) –2 2/3, h) 2.775; 3a) 24, b) –630, c) 0, d) –112 ½, e) 744.48; 4) 4°F*

Mini-Lecture 9.4
Order of Operations with Signed Numbers

Learning Objectives:

1. Use order of operations (integers only).
2. Use order of operations (integers, fractions, and decimals).
3. Use order of operations (exponents).
4. Application problems.

Examples:

1. Perform the indicated operations in the proper order.

   a) $5 + (-5) + (-8)$

   b) $7(-4) + 4$

   c) $3(-8) + 5(4)$

   d) $8 \div 4(-3) + (-8)$

   e) $64 - 5(6) + (-21) \div 3$

   f) $-9 - (-5)(-6) + (-36) \div (-4)$

2. Perform the indicated operations in the proper order.

   a) $\dfrac{8(-3) - 4 + 10}{-90 \div 5}$

   b) $\dfrac{-4 - (-8)}{30 - 30 \div 5}$

   c) $\dfrac{1}{4} - \dfrac{1}{2} \div \dfrac{4}{5}$

   d) $2.8(-3) + 6(5.1)$

   e) $\dfrac{1}{3} \div \left(-\dfrac{2}{5}\right)\left(-\dfrac{5}{6}\right) + (-18)$

3. Perform the indicated operations in the proper order.

   a) $-9 - 3^2 - (-6)$

   b) $7(-5) + (3 - 5)^2$

   c) $6^2 - 4(3) + 24 \div 8$

   d) $\left(\dfrac{1}{2}\right)^2 + \dfrac{2}{5}\left(-\dfrac{3}{4}\right)$

   e) $-3.2 - (2.2)^2 - (-4.2)$

4. After 1 week of dieting, Pedro lost 2.1 pounds. The second week he lost twice as many as the first week, and at the end of the third week he had lost a total of 9.4 pounds. How many pounds did Pedro lose during the third week?

Teaching Notes:

- Many students find this section difficult.
- Many students do not understand the difference between -3^2 and $(-3)^2$.
- Refer students to the *Order of Operations for Signed Numbers* chart in the textbook.

Answers: 1a) –8, b) –24, c) –4, d) –14, e) 27, f) –30; 2a) 1, b) 1/6, c) –3/8, d) 22.2, e) –17 11/36; 3a) –12, b) –31, c) 27, d) –1/20, e) –3.84; 4) 3.116 lb

Mini-Lecture 9.5
Scientific Notation

Learning Objectives:

1. Change numbers in standard notation to scientific notation.
2. Change numbers in scientific notation to standard notation.
3. Add and subtract numbers in scientific notation.
4. Application problems.

Examples:

1. Write in scientific notation.

   a) 96

   b) 632

   c) 102.345

   d) 730,000

   e) 0.054

   f) 0.000657

   g) 0.000000091

   h) 0.023664

2. Write in standard notation.

   a) 2.43×10^3

   b) 8.7794×10^6

   c) 3.2×10^{-2}

   d) 5.332×10^{-5}

   e) 8.0926×10^{-7}

   f) 4.5×10^{12}

3. Perform the indicated operation.

   a) $3.49 \times 10^7 + 5.67 \times 10^7$

   b) $8.32 \times 10^8 - 5.39 \times 10^8$

   c) $6.42 \times 10^5 + 3.2 \times 10^6$

   d) $7.553 \times 10^4 - 9.92 \times 10^5$

4. a) The land area of China is 3.692×10^6 square miles, and that of India is 1.18×10^6 square miles. What is the total land area of China and India expressed in standard notation?

   b) One particle of dust was found to have a mass of 7.13×10^{-14} grams. Another particle of dust was found to have a mass of 6.54×10^{-14} grams. What was the difference in the masses of the two dust particles?

Teaching Notes:

- Some students are confused about whether to put a positive or negative exponent on a number that is changed to scientific notation.
- Many students do not realize that the numbers in example 3 must have the same power of 10 before their decimal parts can be added.

Answers: 1a) $9.6x10^1$, b) $6.32x10^2$, c) $1.02345x10^2$, d) $7.3x10^5$, e) $5.4x10^{-2}$, f) $6.57x10^{-4}$, g) $9.1x10^{-8}$, h) $2.3664x10^{-2}$; 2a) 2430, b) 8,779,400, c) 0.032, d) 0.00005332, e) 0.00000080926, f) 4,500,000,000,000; 3a) $9.16x10^7$, b) $2.93x10^8$, c) $3.842x10^6$, d) $-9.1647x10^5$; 4a) 4,872,000 mi^2, b) $5.9x10^{-15}$ g

Mini-Lecture 10.1
Variables and Like Terms

Learning Objectives:

1. Recognize the variable in an equation or a formula.
2. Write an equation without multiplication signs.
3. Combine like terms (no fractions).
4. Combine like terms (with fractions).

Examples:

1. Name the variables in each equation.

   a) $p = 4s$

   b) $y = 2x + 3$

   c) $A = \dfrac{1}{2}bh$

2. Write each equation without multiplication signs.

   a) $C = 2 \times \pi \times r$

   b) $T = 4 \times f - 5 \times t$

   c) $p = 7 \times m - 2 \times n$

3. Combine like terms.

   a) $4x + 3x$

   b) $-7x + 4x + x$

   c) $5x + 9x - 6x$

   d) $7x - 4 - 4x + 9$

   e) $-15x + 3y - 5x + y$

   f) $2.4x + 2 - 7x - 0.8$

   g) $-3x + 0.4y + 0.3x + 2y$

   h) $4a - 6b - 2b + 3a$

   i) $6.5a + 3.3b - 4.3a$

4. Combine like terms.

   a) $\dfrac{1}{2}x + \dfrac{2}{3}x$

   b) $-\dfrac{5}{8}x + \dfrac{3}{5} + \left(-\dfrac{3}{8}x\right)$

   c) $\dfrac{5}{6}x + \dfrac{7}{8}y - \dfrac{2}{3}x$

Teaching Notes:

- Some students do not realize that $a \times b$ is the same as ab.
- Emphasize the importance of knowing what the word "term" means.
- Some students do not know that a variable without a numerical coefficient, as in 3b), actually has a coefficient of 1.

Answers: 1a) p,s, b) x,y, c) A,b,h; 2a) C=2πr, b) T=4f-5t, c) p=7m-2n; 3a) 7x, b) –2x, c) 8x, d) 3x+5, e) –20x+4y, f) –4.6x+1.2, g) –2.7x+2.4y, h) 7a-8b, i) 2.2a+3.3b; 4a) (7/6)x, b) –x+(3/5), c) (1/6)x+(7/8)y

Mini-Lecture 10.2
The Distributive Property

Learning Objectives:

1. Remove parentheses using the distributive property.
2. Simplify expressions by removing parentheses and combining like terms.
3. Application problems.

Examples:

1. Simplify.

    a) $2(x+6)$

    b) $3(4x-2)$

    c) $(-2)(x+6)$

    d) $(-5)(-3a-4b)$

    e) $(7m-3n)(4)$

    f) $5(2p+4q-1)$

    g) $(-1)(2.3x-4.5y)$

    h) $2\left(\dfrac{3}{4}x+\dfrac{5}{6}\right)$

    i) $\dfrac{1}{3}\left(6x+7y-\dfrac{1}{2}\right)$

2. Simplify.

    a) $4(3x+y)+2(x+y)$

    b) $3(5x-y)-2(x-y)$

    c) $6(2.5x+1)-2(x+2.3)$

    d) $6(5x+1.9y)+3.2(x+4y)$

    e) $-6(5x-2y)-(x-4y)$

    f) $3(x+2y-z)-2(3x-y+3z)$

3. Illustrate the distributive property using the area of two rectangles:

a
$b \qquad c$

Teaching Notes:

- Some students need to rewrite subtraction as adding the opposite when they first start learning how to distribute.
- Many students make sign errors when distributing a negative number.
- Some students need to write a 1 in front of the second parentheses in 2e) in order to distribute correctly.
- Refer students to the ***Distributive Properties of Multiplication over Addition*** chart in the textbook.

Answers: *1a) 2x+12, b) 12x-6, c) −2x-12, d) 15a+20b, e) 28m-12n, f) 10p+20q-5, g) −2.3x+4.5y, h) (3/2)x+(5/3), i) 2x+(7/3)y-(1/6); 2a) 14x+6y, b) 13x-y, c) 13x+1.4, d) 33.2x+24.2y, e) −31x+16y, f) −3x+8y-9z; 3) a(b+c)=ab+ac*

Mini-Lecture 10.3
Solving Equations Using the Addition Property

Learning Objectives:

1. Solve equations using the addition property once.
2. Solve equations using the addition property more than once.
3. Solve equations using the addition property (fractions or decimals).

Examples:

1. Solve for the variable.

   a) $a - 4 = 16$

   b) $14 = b - 12$

   c) $a + 15 = 18$

   d) $-19 = b + 16$

   e) $21 = -16 + n$

   f) $t - (-6) = 18$

2. Solve for the variable.

   a) $8p + 7 = 9p - 6$

   b) $2m - 8 = 3m - 11$

   c) $4x + 3 = 3x - 1$

   d) $5 + 15x = 14x - 6$

   e) $2x + 8 = x + 24$

   f) $8x - 9 = 7x - 7$

3. Solve for the variable.

   a) $\dfrac{1}{4} + x = 10$

   b) $\dfrac{4}{3} + y = -4$

   c) $c - \dfrac{1}{5} = 0$

   d) $x - \dfrac{9}{23} = -\dfrac{6}{23}$

   e) $-2.2 + x = 16$

   f) $6.3 = 19.2 - x$

Teaching Notes:

- Encourage students to use the addition property in such a way that the variable ends up with a positive coefficient.
- Some students prefer to see the addition property steps written horizontally, while others prefer to see them written under the like term on the other side of the equation.
- Encourage students to write out all of the addition property steps, and to avoid using shortcuts until they have mastered these types of equations.
- Encourage students to write the steps for solving the equations in a neat and organized manner. This habit will help immensely when the equations become more complex.
- Refer students to the *Addition Property of Equations* chart in the textbook.

Answers: 1a) 20, b) 26, c) 3, d) −35, e) 37, f) 12; 2a) 13, b) 3, c) −4, d) −11, e) 16, f) 2; 3a) 39/4, b) −16/3, c) 1/5, d) 3/23, e) 18.2, f) 12.9

Mini-Lecture 10.4
Solving Equations Using the Division or Multiplication Property

Learning Objectives:

1. Solve equations using the division property.
2. Solve equations using the multiplication property.
3. Solve equations using the division or multiplication property.

Examples:

1. Solve for the variable.

   a) $6a = -30$

   b) $-64 = 8k$

   c) $-21 = -3c$

   d) $-5x = -45$

   e) $-3t = 48.9$

   f) $-57.4 = 7m$

2. Solve for the variable.

   a) $\dfrac{3}{7}x = 3$

   b) $\dfrac{2}{8}y = 4$

   c) $\dfrac{1}{4}x = 6$

   d) $\dfrac{2}{15}m = \dfrac{1}{3}$

   e) $\dfrac{7}{8}x = -\dfrac{3}{5}$

   f) $\dfrac{8}{9}y = -\dfrac{4}{7}$

   g) $\dfrac{1}{4}y = -3\dfrac{3}{8}$

   h) $1\dfrac{3}{4}z = 7$

   i) $3\dfrac{1}{2}m = 49$

3. Solve for the variable.

   a) $18k = -36$

   b) $-2.5 = 5.5x$

   c) $3 = \dfrac{9}{11}y$

Teaching Notes:

- Remind students that these equations are very similar to proportion equations such as $\dfrac{n}{20} = \dfrac{3}{4}$.
- Some students prefer to use two steps for the fraction type problems. First, multiply both sides by the denominator near the variable, then divide both sides by the remaining coefficient of the variable.
- Refer students to the ***Division/Multiplication Property of Equations*** charts in the textbook.

Answers: 1a) −5, b) −8, c) 7, d) 9, e) −16.3, f) −8.2; 2a) 7, b) 16, c) 24, d) 5/2 or 2 ½, e) −24/35, f) −9/14, g) −27/2 or −13 ½, h) 4, i) 14; 3a) −2, b) −0.4̄5̄, c) 11/3 or 3 2/3

Mini-Lecture 10.5
Solving Equations Using Two Properties

Learning Objectives:

1. Check whether a given answer is the solution to an equation.
2. Use two properties to solve an equation.
3. Solve equations where the variable is on both sides of the equal sign.
4. Solve equations with parentheses.

Examples:

1. Check to see whether the given answer is a solution to the equation.

   a) Is 10 a solution to $2(2m-2) = 3(m+2)$?
   b) Is 2 a solution to $2(2m-2) = 3(m+2)$?

2. Solve.

   a) $10r + 7 = 107$ b) $7n - 8 = 27$ c) $33 = 6x - 3$

   d) $164 = 15x + 14$ e) $\dfrac{1}{2}x - 8 = -2$ f) $-\dfrac{2}{3}x - 8 = -32$

3. Solve.

   a) $8w + 1 = 7 + 9w$ b) $-3y + 3 = 8 + 9y$ c) $3w - 7 = -8 + 7w - 2w$

4. Solve.

   a) $6(2x - 1) = 30$ b) $9p = 6(5p + 7)$ c) $4(y + 7) = 5(y - 3)$

   d) $7x - 3(x - 8) = 3x + 24$ e) $5(x - 3) + 4(2x + 2) = 4(x + 2) + 3$

Teaching Notes:

- Encourage students to check their solutions, as in example 1.
- In example 3, some students prefer to always end up with the variable on the left, while others prefer to always end up with a positive coefficient in front of the variable.
- Some students confuse the different properties and try to subtract the coefficient from the variable instead of dividing it off.
- Some students do not collect the like terms before trying to solve 3a).
- Refer students to the *Procedure to Solve Equations* chart in the textbook.

Answers: *1a) yes, b) no; 2a) 10, b) 5, c) 6, d) 10, e) 12, f) 36; 2a) −6, b) −5/12, c) ½; 4a) 3, b) −2, c) 43, d) 0, e) 2*

Mini-Lecture 10.6
Translating English to Algebra

Learning Objectives:

1. Translate English into mathematical equations using two given variables.
2. Use two properties to solve an equation.
3. Write algebraic expressions for several quantities using one given variable.

Examples:

1. Translate the English sentence into an equation using the given variables.

   a) Kerri's apartment building has 6 more floors than Eric's building. Use k for the number of floors in Kerri's building and e for the number of floors in Eric's building.

   b) The temperature on Friday showed a decrease of 5 degrees compared to the temperature two days before on Wednesday. Use f for the number of degrees on Friday and w for the number of degrees on Wednesday.

   c) The length of a rectangle is 3 centimeters greater than five times the width. Use L for the length and W for the width of the rectangle.

   d) The length of the second side of a triangle is 8 inches shorter than twice the first side of the triangle. Use f to represent the length of the first side of the triangle and s to represent the length of the second side of the triangle.

2. Write algebraic expressions for each quantity using the given variable.

   a) Rasheed's monthly salary is $100 more than Fred's monthly salary. Use the letter f.

   b) Lake Regina has 190,000 fewer square feet of surface area than Lake Montrose. Use the letter m.

   c) The second angle of a triangle is 5° smaller than the first. The third angle is triple the size of the first angle. Use the letter f.

Teaching Notes:

- Many students find these translations difficult at first.
- Refer students to the diagram, at the beginning of this section, which shows common English phrases and the mathematical symbols with which they can be replaced.

Answers: *1a) k=e+6, b) f=w-5, c) L=5W+3, d) s=2f-8; 2a) f, f+100, b) m, 190,000-m, c) f, f-5, 3f*

Mini-Lecture 10.7
Solving Applied Problems

Learning Objectives:

1. Solve problems involving comparisons.
2. Solve problems involving geometric formulas.
3. Solve problems involving rates and percents.

Examples:

1. Solve the following comparison problems using an equation.

   a) A 22-ft pipe is cut into two pieces. The shorter piece is 7 ft shorter than the longer piece. What is the length of the longer piece?

   b) For three days in a row, volunteers picked up trash on a particular beach. They picked up a total of 813 pounds. On the second day they collected 15 pounds more than on the first day. On the third day, they picked up 27 pounds less than on the first day. How many pounds of trash did they pick up on the first day?

2. Solve the following geometric concept problems using an equation.

   a) To trim the edges of a rectangular table cloth, 36 feet of lace are needed. The length of the table cloth is exactly one-half its width. What are the dimensions of the table cloth?

   b) A triangle has three angles, R, S, and T. Angle T is 18° greater than angle S. Angle R is 4 times angle S. What is the measure of each angle?

3. Solve the following rate/percent problems.

   a) A salesman in an exclusive clothing store earns $2300 per month base pay plus a 7% commission on sales. One month he earns $5023. What were his sales that month?

   b) The number of dogs licensed in a particular city this year is 1283. This is a 2% increase over last year. How many dog licenses were on record last year? Round to the nearest whole number.

Teaching Notes:

- Encourage students to write down what they let the variable equal.
- Encourage students to check their final answers.
- Encourage students to draw and label a diagram when they are uncertain where to start.
- Refer students to the *Mathematics Blueprint For Problem Solving* chart in the textbook.

Answers: *1a) 14.5 ft, b) 275 lb; 2a) 12 ft width, 6 ft length, b) R=108°, S=27°, T=45°; 3a) $38,900, b) 1258 dogs*

SKILL BUILDER 1.1
Understanding Whole Numbers

Place Value System

Example: 37,892

Hundred Millions	Ten millions	Millions	Hundred Thousands	Ten thousands	Thousands	Hundreds	tens	ones
				3	7	8	9	2

- Standard Notation: 37,892
- Expanded notation: $30,000 + 7,000 + 800 + 90 + 2 = 37,892$
- Word Name: thirty-seven thousand, eight hundred ninety-two

Write each number in expanded notation.

1) 4,965   2) 405,761   3) 46,115,002   4) 7,903,001

Write each number in standard notation.

5) $800 + 30 + 7 =$ _____   6) $2000 + 800 + 20 + 1 =$ _____

7) $8,000,000 + 200,000 + 7,000 + 400 + 90 =$ _____

Write a word name for each number.

8) 72   9) 4,627   10) 61,205,552   11) 62,004

12) Jason bought a new computer for $1073.99. What word name should Jason write on his check?

SKILL BUILDER 1.2
Adding Whole Numbers

Basic Addition Facts

- Addends: numbers being added.
- Sum: result of numbers being added.
- Identity property of zero: when zero is added to a number, the sum is that number.
- Commutative Property of Addition: two numbers can be added in any order.
- Associative Property of Addition: when we add three numbers, we can group them in any way.

Add from the top. If necessary, rewrite the problem vertically, be sure to group ones, tens, etc. Check by adding in the reverse order.

1) $\begin{array}{r} 67 \\ +21 \end{array}$

2) $\begin{array}{r} 11 \\ 42 \\ 92 \\ +\ 38 \end{array}$

3) $\begin{array}{r} 5789 \\ 1832 \\ +\ 709 \end{array}$

4) $\begin{array}{r} 28,391 \\ +\ 2,999 \end{array}$

5) $\begin{array}{r} 27,305 \\ +\ 898 \end{array}$

6) $27,893 + 385 + 4,208 + 523,987 = $ _____

7) $\begin{array}{r} 25 \\ 83 \\ 6 \\ 19 \\ +\ 4 \end{array}$

8) $\begin{array}{r} 6,002,978 \\ 2,456,081 \\ +\ 4,803,255 \end{array}$

9) $\begin{array}{r} 6,327 \\ 783,411 \\ +\ 29,979 \end{array}$

10) $\begin{array}{r} 376 \\ 1098 \\ 26 \\ +\ 573 \end{array}$

Applying Addition to Real-Life Situations

- Understand the problem
- Calculate and state the answer
- Check

11) Joseph and Alexandra wanted to build a fence around their back yard. The yard is 189 feet long and 144 feet wide. What is the total number of feet of fencing they will need for their back yard?

12) Samantha and Nicholas went to the pet store to by supplies for their cat Ariel. They purchased cat food for $5.32, kitty litter for $2.99, a cat brush for $1.99, and a flea collar for $1.49. How much money did they spend?

SKILL BUILDER 1.3
Subtracting Whole Numbers

Subtraction: (minuend) - (subtrahend) = (difference)

 We check subtraction with addition: $9 - 3 = 6$; check: $6 + 3 = 9$

Subtracting Whole Numbers
- Line up the ones column, the tens column, the hundreds column, and so on.
- Begin subtracting from right to left.
- If a digit in the lower number is greater than the digit in the upper number, we need to "borrow" from the digit to the left.

Subtract. Check your answers with addition.

1) 58 Check:
    - 22

2) 149 Check:
    - 14

3) 44,763 Check:
    - 2,321

4) 20,342 Check:
    - 4,297

5) 29,791 Check:
    - 8,432

6) 167,002 Check:
    - 89,370

7) 100,000 Check:
    - 8,934

8) 8,061 Check:
    - 278

9) 1,243,581 Check:
    - 67,490

Applying Subtraction to Real-Life Situations

10) The results from a recent Student Senate election on campus are as follows:

Candidate's Name	# of Votes Received
Anastasia	873
Dave	482
Raymond	627

How many more votes did Anastasia receive than Dave?

How many more votes did Raymond receive than Dave?

How many students participated in this election?

SKILL BUILDER 1.4
Multiplying Whole Numbers

Basic Multiplication Facts

- (factor) x (factor) = product
- Multiplication property of zero: $3 \times 0 = 0$
- Identity element for multiplication: $2 \times 1 = 2$
- Commutative property of multiplication: 3 x 2 is the same product as 2 x 3.
- Associative property of multiplication: 2 x (5 x 3) is the same product as (2 x 5) x 3
- Distributive property of multiplication over addition: 3 x (10 + 2) = (3 x 10) + (3 x 2)

Find the product. Don't forget, when multiplying by powers of ten, count the number of zeros in the power of 10 and attach that number of zeros to the right side of the other whole number.

1) $\begin{array}{r} 43 \\ \times\ 5 \\ \hline \end{array}$

2) $\begin{array}{r} 402 \\ \times\ 6 \\ \hline \end{array}$

3) $\begin{array}{r} 823 \\ \times\ 4 \\ \hline \end{array}$

4) $\begin{array}{r} 20{,}609 \\ \times\ \ \ 6 \\ \hline \end{array}$

5) $\begin{array}{r} 38{,}294 \\ \times\ \ \ 0 \\ \hline \end{array}$

6) $\begin{array}{r} 231 \\ \times\ 10 \\ \hline \end{array}$

7) $\begin{array}{r} 4923 \\ \times\ 10 \\ \hline \end{array}$

8) $\begin{array}{r} 892 \\ \times\ 27 \\ \hline \end{array}$

9) $\begin{array}{r} 6309 \\ \times\ 415 \\ \hline \end{array}$

10) $\begin{array}{r} 380 \\ \times\ 30 \\ \hline \end{array}$

11) $\begin{array}{r} 403 \\ \times\ 268 \\ \hline \end{array}$

12) $\begin{array}{r} 1894 \\ \times\ 576 \\ \hline \end{array}$

13) $20 \cdot 8 \cdot 2 = \underline{\hspace{2cm}}$

14) $13 \cdot 5 \cdot 5 = \underline{\hspace{2.5cm}}$

Applying Multiplication to Real-Life Situations

15) The average weekly salary of a restaurant worker is $289.35. There are 27 employees. What is the weekly payroll?

16) What is the area of a rectangular room that measures 12 feet long by 15 feet wide?

SKILL BUILDER 1.5
Dividing Whole Numbers

$$\overset{\textit{quotient}}{\textit{divisor}\,)\overline{\textit{dividend}}}$$

(divisor × quotient) + remainder = dividend

Dividing Whole Numbers

- Any nonzero number divided by itself equals 1: $5 \div 5 = 1$
- Any number divided by 1 equals itself: $6 \div 1 = 6$
- Zero divided by any number equals zero: $0 \div 3 = 0$
- Division by zero is undefined: $7 \div 0$ or $\dfrac{7}{0}$ is undefined
- When performing long division, be careful to line up all digits in the correct place value.
- Don't forget to check your division with multiplication!!!

Divide. Be sure to show remainder by using the letter R. Check your answer with multiplication.

1) $9\overline{)81}$ Check:

2) $8\overline{)56}$ Check:

3) $2\overline{)0}$ Check:

4) $5\overline{)35}$ Check:

5) $78 \div 7 =$ ____
     Check:

6) $27 \div 0 =$ _____
     Check:

7) $6\overline{)102}$ Check:

8) $7\overline{)163}$ Check:

9) $3\overline{)413}$ Check:

10) $8\overline{)1325}$ Check:

11) $5\overline{)2765}$ Check:

12) $21\overline{)2063}$ Check:

13) $14\overline{)1878}$ Check:

14) $41\overline{)8671}$ Check:

15) $17\overline{)8762}$ Check:

16) A group of six friends purchased tickets to a concert for a total bill of $525.90. How much did each concert ticket cost?

SKILL BUILDER 1.6
Exponents and the Order of Operations

Exponents

- $BASE^{exponent}$
- "Shorthand" way of writing multiplication of the same number
- $7^4 = 7 \times 7 \times 7 \times 7 = 2,401$
- Any whole number (not zero) raised to the zero power equals 1

Write each product in exponent form.

1) $3 \times 3 \times 3 \times 3 \times 3 =$ _____   2) $6 \times 6 \times 6 =$ _____   3) $10 \times 10 \times 10 \times 10 =$ _____

Find the value of each expression.

4) $6^2 =$ _____   5) $8^3 =$ _____   6) $10^7 =$ _____   7) $14^0 =$ _____

8) $2^3 + 4^3 + 8^2 =$ _____   9) $6^0 + 1^5 + 13^0 =$ _____

Order of Operations

- 1st: Perform operations in parentheses or any grouping symbols.
- 2nd: Simplify any expressions with exponents.
- 3rd: Multiply or divide from left to right.
- 4th: Add or subtract from left to right.

Using correct order of operations, evaluate the following expressions.

10) $3 \times 8 + 4 - 3 =$ _____   11) $9 \times 3 - 14 \div 2 =$ _____   12) $5 \times 2^3 - 4 \times (14 \div 7) =$ ____

13) $50 \div 5 \times 2 + (11 - 8)^2 =$ _____   14) $9^2 + 4^2 \div 2^2 - 4^4 \div 2^2 =$ _____

SKILL BUILDER 1.7
Rounding and Estimation

Rounding a Whole Number

- If the first digit to the right of the round-off place is less than 5, we make no change to the digit in the round-off place; all digits to the right of the round-off place change to zeros.
- If the first digit to the right of the round-off place is equal to 5 or more than 5, we increase the digit in the round-off place by 1; all digits to the right of the round-off place change to zeros.

Round the exact number to the place stated in each column.

	Exact Number	Tens	Hundreds	Thousands
1	14,342			
2	18,608			
3	209,355			
4	9,999			

Estimation

- Round the numbers so that there is only one, nonzero digit.
- Perform the calculation with the rounded numbers.
- Use the symbol ≈ to mean *approximately equal to*.

Using estimation, find an approximation for each calculation.

5) $712 + 598 + 198 \approx$ _____

6) $41{,}276 - 9{,}878 \approx$ _____

7) $51 \times 47 \approx$ _____

8) $39{,}042 \times 5{,}902 \approx$ _____

9) $392{,}406 \div 102{,}380 \approx$ _____

10) $2081 \div 1977 \approx$ ___

11) Allison determined that she had spent $19 on cat food each week last year. Estimate how much she spent on cat food over the entire year.

SKILL BUILDER 1.8
Applied Problems

Solving Applied Problems

MATHEMATICS BLUEPRINT FOR PROBLEM SOLVING

Gather the Facts	What Am I Asked to Do?	How Do I Proceed?	Key Points to Remember
Find the numbers that you will need to use in your calculations.	Are you finding an area? Volume? Cost? Total number? What is it that you need to find?	Do you need to add items together? Do you need to multiply or divide? What types of calculations are required?	Write down things you might forget. For example: units of measure, conversions, etc.

Using the Mathematics Blueprint for Problem Solving, solve the following word problems.

1. Amy planned a two-day trip of 1137 miles to Florida. On the first day, Amy traveled 673 miles. How many miles must Amy travel on day two to complete her trip?

2. Ari purchased four books at the local bookstore. The cost of each book was: $3.95, $7.95, $4.85, and $10.95. How much did Ari spend at the bookstore?

3. Juan began a trip to New York City on a full tank of gas. His odometer read 21,903. When he arrived in New York City, his odometer read 22,103. He filled his car's gas tank and it took 8 gallons of gas. How many miles per gallon did he get?

4. Four students rented a car for six days. The cost to rent a car was $21.90 per day. How much did each student have to pay?

5. Mrs. Robichaud had a balance of $257.82 in her checking account when she went shopping. She bought 2 blouses for $29 each, a pair of jeans for $49, a pair of sandals for $24, and a jacket for $49. Assuming no sales tax, how much money did she have left in her checking account?

6. Twelve friends agreed to equally divide a $395.40 bill for dinner. How much did each of them have to pay?

7. A bag of cookies contain 35 cookies and cost $3.85. How much does each cookie cost?

SKILL BUILDER 2.1
Understanding Fractions

Understanding Fractions

- $\dfrac{numerator}{denominator}$; (numerator) ÷ (denominator) ; $denominator\,)\overline{numerator}$

- Any nonzero number divided by itself is 1: $\dfrac{3}{3} = 1$

- Any number divided by 1 remains that number: $\dfrac{14}{1} = 14$

- Zero divided by any nonzero number is always zero: $\dfrac{0}{6} = 0$

- Division by zero is undefined: $\dfrac{5}{0} = undefined$; $\dfrac{0}{0} = undefined$

Use a fraction to represent the shaded part of the object.

1)

2)

3)

4)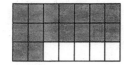

5)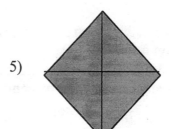

Draw a sketch to illustrate each fractional part.

6) $\dfrac{3}{5}$ of an object

7) $\dfrac{7}{15}$ of an object

8) $\dfrac{0}{12}$ of an object

9) In the parking lot, there were 15 black cars, 12 white cars, 14 blue cars, and 21 other colored cars. What fractional part of the cars were blue?

SKILL BUILDER 2.2
Simplifying Fractions

Simplifying Fractions

- Prime number: whole number greater than one that can only be divided by itself and 1.
- Composite number: whole number greater than 1 that can be divided by whole numbers other than 1 and itself.
- Divisibility tests
  - Divisible by 2: last digit is 0, 2, 4, 6, 8
  - Divisible by 3: sum of digits is divisible by 3
  - Divisible by 5: last digit is 0 or 5
- Prime Factorization: writing a number as a product of prime factors.
  - Example: $36 = 2 \times 2 \times 3 \times 3 = 2^2 \times 3^2$

1) List the first 12 prime numbers: ___ , ___, ___, ___, ___, ___, ___, ___, ___, ___, ___, ___

Write each number as a product of <u>prime factors</u>. Be sure to use exponents when necessary.

2) 21   3) 45   4) 16   5) 72

Reducing a Fraction

- Common factor method: Divide both numerator and denominator by a common factor. Repeat until no common factors are left
- Prime Factorization: Write the prime factorization of both numerator and denominator. Divide both numerator and denominator by common prime factors.
- Equality test for fractions: if $\dfrac{a}{b} = \dfrac{c}{d}$, then $a \times d = b \times c$ (Cross products)

Reduce each fraction by finding a <u>common factor</u> in the numerator and in the denominator and viding by the common factor.

6) $\dfrac{5}{25}$ 7) $\dfrac{33}{55}$ 8) $\dfrac{24}{32}$ 9) $\dfrac{18}{27}$

Reduce each fraction by the method of prime factors.

10) $\dfrac{22}{36}$ 11) $\dfrac{21}{28}$ 12) $\dfrac{12}{33}$ 13) $\dfrac{45}{63}$

Are the following fractions equal? Why or why not?

14) $\dfrac{7}{11} = \dfrac{56}{88}$????   15) $\dfrac{21}{28} = \dfrac{15}{20}$?????

SKILL BUILDER 2.3
Improper Fractions and Mixed Numbers

Changing a Mixed Number to an Improper Fraction

- Step 1: Multiply the whole number by the denominator of the fraction.
- Step 2: Add the numerator of the fraction to the product found in step 1.
- Step 3: Write the sum found in step 2 over the denominator of the fraction.

Example: Change $4\frac{2}{3}$ to an improper fraction.

$$\frac{(4 \times 3) + 2}{3} = \frac{14}{3}$$

Change each mixed number to an improper fraction.

1) $2\frac{1}{2} = $ _____

2) $3\frac{2}{3} = $ _____

3) $6\frac{4}{11} = $ _____

4) $28\frac{11}{14} = $ _____

Changing an Improper Fraction to a Mixed Number

- Step 1: Divide the numerator by the denominator.
- Step 2: Write the quotient followed by the fraction with the remainder over the denominator.
- Step 3: Be sure final answer is in completely reduced form.

Example: Change $\frac{36}{5}$ to a mixed number.

$$5\overline{)36}^{\,7R1} = 7\frac{1}{5}$$

Change each improper fraction to a mixed number or a whole number.

5) $\frac{42}{5} = $ _____

6) $\frac{72}{8} = $ _____

7) $\frac{102}{7} = $ _____

8) $\frac{231}{6} = $ _____

9) $\frac{405}{10} = $ _____

10) $\frac{3125}{50} = $ _____

SKILL BUILDER 2.4
Multiplication of Fractions and Mixed Numbers

Multiplication of Fractions

- Multiplying two proper or improper fractions: $\dfrac{multiply \ \ numerators}{multiply \ \ deno\min ators}$, then simplify.

- Multiplying a whole number by a fraction: express whole number as a fraction with a denominator of 1. Multiply as two proper/improper fractions.
- Multiplying mixed numbers: change each mixed number to an improper fraction, then multiply as two proper/improper fractions..

Multiply. Make sure all fractions are simplified in the final answer. Use above rules.

1) $\dfrac{2}{7} \times \dfrac{3}{5} =$ _____

2) $\dfrac{1}{4} \times \dfrac{5}{7} =$ _____

3) $\dfrac{6}{5} \times \dfrac{7}{11} =$ _____

4) $\dfrac{5}{6} \times \dfrac{3}{4} =$ _____

5) $\dfrac{8}{15} \times 5 =$ _____

6) $\dfrac{9}{16} \times \dfrac{2}{3} =$ _____

7) $12 \times \dfrac{7}{8} =$ _____

8) $\dfrac{4}{3} \times \dfrac{1}{2} \times \dfrac{6}{7} =$ _____

9) $\dfrac{55}{72} \times \dfrac{18}{77} =$ _____

10) $2\dfrac{4}{5} \times \dfrac{1}{7} =$ _____

11) $1\dfrac{1}{3} \times 2\dfrac{3}{8} =$ _____

12) $6 \times 3\dfrac{1}{6} =$ _____

13) $3\dfrac{3}{10} \times 1\dfrac{2}{3} =$ _____

14) $\dfrac{9}{9} \times 3\dfrac{7}{11} =$ _____

15) $0 \times 5\dfrac{1}{2} =$ _____

16) A rectangular room measures $13\dfrac{1}{2}$ feet long by $22\dfrac{1}{4}$ feet wide. Find the area of the room. Remember, area = length × width.

SKILL BUILDER 2.5
Dividing Fractions and Mixed Numbers

Dividing Fractions

- Dividing two fractions: invert the second fraction and multiply.
- Dividing a whole number and a fraction: express the whole number with a 1 in the denominator. Invert second fraction and multiply.
- Dividing mixed numbers: convert to improper fractions, invert the second fraction, and multiply.

Divide.

1) $\dfrac{1}{4} \div \dfrac{3}{4} = $ _____

2) $\dfrac{4}{15} \div \dfrac{2}{5} = $ _____

3) $\dfrac{15}{17} \div 5 = $ _____

4) $1 \div \dfrac{5}{8} = $ _____

5) $\dfrac{3}{8} \div \dfrac{1}{6}$ _____

6) $\dfrac{7}{13} \div \dfrac{7}{13} = $ _____

7) $0 \div \dfrac{5}{11} = $ _____

8) $\dfrac{8}{15} \div 4 = $ _____

9) $\dfrac{11}{25} \div 0 = $ _____

10) $3000 \div \dfrac{15}{17} = $ _____

11) $2\dfrac{2}{3} \div \dfrac{2}{5} = $ _____

12) $3\dfrac{1}{3} \div 5 = $ _____

13) $\dfrac{4\frac{1}{2}}{\frac{3}{4}} = $ _____

14) $\dfrac{\frac{5}{12}}{7\frac{1}{2}} = $ _____

15) $\dfrac{6\frac{1}{2}}{2\frac{1}{4}} = $ _____

16) Find the value of x : $x \div \dfrac{2}{3} = \dfrac{9}{10}$

SKILL BUILDER 2.6
The Least Common Denominator and Creating Equivalent Fractions

Finding the Least Common Denominator

- Step 1: Write each denominator as the product of prime factors.
- Step 2: List all the prime factors that appear in either product.
- Step 3: Form a product of those prime factors, using each factor the greatest number of times it appears in any one denominator.

  Example: Find the LCD for $\dfrac{3}{4}$ and $\dfrac{1}{6}$

  Step 1: $4 = 2 \times 2$; $6 = 2 \times 3$

  Step 2: LCD will contain the factors 2, 3

  Step 3: $\text{LCD} = \overbrace{2 \times 2}^{4} \underbrace{\times 3}_{6} = 12$

Find the LCD for each set of fractions.

1) $\dfrac{2}{7}$ and $\dfrac{3}{14}$

2) $\dfrac{1}{5}$ and $\dfrac{3}{4}$

3) $\dfrac{1}{12}$ and $\dfrac{1}{4}$

4) $\dfrac{11}{30}$ and $\dfrac{3}{40}$

5) $\dfrac{5}{36}$ and $\dfrac{8}{45}$

6) $\dfrac{7}{18}, \dfrac{11}{30}, \dfrac{5}{72}$

Building Up Fractions

- Step 1: Find LCD for the fractions involved
- Step 2: Create equivalent fractions by multiplying numerator and denominator by the same value: $\dfrac{a}{b} = \dfrac{a}{b} \times 1 = \dfrac{a}{b} \times \dfrac{c}{c} = \dfrac{a \times c}{a \times c}$

Find the LCD. Build up the fractions to equivalent fractions having the LCD as the denominator.

7) $\dfrac{1}{3}$ and $\dfrac{5}{12}$

8) $\dfrac{7}{8}$ and $\dfrac{17}{48}$

9) $\dfrac{7}{24}$ and $\dfrac{11}{16}$

10) $\dfrac{3}{7}, \dfrac{11}{63}, \dfrac{1}{9}$

11) $\dfrac{5}{6}, \dfrac{8}{15}, \dfrac{1}{18}$

12) $\dfrac{3}{10}, \dfrac{5}{28}, \dfrac{11}{35}$

SKILL BUILDER 2.7
Adding and Subtracting Fractions

Adding and Subtracting Fractions

- With a common denominator: Add or subtract numerator, keep common denominator.
- Without a common denominator:
  - Step 1: Find the LCD.
  - Step 2: Build up each fraction so that its denominator is the LCD.
  - Step 3: Add or subtract numerators, keep common denominator. Simplify.

Add or subtract. Simplify all answers.

1) $\dfrac{3}{5} + \dfrac{1}{10} = $ _____

2) $\dfrac{1}{4} + \dfrac{1}{3} = $ _____

3) $\dfrac{5}{14} + \dfrac{1}{2} = $ _____

4) $\dfrac{5}{6} + \dfrac{1}{8} = $ _____

5) $\dfrac{19}{100} + \dfrac{7}{10} = $ _____

6) $\dfrac{7}{25} + \dfrac{12}{45} = $ _____

7) $\dfrac{31}{45} - \dfrac{2}{15} = $ _____

8) $\dfrac{8}{9} - \dfrac{5}{36} = $ _____

9) $\dfrac{3}{5} - \dfrac{12}{20} = $ _____

10) $\dfrac{5}{8} - \dfrac{1}{12} = $ _____

11) $\dfrac{3}{4} - \dfrac{11}{20} = $ _____

12) $\dfrac{5}{12} - \dfrac{15}{42} = $ _____

13) $\dfrac{1}{8} + \dfrac{2}{3} + \dfrac{3}{24} = $ _____

14) $\dfrac{23}{42} + \dfrac{1}{7} + \dfrac{1}{6} = $ _____

15) $\dfrac{11}{28} + \dfrac{3}{4} + \dfrac{6}{7} = $ ___

SKILL BUILDER 2.8
Adding and Subtracting Mixed Numbers and the Order of Operations

Adding Mixed Numbers

- Add the fractions together. Build up the fraction parts to obtain a common denominator, if necessary.
- Add the whole numbers together.
- If the sum of the fractions is an improper fraction, we convert it to a mixed number and add the whole numbers together.

Add. Express the answer as a mixed number. Simplify all answers.

1) $\quad 2\dfrac{1}{7}$

$\quad + \; 4\dfrac{3}{7}$

2) $\quad 7\dfrac{1}{6}$

$\quad + \; 5\dfrac{5}{12}$

3) $\quad 3\dfrac{5}{6}$

$\quad + \; 1\dfrac{1}{3}$

4) $\quad 8\dfrac{11}{20}$

$\quad + \; 4\dfrac{4}{5}$

Subtracting Mixed Numbers

- Subtract the fractions. Build up the fraction parts to obtain a common denominator, if necessary.
- If you cannot subtract, you will need to borrow "1" from the whole number part.
- Subtract the whole number part. Be sure all fractions are completely simplified.

5) $\quad 2\dfrac{7}{10}$

$\quad - \; 1\dfrac{1}{10}$

6) $\quad 7\dfrac{2}{3}$

$\quad - \; 4\dfrac{3}{5}$

7) $\quad 6\dfrac{1}{3}$

$\quad - \; 3\dfrac{5}{6}$

8) $\quad 4$

$\quad - \; 2\dfrac{3}{8}$

Order of Operations

- Perform operations inside the parentheses.
- Simplify any expressions with exponents.
- Multiply or divide from left to right.
- Add or subtract from left to right.

Evaluate using the correct order of operation.

9) $\dfrac{1}{3} + \dfrac{4}{5} \times \dfrac{1}{2} = $ _____

10) $\dfrac{3}{2} \div \left(\dfrac{3}{4} - \dfrac{1}{6} \right) + \dfrac{3}{7} = $ _____

11) $\left(\dfrac{3}{8} \right)^2 \div \dfrac{15}{8} = $ _____

SKILL BUILDER 2.9
Solving Applied Problems Involving Fractions

Solving Applied Problems

- Understand the problem: Read the problem carefully, draw a picture, fill in the Mathematics Blueprint (Section 1.8).
- Solve: Perform the calculations; state the answer, including the unit of measure.
- Check: Estimate the answer, round fractions to the nearest whole number.
      Compare the exact answer with the estimate to see if your answer is reasonable.

Use the above steps for solving the following applied problems. Be sure to use the Mathematics Blueprint to assist you.

1. The local pizza parlor used $27\frac{1}{4}$ pounds of pizza dough on Monday, $23\frac{2}{3}$ pounds on Tuesday, and $25\frac{1}{2}$ pounds on Wednesday. How many pounds of pizza dough were used over the three days?

2. During the month of June, Karen work the following hours:
   Week 1: $32\frac{1}{4}hrs$; Week 2: $39\frac{1}{2}hrs$; Week 3: $40hrs.$; Week 4: $37\frac{1}{3}$
   If Karen makes \$11/hour, how much money did Karen earn during the month of June?

3. A family began their vacation on Monday morning. They left their home at 8 a.m. and traveled until lunchtime at 1 p.m. They began driving again at 2 p.m. and continued driving until 8 p.m. At this point, they stopped at a motel to sleep. They began driving Tuesday morning at 7 a.m. and drove until lunchtime at 12:30 p.m. They began driving again at 2 p.m. and continued driving until 8:30 p.m. Finally, on the Wednesday, they left at 7:30 a.m. and drove until Noon. They stopped for lunch and began the final part of their trip at 2:30. They arrived at their destination at 6 p.m. They had traveled a total of 1,457 miles. What was their average speed in miles per hour?

4. How many $\frac{3}{4}$-pound bags of coffee can be made from 30 pounds of coffee?

SKILL BUILDER 3.1
Using Decimal Notation

Reading Decimal Numbers

- Left of decimal point is read as a whole number
- Decimal point is read as *"and"*
- Right of decimal point is read as an ordinary whole number but finish with the place value name of the digit to the right, end in *"ths"*

Complete the following chart: (Write each fraction or mixed number in lowest terms.)

	FRACTION	DECIMAL	WORD NAME
1	$\dfrac{7}{10}$		
2		0.351	
3	$18\dfrac{45}{1000}$		
4			Eight and sixty-two ten-thousandths
5		0.50	
6	$\dfrac{73}{1000}$		
7			Sixty two and four ten thousandths

	DECIMAL	WORD NAME
8	$491.62	
9		Three hundred thirty one and $\dfrac{27}{100}$ dollars

SKILL BUILDER 3.2
Comparing, Ordering, and Rounding Decimals

Comparing Two Numbers in Decimal Notation

- Start at the left and compare <u>corresponding</u> digits. If the digits are the same, move one place to the right. If the digits are different, the larger number is the one with the larger digit.
- 1.83 < 1.87 because the digits in the ones and tenths place are the same. The digits in the hundredths place are different. So 3 < 7, then 1.83 < 1.87.

Fill in the blank with one of the symbols $<$, $=$, or $>$.

1) 1.75 _____ 1.7

2) 0.0003 _____ 0.003

3) 408.603 _____ 408.605

4) $4\frac{7}{100}$ ____ 4.08

5) 6.13 ____ 6.13000

6) 23.0097 ____ 23.009

Rounding Decimals

- Draw a line after the place to be rounded to.
- Look at the next digit.
- If the digit is less than 5, drop it and all digits to the right of it.
  If the digit is 5 or more, increase the number in the given place value by one. Drop all digits to the right of this place.
- You can use the "$\approx$" sign to indicate that this value is "approximately equal to."

7) Round 13.574301 to the nearest thousandth: _____

8) Round 2.7093 to the nearest tenth: _____

9) Round 9.60325 to the nearest ten-thousandth: _____

10) Round $ 0.995 to the nearest cent: _____

11) Round $37.45 to the nearest dollar: _____

12) Round 0.003275 to the nearest hundred thousandths _____

13) Arrange in order from smallest to largest.

$$2\frac{4}{10}, \quad 2.042, \quad 2.004, \quad 2.41, \quad 2.0042$$

SKILL BUILDER 3.3
Adding and Subtracting Decimals

Adding and Subtracting Decimals

- Write numbers vertically, line up decimal point
- Write 0's so all values have the same number of decimal places.
- Add or subtract from right to left.
- Place the decimal point in line with the decimal points of the numbers added or subtracted.

Add or subtract as indicated.

1) 5.25 + 3.41 = _____

2) 42.367 - 23.01 = _____

3) 27.0 + 1.435 + 41.78 = _____

4) $19.39 + $2.70 + $ 0.37 = _____

5) 4.23 – 2.12 = _____

6) 0.278 – 0.1999 = _____

7) 103.02
    - 22.91

8) 921.07
    + 38.204

9) 10
    - 4.9607

10) (102.37 - 81.99) + (1.003 + 3.02) = _____

11) At the local restaurant, Alicia bought a soda for $0.99, a medium French fry for $1.29, and a chicken sandwich for $2.89. How much did Alicia pay for her meal?

12) Raymond had $30 to buy groceries. He brought the following items to the cashier:

Lettuce: $1.89; Soda: $4.99; Tomatoes: $1.99; Chicken: $6.39;
Cucumbers: $1.49; Steak: $6.89; Ice Cream: $2.99

Did Raymond have enough money for this purchase? _____
If Raymond had more money than necessary, how much change did he receive back?
_____

SKILL BUILDER 3.4
Multiplying Decimals

Multiplying Decimals

- Ignore decimal point. Multiply like whole numbers
- Count the total number of decimal places in both factors.
- Using above number, count from right that many decimal places and place decimal point. You may need 0's on left side to get correct number of places.
- Remember: When multiplying a decimal by a power of 10, move the decimal point to the right the same number of places as the number of zeros in the power of 10.

Multiply.

1)   0.027
   x   4.2

2)   67 .37
   x   0.6

3)   8.239
   x   4.9

4) $6.32
   x   10

5)   673.45
   x   100

6)   7890.456
   x   10000

7)   0.00067
   x   5.39

8) $723.4070 \times 10^3 =$ _____

9)   Amy pays $37.50 / month for her cell phone. How much will she pay for the year?

10)   How many inches are in 50 meters? Remember, one meter is about 39.36 inches.

SKILL BUILDER 3.5
Dividing Decimals

$$\text{divisor} \overline{\smash{)}\text{dividend}}^{\text{quotient}}$$

Dividing Decimals by Whole Numbers

- Write decimal point in the quotient directly above the decimal point in the dividend.
- Divide as if both numbers were whole numbers.
- Check: (quotient) x (divisor) = dividend

1) $5\overline{\smash{)}58.5}$

2) $16\overline{\smash{)}259.84}$

3) $\dfrac{0.37892}{4}$

4) $3.25 \div 0.05 = $ _____

5) $36.935 \div 0.83 = $ _____

Dividing by Decimals

- Count the number of decimal places in the divisor and move the decimal point that many places to the *right*.
- Move the decimal point in the dividend the same number of places to the *right*. Use extra 0s if necessary.
- Write the decimal point in the quotient directly above the decimal point in the dividend. Divide as usual.

Round to the nearest hundredth if necessary

6) $0.4\overline{\smash{)}112.34}$

7) $1.32\overline{\smash{)}234.5}$

8) $\dfrac{4.93488}{0.023}$

Find the value of n.

9) $0.7 \times n = 175.98$

10) $1.3 \times n = 93.6$

11) $0.5 \times n = 0.0615$

12) Allison borrowed $1359 from her best friend Mikaela. She promised to pay her back the money in 12 equal monthly payments. How much should Allison pay Mikaela each month?

SKILL BUILDER 3.6
Converting Fractions to Decimals and the Order of Operations

Converting a Fraction to an Equivalent Decimal

- $\dfrac{numerator}{denomiator} = denominator\overline{\smash{)}numerator}$
- Divide the denominator into the numerator until the remainder becomes zero, the remainder repeats itself, or the desired number of decimal places is achieved.
- Remember, place the bar over the repeating group of digits. Example: $\dfrac{1}{3} = 0.\overline{3}$.

Fill in the missing value. If necessary, round to the nearest thousandth .

1) $\dfrac{3}{5} = $ _____

2) $16\dfrac{1}{5} = $ _____

3) $4\dfrac{39}{40} = $ _____

4) $\dfrac{11}{7} = $ _____

5) $\dfrac{35}{23} = $ _____

6) $\dfrac{3}{19} = $ _____

Write as an equivalent decimal. If a repeating decimal is obtained, use appropriate notation.

7) $27\dfrac{1}{3} = $ _____

8) $\dfrac{21}{50} = $ _____

9) $\dfrac{4}{11} = $ _____

Order of Operations

- Step 1: Perform operations inside parentheses
- Step 2: Simplify any expressions with exponents
- Step 3: Multiply or divide from left to right
- Step 4: Add or subtract from left to right

Evaluate:

10) $15 \div 0.3 - 175 \div (3.21 + 1.79)^2 = $ _____

11) $(2.3)^3 + (14 - 7.62) \div (0.8 - 0.6) = $ _____

12) $(6.7 - 2.5)^2 - (3.2 - 1.1)^2 \div 0.3 = $ _____

SKILL BUILDER 3.7
Estimating and Solving Applied Problems Involving Decimals

Estimating: To determine if an answer is reasonable, use "one nonzero digit" rounding to determine if your answer is logical. This is one of many different methods of estimating.

Example: $18,347 + 4,230 =$ _____

    Estimate -- $20,000 + 4,000 = 24,000$
    Exact   -- $18,247 + 4,230 = 22,477$

In the following examples, round to one nonzero digit. Estimate the result of the calculation then find the exact value.

1) $495,327 + 62,382 =$ _____ ; _____
                                  estimate   exact

2) $4,117 \times 0.576 =$ _____ ; _____
                                  estimate   exact

3) $272,622 \div 1532 =$ _____ ; _____
                                  estimate   exact

4) $3949.25 - 1973.57 =$ _____ ; _____
                                  estimate   exact

Solving Applied Problems

- Gather the facts.
- What am I asked to do?
- How do I proceed?
- Key points to remember.

Solve the following applied problems. Be sure to use the four steps listed above.

5) Denise made her weekly trip to the candy store. She bought 3.2 pounds of sour drops for $2.89 per pound and 4.3 pounds of sugar free hard candy at $5.13 per pound. How much did she spend for candy? Round to the nearest cent if necessary.

6) Matthew worked 35 hours last week. His pay check was for $309.75. How much was he paid per hour?

7) Andrea opened a savings account with $300. During the month, she went shopping and spent $123.49 on clothing and $89.23 on groceries. At this point, Andrea really wanted to purchase a new CD player for $99.99. Does she have enough money? Explain.

SKILL BUILDER 4.1
Ratio and Rates

Ratio: comparison of two quantities that have the *same units*. Always express a ratio in simplest form - no common factor and both numbers are whole numbers.

Example: ratio of 20 hours to 30 hours $\longrightarrow$ 20:30 $\longrightarrow$ $\dfrac{20}{30} = \dfrac{2}{3}$

Write the ratio in simplest form. Express your answer as a fraction.

1)   5 : 15

2)   28 : 14

3)   56 to 40

4)   27 to 99

5)   40 years to 75 years

6)   228 yards to 12 yards

7) $3\dfrac{1}{3}$ tons to $2\dfrac{1}{3}$ tons

Rates: comparison of two quantities with *different units*.   Express a rate as a fraction with the units included. A rate in which the denominator is 1 is a unit rate.

Example: A car traveled 148 miles in 4 hours. Find the unit rate.

$\dfrac{148\,miles}{4\,hours} = \dfrac{37\,miles}{1\,hour}$ Since the denominator is 1, we can write 37 miles/hour

Write as a rate in simplest form.

8) $60 for 2 books

9) $68 for 28 coffees

10) 13 pizzas for 104 people

Write as a unit rate.

11)   Travel 480 miles on 15 gallons of gas.

12)   Earn $720 in 40 hours

13) $18, 081 was spent on 123 shares of Robigrim stock. Find the cost per share.

14)   A retailer purchased 15 washing machines for $3525. He sold them for $5,700. How much profit did he make per washing machine?

SKILL BUILDER 4.2
The Concept of Proportions

Proportions: States that two ratios or two rates are equal.

Equality Test for Fractions: For any two fractions where b $\neq 0$ and d $\neq 0$,

Use cross products to show equality: 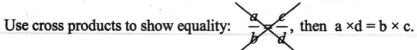, then a $\times$ d = b $\times$ c.

Write a proportion.

1) 21 is to 7 as 3 is to 1.   2)   28 is to 32 as 7 is to 8   3) 3.2 is to 11 as 16 is to 55

4)   When Karla makes popcorn, she uses 1 cup of popcorn with 2 tablespoons of oil. To make 6 cups of popcorn, she needs 12 tablespoons of oil.

5)   There are 2 computers for every 5 students. If we have 300 students, then we will have 120 computers.

6) If 3 containers of pool chemicals will treat 45,000 gallons of water, then 75,000 gallons of water will need 5 containers.

Determine which equations are proportions.

7) $\dfrac{6}{10} \overset{?}{=} \dfrac{15}{25}$ 8) $\dfrac{16}{5} \overset{?}{=} \dfrac{22}{7}$ 9) $\dfrac{2\frac{1}{3}}{3} \overset{?}{=} \dfrac{11\frac{2}{3}}{15}$ 10) $\dfrac{3}{8} \overset{?}{=} \dfrac{18.6}{48.8}$

11) $\dfrac{38 \ miles}{4 \ miles} \overset{?}{=} \dfrac{228 \ miles}{24 \ miles}$ 12) $\dfrac{49 \ points}{56 \ games} \overset{?}{=} \dfrac{7 \ points}{9 \ games}$

13) In the 8 a.m. section of mathematics, there are 12 female students and 16 male students enrolled. In the 1 p.m. section of mathematics, there are 12 male students and 9 female students enrolled. Is the ratio of male students to female students the same in both mathematics classes?

SKILL BUILDER 4.3
Solving Proportions

Solving Proportions

- Find the cross products.
- Divide each side of the equation by the number multiplied by n.
- Simplify the result.
- Check your answer.

Solve for n.

1) $8 \times n = 280$

2) $n \times 9 = 20.7$

3) $13 \times n = 156$

4) $\dfrac{3}{8} \times n = 15$

Find the value of n. Check your answer.

5) $\dfrac{n}{15} = \dfrac{2}{5}$

6) $\dfrac{8}{36} = \dfrac{n}{9}$

7) $\dfrac{42}{n} = \dfrac{35}{100}$

8) $\dfrac{27}{300} = \dfrac{18}{n}$

9) $\dfrac{14}{56} = \dfrac{n}{12}$

10) $\dfrac{2}{5} = \dfrac{11}{n}$

11) $\dfrac{1.3}{n} = \dfrac{2.6}{4}$

12) $\dfrac{5}{7} = \dfrac{n}{8.4}$

13) $\dfrac{12\frac{3}{5}}{100} = \dfrac{n}{5}$

14) $\dfrac{n \ grams}{200 \ liters} = \dfrac{7.5 \ grams}{40 \ liters}$

15) $\dfrac{24 \ quarters}{6 \ dollars} = \dfrac{97 \ quarters}{n \ dollars}$

SKILL BUILDER 4.4
Solving Applied Problems Involving Proportions

Solving Applied Problems Using Proportions

Example: Alicia's car can go 160 miles on 5 gallons of gas. How many gallons of gas are needed for a trip of 288 miles?

MATHEMATICS BLUEPRINT FOR PROBLEM SOLVING

Gather the Facts	What Am I Asked to Do?	How Do I Proceed?	Key Points to Remember
160 miles on 5 gallons of gas 288 miles for a trip	How many gallons of gas are needed to go 288 miles.	Set up a proportion comparing miles to gallons of gas.	$\dfrac{miles}{gallons}$

Solution: $\dfrac{160\,miles}{5\,gallons} = \dfrac{288\,miles}{n}$ $\longrightarrow$ $160 \times n = 5 \times 288$

$$n = \frac{5 \times 288}{160} = 9\,gallons$$

1) A shipment of 245 cameras had 7 defective cameras. How many defective cameras would you expect, at the same rate, in a shipment of 2275 cameras?

2) Andy's car can travel 330 miles on 22 gallons of gas. How many miles can he travel on 30 gallons of gas?

3) A recent survey showed that 7 out 10 people chewed Hi-Sugah chewing gum. If you surveyed 890 people, how can you expect to choose this brand of gum?

4) On a map, the distance from one city to another is 7 inches. If the actual distance is 315 miles, what is the actual distance between two other cities that are 11 inches apart on the map?

5) The Pizza Express sold 78 pizzas on Friday night when 110 customers were served. Next Friday, they expect 275 customers. How many pizzas should they be prepared to serve?

6) A profession basketball player who stands 7.5 feet tall casts a 6-foot shadow. At the same time, he is standing next to a building that casts a shadow 185 feet. How tall is the building? Round your answer to the nearest tenth.

SKILL BUILDER 5.1
Understanding Percent

Percent: means per 100.   Example: $17\% = 17$ parts per one hundred $= \dfrac{17}{100}$

Write a percent to express each of the following.

1) $\dfrac{41}{100} =$ _____

2) $\dfrac{4}{100} =$ _____

3) $\dfrac{75}{100} =$ _____

4) $\dfrac{310}{100} =$ _____

5) $\dfrac{2.7}{100} =$ _____

6) $\dfrac{0.013}{100} =$ _____

7) 47 people out 100 are sick.

8) 36 out 100 cars sold were Ford Explorers.

Changing a Percent to a Decimal

- Drop the % symbol.
- Move the decimal point two places to the left.

Write as a decimal.

9) $57\% =$ _____

10) $5\% =$ _____

11) $73.4\% =$ _____

12) $0.05\% =$ _____

13) $0.83\% =$ _____

14) $372\% =$ _____

Changing a Decimal to a Percent

- Move the decimal point two places to the right.
- Then write the % symbol at the end of the number.

Write as a percent.

15) $0.92 =$ _____

16) $0.08 =$ _____

17) $0.30 =$ _____

18) $0.389 =$ _____

19) $0.00076 =$ _____

20) $5.04 =$ _____

SKILL BUILDER 5.2
Changing Between Percents, Decimals, and Fractions

Changing a Percent to a Fraction

- Remove the percent symbol and write the number over 100.
- Simplify the resulting fraction, if necessary.
- In some cases, write the percent as a decimal before you write it as a fraction in simplest form.

Write as a fraction or as a mixed number.

1) 11% = _____

2) 65% = _____

3) 15% = _____

4) 4% = _____

5) 7.3% = _____

6) 78.5% = _____

7) 275% = _____

8) $3\frac{1}{2}$% = _____

9) $15\frac{2}{5}$% = _____

Changing a Fraction to a Percent

- Write the fraction in decimal form. (Don't forget to use long division!)
- Convert the decimal to a percent.

Write as a percent. Round to the nearest hundredth of a percent when necessary.

10) $\frac{2}{4}$ = _____ %

11) $\frac{13}{20}$ = _____ %

12) $\frac{19}{40}$ = _____ %

13) $\frac{8}{5}$ = _____ %

14) $3\frac{5}{6}$ = _____ %

15) $\frac{47}{15}$ = _____ %

Complete the table of equivalents. Simplify all fractions.

	Fraction	Decimal	Percent
16	$\frac{7}{500}$		
17			38%
18		0.035	

SKILL BUILDER 5.3A
Solving Percent Problems Using Equations

Solving a Percent Problem by Solving an Equation

- Amount = percent × base
- Word to Mathematical Symbol Chart

Word	Mathematical Symbol
of	multiplication: × or ( ) or ·
is	=
what	Any letter: n
find	n =

Solve.

1) What is 10% of 50? _____

2) 25 is what percent of 200? _____

3) 30% of what is 27? _____

4) Find 175% of 500 . _____

5) What is 40% of 110? _____

6) 28 is 0.4% of what? _____

7) 0.7% of what is 210? _____

8) 95 is what percent of 25? _____

9) Raymond's bill for new brakes on his car was $120. Of this amount, $30 was charged for labor and $90 was charged for parts. What percent of the bill was for parts?

10) A recent study claimed that 64% of students enrolled at a local college lived on campus. If there are 800 students enrolled, how many of these students live on campus?

SKILL BUILDER 5.3B
Solving Percent Problems Using Proportions

Percent Proportion

• $\dfrac{amount}{base} = \dfrac{p}{100}$

• p - percent number (remove the percent symbol).
   $base - (b)$ the entire quantity that follows the word *of*.
   $amount - (a)$ part being compared to the whole.

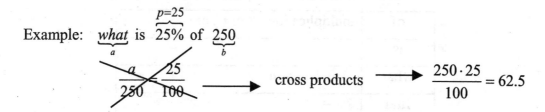

Example: $\underset{a}{\underbrace{what}}$ is $\overset{p=25}{\overbrace{25\%}}$ of $\underset{b}{\underbrace{250}}$

$\dfrac{a}{250} = \dfrac{25}{100}$ → cross products → $\dfrac{250 \cdot 25}{100} = 62.5$

Solve for the amount a.

1) 25% of 275 is what?   2) Find 320% of 80.   3) 0.6% of 400 is what?

Solve for the base b.

4) 30 is 40% of what?   5) 155% of what is 310?   6) 2000 is 0.5% of what?

Solve for the percent p.

7) 42 is what percent of 60?   8) What percent of 150 is 75?   9) What percent of 560 is 28?

Mixed Practice.

10) Find 0.5% of 650.   11) 300% of what is 165?   12) 102 is 48% of what?

13) A car salesman sells a car for $35,750. He gets a commission of 4% on the sale. What is his commission?

SKILL BUILDER 5.4
Solving Applied Percent Problems

__Method A:__ Translate to the equation "$p\%$ of b is a"

__Method B:__ Use the percent proportion $\dfrac{a}{b} = \dfrac{p}{100}$

Whether you use Method A or Method B, it may be helpful to use the Mathematics Blueprint.

MATHEMATICS BLUEPRINT FOR PROBLEM SOLVING

Gather the Facts	What Am I Asked to Do?	How Do I Proceed?	Key Points to Remember
Identify $p\%$, b-base, and a-amount, if possible. Can you make an estimate?	Find the question. (Hint: Find the "?".) Is it a part of the percent proportion? Discount? Etc.	Use: $\dfrac{a}{b} = \dfrac{p}{100}$ Remember: *is, of, what, find.*	Were percents added? Discount? Any extra information should be noted.

Solve. Round to the nearest hundredth when necessary.

1) The Snappy Potato Chip company found that 42 out of 500 bags inspected were under the weight advertised. What percent of the bags of chips inspected were under weight?

2) Allison bought a new CD player. The sales tax in her state is 5%, and she paid $4.50 in tax. What was the price of the CD player before tax?

3) In a recent survey on campus, 82% of the students claimed that they used the library to study at least 3 times per week. If there are 850 students on campus, how many students use the library to study at least 3 times per week?

4) Alicia earns $908 per month. Her cell phone bill for one month was $137. What percent of her total income goes toward paying her cell phone bill?

5) The nutrition label on a box of crackers reads: "Calories – 80; Calories from Fat – 30". What percent of the calories in a serving of cookies is from fat?

SKILL BUILDER 5.5
Solving Commission, Percent of Increase or Decrease, and Interest Problems

Solving Commission Problems

- Commission = commission rate × value of sales

Solve the following commission word problems.

1) A real estate agent sells a home for $365,000. The agent has a commission rate of 16%. What is the agent's commission?

2) Amy works for a telemarketing firm selling magazine subscriptions. She is paid $400 per month and 3% of her total sales. Last month, she sold $4,800 in magazine subscriptions. What was her total income for the month?

3) A salesperson earns a commission rate of 19%. How much commission would be paid if the salesperson sold $6800 in merchandise?

Solving Percent-of –Increase/Percent-of-Decrease Problems

- % of decrease = $\dfrac{amount\ of\ decrease}{original\ amount}$; % of increase= $\dfrac{amount\ of\ increase}{original\ amount}$

Solve the following percent-of-increase/decrease problems.

4) A car originally sold for $32,000. On Sunday only, the car sold for $24,000. What was the percent of decrease?

5) The enrollment in the Evening Division of a local college increased from 4200 to 5544 students per semester. What was the percent of increase?

6) The Dempsey family purchased a new stereo system. The list price was $875. They received a special 15% discount. How much did they pay for the new stereo system?

Solving Simple Interest Problems

- Interest = principal × rate × time $\longrightarrow$ I = P × R × T

Solve the following simple interest problems.

7) Find the simple interest on a loan of $8500 borrowed at 12% for one year.

8) Ray placed $1750 in a one-year CD at the bank. The bank is paying simple interest of 6.5% for one year on the CD. How much interest will Ray earn in one year?

9) Maria deposited $2800 in her savings account for one year. Her account earns 3.6% interest annually. She did not add any more money within the year. At the end of the year, how much interest did she earn? How much money did she have total in the bank?

SKILL BUILDER 6.1
American Units

Converting from One Unit of Measure to Another

- When multiplying by a unit fraction, the unit we want to change to should be in the numerator. The unit we start with should be in the denominator. This unit will divide out.

  Example: Convert 14,080 $\underbrace{yards}_{denominator}$ to $\overbrace{miles}^{numerator}$

  $$14{,}080 \text{ yards} \times \frac{1 \ mile}{1760 \ yards} = \frac{14{,}080}{1760} miles = 8 \ miles$$

Convert. When necessary, express your answer as a decimal.

1) 36 feet = _____ yards

2) 264 inches = _____ feet

3) 6 miles = _____ yards

4) 15,480 yards = _____ miles

5) 3 miles = _____ feet

6) 400 ounces = _____ pounds

7) 32 pounds = _____ ounces

8) 7.25 tons = _____ pounds

9) 11,0000 pounds = _____ tons

10) 15 minutes = _____ seconds

11) $8\frac{1}{2}$ hours = _____ minutes

12) 49 weeks = _____ days

13) 8 pints = _____ cups

14) 14 quarts = _____ gallons

15) 78 fluid ounces = _____ cups

16) 200 cups = _____ gallons

SKILL BUILDER 6.2
Metric Measurements: Length

Commonly Used Metric Lengths

    1 kilometer (km) = 1000 meters
    1 meter (m)
    1 centimeter (cm) = 0.01 meter
    1 millimeter (mm) = 0.001 meter

Perform the following conversions.

1)   36 centimeters = _____ millimeters

2)   890 millimeters = _____ centimeters

3)   3800 meters = _____ kilometers

4)   11.5 kilometers = _____ meters

5)   1.5 meters = _____ millimeters

6)   0.0815 meters = _____ centimeters

7)   65,000 mm = _____ km

8)   75 mm = _____ meters

9)   14 centimeters = _____ meters

10)   70 meters = _____ centimeters

11)   1200 meters = _____ kilometers

12)   3.2 kilometers = _____ meters

13)   80 meters = _____ millimeters

14)   0.5 kilometers = _____ meters

15)   137 centimeters = _____ meters

16)   10.2 centimeters = _____ millimeters

17) 43,000 millimeters = _____ meters

18)   71 meters = _____ millimeters

19)   4.75 km + 60 m + 832 cm = _____ meters

20)   2.3 m + 14 cm + 3020 mm = _____ centimeters

SKILL BUILDER 6.3
Metric Measurements: Volume and Weight

Common Metric Volume Measurements

1 kiloliter (kL) = 1000 liters
1 liter (L)
1 milliliter (mL) = 0.001 liter
1000 cc = 1 liter

Perform each conversion.

1) 32 kL = _____ L

2) 130 L = _____ kL

3) 13 L = _____ mL

4) 445 mL = _____ L

5) 0.003 kL = _____ mL

6) 756 mL = _____ cm^3

7) 1,567 cm^3 = _____ L

8) Add: 15 L + 0.07 kL + 20000 mL = _____ L

Common Metric Weight Measurements

1 metric ton (t) = 1,000,000 grams
1 kilogram (kg) = 1000 grams
1 gram (g)
1 milligram (mg) = 0.001 gram

9) 4310 g = _____ kg

10) 5.62 kg = _____ g

11) 0.098 g = _____ mg

12) 732 mg = _____ g

13) 76 t = _____ kg

14) 0.054 t = _____ kg

15) 43,000 mg = _____ kg

16) Add: 320 g + 8 kg + 870 mg = _____

SKILL BUILDER 6.4
Converting Units

	American to Metric	Metric to American
Length	1 mile ≈1.61 km 1 yard ≈0.914 m 1 foot ≈0.305 m 1 inch = 2.54 cm	1 km ≈0.62 mile 1 m ≈3.28 feet 1 m ≈1.09 yards 1 cm ≈0.394 inch
Volume	1 gallon ≈3.79 L 1 quart ≈0.946 L	1 L ≈0.264 gallon 1 L ≈1.06 quarts
Weight	1 pound ≈0.454 kg 1 ounce ≈28.35 g	1 kg ≈2.2 pounds 1 g ≈0.0353 ounce

Perform each length conversion. Round to the nearest hundredth when necessary.

1)   3 feet ≈_____ m

2) 8 inches ≈_____ cm

3)   22 m ≈_____ yards

4)   8 miles ≈_____ km

5)   14 yards ≈_____ m

6)   11.2 cm ≈_____ inches

7)   100 km ≈_____ miles

8)   304.8 cm ≈_____ inches ≈_____ feet

Perform each volume conversion. Round to the nearest hundredth when necessary.

9) 8 quarts ≈_____ L

10) 2.5 quarts ≈_____ L

11) 27 L ≈_____ quarts

12) .98 L ≈_____ gallons

13) 5 L ≈_____ gallons

14) 0.45 L ≈_____ quarts

Perform each weight conversion. Round to the nearest hundredth when necessary.

15) 27 ounces ≈_____ grams

16) 50 grams ≈_____ ounces

17) 10 pounds ≈_____ kg

Celsius to Fahrenheit	Fahrenheit to Celsius
$F = 1.8 \times C + 32$ C is the number of Celsius degrees F is the number of Fahrenheit degrees	$C = \dfrac{5 \times F - 160}{9}$

18)   125° C to Fahrenheit

19) 221° F to Celsius

SKILL BUILDER 6.5
Solving Applied Measurement Problems

Solving Applied Problems

- Use the Mathematics Blueprint for solving applied problems.
- Be sure that you are working in the same unit of measurement.

Example: A lab assistant must use 18.06 liters of solution to fill 35 jars. How many milliliters of the solution will go into each jar?

MATHEMATICS BLUEPRINT FOR PROBLEM SOLVING

Gather the Facts	What Am I Asked to Do?	How Do I Proceed?	Key Points to Remember
We have 18.06 L of solution. Divide solution into 35 jars.	Find out how many milliliters will go into each jar.	Get all measurements into milliliters. Divide that result by 35.	1 L = 1000 ml (move decimal to the right three places)

Solve. Round to the nearest hundredth.

1. A leaky pipe drips 2 pints of water per hour. How many gallons of water is this per week?

2. A rectangular window measures 28 inches × 54 inches. Window insulation is applied along all four sides. The insulation costs $6.00 per meter. What will it cost to insulate the window?

3. A piece of rope measures 30.5 meters. It needs to be cut into 5 equal pieces. How many centimeters long will each piece be?

4. A swimming pool's thermometer reads 30°C. Allison exclaimed "I cannot go in that pool, I have to have the temperature at least 82°F!" Can Allison swim in this pool?

5. An amusement park ride had a sign posted that said you must be at least 4 feet tall to ride. Nicholas measures 145 cm tall. Can Nicholas go on the ride?

6. A swimming pool is being filled at the rate of 11 quarts per minute. How many gallons per hour is this?

SKILL BUILDER 7.1
Angles

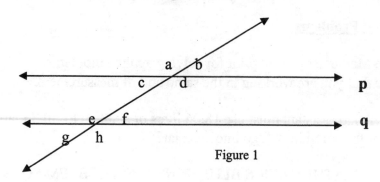

Figure 1

Refer to Figure 1 for questions 1 - 8. Given : p ∥ q, $\angle$ a = 112°, find the measure for the following angles.

1) $\angle b$ = _____

2) $\angle c$ = _____

3) $\angle d$ = _____

4) $\angle e$ = _____

5) $\angle f$ = _____

6) $\angle g$ = _____

7) $\angle h$ = _____

8) $\angle a + \angle b$ = _____

Sketch the following.

9) Sketch a 90° angle. Label the side and vertex.

10) Sketch an acute angle. Label the degree measure.

11) Sketch an obtuse angle. Label the degree measure.

12) Sketch and label adjacent angles.

SKILL BUILDER 7.2
Rectangles and Squares

Rectangles

- Perimeter: $P = 2l + 2w$
- Area: $A = lw$

Find the perimeter and the area of the following rectangles. Round to the nearest hundredth.

1) Length: 15 inches

   Width: 9 inches

   Perimeter = _____

   Area = _____

2) Length: $12\frac{1}{3}$ meters

   Width: $7\frac{1}{3}$ meters

   Perimeter = _____

   Area = _____

3) Length: 27.25 yards

   Width: 13.5 yards

   Perimeter = _____

   Area = _____

Squares

- Perimeter: $P = 4s$
- Area: $A = s^2$

Find the perimeter and the area of the following squares. Round to the nearest hundredth

4) Side: 37 miles

   Perimeter: _____

   Area: _____

5) Side: $6\frac{3}{4}$ feet

   Perimeter: _____

   Area: _____

6) Side: 42.38 centimeters

   Perimeter: _____

   Area: _____

7) The rectangular swimming pool at the health club measures 30 feet wide and 60 feet long. A new pool cover is needed and costs $0.75 per square foot. If you purchase exactly what is needed, how much is this going to cost?

SKILL BUILDER 7.3
Parallelograms, Trapezoids, and Rhombuses

Parallelograms

- Four-sided figure in which both pairs of opposite sides are parallel and equal in length.
- Perimeter: add the lengths of all sides of the figure.
- Area: $A = bh$ (*b-base:* any side of parallelogram; *h-height*: shortest distance between the base and side opposite the base).

1) Find the perimeter of a parallelogram with one side measuring 5.6 meters and a second side that measures 34.6 meters.

2) Find the area of a parallelogram with base measuring 42.6 yards, and the height is 63.75 yards.

3) Find the area of a lawn shaped like a parallelogram. Its base is 504 feet and its height is 112 feet.

Trapezoid

- Four sided figure with two parallel sides.
- Perimeter: sum of the lengths of all of its sides.
- Area: $\dfrac{h(b + B)}{2}$; (h – height: distance between the two parallel sides; b-shorter base; B-longer base).

4) Find the perimeter of a trapezoid with four sides measuring: 260 in., 140 in., 520 in., and 80 in.

5) Find the area of the trapezoid with a height of 45 meters and the bases are 21 meters and 44.5 meters.

Rhombus

- Parallelogram with all four sides equal.
- Perimeter: $P = 4s$
- Area: $A = bh$

6) An inlaid piece of colored glass in a window is in the shape of a rhombus. This piece of glass has a base of 84 cm. and a height of 56 cm. Find the perimeter and area of the piece of inlaid glass.

SKILL BUILDER 7.4
Triangles

Triangles

- Three-sided figure with 3 angles
- Sum of the measures of the 3 angles equals 180°
- Perimeter = $s_1 + s_2 + s_3$; sum of all three sides
- Area = $\dfrac{bh}{2}$; b – base: perpendicular to height; h – height: distance of a line drawn from a vertex perpendicular to the opposite side or an extension of the opposite side.

1) Find the measure of the missing angle of a triangle with two angles that measure 42° and 37°.

2) Find the measure of the three angles of an equilateral triangle.

3) Find the measure of the angles for a right triangle that has one angle measuring 19°.

4) Find the perimeter of a triangle whose sides measure: 142 m, 130 m, and 164 m.

5) Find the area of a triangle whose base is 52 feet and the height is 28.5 feet.

6) Find the area of the following triangle.

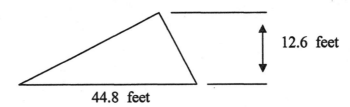

12.6 feet

44.8 feet

7)   A triangular study room needs new carpet.   Together, Allison and Alicia notice that the room forms a right triangle.   The length of the walls of the study room measure: 27 feet, 27 feet, and 38.2 feet.   Allison and Alicia have priced carpet and find that the carpet they want costs $8.99/ square *yard*. How much will it cost to carpet the study room (if necessary, round to the nearest cent)?

SKILL BUILDER 7.5
Square Roots

Square Roots

- If a number is a product of two identical factors, then either factor is called a square root.
- Example: $\sqrt{81}$ (read square root of 81) = 9 because (9)(9) = 81

Find each square root. Do not use a calculator or a square root table.

1) $\sqrt{4}$ = _____

2) $\sqrt{36}$ = _____

3) $\sqrt{49}$ = _____

4) $\sqrt{9}$ = _____

5) $\sqrt{0}$ = _____

6) $\sqrt{144}$ = _____

7) $\sqrt{100}$ = _____

8) $\sqrt{16}$ = _____

9) $\sqrt{121}$ = _____

10) $\sqrt{64}$ = _____

11) $\sqrt{1}$ = _____

12) $\sqrt{25}$ = _____

Evaluate the square roots first, then add or subtract the results. Do not use a calculator or a square root table.

13) $\sqrt{25} + \sqrt{1}$ = _____

14) $\sqrt{121} - \sqrt{36}$ = _____

15) $\sqrt{144} + \sqrt{0}$ = _____

Use a calculator to approximate to the nearest thousandth.

16) $\sqrt{83}$ = _____

17) $\sqrt{99}$ = _____

18) $\sqrt{17}$ = _____

SKILL BUILDER 7.6
The Pythagorean Theorem

Pythagorean Theorem

leg | hypotenuse (always side opposite right angle)

leg

- Hypotenuse = $\sqrt{(leg)^2 + (leg)^2}$
- Leg = $\sqrt{(hypotenuse)^2 - (leg)^2}$

Find the unknown side of the right triangle. Round to the nearest thousandth, if necessary.

1) leg = 9, leg = 6

2) leg = 4, hypotenuse = 9

3) leg = 3, leg = 3

Special Right Triangles

- $30° - 60° - 90°$ triangle: The length of the leg opposite the 30° angle is ½ the length of the hypotenuse.
- $45° - 45° - 90°$ triangle: Sides opposite the 45° angles are equal. The length of the hypotenuse is equal to $\sqrt{2} \times$ the length of either leg.

Find the length of the unknown sides. Round to the nearest tenth.

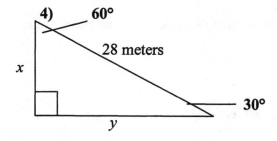

x = _____ , y = _____

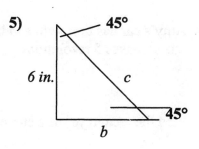

b = _____ , c = _____

SKILL BUILDER 7.7
Circles

Circles

- $C = \pi d$; C = circumference, d = 2 × radius
- $A = \pi r^2$; A = area; r = radius

Solve the following. Use $\pi \approx 3.14$. Round all answers to the nearest hundredth.

1) The radius of a circle is 14 inches. Find the circumference and area of the circle.

2) The diameter of the top of a round table is 38 inches. Find the circumference and the area of the tabletop.

3) A decorative round window has a radius of 14 inches. What is the length of the insulation strip that encircles the window and keeps out the wind and moisture?

4) A radio station sends out radio waves in all directions from a tower a the center of the circle of broadcast range. Determine how large an area can be reached if the diameter of the circle of broadcast is 180 miles.

5) Raymond bought a circular piece of marble to use as a table in his living room. The marble piece was 4.5 ft in diameter. Find the cost at $85 per square yard of marble.

6) Amy's car has tires with a radius of 21 inches. How many feet does her car travel if the wheel makes 5 revolutions.?

7) Find the area in yd^2 of a circle with a diameter of 30 feet.

8) A circular burner on a stove has an area of 28.3 square inches. Marie wants to place a 12-inch diameter fry pan on the burner. Is this a good choice? Why or why not?

SKILL BUILDER 7.8
Volume

Finding the Volume

- Rectangular Solid: $V = lwh$; V = volume, l = length, w = width, h = height

- Cylinder: $V = \pi r^2 h$; r = radius, h = height

- Sphere: $V = \dfrac{4\pi\, r^3}{3}$; r = radius

- Cone: $V = \dfrac{\pi\, r^2 h}{3}$; r = radius, h = height

- Pyramid: $V = \dfrac{Bh}{3}$; B = base of the pyramid; h = height

Solve the following. Use $\pi \approx 3.14$. Round to the nearest tenth when necessary.

1) Find the volume of a shoebox of width 12 in., length 14 in., and height 4 in.

2) Find the volume of an oil barrel of radius 15 in. and height 45 in..

3) Find the volume of a ball with radius 18 in.

4) Find the volume of a cone of radius 2.7 ft and height 3 ft.

5) Find the volume of a pyramid with height 300 m, length of base 1400 m, width of base 160 m.

6) Jenny and Nicki are constructing a sandbox. The have built a frame that is 6 in. in height, 2 yd wide and 3 yd long. How many cubic yards of sand is needed to fill their sandbox?

7) A pyramid of height 24 m and with a square base of side 16 m.

8) A farm silo in the shape of a cylinder is 42.5 ft. high, and its circular base has a radius of 15 ft. Find its volume.

SKILL BUILDER 7.9
Similar Geometric Figures

Similar Triangles

- Corresponding angles of similar triangles are equal.
- Corresponding sides of similar triangles have the same ratio.
- Perimeters of similar triangles have the same ratio as the corresponding sides.

For each pair of similar triangles, find the missing side *n*. Round to the nearest tenth when necessary.

1)

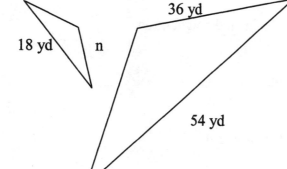

3 in n 8 in 16 in

2)   5 cm 3 cm 12.5 cm n

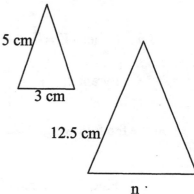

3)   18 yd   n   36 yd   54 yd

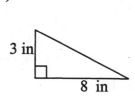

Similar Geometric Figures

- Corresponding sides of similar geometric figures have the same ratio.
- Perimeters of similar figures have the same ratio as their corresponding sides.
- Special case: *All* circles are similar.

Find the missing side for the pair of similar figures. Round to the nearest tenth if necessary.

4)   n   6 in   21 in   15 in

5   12.3 mm   20 mm   1mm   n

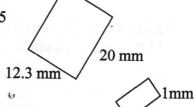

SKILL BUILDER 7.10
Applied Problems Involving Geometry

Solving Applied Problems Involving Geometric Shapes

MATHEMATICS BLUEPRINT FOR PROBLEM SOLVING

Gather the Facts	What Am I Asked to Do?	How Do I Proceed?	Key Points to Remember
List all measurements. List all geometric shapes involved in the problem.	What are you trying to find? Area? Perimeter? Volume? etc.	List the steps needed to accomplish what you are asked to do.	Formulas that apply to area, perimeter, volume, etc.

Using the Mathematics Blueprint for Problem Solving, solve the following applied problems.

1) A professional painter can paint 16 ft^2 per 10 minutes. He will be painting the four, rectangular, outside walls of a house. Two walls measure 48 feet long by 16 feet high and the two other walls measure 24 feet by 16 feet high.   How many hours will it take to paint all four walls?

2) The floor area of an exercise room at Tinnie's house is shown in the following drawing. How much will it cost to carpet the room if the carpet costs $9 per square yard. (Note: the shape of the exercise floor is a trapezoid.)

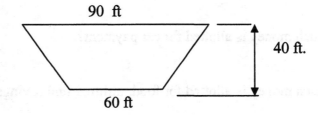

3) As a fund-raiser, the Student Senate on campus sell decorated boxes of candy. Each box measures 6 in. wide × 8 in. long × 4 in. high. The group has projected that they will be able to sell 450 decorated boxes of candy. If one bag of candy cost $1.99 and can fill 240 cubic inches, how much will it cost to purchase the candy for the fundraiser?

SKILL BUILDER 8.1
Circle Graphs

Reading a Circle Graph

- <u>Statistics</u>: branch of mathematics that collects and studies data.
- <u>Graphs</u>: a visual representation of the data that is easy to read.
- <u>Circle graphs</u>: shows relationships of parts to a whole, the entire circle represents 100%

The following circle graph displays Anna and Dave Rosi's monthly $3700 family budget. Use the circle graph to answer the following questions.

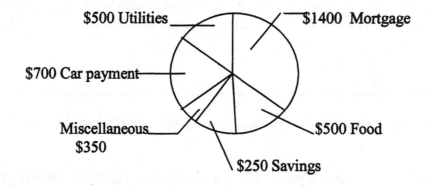

$500 Utilities _____ _____ $1400 Mortgage

$700 Car payment

Miscellaneous _____ $350

$250 Savings

$500 Food

1) Which category takes the most amount of the budget?

2) Which category takes the least amount of the budget?

3) Which 2 categories use the same amount of the budget each month?

4) How much money is allotted for car payment?

5) How much money is allotted for food, utilities, and savings?

6) What is the ratio of money spent on utilities to the total amount of the monthly budget?

7) What percent of the monthly family budget is the mortgage? Round to the nearest hundredth.

8) What is the ratio of car payment to mortgage?

SKILL BUILDER 8.2
Bar Graphs and Line Graphs

Reading and Interpreting a Bar and Line Graphs

- <u>Bar graphs</u>: helpful for seeing changes over a period of time.
- <u>Double-bar graphs</u>: useful for making comparisons.
- <u>Line graph</u>: useful for showing trends over a period of time.
- <u>Comparison line graph</u>: show two or more line graphs together.

The following bar graph shows the number of textbooks Joe, Angela and Anna sold each quarter during a year. Use the graph to approximate the following questions.

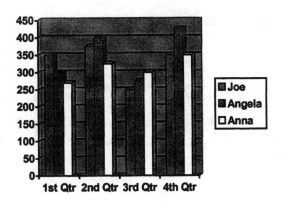

1) How many textbooks did Joe sell during the 1st quarter?

2) How many textbooks did Angela sell the entire year?

3) Who sold the most amount of books during any one quarter?

4) Who sold the most amount of books over the entire year?

5) Who sold the least amount of books during any one quarter?

6) How many more books did Joe sell than Anna during the 2nd quarter?

7) How many textbooks were sold during the entire year?

SKILL BUILDER 8.3
Histograms

Constructing a Histogram from Raw Data

- Select data class intervals of equal width for the data.
- Make a table with class intervals and a tally (count) of how many numbers occur in each interval. Add up the tally to find the class frequency for each class interval.
- Draw the histogram.

The following lists the number of miles hiked by each member of the Quinsigamond Hiking Club.
Determine the frequencies of the class intervals for this data.

31	27	14	35	42	35	40
22	27	32	25	22	23	16
44	46	35	38	15	21	16
28	30	53	22	45	23	25

Miles Hiked
Class Interval Tally   Frequency

1) 14 – 18 miles _____ _____

2) 19 - 23 miles _____ _____

3) 24 – 28 miles _____ _____

4) 29 - 33 miles _____ _____

5) 34 – 38 miles _____ _____

6) 39 – 43 miles _____ _____

7) 44 – 48 miles _____ _____

8) 49 – 53 miles _____ _____

9) Using the table of information above, construct a histogram.

SKILL BUILDER 8.4
Mean, Median, and Mode

Finding the Mean, Median, and Mode

- Mean: sum of the values divided by the number of values.
- Median: value that has the same number of values above it as below it.
- Mode: number or numbers that occur most often.

Find the mean of the following sets of data. Round to the nearest tenth when necessary.

1) The number of students who were served at the cafeteria during lunchtime in the past five days were as follows: 375, 420, 325, 390, 410.

2) The number of miles jogged by a student over 7 days were: 14, 18, 12, 8, 15, 13, 13.

Find the median value.

3) The salaries of employees of a local restaurant are $21,000, $14,500, $32,450, $11,500, $22,000.

4) The cellular phone bills for Alicia over the last six month's were as follows: $110, $95, $115, $145, $120, $105.

Find the mode.

5) Exam scores for math test were: 85, 79, 83, 85, 100, 95, 85, 100, 83, 62, 71.

6) The number of people attending an art show during the last ten days were: 245, 325, 250, 245, 190, 275, 250, 185, 245, 250.

7) At the end of the semester, a student decided to find the "middle value" of her grades. On five different exams, she scored: 84, 94, 97, 81, 89, 89. Find the mean of the student's scores.

SKILL BUILDER 9.1
Adding Signed Numbers

Addition Rule for Two Numbers with the Same Sign

- Add the absolute value of the numbers.
- Use the common sign in the answer.

Add each pair of signed numbers that have the same sign.

1) -5 + (-3) = _____

2) -10 + (-12) = _____

3) 8.2 + 2.3 = _____

4) $-\dfrac{1}{2}+\left(-\dfrac{1}{3}\right)=$ _____

5) -9.72 + (-12.34) = _____

6) $\dfrac{6}{11}+\dfrac{3}{22}=$ _____

Addition Rule for Two Numbers with Different Signs

- Subtract the absolute value of the numbers.
- Use the sign of the number with the larger absolute value.

Add each pair of signed numbers that have different signs.

7) 5 + (-15) = _____

8) -20 + 11 = _____

9) $-\dfrac{1}{5}+\left(\dfrac{3}{5}\right)=$ _____

10) 14.2 + (-36.3) = _____

11) (-68) + 15 = _____

12) (-110) + (213) = _____

Mixed Practice. Add.

13) -35 + (-3) = _____

14) (-14) + (19) = _____

15) 32 + (-113) = _____

16) (-3) + (-8) + (-21) + 31 = _____

17) (-5) + 5 = _____

18) $\dfrac{4}{15}+(-\dfrac{11}{12})=$ _____

19) (-18) + (14) + (-27) + (-43) + 63 + (-12) = _____

S-54

SKILL BUILDER 9.2
Subtracting Signed Numbers

Subtraction of Signed Numbers

- "Add the opposite"
- The first number does not change
- Subtraction sign is changed to addition
- Write the opposite of the second number.

Subtract the signed numbers by adding the opposite of the second number to the first number.

1) 6 - 8 = _____

2) 8 - 19 = _____

3) 17 - 27 = _____

4) -42 - (-25) = _____

5) (-5.6) - 9.03 = _____

6) 530 – (-220) = _____

7) (-201) – 32 = _____

8) $\dfrac{2}{7} - \dfrac{18}{21} =$ _____

9) (-80.09) – (- 76.8) = _____

10) $-\dfrac{11}{15} - \left(-\dfrac{1}{2}\right) =$ _____

11) 6 – (-9) – (-10) –13 = _____

12) -123 – (-123) = _____

13) -30 + 12 – (-15) – 8 = _____

14) Tinnie overdrew her checking account by $25.32. Quickly, she ran to the bank and deposited her paycheck of $214.78. What is the balance of her checking after her deposit?

SKILL BUILDER 9.3
Multiplication and Division of Signed Numbers

Multiplication and Division of Different Signed Numbers

- To multiply or divide two numbers with different signs, multiply or divide the absolute values. The result is *negative*.

Multiplication and Division Rule for Two Numbers with the Same Sign

- To multiply or divide two numbers with the same sign, multiply or divide the absolute values. The sign of the result is *positive*.

Multiply or Divide.

1) (13)(4) = _____

2) (-30)(-5) = _____

3) (-120)(-13) = _____

4) (5)(-3) = _____

5) (15.2)(-19.3) = _____

6) (174)(-45) = _____

7) (100) ÷ (-25) = _____

8) (-87) ÷ (-3) = _____

9) $\dfrac{-49}{-7}$ = _____

10) $\dfrac{-144}{12}$ = _____

11) $\dfrac{11}{16} \div \dfrac{33}{40}$ = _____

12) 27.5 ÷ (-0.5) = _____

13) $5(-3)(-2)\left(\dfrac{2}{15}\right)$ = _____

14) (-9)(0)(-4)(10) = _____

SKILL BUILDER 9.4
Order of Operations with Signed Numbers

Order of Operations for Signed Numbers

Do First   Perform operations inside the parentheses.

Simplify any expressions with exponents, and find any square roots.

Multiply or divide from left to right.

Do Last   Add or subtract from left to right.

Perform the indicated operations in the proper order.   If necessary, simplify the numerator and denominator first. Reduce all fractions.

1) $15 + (-30) \div (-5) =$ _____

2) $5(-3) + 7(-1) - (-21) =$ _____

3) $12 (-5) - 3(12) =$ _____

4) $8 - 20 \div 2 =$ _____

5) $-63 \div 9 + 12 =$ _____

6) $(-48) \div 6 + (90)\left(-\dfrac{3}{10}\right) =$ _____

7) $\dfrac{9 - 12 - 3}{5 + 8 - 15} =$ _____

8) $\dfrac{4(-8) - 2(5)}{27 \div 9(-2)} =$ _____

9) $\dfrac{36 \div 6 + (-2)(3)}{8 - 8 \div (-2)} =$ _____

10) $\dfrac{60 \div 6 + (8)(-2)}{72 \div 9 + (-2)} =$ _____

11) $8(-3) + 5^2 =$ _____

12) $-90 \div 3^2 + (5 - 3)^3 =$ _____

13) $1.69 - (-0.7)(3) =$ _____

14) $\left(\dfrac{3}{4}\right)^2 - \left(\dfrac{1}{2}\right)^2 =$ _____

SKILL BUILDER 9.5
Scientific Notation

Scientific Notation

- Of the form $a \times 10^n$ where "a" is a number greater than (or equal to) 1 and less than 10, and n is an integer.

- Example: Write 1,200 in scientific notation. $1,200 = 1.2 \times 10^3$
  Write 0.00032 in scientific notation. $0.00032 = 3.2 \times 10^{-4}$

Complete the table with equivalent values.

	Scientific Notation	Standard Notation
1		1,200
2	2.47×10^5	
3	6.3×10^{-4}	
4		0.00000998
5	3.72×10^{12}	
6		0.0000546
7		3,000,000,000,000
8	$9.32 \times^{-9}$	

Add or subtract as indicated.

9) $6.0 \times 10^3 + 2.0 \times 10^3 =$ _____

10) $9.3 \times 10^{-2} - 3.1 \times 10^{-2} =$ _____

11) $5.326 \times 10^8 + 2.439 \times 10^8 =$ _____

12) $9.702 \times 10^{-3} - 3.999 \times 10^{-3} =$ _____

SKILL BUILDER 10.1
Variables and Like Terms

Variables

- A symbol, usually a letter of the alphabet, that stands for a number.
- Note: $V = lwh$ is the same as $l \times w \times h$

Write each equation without multiplication signs.

1) $A = b \times h$ 2) $r = 5 \times \times m + 6n$ 3) $p = 4 \times a \times b \times c$

Like Terms

- Term: a number, a variable, or a product of a number and one or more variables separated from other terms by a "+" sign or a "-" sign.
- Like terms: terms that have identical variables and identical exponents
- Numerical coefficients: numbers that are directly in front of the terms

Combine like terms.

4) $5x + 4x + 8x$ 5) $x + 4x - 8x$

6) $1.2x + 13 - 5.3x - 8.2x$ 7) $14y + 32y - (-8y)$

8) $3x + 2y - 6x - 4y + 9x$ 9) $9a + 12b - 3c - a - 6b - 4c$

10) $\dfrac{1}{3}x - \dfrac{1}{4}y - \dfrac{2}{3}x + \dfrac{3}{4}y$ 11) $1.2x + 2.3y - 6.2z - 2.1x - 6.3y + 8.3z$

Find the perimeter of each figure.

12)

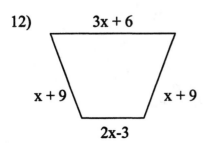

3x + 6

x + 9   x + 9

2x - 3

13)

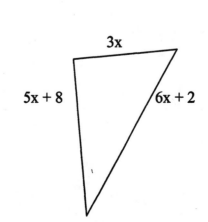

3x

5x + 8   6x + 2

SKILL BUILDER 10.2
The Distributive Property

Distributive Properties of Multiplication over Addition

- If a, b, and c are signed numbers, then $a(b + c) = ab + ac$ and $(b + c)a = ba + ca$

Simplify.   Be sure to combine like terms.

1) $3 (2x - 2)$

2) $5 (7x - 3)$

3) $(-5) (a + b)$

4) $(-2x + 7y) (-9)$

5) $(-10)(2x - 3y - 4z)$

6) $2(3.5x - 2.3y)$

7) $9(-3x - 4)$

8) $(-1)(6x - 9)$

9) $4(2x - 2y)$

10) $5\left(\dfrac{2}{3}x + 4y\right)$

11) $12(-14x - 18y - 21z)$

12) $(-8)(6.2x - 9.1y)$

13) $\dfrac{1}{5}\left(3x - 2y - \dfrac{5}{7}z + \dfrac{1}{3}\right)$

14) $0.2(-x - 2.1y + 5)$

15) $3(5x - 2) + 3(x - 2)$

16) $2(3y - 4) + 8(y - 7)$

17) $4(x + 2y) - 3(x + 9)$

18) $\dfrac{1}{7}\left(\dfrac{7}{3}x - 4\right) + 2\left(\dfrac{1}{3}x - \dfrac{1}{7}\right)$

SKILL BUILDER 10.3
Solving Equations Using the Addition Property

Addition Property of Equations

- You may add the same number to each side of an equation to obtain an equivalent equation.

Solve for the variable.

1) $x - 8 = 10$

2) $x - 10 = 12$

3) $y - 9 = 0$

4) $y + 3 = 10$

5) $x + 5 = 15$

6) $y + 7 = 23$

7) $-13 + x = 4$

8) $-12 + a = -4$

9) $-2 + x = -9$

10) $x - 2.3 = 5.7$

11) $y - 9.3 = -2.2$

12) $-3.7 + y = 6.9$

13) $x + \dfrac{2}{5} = \dfrac{4}{5}$

14) $y - \dfrac{4}{7} = \dfrac{6}{7}$

15) $\dfrac{2}{3} + y = -\dfrac{11}{12}$

16) $4x - 8 = 3x + 2$

17) $5x + 8 = 4x - 2$

18) $16x + 52 = 15x - 13$

SKILL BUILDER 10.4
Solving Equations Using the Division or Multiplication Property

Division or Multiplication Property

- You may divide each side of an equation by the same nonzero number to obtain an equivalent equation.
- You may multiply each side of an equation by the same nonzero number to obtain an equivalent equation.

Solve for the variable. Use the division or multiplication property of equations.

1) $5x = 15$

2) $3x = 12$

3) $9x = 81$

4) $9x = 27$

5) $-6y = 36$

6) $-8y = -48$

7) $-72 = 9y$

8) $-110x = 220$

9) $-40 = 10x$

10) $3.3z = 9.9$

11) $8.1\,y = -18.63$

12) $-0.3y = 8.4$

13) $\dfrac{1}{2}x = 4$

14) $15 = -\dfrac{3}{4}y$

15) $-2\dfrac{1}{3}x = 21$

SKILL BUILDER 10.5
Solving Equations Using Two Properties

Solving Equations

- Remove any parentheses by using the distributive property.
- Collect like terms on each side of the equation.
- Use Addition Property of Equations (Section 10.3)
- Use Division Property of Equations (Section 10.4)
- Check by substituting the solution back into the original equation.

Solve.

1) $14x - 24 = 4$

2) $13x - 12 = 27$

3) $4x - 12 = 4$

4) $7x + 3 = 59$

5) $10 - 3x = 2x + 25$

6) $21 + 3y = 2y$

7) $-25 - 2y + 15 = 3y - 20$

8) $\dfrac{2}{5}x - 8 = 12$

9) $\dfrac{5}{12}x - 6 = 24$

10) $2y - 20 + 9y + 50 = -116 - 3y$

11) $3(x - 5) = 2x + 1$

12) $14x - 3(x + 6) = 3(x + 2)$

SKILL BUILDER 10.6
Translating English to Algebra

SYMBOL	+	-	×	2×	3×	÷	=
ENGLISH	greater than increased by more than added to sum of	less than decreased by smaller than fewer than shorter than difference of	multiplied by of product of times	double	triple	divided by ratio of quotient of	is was has costs equals represents amounts to

Translate the English sentence into an equation using the variable indicated.

1) Alicia is 5 inches taller than Allison. Use h for Alicia's height and r for Allison's height.

2) The length of the rectangle is 5 meters longer than twice the width. Use l for the length and w for the width of the rectangle.

3) The combined number of hours Amy and Bill study per school day is 9 hours. Use a for the number of hours Amy studies and b for the number of hours Bill studies.

4) The product of your hourly wage and the amount of time worked is $300. Let h = the hourly wage and t = the number of hours worked.

Write algebraic expressions for each quantity using the given variable.

5) Matt's car trip was 247 miles longer than Andrea's car trip. Use the letter t.

6) Anastasia and Elias were raising money for the Diabetes Foundation. Anastasia collected $540 more in donations that Elias. Nicholas made $60 less than Elias. Use the letter e.

SKILL BUILDER 10.7
Solving Applied Problems

Solving Applied Problems

- Understand the Problem: Read and re-read the problem. Draw a picture or diagram.
- Write an equation
- Solve and state the answer.
- Check: Be sure to verify the solution.

Solve using an equation. Show what you let the variable equal.

1) A 45-foot rope is cut into two pieces. The longer piece is 15 feet longer than the shorter piece. What is the length of each piece?

2) Mr. Exarchos has 527 cars on his used-car lot. He has 52 more luxury vehicles than compact. He also has 50 fewer mini-vans than compact vehicles. How many of each type of vehicle (luxury, compact, mini-vans) are on his lot?

3) The perimeter of a rectangle is 450 inches. The length is 25 inches more that 3 times the width. What are the dimensions of the rectangle?

4) This month's salary for an appliance salesman was $5000. This includes her base monthly salary of $3600 plus a 7% commission on total sales. Find the total sales for the month.

5) The perimeter of a square is 64 feet. Each side is tripled, what will be the perimeter of the larger square?

- 1 -ANSWERS TO SKILL BUILDERS

Chapter 1

Section 1.1: 1) four thousand, nine hundred sixty-five; 2) four hundred five thousand, seven hundred sixty-one; 3) forty-six million, one hundred fifteen thousand, two; 4) seven million, nine hundred three thousand, one; 5) 837; 6) 2,821; 7) 8,207,490; 8) seventy-two; 9) four thousand, six hundred twenty-seven; 10) sixty-one million, two hundred five thousand, five hundred fifty-two; 11) sixty-two thousand, four; 12) one thousand seventy-three and 99/100 dollars.

Section 1.2: 1) 88; 2) 183; 3) 8,330; 4) 31,390; 5) 28,203; 6) 556,473; 7) 137; 8) 13,262,314; 9) 819,717; 10) 2,073; 11) 666 feet; 12) $11.79.

Section 1.3: 1) 36; 2) 135; 3) 42,442; 4) 16,045; 5) 21,359; 6) 77,632; 7) 91,066; 8) 7,783; 9) 1,776,091; 10) 391, 145, 1982

Section 1.4: 1) 215, 2) 2,412; 3) 3,292; 4) 123,654; 5) 0; 6) 2310; 7) 49,230; 8) 24,084; 9) 2,618,235; 10) 11,400; 11) 108,004; 12) 1,090,944; 13) 320; 14) 325; 15) $7,812.45; 16) 180 square feet.

Section 1.5: 1) 9; 2) 7; 3) 0; 4) 7; 5) 11r1; 6) undef.; 7) 17; 8) 23r2; 9) 137r2; 10) 165r5; 11) 553; 12) 98r5; 13) 134r2; 14) 211r20; 15) 515r7; 16) $87.65

Section 1.6: 1) 3^5; 2) 6^3; 3) 10^4; 4) 36; %) 512; 6) 10,000,000; 7) 1; 8) 136; 9) 3; 10) 25; 11) 20; 12) 32; 13) 29; 14) 21

Section 1.7: 1) 14340, 14300, 14000; 2) 18610, 18600, 19000; 3) 209360, 209400, 209000; 4) 10000, 10000, 10000; 5) 1,500; 6) 30,000; 7) 2,500 8) 240,000,000; 9) 4; 10) 1; 11) $1,000.

Section 1.8: 1) 464 miles; 2) $27.70; #) 25 miles/gallon; 4) $32.85; 5) $77,82; 6) $32.95; 7) $0.11/cookie

Chapter 2

Section 2.1: 1) 3/10; 2) ½; 3) 4/8; 4) 16/21; 5) 4/4; 6) – 8) answers will vary; 9) 14.62

Section 2.2: 1) 2, 3, 5, 7, 11, 13, 17, 19, 23, 29, 31, 37; 2) 3x7; 3) 3^2x5; 4) 2^4; 5) 2^3x3^2; 6) 1/5; 7) 3/5; 8) ¾; 9) 2/3; 10) 11/18; 11) ¾; 12) 4/11; 13) 5/7; 14) yes; 15) yes

Section 2.3: 1) 5/2; 2) 11/3; 3) 70/11; 4) 403/14; 5) 8 2/5; 6) 9; 7) 14 4/7; 8) 38 ½; 9) 40 ½; 10) 62 ½

Section 2.4: 1) 6/35; 2) 5/28; 3) 42/55; 4) 5/8; 6) 2 2/3; 6) 3/8; 7) 10 ½; 8) 4/7; 9) 10/56; 10) 2/5; 11) 19/6; 12) 19; 13) 5 ½; 14) 3 7/11; 15) 0; 16) 300 3/8 square feet.

Section 2.5: 1) ½; 2) 2/3; 3) 3/17; 4) 1 3/5; 5) 2 ¼; 6) 1; 7) 0; 8) 2/15; 9) undef.; 10) 3400; 11) 6 2/3; 13) 2/3; 13) 6; 14) 1/6; 15) 2 8/9; 16) 3/5

Section 2.6: 1) 14; 2) 20; 3) 12; 4) 120; 5) 180; 6) 360; 7) 4/12, 5/12; 8) 42/48, 17/48; 9) 14/48, 33/48; 10) 27/63, 1/63, 7/63; 11) 15/90, 48/90, 5/90; 12) 42/140, 25/140, 44/140

Section 2.7: 1) 7/10; 2) 7/12; 3) 6/7; 4) 23/24; 5) 89/100; 6) 41/75; 7) 5/9; 8) ¾; 9) 0; 10) 13/24; 11) 1/5; 12) 5/84; 13) 11/12; 14) 6/7; 15) 2

Section 2.8: 1) 6 4/7; 2) 12 7/12; 3) 5 1/6; 4) 13 7/20; 5) 1 3/5; 6) 3 1/15) 7) 2 2/1/2; 8) 1 5/8; 9) 11/15; 10) 3; 11) 3/40

Section 2.9: 1) 76 5/12 pounds; 2) $1641.75; 3) 47 mph; 4) 40 bags

Chapter 3

Section 3.1: 1) 0.7, seven tenths; 2) 351/1000, three hundred fifty-one thousandths; 3) 10.045, eighteen and forty-five thousandths; 4) 8 31/5000, 8.0062; 5) ½, five tenths; 6) 0.073, seventy-three thousandths; 7) 62 1/2500; 62.0004; 8) four hundred ninety-one and 62/100 dollars; 9) $331.27

Section 3.2: 1) >; 2) <; 3) < ; 4) <; 5) =; 6) >; 7) 13.574; 8) 2.7; 9) 9.6033; 10) $1.00; 11) $37; 12) 0.00328; 13) 2.004, 2.0042, 2.042, 2 4/10, 2.41

Section 3.3: 1) 8.66; 2) 19.357; 3) 70.215; 4) $22.46; 5) 2.11; 6) 0.0781; 7) 80.11; 8) 959.274; 9) 5.0393; 10) 24.403; 11) $5.17; 12) yes, $3.37

Section 3.4: 1) 0.1134: 2) 40.442; 3) 40.3711; 4) 63.20; 5) 67,345; 6) 78,904,560; 7) 0.0036113; 8) 723,407.0 ; 9) $450; 10) 1968 inches

Section 3.5: 1) 11.7; 2) 16.24; 3) 0.09473; 4) 65; 5) 44.5; 6) 280.85; 7) 177.65; 8) 214.56; 9) 251.4; 10) 72; 11) 0.123; 12) $113.25

Section 3.6: 1) 0.6; 2) 16.2; 3) 4.975; 4) 1.571; 5) 1.522; 6) 0.158; 7) $27.\overline{3}$; 8) 0.42; 9) $0.\overline{36}$; 10) 43; 11) 44.067; 12) 2.94

Section 3.7: 1) 560000, 557709; 2) 2400, 2371.392; 3) 150, 177.952; 4) 2000, 1975.68; 5) $31.31; 6) $8.85/hr.; 7) no, answers will vary

Chapter 4

Section 4.1: 1) 1/3; 2) 2/1; 3) 7/5; 4) 3/11; 5) 8/15; 6) 19/1; 7) 10/7; 8) $30/book; 9) $17/7 coffees; 10) 1 pizza/8 people; 11) 32 miles/gallon; 12) $18/hr.; 13) $147/share; 14) $145/machine

Section 4.2: 1) 21/7 = 3/1; 2) 28/32 = 7/8; 3) 3.2/11 = 16/55; 4) ½ = 6/12; 5) 2/5 = 120/300; 6) 3/45000 = 5/75000; 7) yes; 8) no; 9) yes; 10) no 11) yes; 12) no; 13) yes

Section 4.3: 1) 35; 2) 2.3; 3) 12; 4) 40; 5) 6; 6) 2; 7) 120; 8) 200; 9) 3; 10) 27.5; 11) 2; 12) 6; 13) 0.63; 14) 3.75; 15) 24.25

Section 4.4: 1) 65 defective; 2) 450 miles; 3) 623 people; 4) 495 miles; 5) 195 pizzas; 6) 231.3 feet

Chapter 5

Section 5.1: 1) 41%; 2) 4%; 3) 75%; 4) 310%; 5) 2.7%; 6) 0.013%; 7) 47%; 8) 36%; 9) 0.57; 10) 0.05; 11) 0.734; 12) 0.0005; 13) 0.0083; 14) 3.72; 15) 92%; 16) 8%; 17) 30%; 18) 38.9%; 19) 0.076%; 20) 504%

Section 5.2: 1) 11/100; 2) 13/50; 3) 3/20; 4) 1/25; 5) 73/1000; 6) 157/200; 7) 2 ¾; 8) 7/200; 9) 77/500; 10) 50%; 11) 65%; 12) 47.5%; 13) 160%; 14) 383%; 15) 313%; 16) 0.014, 1.4%; 17) 19/50, 0.38; 18) 7/200 , 3.5%

Section 5.3A: 1) 5; 2) 12.5%; 3) 90; 4) 875; 5) 44; 6) 7000; 7) 30,000; 8) 380%; 9) 75% ; 10) 512

Section 5.3B: 1) 68.75; 2) 256; 3) 2.4; 4) 75; 5) 200; 6) 400,000; 7) 70%; 8) 50%; 9) 5%; 10) 3.25; 11) 55; 12) 212.50; 13) $1,430

Section 5.4: 1) 8.4%; 2) $90; 3) 697 students; 4) 15.1%; 5) 37.5%

Section 5.5: 1) $58,400; 2) $544; 3) $1292; 4) 25%; 5) 32%; 6) $743.75; 7) $1020; 8) $113.75; 9) $100.80, $2900.80

Chapter 6

Section 6.1: 1) 12; 2) 22; 3) 10,560; 4) 9; 5) 15,840; 6) 25; 7) 25; 8) 14,500; 9) 5.5; 10) 900; 11) 510; 12) 343; 13) 16; 14) 3.5; 15) 9.75; 16) 12.5

Section 6.2: 1) 360; 2) 89.0; 3) 3.8; 4) 11,500; 5) 1500; 6) 8.15; 7) 0.065; 8) 0.075; 9) 0.14; 10) 7000; 11) 1.2; 12) 3200; 13) 80,000; 14) 500 ; 15) 1.37; 16) 102; 17) 43.0; 18) 71,000; 19) 4818.32; 20) 546

Section 6.3: 1) 32,000; 2) 0.13; 3) 13,000; 4) 0.445; 5) 3000; 6) 756; 7) 1.567; 8) 105; 9) 4.31; 10) 5620; 11) 98; 12) 0.732; 13) 76,000; 14) 54; 15) 0.043; 16) 8320.87

Section 6.4: 1) 0.915; 2) 20.32; 3) 23.98; 4) 12.88; 5) 12.8; 6) 9; 7) 62; 8) 120, 10; 9) 7.568; 10) 2.365; 11) 28.54; 12) 0.26; 13) 1.32; 14) 0.48; 15) 765.45; 16) 1.76; 17) 4.55; 18) 257°F; 19) 105°C

- 4 -ANSWERS TO SKILL BUILDERS

Section 6.5: 1) 42 gallons; 2) 4.17 in.; 3) 610 cm; 4) yes; 5) yes; 6) 165 gal/hr

Chapter 7

Section 7.1: 1) 68° ; 2) 68° ; 3) 112°; 4) 112° ; 5) 68° ; 6) 68°; 7) 112° ; 8) 180° ;
9) – 12) Answers will vary.

Section 7.2: 1) 48 in, 135 in^2; 2) 39 1/3 m, 90 4/9 m^2; 3) 81.5 yds, 367.88 yd^2 ; 4) 148 miles, 1369 square miles; 5) 27 ft., 45.56 ft^2 ; 6) 169.52 cm, 1796.06 square cm; 7) $1350

Section 7.3: 1) 1) 80.4 m; 2) 2715.75yds^2; 3) 56,448 ft^2.; 4) 1000 in. 5) 1473.75 m^2;
   6) 336 cm., 4704 cm^2

Section 7.4: 1) 101° ; 2) 60° ; 3) 71° ; 4) 436 m; 5) 71 ft^2; 6) 282.24 ft^2 ; 7) $364.10

Section 7.5: 1) 2; 2) 6; 3) 7; 4) 3; 5) 0; 6) 12; 7) 10; 8) 4; 9) 11; 10) 8; 11) 1; 12) 5; 13) 6; 14) 5; 15) 12; 16) 9.110; 17) 9.950; 18) 4.123

Section 7.6: 1) 10.817; 2) 8.062; 3) 4.243; 4) 14 m; 24.2 m; 5) 6 in., 8.5 in.

Section 7.7: 1) 87.92 in., 615.44 in^2; 2) 119.32 in, 1133.54; 3) 87.92 in.; 4) 565.2 miles; 5) $150.45; 6) 27.5 ft.; 7) 78.5 ft.; 8) No, answers will vary

Section 7.8: 1) 672 in^3; 2) 31,792.5 in^3; 3) 24,416.6 in^3 ; 4) 22.9 ft^3; 5) 22,400,000 m^3 ;
6) 1 yd^3 ; 7) 2048 m^3 ; 8) 30,026.3 ft^3

Section 7.9: 1) 6 ; 2) 7.5 ; 3) 12 ; 4) 8.4 in ; 5) 0.615 mm

Section 7.10: 1) 24 hrs.; 2) $3150   3) $716.40

Chapter 8

Section 8.1: 1) mortgage; 2) miscellaneous; 3) utilities and food; 4) $700; 5) $1250;
6) 5/37; 7) 37.8%; 8) ½

Section 8.2: 1) 350; 2) 1400; 3) Angela; 4) Angela; 5) Joe; 6) 50 ; 7) 3975

Section 8.3: 1) 4; 2) 6; 3) 5; 4) 3; 5) 4; 6) 2; 7) 3; 8) 1 ;

Section 8.4: 1) 384; 2) 13.3; 3) $21,000 ; 4) $112.50 ; 5) 85 ; 6) 245,250; 7) 89

Chapter 9

Section 9.1: 1) -8 ; 2) -22 ; 3) 10.5 ; 4) -5/6 ; 5) -22.06 ; 6) 15/22; 7) -10 ; 8) -9 ;
9) 2/5; 10) -22.1 ; 11) -53 ; 12) 103; 13) -38 ; 14) 5 ; 15) -81 ; 16) -1 ; 17) 0 ;
18) -12/20 ; 19) -23

<u>Section 9.2</u>: 1) -2 ; 2) -11 ; 3) -10 ; 4) -17 ; 5) -14.63 ; 6) 750 ; 7) -233 ; 8) -12/21 ; 9) -3.29 ; 10) -7/30 ; 11) 12 ; 12) 0 ; 13) -11 ; 14) $189.46

<u>Section 9.3</u>: 1) 2 ; 2) 150 ; 3) 1560 ; 4) -15 ; 5) -293.36 ; 6) -7830 ; 7) -4 ; 8) 29; 9) 7 ; 10) -12 ; 11) 5/6 ; 12) -55 ; 13) 4 ; 14) 0

<u>Section 9.4</u>: 1) 21 ; 2) -1; 3) -96 ; 4) -2 ; 5) 5 ; 6) -35 ; 7) 3; 8) 7 ; 9) 0 ; 10) -1 ; 11) 1; 12) -2 ; 13) 1.9 ; 14) 5/16

<u>Section 9.5</u>: 1) 1.2×10^3 ; 2) 247,000 ; 3) 0.00063 ; 4) 9.98×10^{-6} ; 5) 3,720,000,000,000 ; 6) 5.46×10^{-5} ; 7) 3.0×10^{12} ; 8) 0.00000000932 ; 9) 8.0×10^3 ; 10) 6.2×10^{-2} ; 11) 7.765×10^8 ; 12) 5.703×10^{-3}

Chapter 10

<u>Section 10.1</u> : 1) A=(b)(h) ; 2) r=5m+6n ; 3) p=4abc ; 4) 17x ; 5) -3x ; 6) -12.3x + 13 ; 7) 54y ; 8) 6x – 2y ; 9) 8a+6b-7c ; 10) –1/3x + 1/2y ; 11) -0.9x –4y + 2.1z ;12) 7x + 21; 13) 14x+10

<u>Section 10.2</u>: 1) 6x-6 ; 2) 35x – 15; 3) -5x-5b ; 4) 18x-63y ; 5) -20x+30y+40z ; 6) 7x – 4.6y ; 7) -27x-36 ; 8) -6x+9 ; 9) 8x-8y ; 10) 10/3x + 2oy ; 11) -168x –216y – 252z ; 12) -49.6x + 72.8y ; 13) 3/5x – 2/5y – 1/7z + 1/15 ; 14) -0.2x-0.42y+1 ; 15) 18x – 12; 16) 14y-64 ; 170 x+8y-27 ; 18) x– 6/7

<u>Section 10.3</u>: 1) 18 ; 2) 22 ; 3) 9 ; 4) 7 ; 5) 10 ; 6) 16 ; 7) 17 ; 8) 8 ; 9) -7 ; 10) 8.0 ; 11) 7.1 ; 12) 10.6 ; 13) 2.5 ; 14) 1 3/7 ; 15) -1 7/12 ; 16) 10 ; 17) -10 ; 18) –65

<u>Section 10.4</u>: 1) 3 ; 2) 4 ; 3) 9 ; 4) 3 ; 5) –6 ; 6) 6 ; 7) –8 ; 8) –2; 9) –4 ; 10) 3 ; 11) -2.3 ; 12) –28 ; 13) 8 ; 14) -20 ; 15) –9

<u>Section 10.5</u> : 1) 2 ; 2) 3 ; 3) 4 ; 4) 8 ; 5) –3 ; 6) –21; 7) 2 ; 8) 50; 9) 72 ; 10) –10 ; 11) 16; 12) 4 4/5

<u>Section 10.6</u>: 1) h = 5+r, r = Allison; 2) l = 5 + 2w ; 3) a + b = 9 hours; 4) ht ; 5) Andrea: t , Matt: 247 + t ; 6) Elias: e , Anastasia e + $540 , Nicholas: e - $60

Activity 1-A
Whole Numbers

Following Oral Directions

Read the following examples to the class, leaving time for students to compute the answers. When all are complete, compare answers and solve as a class.

1. Start with 6; double it; add 3; divide by 5; the answer is _____ .

2. Start with 13; subtract 3; add 5; add 3; divide by 6; the answer is ____ .

3. Start with 10; add 15; divide by 5; multiply by 4; add 8; divide by 4; the answer is ___.

4. From a number that is 5 larger than 12, add 5; divide by 2, subtract 4; the answer is ___.

5. From a number that is 2 smaller than 7, add 6; add 7; multiply by 2; divide by 3; the answer is _____.

6. Add 6 to 10; subtract 4; add 10; subtract 13; double it; the answer is ____.

7. Add 4 to 8; add 9; add 7; add 9; add 9; divide by 2; the answer is _____.

8. Subtract 6 from 13; add 5; multiply by 5; subtract 20; subtract 10; add 1; the answer is___.

9. From a number that is 14 larger than 6, add 5; divide by 5, multiply by 3; add 1; the answer is _____ .

10. Take the square root of 16; add 5; add 16; divide by 5; add 3; divide by 2; the answer is ____

11. From a number that is 5 larger than 3; subtract 3; add 2; add 3; add 8; divide by 2; the answer is _____ .

12. In the series of numbers, 4-9-8-3-9-12, the first three numbers were _____.

13. In the series of numbers, 2-6-7-9-7-6-8, the sum of the first three numbers is ____.

14. In the series of numbers, 11-9-4-8-7-9-6-12, the lowest odd number is _____.

15. In the series of number, 4-6-7-3-6-1-3-9, the sum of these numbers is _____.

Activity 1-B
Whole Numbers

Multiplication Table

Complete the multiplication table. Use it to help practice your multiplication facts.

x	0	1	2	3	4	5	6	7	8	9	10	11	12
0													
1													
2													
3													
4													
5													
6													
7													
8													
9													
10													
11													
12													

Activity 2-A
Fractions

How Much Pudding Do You Need?

You have decided to make Indian Pudding for three different holiday parties you will be attending. The table below shows how many servings of the pudding you will need for each party. The recipe you found shows the ingredients for 16 servings of pudding.

In this activity you will calculate the ingredient measurements for the other two parties and fill in the table.

Ingredient	Party #1 16 Servings	Party #2 8 Servings	Party #3 24 Servings
Milk	8 cups		
Cream of Wheat Cereal	1 ½ cup		
Butter	4 tbsp		
Light Molasses	1 cup		
Egg	2		
Firmly packed light brown sugar	1/2 cup		
Ground cinnamon	1 ½ tsp		
Ground ginger	¾ tsp		

Try It At Home!

In a large saucepan, over medium heat, bring milk to a boil; gradually sprinkle in cereal, stirring constantly. Heat to a boil, stirring constantly; reduce heat. Cook 5 minutes for regular, 3 to 4 minutes for quick, and 2 to 3 minutes for instant cereal, stirring occasionally until thickened. Remove from heat, stir in margarine, molasses, egg, brown sugar, cinnamon, and ginger.

Spoon mixture into 16 greased custard cups (6-oz size). Bake at 350° F for 20 minutes. Serve warm with frozen yogurt, if desired.

Activity 2-B
Fractions

Fraction Puzzle-Carefully cut the pieces apart. Put the puzzle back together matching the correct improper fraction with the correct proper fraction. Be sure to simplify!

$\dfrac{1}{11}$	10	$3\dfrac{1}{9}$	$\dfrac{11}{12}$
14 $\qquad$ $\dfrac{13}{3}$	$4\dfrac{1}{3}$ $\qquad$ $2\dfrac{1}{5}$	$\dfrac{132}{60}$ $\qquad$ $\dfrac{36}{5}$	$7\dfrac{1}{5}$ $\qquad$ $\dfrac{2}{13}$
$\dfrac{48}{32}$	$\dfrac{20}{5}$	$8\dfrac{5}{20}$	$\dfrac{38}{5}$
$1\dfrac{1}{2}$	4	$\dfrac{33}{4}$	$7\dfrac{3}{5}$
$8\dfrac{2}{3}$ $\qquad$ $\dfrac{15}{12}$	$1\dfrac{1}{4}$ $\qquad$ $9\dfrac{6}{8}$	$\dfrac{39}{4}$ $\qquad$ $\dfrac{38}{11}$	$3\dfrac{5}{11}$ $\qquad$ $\dfrac{4}{9}$
$\dfrac{137}{137}$	0	$7\dfrac{2}{20}$	$8\dfrac{1}{5}$
1	$\dfrac{0}{4}$	$\dfrac{71}{10}$	$\dfrac{41}{5}$
$3\dfrac{5}{6}$ $\qquad$ $8\dfrac{1}{7}$	$\dfrac{57}{7}$ $\qquad$ $\dfrac{29}{10}$	$2\dfrac{9}{10}$ $\qquad$ $\dfrac{44}{7}$	$6\dfrac{2}{7}$ $\qquad$ $\dfrac{1}{7}$
$1\dfrac{1}{4}$	$3\dfrac{1}{6}$	$2\dfrac{4}{7}$	$\dfrac{23}{11}$
$\dfrac{10}{8}$	$\dfrac{19}{6}$	$\dfrac{18}{7}$	$2\dfrac{1}{11}$
$8\dfrac{7}{10}$ $\qquad$ $\dfrac{100}{24}$	$4\dfrac{1}{6}$ $\qquad$ $\dfrac{9}{8}$	$1\dfrac{3}{24}$ $\qquad$ $\dfrac{90}{11}$	$8\dfrac{2}{11}$ $\qquad$ $3\dfrac{8}{11}$
$\dfrac{2}{9}$	10	$\dfrac{1}{90}$	$\dfrac{4}{0}$

Activity 3-A
Decimals

<u>Which One Doesn't Belong?</u>

In each row, circle the item that does not belong. Be prepared to give the reason for your answer. Reasons may vary.

	A	B	C	D
1	4 ½	$\frac{9}{2}$	4.5	9.2
2	$\frac{21}{28}$	0.75	$\frac{30}{40}$	$\frac{16}{64}$
3	$\frac{1}{5}, \frac{4}{5}$	$\frac{2}{5}, 0.6$	0.34, 0.66	$\frac{4}{9}, \frac{6}{9}$
4	$1.04 \div 0.02$	$1.28 \div 0.04$	$\frac{312}{6}$	$1.56 \div 0.03$
5	$2.76 + 0.45$	$12.91 - 9.7$	$8.21 - 5.49$	$3\frac{21}{100}$
6	0.125	0.875	0.555	0.375
7	0.06	$\frac{3}{5}$	0.6	$\frac{9}{15}$
8	$(0.05)(8)$	$\left(\frac{1}{2}\right)\left(\frac{1}{4}\right)$	$\frac{1}{16} \times 2$	$(2.5)(0.05)$

Create your own problem where one item does not belong. Be ready to discuss your example.

	A	B	C	D
9				

Activity 3-B
Decimals

Who's Greater?

In each row write:
  A if the first item is greater
  B if the second item is greater
  C if they are equal
  D if there's not enough information to decide

	FIRST ITEM	SECOND ITEM	RESPONSE
1	$\frac{1}{2} \times 18.2$	4.5×2	
2	0.666	$\frac{2}{3}$	
3	$0.5 + 0.2 + 0.8$	0.15	
4	8.2×1000	820×100	
5	$(0.7)^3$	$(0.7)^2$	
6	3.06×10^4	30.6×10^3	
7	$1 \div 0.1$	$0.1 \div 1$	
8	5/8 of a pizza	0.625 of a pizza	

Extension: Select any problem on this page and explain your thinking in arriving at the response you selected.

Activity 4-A
Ratio and Proportion

Writing with Ratios and Proportions

Write one or more complete sentences to answer each question. Answers may vary.

1. When writing a ratio, how do you decide which value is the numerator and which value is the denominator?

2. How do you write the ratio of 6 quarts to 6 gallons?

3. Would you prefer that the ratio of your income (money earned) to your expenses be   1 to 4 or   4 to 1?

4. Find a sales flyer for a local clothing store.   Find two items that are similar and discuss which item is the better buy and why.   Be sure to include unit rates.

5. Allison worked 5.5 hours and cleaned 110 appliances.   Amy cleaned 148 appliances in 9 hours.   To see whether the employees worked equally fast, Ray (the supervisor) set up this proportion:

$$\frac{5.5}{110} = \frac{148}{9}$$

Is this proportion true or false? Write one or more sentences discussing your decision.

Activity 4-B
Ratio and Proportion

Be a Bargain Shopper!

In each row, write A if the first item is the better bargain or B if the second item is the better bargain. Be sure to explain your reasoning. Round to the nearest cent, if necessary.

	FIRST ITEM A	SECOND ITEM B	RESPONSE
1	50 CD's for $8.29	10 CD's for $2	
2	12 pack of soda for $2.99	$5.75 for 25 cans of soda	
3	3 pounds of ground beef for $4.47	$1.47/pound of ground beef	
4	10.2 ounce package of candy for $2.50	6 ounce candy bar $0.99	
5	2 pack of light bulbs (no special) for $0.44	4 pack of light bulbs for $1.99 Special: Buy 1 pack get 1 pack free!	
6	2-6 ounce tubes of toothpaste for $4	1-10 ounce tube of toothpaste for $2.99	
7	38 ounce bottle of mouthwash for $1.89	2-12 ounce bottles of mouthwash for $1.29	
8	Package of 20 Cold & Sinus Medication for $6.40	2 packages of 15 tablets each for $4.80/package	

Activity 5-A
Percent

What's Missing?

Write a complete sentence to provide the additional piece(s) of information needed to solve each problem. Finally, solve the problem. Answers will vary.

Example: The price of a DVD decreased 10%. What was the new price?
Answer: *The original price of the DVD was $20.00. Solution: $18.00*

1. Geraldo purchased a sweatshirt and paid $1.50 in sales tax. What was the rate of tax?

2. A store was offering a discount on CDs listed at $19.00. What was the sale price of the CDs?

3. In a music store containing New Age and Pop CD's, 32% of the CDs are New Age. How many Pop CDs are in the store?

4. Jackie can burn CD's at the rate of 6 tracks per minute. How long will it take him to copy his CD collection?

5. On an average day, 72% of the people entering an eyeglass shop purchase at least one pair of eyeglasses. How many people purchased eyeglasses yesterday?

Extra: Select any problem on this page and explain why you feel the information you provided was necessary to complete the problem.

Activity 5-B
Percent

Comparing Percents

In each row, write A if the first item is greater, B if the second item is greater, C if they are equal, and D if there's not enough information to decide.

	FIRST ITEM	SECOND ITEM	RESPONSE
1	25% of 178	¼ of 178	
2	The cost of a $125 radio at 10% off	The cost of a $125 radio at $12 off	
3	15½% of 30	2.5	
4	25% of 75	75% of 25	
5	50% of 350	5% of 35	
6	10% of 250 + 10% of 250	20% of 250	
7	$200 increased by 20%	$220 decreased by 20%	
8	350% of 8	0.35×8	

Activity 6-A
Measurement

Working with Metric Length Units

1. Which of the following items are about 1 m long?

   pen
   wiffleball bat
   height of length from floor to doorknob
   height of a telephone pole
   basketball player's arm length

2. Which is the most reasonable metric unit for each of the following measurements?

   The woman's height was 166 _____.
   A postage stamp is 21 _____ wide.
   The man paddled 3 _____ down the river.
   Pencil lead is 0.7 _____ thick.
   The classroom was 13 _____ long.

3. Converting between metric length units using the metric conversion line:

   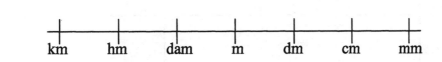

   Step 1 Find the unit you are given on the metric conversion line.

   Step 2 Count the number of places to get from the unit you are given to the unit you want in the answer.

   Step 3 Move the decimal point the **same number of places** and in the **same direction** as you did on the conversion line.

   Use the conversion line to make the following unit conversions:

   a) 8 m to cm

   b) 42 mm to m

   c) 9.3 km to m

   d) 509 cm to m

   e) 25 mm to cm

   f) 63.4 m to mm

Activity 6-B
Measurement

Around the Room

Materials needed: Ruler with American units.

Measure items in your classroom. Convert the measurement into an appropriate metric unit.
Fill out the questions below. Note: The first one is done for you.

	ITEM	AMERICAN UNITS	METRIC UNITS
1	Pencil	7 inches	17.78 centimeters
2			
3			
4			
5			
6			
7			
8			
9			

Activity 7-A
Geometry

Using Geometric Formulas

Materials needed: 1 ruler per group (preferably with cm markings)

1. Calculate the area of the shape shown below by following steps 1 to 3:

   a) Write the formula you will use.

   b) What values need to be measured so that you have numbers to plug into the formula? Use a ruler to make the measurements. Record the measurements here, and write the measurements where they belong on the shape.

   c) Calculate the area (show work).

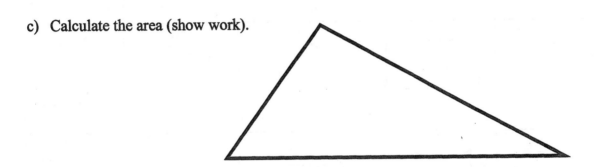

2. Calculate the area of the shape shown below by following steps 1 to 3:

   a) Write the formula you will use.

   b) What values need to be measured so that you have numbers to plug into the formula? Record the measurements here, and write the measurements where they belong on the shape.

   c) Calculate the area (show work).

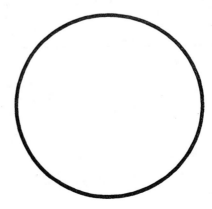

Activity 7-B
Geometry

Which One Does Not Belong?

In each row, circle the item that does not belong. Be prepared to give the reason for your answer. Answers may vary.

	A	B	C	D
1				
2				
3				
4	$P = 2l + 2w$	$A = lw$	$A = bh$	$A = \dfrac{bh}{2}$
5	$23° + 67°$		$47° + 43°$	$90°$

Activity 8-A
Statistics

Internet Activity – Hometown Population Trends

Gather the information needed to answer the questions below by using the internet or by using reference materials at a library.

1. In the space provided below, construct a bar graph that shows the population in your hometown for the years 1940, 1960, 1980, and 2000.

2. In the space provided below, construct a line graph that shows the same information as in question 1.

3. Discuss the population trends in your hometown. What do you predict the population will be in the year 2020 if the trend continues? Be prepared to share your answer with the class.

Activity 8-B
Statistics

Statistics Around Us

Look through any newspaper, magazine, periodical, journal, etc. Find a circle graph, line graph, or bar graph. Cut out the graph. Read the article(s) associated with the graph and write 5 questions that could be asked about the graph. Be sure to have the answers available with the questions.

Attach graph here

Question 1:

Question 2:

Question 3:

Question 4:

Question 5:

Writing with Signed Numbers

Write a word problem to accompany the mathematical expression. Be sure to include the answer in your word problem. Answers will vary.

1. 13 (18)

    Alex ate 13 crackers with 18 calories in each. How many calories did Alex eat? (234 calories)

2. $423.18 + $85.50 + (- $22.23) + (-$49.50)

3. 25° - 12° - 7°

4. ($415)(5) + (.06)($1475) - $45

5. (-22) + (-37) + (-34)

6. 17(-$3.50)

Activity 9-B
Signed Numbers

Which One Is Greater?

In each row, evaluate the expressions. In the last column, use < or > to indicate the smaller value.

	Expression A	Expression B	< or >
1	$7 - 8 - 14 + (-3)$	$-3 + (-2) + (-16)$	
2	$5 \div \left(-\dfrac{5}{7}\right)$	$\left(-\dfrac{1}{2}\right)\left(\dfrac{8}{2}\right)$	
3	$-6 \cdot 3 \div 9 \cdot (-2)$	$-55 \div (-11)$	
4	$-13 + 13$	$-14 + 13$	
5	$-11.9 - (-4.3) + 8.6$	$-\dfrac{2}{3} - \left(-\dfrac{5}{12}\right) + \dfrac{1}{4}$	
6	$\left(-\dfrac{1}{3}\right)(15)$	$(-3)\left(\dfrac{1}{15}\right)$	
7	$-6 + (-5) \cdot (9 - 14)$	$(-1)(-8)(-2)(-1)$	
8	$(-4) \div \left(-\dfrac{1}{25}\right)$	$\left(-\dfrac{1}{4}\right) \div \left(-\dfrac{1}{25}\right)$	

Activity 10-A
Introduction to Algebra

Linear Equation Exploration – How Many Solutions Are There?

Consider the equation: $2(x + 3) = 2x + 6$

1. Is $x = 4$ a solution to the equation? Check by substituting 4 in for x and seeing whether the two sides of the equation come out equal. Show your work.

2. Is $x = -2$ a solution? Show your work.

3. Is $x = 1/3$ a solution? Show your work.

4. Choose another value for x and check if it is a solution. Show your work.

5. Solve the equation by clearing parentheses and isolating the x. Show your work.

    $2(x + 3) = 2x + 6$

6. How many solutions do you think this equation has? Write a sentence or two explaining your answer.

Activity 10-B
Introduction to Algebra

Family Room Renovation

You have been hired to renovate a family room. Instead of measuring the length and width of the room, the owners told you:

"The length of the family room is 5 less than twice the width.
The perimeter is 80 feet."

1) Find the length and width of the room.

2) The carpet that is needed costs $12 per square yard.

3) The walls are 8 feet high. One gallon of paint can cover 200 square feet. You need to paint all four walls. (We are not going to worry about the door and windows!) One gallon of paint costs $14.99. We will have leftover paint.

4) One-foot-square ceiling tiles are sold in packages of 50. One package of ceiling tiles cost $39.99. We will have leftover ceiling tiles.

5) Miscellaneous supplies will cost $28.

How much will it cost, in supplies, to re-do this family room?

Answers to Activities

Activity 1-A: 1) 3, 2) 3, 3) 7, 4) 7, 5) 12, 6) 18, 7) 23, 8) 31, 9) 16, 10) 4, 11) 9, 12) 4,9,8, 13) 15, 14) 7, 15) 39

Activity 1-B:

x	0	1	2	3	4	5	6	7	8	9	10	11	12
0	0	0	0	0	0	0	0	0	0	0	0	0	0
1	0	1	2	3	4	5	6	7	8	9	10	11	12
2	0	2	4	6	8	10	12	14	16	18	20	22	24
3	0	3	6	9	12	15	18	21	24	27	30	33	36
4	0	4	8	12	16	20	24	28	32	36	40	44	48
5	0	5	10	15	20	25	30	35	40	45	50	55	60
6	0	6	12	18	24	30	36	42	48	54	60	66	72
7	0	7	14	21	28	35	42	49	56	63	70	77	84
8	0	8	16	24	32	40	48	56	64	72	80	88	96
9	0	9	18	27	36	45	54	63	72	81	90	99	108
10	0	10	20	30	40	50	60	70	80	90	100	110	120
11	0	11	22	33	44	55	66	77	88	99	110	121	132
12	0	12	24	36	48	60	72	84	96	108	120	132	144

Activity 2-A: Party #2) 4 cups milk, ¾ cups cream of wheat, 2 tbsp butter, ½ cup molasses, 1 egg, ¼ cup brown sugar, ¾ tsp cinnamon, 3/8 tsp ginger, Party #3) 12 cups milk, 2 ¼ cups cream of wheat, 6 tbsp butter, 1 ½ cups molasses, 3 eggs, ¾ cup brown sugar, 2 ¼ tsp cinnamon, 1 1/8 tsp ginger

Activity 2-B: master copy of activity is answer key

Activity 3-A: 1) D, 2) D, 3) D, 4) B, 5) C, 6) C, 7) A, 8) A, 9) Answers will vary

Activity 3-B: 1) A, 2) B, 3) A, 4) B, 5) B, 6) C, 7) A, 8) C

Activity 4-A: 1) – 4) Answers will vary, 5) False

Activity 4-B: 1) A, 2) B, 3) B, 4) B, 5) A, 6) B, 7) A, 8) neither, =

Activity 5-A: 1) – 5) Answers will vary

Activity 5-B: 1) C, 2) B, 3) A, 4) C, 5) A, 6) C, 7) A, 8) A

Activity 6-A: 1) wiffleball bat, height of length from floor to doorknob, basketball player's arm length, 2) cm, mm, km, mm, m, 3a) 800 cm, b) 0.042 m, c) 9300 m, d) 5.09 m, e) 2.5 cm, f) 63,400 mm

Activity 6-B: Answers will vary.

Activity 7-A: 1a) A = ½ bh, b) h ≈ 3.4 cm, b ≈ 8.9 cm, c) A ≈ 15.1 cm^2, 2a) A = πr^2, b) r ≈ 2.5 cm, c) A ≈ 19.6 cm^2

Activity 7-B: Answers will vary.

Activity 8-A: Answers will vary

Activity 8-B: Answers will vary.

Activity 9-A: Answers will vary

Activity 9-B: 1) A>B, 2) A<B, 3) A<B, 4) A>B, 5) A>B; 6) A<B; 7) A>B; 8) A>B

Activity 10-A: 1) yes, 2) yes, 3) yes, 4) values vary, yes-solution, 5) x = x, or 0 = 0, for example, 6) infinite solutions

Activity 10-B: $907.88

1.1 Understanding Whole Numbers _____ *Free Response*

1. Write 352 in expanded form.

2. Write 85,264 in expanded form.

3. Write $80,000 + 7000 + 300 + 6$ in standard notation.

4. Write $100,000 + 30,000 + 4000 + 600 + 80 + 9$ in standard notation.

5. For the number 16,256, which number is in the thousands place? _____

   For the same number, which number is in the tens place? ____

6. For the number 2,766,939, which number is in the hundred thousands place? ___

   For the same number, which number is in the tens place? ____

7. In the number 19,325, identify the value of the digit 3.

8. What is the word name for 235,060?

9. What is the word name for 64,658,009?

10. Cheryl bought new windows for her house for $7092. How will she write out $7092 in words on the check?

1.1 Understanding Whole Numbers _____ *Multiple Choice*

1. Write 135,060 in words.
   - **a.** One hundred thirty-five thousand, sixty
   - **b.** Thirteen thousand, five hundred six
   - **c.** Thirteen thousand, five hundred sixty
   - **d.** One million, thirty-five thousand, sixty

2. Write for 9,300,695 in words.
   - **a.** Nine million, thirty thousand, six hundred ninety-five
   - **b.** Nine million, three thousand, six hundred ninety-five
   - **c.** Ninety-three thousand, six hundred ninety-five
   - **d.** Nine million, three hundred thousand, six hundred ninety-five

3. Write the number 32,501,002 in expanded form.
   - **a.** $30,000,000 + 200,000 + 50,000 + 1000 + 2$
   - **b.** $32,000,000 + 501,000 + 2$
   - **c.** $30,000,000 + 2,000,000 + 5000,000 + 100 + 2$
   - **d.** $30,000,000 + 2,000,000 + 500,000 + 100 + 2$

4. Write the number $7000 + 500 + 40 + 9$ in standard notation.
   - **a.** 9457
   - **b.** 7549
   - **c.** $7000 + 549$
   - **d.** $9000 + 457$

5. For the number 4,869,734, what number is in the millions place? The thousands place?
   - **a.** Millions: 8, thousands: 9
   - **b.** Millions: 4, thousands: 6
   - **c.** Millions: 7, thousands: 3
   - **d.** Millions: 4, thousands: 9

6. For the number 93,872, what number is in the ten thousands place? The hundreds place?
   - **a.** Ten thousands: 9, hundreds: 3
   - **b.** Ten thousands: 9, hundreds: 8
   - **c.** Ten thousands: 7, hundreds: 8
   - **d.** Ten thousands: 3, hundreds: 2

7. Write eight thousand, one hundred sixty-seven in standard form.
   - **a.** 8167
   - **b.** 81,067
   - **c.** 800,167
   - **d.** 810,067

8. Write ten million, three hundred fifty-four thousand, two hundred three in standard form.
   - **a.** 135,423
   - **b.** 1,354,203
   - **c.** 10,354,203
   - **d.** 1,354,230

Use the following chart to answer questions 9 and 10.

Estimated Population of Four States from 1910 to 1990 (in millions)

State	1910	1920	1930	1940	1950	1960	1970	1980	1990
California	2	3	6	7	11	16	20	24	30
Florida	1	1	1	2	3	5	6	10	13
Illinois	5	6	8	8	9	10	11	11	11
New York	9	10	13	13	15	17	18	18	18

Source: US Bureau of Census

9. What was the population of California in 1960?
   - **a.** 1,600,000
   - **b.** 16,000,000
   - **c.** 16
   - **d.** 1.6×10^{10}

10. What was the estimated population of New York in 1980?
   - **a.** 18
   - **b.** 1,800,000
   - **c.** 18,000,000
   - **d.** 1.8×10^{10}

1.2 Addition of Whole Numbers _____ *Free Response*

1. Add: 8
             7
             2
          + 9

2. Add: 26
             39
             41
          + 89

3. Add: 1652
             2139
              714
               82
                5
          + 9673

4. Add: 9,216,823
             4,781,244
          +   17,558

5. Add: $11,296 + 81,619 + 42,543 + 692$

6. Add: $84 + 197 + 1933 + 16,467$

7. Last year a company had 5876 employees. This year the number of employees increased by 1386. How many employees does the company have now?

8. A town's population in 1976 was 158,111. By the year 2000, it had increased by 27,826. How many people lived there in 2000?

9. Jesse is installing an invisible fence in his back yard that has different measurements on each side: 101 feet, 66 feet, 87 feet, and 98 feet. How many feet of wiring are needed to enclose his yard?

10. A store sold 38 CD players on Monday, 16 on Tuesday, and 27 on Wednesday. How many CD players did the store sell in all?

1.2 Addition of Whole Numbers _____ *Multiple Choice*

1. Add: 12
          13
        + 12

   a. 73   **b.** 46
   c. 64   **d.** 37

2. Add: 59
            755
           4693
        + 16,123

   a. 21,610   **b.** 21,630
   c. 21,530   **d.** 20,630

3. Add: 2,440,220
         4,286,842
       + 4,003,454

   a. 10,720,516   **b.** 10,730,526
   c. 10,730,516   **d.** 9,730,516

4. Add: $7963 + 740 + 26 + 5183$

   a. 12,902   **b.** 13,912   **c.** 12,812   **d.** 13,802

5. Add: $11,222 + 22,333 + 23,111$

   a. 56,486   **b.** 66,566   **c.** 56,666   **d.** 46,766

6. Add: 6294
          800
           80
         6356
       + 4069

   a. 17,599   **b.** 16,589
   c. 16,499   **d.** 17,489

7. Add: 432
          66
        7620
          37
         877
       + 1965

   a. 13,190   **b.** 32,975
   c. 4399   **d.** 10,997

8. Isabelle went shopping for holiday presents for her family. She spent $303 on Monday, $320 on Tuesday, and $213 on Wednesday. What is the total amount of money that she spent on gifts?

   a. $736   **b.** $836   **c.** $826   **d.** $926

9. An election of student body president was held over 3 days. On the first day Todd received 206 votes and Bonnie received 138 totes. on the second day Todd received 298 votes and Bonnie received 346 votes. On the third day Todd received 219 votes and Bonnie received 169 votes. How many votes did Bonnie receive?

   a. 813   **b.** 723   **c.** 653   **d.** 863

10. Is it 91 miles from Waterton to Hartford. It is 83 miles from Hartford to Cayfield. Driving directly, it is 137 miles from Waterton to Cayfield. It is 48 miles from Cayfield to Morland. If Juan drives from Waterton to Hartford, then from Hartford to Cayfield, and finally home to Waterton, how many miles does he drive?

    a. 321   **b.** 359   **c.** 276   **d.** 311

1.3 Subtraction of Whole Numbers _____ *Free Response*

1. Subtract: 689
               − 213

2. Subtract: 8923
               − 2711

3. Subtract: 841
               − 153

4. Subtract: 70,000
               − 26,815

5. Subtract: 703,196
               − 215,589

6. Solve: $x + 19 = 47$

7. Solve: $73 + x = 152$

8. Janet has a total of $3301 in her checking account. If she writes a check for each of the items below, how much money will be left in her account?

    Phone $48
    Rent $750
    Car $429

9. Svetlana is trading her car in on a new car. The new car costs $25,025. The car is worth $7998. How much money does she need to buy the new car?

10. The population of Marion County is 664,446. The population of Farmington County is 295,129. The population of Cross County is 283,945. How much greater is the population of Marion County than Cross County?

1.3 Subtraction of Whole Numbers _____ *Multiple Choice*

1. Subtract: 95
            − 12

    a. 107   **b.** 79
    c. 83   **d.** 143

2. Subtract: 6875
            − 2133

    a. 4742   **b.** 4736
    c. 4676   **d.** 6742

3. Subtract: 80,000
            − 32,681

    a. 102,681   **b.** 52,681
    c. 110,649   **d.** 47,319

4. Subtract: 7020
            − 4562

    a. 4568   **b.** 3568
    c. 2458   **d.** 3542

5. Subtract: 600,152
            − 206,985

    a. 403,167   **b.** 393,167
    c. 393,067   **d.** 392,067

6. Subtract: 470,884
            − 136,836

    a. 333,948   **b.** 334,048
    c. 335,048   **d.** 434,048

7. Is the subtraction correct?   579
                                  − 210
                                  ─────
                                    369

    a. Correct
    b. Correct answer is 469.
    c. Correct answer is 379.
    d. Correct answer is 479.

8. Is the subtraction correct?   474
                                  −   53
                                  ─────
                                    431

    a. Correct
    b. Correct answer is 419.
    c. Correct answer is 413.
    d. Correct answer is 421.

Population of Four States from 1960 to 2000

State	1960	1970	1980	1990	2000
Illinois	10,081,158	11,102,853	11,427,409	11,430,602	12,051,683
Michigan	7,823,194	8,881,826	9,262,044	9,295,297	9,679,052
Indiana	4,662,498	5,195,392	5,490,212	5,554,159	6,045,521
Minnesota	3,413,864	3,806,103	4,075,970	4,375,099	4,830,784

Source: US Census Bureau

9. Using the above chart, how much did the population of Illinois increase from 1960 to 1990?
    a. 321,317   **b.** 320,317   **c.** 1,342,444   **d.** 1,343,444

Year	Population in Hatsburg
1999	76
2000	143
2001	111

10. Using the above chart, what was the increase in the number of new residents in Hatsburg from 1999 to 2000?
    a. 69   **b.** 52   **c.** 67   **d.** 42

1.4 Multiplication of Whole Numbers _____ *Free Response*

1. Multiply: 1892
    $\times$ 7

2. Multiply: 7039
    $\times$ 40

3. Multiply: 6492
    $\times$ 100

4. Multiply: 483
    $\times$ 691

5. Multiply: 3904
    $\times$ 705

6. Multiply: $14 \cdot 3 \cdot 2 \cdot 5$

7. Find the value for x in the equation $72 = 24(x)$

8. The textbook for a history class costs $63. There are 23 students in the class. Find the total cost of the history books for the class.

9. The seats in a lecture hall are arranged in 17 rows with 9 seats in each row. Find how many seats are in this room.

10. A case of candy bars has 2 layers of candy bars. In each layer are 8 rows with 14 candy bars in each row. Find how many candy bars are in a case.

1.4 Multiplication of Whole Numbers _____ *Multiple Choice*

1. Multiply: $\begin{array}{r} 15,815 \\ \times \quad 8 \\ \hline \end{array}$
   - **a.** 126,480
   - **b.** 126,510
   - **c.** 126,620
   - **d.** 126,520

2. Multiply: $\begin{array}{r} 6010 \\ \times \quad 70 \\ \hline \end{array}$
   - **a.** 420,700
   - **b.** 419,700
   - **c.** 421,700
   - **d.** 430,700

3. Multiply: $\begin{array}{r} 7900 \\ \times \quad 600 \\ \hline \end{array}$
   - **a.** 4,741,000
   - **b.** 4,739,000
   - **c.** 4,740,000
   - **d.** 4,739,501

4. Multiply: $\begin{array}{r} 9829 \\ \times \quad 454 \\ \hline \end{array}$
   - **a.** 4,461,366
   - **b.** 4,472,366
   - **c.** 4,462,366
   - **d.** 4,462,466

5. Multiply: $\begin{array}{r} 9401 \\ \times \quad 32 \\ \hline \end{array}$
   - **a.** 47,005
   - **b.** 300,832
   - **c.** 28,213
   - **d.** 282,032

6. Multiply: $6 \cdot 4 \cdot 9 \cdot 3$
   - **a.** 219
   - **b.** 216
   - **c.** 22
   - **d.** 648

7. A rectangular plot of land measures 90 feet by 160 feet. Find its area.
   - **a.** 14,400 sq ft
   - **b.** 1440 sq ft
   - **c.** 500 sq ft
   - **d.** 250 sq ft

8. In a distant solar system the diameter of Plant A is 6 times as great as the diameter of Planet B. The diameter of Planet B is 677 miles. Find the diameter of Planet A.
   - **a.** 4056 mi
   - **b.** 4062 mi
   - **c.** 3962 mi
   - **d.** 4052 mi

9. A company rents a mid-size car at $295 per month for twelve months. What is the cost for the car rental during this time?
   - **a.** $307
   - **b.** $3540
   - **c.** $3489
   - **d.** $3272

10. There are 78 kittens in a room with an assortment of black and white ears and paws. 15 kittens have totally black ears and 3 white paws, 22 have 1 black ear and 2 white paws, and 41 have no black ears and 1 white paw. How many black paws are in the room?
    - **a.** 133
    - **b.** 130
    - **c.** 181
    - **d.** 182

1.5 Division of Whole Numbers _____ *Free Response*

1. Divide: $8\overline{)72}$

2. Divide: $3\overline{)2700}$

3. Divide: $53\overline{)51,251}$

4. Divide: $6\overline{)1946}$

5. Divide: $16\overline{)15,773}$

6. Divide: $5463 \div 24$

7. For the equation $3393 \div 261 = x$, what is the value of x?

8. Amy teaches Chinese lessons for $65 per student for a 6-week session. From one group of students, she collects $1820. Find how many students are in the group.

9. One ticket won a prize of $9,338,000. The winning ticket was purchased by 29 people who had pooled their money. Find how many dollars each person received if each receive an equal share.

10. In a distant galaxy the gravity of Planet A is 218 times as strong as the gravity of Planet B, so objects on Planet A weigh 218 times as much as they weigh on Planet B. If the object weighs 33,572 pounds on Planet A, how much does it weigh on Planet B?

1.5 Division of Whole Numbers _____ *Multiple Choice*

1. Divide: $3\overline{)408}$

    a. 138   b. 136
    c. 139   d. 134

2. Divide: $4\overline{)7685}$

    a. 1922   b. 1921
    c. 1921 R3   d. 1921 R1

3. Divide: $47\overline{)80,511}$

    a. 1713   b. 1703
    c. 1723 R17   d. 1718 R9

4. Divide: $15,773 \div 16$

    a. 985 R7   b. 985
    c. 985 R13   d. 13

5. Divide: $135\overline{)3919}$

    a. 139   b. 136 R4
    c. 29 R4   d. 29

6. For the equation $2565 \div 171 = x$, what is the value of x?

    a. 2736   b. 438,615   c. 13   d. 15

7. Mr. Losch has a piece of rope 170 feet long that he cuts into pieces for an experiment in his first-grade class. Each piece of rope is to be 6 feet long. How many 6-foot-long pieces of rope can he cut from the original piece of rope?

    a. 29 pieces of rope   b. 28 pieces of rope   c. 2 pieces of rope   d. 30 pieces of rope

8. A dairy produces 620,000 quarts of milk each day. There are 4 quarts in a gallon. How many gallons of milk are produced each day?

    a. 155,000 gal   b. 15,500gal   c. 1,550,000 gal   d. 12,480,000 gal

9. Karl wishes to pay off a car loan of $5016 in 24 months. How large will his monthly payment be?

    a. $191   b. $200   c. $209   d. $2508

10. County records list a rectangular parcel of land as measuring 48,006 square yards. A surveyor measures the length of the parcel of land as 254 yards. What is the width of the parcel?

    a. 189 yards   b. 47,752 yards   c. 182 yards   d. 198 yards

1.6 Exponents and Order of Operations _____ *Free Response*

1. Rewrite using exponents: $6 \times 6 \times 6 \times 6$

2. Rewrite using exponents: $9 \times 9 \times 9$

3. Evaluate: 2^6

4. Evaluate: 3^5

In problems 5-10, simplify using the correct order of operations.

5. $240 \div 6 - 2$

6. $10^2 - 5 \times 8$

7. $18 \times 8 + 5 \times 3$

8. $4^3 + 2^2 - 48 + 30$

9. $12 + 12 \div 4 + 6 \times 8$

10. $2 \times 5 + 9(9 + 7) + 7$

1.6 Exponents and Order of Operations _____ *Multiple Choice*

1. Rewrite using exponents: $15 \times 15 \times 15 \times 15 \times 15$
    a. 15^5 b. 5^{15} c. $5 \cdot 15$ d. 5×5^{15}

2. Rewrite using exponents: $7 \times 7 \times 7 \times 7$
    a. 28   b. 7^2 c. 7^4 d. 4^7

3. Evaluate: 8^4
    a. 512   b. 32   c. 65,536   d. 4096

4. Evaluate: 4^5
    a. 20   b. 1024   c. 625   d. 4096

5. Evaluate: $8 \times 3 + 2 \times 6 + 3$
    a. 291   b. 360   c. 117   d. 39

6. Evaluate: $6^3 \times 13^2 + (7 - 5) \times 3$
    a. 36,510   b. 36,540   c. 474   d. 474,558

7. Evaluate: $644 \div (28 \div 4)$
    a. 23   b. 92   c. 28   d. 4

8. Evaluate: $9^2 + 9^2 + (27 - 24) \times 4$
    a. 93   b. 6573   c. 147   d. 660

9. Evaluate: $7^2 - 2^2 + 6 \times 9$
    a. 99   b. 459   c. 79   d. −9

10. Evaluate: $7 \times 24 - 20 \div 4 + 7^2$
    a. 222   b. 56   c. 196   d. 212

1.7 Rounding and Estimation _____ *Free Response*

1. Round 8867 to the nearest ten.

2. Round 5023 to the nearest hundred.

3. Round 83,619 to the nearest thousand.

4. A publishing company sold 27,266,591 books in 2003 Round the number of books sold to the nearest ten-million.

In problems 5 and 6, use the principle of estimation to find an estimate for the calculation.

5. $897,248 - 340,002$

6. $10^2 - 5 \times 33,892 \times 61$

7. Estimate the result of the calculation. Use your result to determine if the calculation appears to be correct or incorrect.

$$
\begin{array}{r}
822,206 \\
-\ 388,671 \\
\hline
433,535
\end{array}
$$

8. The Pan family took a trip and traveled 365 miles, 449 miles, 639 miles, 798 miles, and 460 miles on five consecutive days. Round each distance to the nearest hundred and estimate the distance they traveled.

9. A local sandwich shop sells 151 sandwiches on an average day. Estimate how many sandwiches they sold in the last 237 days. Round the number of sandwiches and the number of days to the nearest ten.

10. Paul traveled for 4 weeks in Africa last year and spent $1847 while he was there. Estimate the average amount he spent each day. Round the number of days to the nearest ten and the amount of money spent to the nearest hundred.

1.7 Rounding and Estimation _____ *Multiple Choice*

1. Round 708 to the nearest ten.

   a. 700   **b.** 720   **c.** 710   **d.** 810

2. Round 95,221 to the nearest hundred.

   a. 95,200   **b.** 95,300   **c.** 95,100   **d.** 95,210

3. Round 496,806 to the nearest ten thousand.

   a. 490,000   **b.** 496,000   **c.** 600,000   **d.** 500,000

4. In 1999 a company spent $593,749,536 on advertising. Round the advertising figure to the nearest hundred-thousand.

   a. 600,000,000   **b.** 593,700,000   **c.** 593,800,000   **d.** 500,000,000

In problems 5 and 6, use the principle of estimation to find an estimate for the calculation.

5. $170,728 + 58,759 + 449,528$

   a. 560,000   **b.** 660,000   **c.** 7,880,100,000   **d.** 7,867,500,000

6. $8,664,116 \div 451$

   a. 18,000   **b.** 22,500   **c.** 180,000   **d.** 2250

In questions 7 and 8, estimate the result of the calculation. Use your result to determine if the calculation appears to be correct.

7.
$$\begin{array}{r} 583 \\ 240 \\ 488 \\ +\ 836 \\ \hline 2147 \end{array}$$

   a. Incorrect. Estimate: 2300   **b.** Incorrect. Estimate: 2200
   c. Incorrect. Estimate: 2000   **d.** Correct. Estimate: 2100

8.
$$\begin{array}{r} 887,291 \\ -\ 225,359 \\ \hline 561,932 \end{array}$$

   a. Incorrect. Estimate: 800,000   **b.** Incorrect. Estimate: 600,000
   c. Incorrect. Estimate: 700,000   **d.** Correct. Estimate: 900,000

9. Andy wants to buy a refrigerator for $799, a stove for $859, and a dishwasher for $449. Round each cost to the nearest hundred to estimate the total cost.

   a. $1900   **b.** $2100   **c.** $2000   **d.** $2200

10. As part of her preparation for lacrosse tryouts, Linda did 79 push-ups each day for 83 days. Estimate how many push-ups she did during that period. Round the number of push-ups and the number of days to the nearest ten.

   a. 15,000   **b.** 64,000   **c.** 6400   **d.** 1500

1.8 Solving Applied Problems _____ *Free Response*

1. A corporate executive picks up a rental car that has an odometer reading of 35,829 miles on it. When she returns it, the odometer reads 36,728 miles. How many miles did she drive the rental car?

2. Matt bought a bag of oranges at a cost of $1.32. The bag contained 12 oranges. What is the cost per orange?

3. An airplane is flying west at an altitude of 33,485 feet. Another plane is flying southwest at an altitude of 30,785 feet. How much above the southwest-bound plane is the west-bound plane when their paths cross?

4. Tom bought 6 books at $19.85 each and 3 CDs at $6.42 each. What was the total of his purchases?

5. Sarah reads one magazine each weekday (Monday-Friday). How many magazines does she read in one year (52 weeks)?

6. Jara had a balance of $59 in his checking account. Since then he made deposits of $147, $484, and $341 and wrote checks for $55, $128, $177, and $357. When all of the deposits are recorded and all of the checks clear, what balance will he have in his checking account?

7. Frank can type 36 words each minute. How many words can he type in a typical 8-hour day?

8. Barbara bought 73 shares of stock for $3504. How much did the stock cost per share?

9. Jorge was just promoted to assistant store manager of a Wal-Mart store. He bought two suits at $250 each, two shirts at $31 each, two pairs of shoes at $75 each, and three ties at $21 each. What was the total cost of his new work wardrobe?

10. Every 60 minutes, the world population increases by 100,000 people. How many people will be born during the next 420 minutes?

1.8 Solving Applied Problems _____ *Multiple Choice*

1. A 16-ounce can of tomato soup is priced at $0.96. What is the unit price per ounce?

    a. $15.36 per ounce   **b.** $0.08 per ounce   **c.** $0.90 per ounce   **d.** $0.06 per ounce

2. A store has gross revenues of $6105, $4571, $7276, and $7014 in its first four weeks of business. What was the gross revenue for those four weeks?

    a. $25,066   **b.** $24,966   **c.** $23,966   **d.** $25,516

3. A store orders 15 cases of snack crackers. Each case contains 102 snack crackers. How many snack crackers did the store order?

    a. 1520   **b.** 1540   **c.** 1530   **d.** 1524

4. Leslie enjoys skiing in the winter. Last year she skied 27 times and spent a total of $756. How much did it cost her each time?

    a. $28   **b.** $29   **c.** $20,412   **d.** $729

5. A plot of land that is up for sale is advertised as 41 acres. If there are 4840 square yards in an acre, how many square yards does the plot of land cover?

    a. 198,030 square yards   **b.** 199,260 square yards

    c. 198,440 square yards   **d.** 4881 square yards

6. The Spring City school system has 2953 high school students, 4018 middle school students, and 6079 elementary school students. How many total students are in the Spring City school system?

    a. 13,105   **b.** 13,050   **c.** 13,010   **d.** 12,958

7. Caitlyn wanted to determine the gas mileage she was getting on her car. She filled the gas tank on her car when the odometer read 25,165 miles. After 9 days, the odometer read 25,354 miles and it took 7 gallons of gas to fill the tank. How many miles to the gallon did Caitlyn's car achieve?

    a. 27 miles per gallon   **b.** 21 miles per gallon

    c. 189 miles per gallon   **d.** 184 miles per gallon

8. Lauren owns 16 acres of land that she rents to a farmer for $2313 per acre per year. Her property taxes are $758 per acre per year. How much profit does she make on the land each year?

    a. $37,788   **b.** $49,136   **c.** $36,250   **d.** $24,880

9. In preparation for his new job, Tristan bought two suits at $184 apiece, four shirts at $27 apiece, two pairs of shoes at $72 a pair, four ties at $27 apiece, and five pairs of socks at $5 a pair. What was the total cost of these items?

    a. $753   **b.** $315   **c.** $775   **d.** $728

10. Louie's Lunchtime Lounge has 27 tables and each table has either 2 or 4 chairs. If there are 96 chairs to go with the 27 tables, how many tables have exactly 4 chairs?

    a. 7   **b.** 6   **c.** 21   **d.** 20

2.1 Understanding Fractions _____ *Free Response*

1. Name the numerator and denominator in the fraction: $\dfrac{7}{11}$

2. Name the numerator and denominator in the fraction: $\dfrac{13}{5}$

3. Use a fraction to represent the shaded part of the figure.

    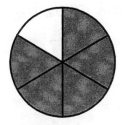

4. Use a fraction to represent the shaded part of the figure.

    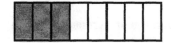

5. Shade portions of the figure to illustrate the fraction $\dfrac{3}{7}$.

6. Shade portions of the figure to illustrate the fraction $\dfrac{2}{5}$.

    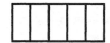

7. Of the 177 students at a university, 48 are juniors. What fraction of the students are juniors?

8. Of the 248 students at a private school, 28 are seniors. What fraction of the students are NOT seniors?

9. Of the 96 executives as a private accounting firm, 88 are women. What fraction of the executives are women?

10. Of the 95 teachers at a school, 68 are men. What fraction of the teachers are NOT men?

2.1 Understanding Fractions _____ *Multiple Choice*

1. Name the numerator and denominator of the fraction: $\frac{8}{3}$
   a. Numerator 8, denominator 3
   b. Numerator 3 denominator 8
   c. Numerator $\frac{3}{8}$, denominator 8
   d. Numerator 11, denominator 1

2. Name the numerator and denominator of the fraction: $\frac{5}{9}$
   a. Numerator 9, denominator 5
   b. Numerator $\frac{5}{9}$, denominator 9
   c. Numerator 14, denominator 9
   d. Numerator 5, denominator 9

For problems 3 and 4, what fraction of the figure is shaded?

3.
   a. $\frac{1}{4}$
   b. $\frac{1}{3}$
   c. $\frac{3}{4}$
   d. $\frac{3}{1}$

4.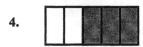
   a. $\frac{3}{2}$
   b. $\frac{2}{5}$
   c. $\frac{3}{5}$
   d. $\frac{2}{3}$

5. Which illustration best represents $\frac{6}{11}$ of an object?

   a.
   b.

   c.
   d.

6. Which illustration best represents $\frac{4}{7}$ of an object?

   a.
   b.

   c.
   d.

7. According to a recent study, 13 out of 20 visits to a hospital emergency room were for an injury. What fraction of emergency room visits were injury-related?
   a. $\frac{7}{13}$
   b. $\frac{20}{13}$
   c. $\frac{13}{7}$
   d. $\frac{13}{20}$

8. According to a recent study, 8 out of 19 visits to a hospital emergency room were for an injury. What fraction of emergency room visits were NOT injury-related?
   a. $\frac{19}{11}$
   b. $\frac{11}{19}$
   c. $\frac{11}{8}$
   d. $\frac{8}{11}$

9. There are 100 centimeters in a meter. What fractional part of a meter does 17 centimeters represent?
   a. $\frac{17}{100}$
   b. $\frac{100}{17}$
   c. $\frac{83}{17}$
   d. $\frac{17}{83}$

10. In a psychology class containing 49 students, there are 7 freshmen, 10 sophomores, 8 juniors, and the rest are seniors. What fraction of the class is comprised of seniors?
    a. $\frac{24}{66}$
    b. $\frac{49}{24}$
    c. $\frac{24}{49}$
    d. $\frac{1}{4}$

2.2 Simplifying Fractions _____ *Free Response*

1. Write as a product of primes: 63

2. Write as a product of primes: 154

For problems 3-5, reduce the fraction by finding a common factor in the numerator and in the denominator and dividing by the common factor.

3. $\dfrac{30}{70}$

4. $\dfrac{22}{36}$

5. $\dfrac{12}{27}$

6. Reduce $\dfrac{42}{66}$ by the method of prime factors.

7. Reduce $\dfrac{24}{84}$ by the method of prime factors.

8. Are the fractions $\dfrac{4}{9}$ and $\dfrac{14}{19}$ equal?

9. There are 5280 feet in a mile. What fraction of a mile is represented by 120 feet? Write the faction in simplest form.

10. A company employs 270,000 employees worldwide. About 25,200 employees work in the United States. What fraction of the employees work in the United States? Write the fraction in simplest form.

2.2 Simplifying Fractions _____ *Multiple Choice*

1. Write 700 as the product of primes.

   a. $5^4 \times 7$ **b.** $2^2 \times 5^2 \times 7$ **c.** $2^4 \times 7$ **d.** $2^3 \times 5^2 \times 7$

2. Write 203 as the product of primes.

   a. 7×29 **b.** 7^2 **c.** $7^2 \times 29$ **d.** 7×27

For problems 3-5, reduce the fraction by finding a common factor in the numerator and in the denominator and dividing by the common factor.

3. $\dfrac{130}{221}$ **a.** $\dfrac{10}{13}$ **b.** $\dfrac{130}{221}$ **c.** $\dfrac{13}{17}$ **d.** $\dfrac{10}{17}$

4. $\dfrac{107}{113}$ **a.** $\dfrac{53}{107}$ **b.** $\dfrac{53}{56}$ **c.** $\dfrac{107}{113}$ **d.** $\dfrac{113}{53}$

5. $\dfrac{318}{393}$ **a.** $\dfrac{131}{106}$ **b.** $\dfrac{393}{318}$ **c.** $\dfrac{318}{393}$ **d.** $\dfrac{106}{131}$

For problems 6 and 7, reduce by the method of prime factors. Then write the fraction in lowest terms.

6. $\dfrac{24}{140}$

   a. $\dfrac{2 \times 2 \times 2 \times 3}{2 \times 2 \times 5 \times 7} = \dfrac{6}{35}$ **b.** $\dfrac{2 \times 2 \times 3}{2 \times 5 \times 7} = \dfrac{6}{35}$

   c. $\dfrac{2 \times 2 \times 3 \times 3}{2 \times 2 \times 5 \times 7} = \dfrac{9}{35}$ **d.** $\dfrac{2 \times 2 \times 2 \times 3}{2 \times 2 \times 2 \times 7} = \dfrac{3}{5}$

7. $\dfrac{55}{88}$

   a. $\dfrac{2 \times 5 \times 11}{2 \times 2 \times 2 \times 11} = \dfrac{15}{22}$ **b.** $\dfrac{3 \times 11}{2 \times 2 \times 11} = \dfrac{33}{8}$

   c. $\dfrac{5 \times 11}{2 \times 2 \times 2 \times 11} = \dfrac{5}{8}$ **d.** $\dfrac{2 \times 2 \times 2 \times 11}{2 \times 5 \times 11} = \dfrac{22}{15}$

8. Are the fractions $\dfrac{63}{70}$ and $\dfrac{72}{90}$ equal?

   a. Yes   **b.** No

9. A company employs 288,000 employees worldwide. About 72,000 employees work in the United Sates. What fraction (in lowest form) of the employees do NOT work in the United States?

   a. $\dfrac{1}{4}$ **b.** $\dfrac{3}{4}$ **c.** $\dfrac{216,000}{288,000}$ **d.** $\dfrac{72,000}{288,000}$

10. There are 17,100 spectators at a ball game. If 5400 are females, what fraction (in lowest terms) of the spectators are females?

    a. $\dfrac{5400}{\text{females}}$ **b.** $\dfrac{13}{19}$ **c.** $\dfrac{13}{6}$ **d.** $\dfrac{6}{19}$

2.3 Improper Fractions and Mixed Numbers _____ *Free Response*

1. Change $5\dfrac{5}{7}$ to an improper fraction.

2. Change $8\dfrac{5}{6}$ to an improper fraction.

3. Change $\dfrac{41}{5}$ to a mixed number.

4. Change $\dfrac{63}{7}$ to a mixed number.

5. Reduce: $\dfrac{147}{70}$

6. Reduce: $\dfrac{132}{44}$

7. Change $\dfrac{550}{90}$ to a mixed number and reduce.

8. Change $\dfrac{396}{28}$ to a mixed number and reduce.

9. By eating right and exercising regularly, Bob lost $6\dfrac{5}{8}$ pounds. Change this number to an improper fraction.

10. The flagpole in front of Jack and Isabelle's house is $21\dfrac{12}{23}$ feet tall. Change this number to an improper fraction.

2.3 Improper Fractions and Mixed Numbers _____ *Multiple Choice*

1. Change $4\frac{3}{4}$ to an improper fraction.

    a. $\frac{19}{3}$ b. $\frac{16}{4}$ c. $\frac{19}{4}$ d. $\frac{16}{3}$

2. Change $12\frac{16}{23}$ to an improper fraction.

    a.   28   b.   192   c. $\frac{192}{23}$ d. $\frac{292}{23}$

3. Change $\frac{85}{7}$ to a mixed number.

    a. $\frac{7}{85}$ b. $12\frac{1}{7}$ c. $85\frac{85}{7}$ d. $85\frac{7}{85}$

4. Change $\frac{215}{4}$ to a mixed number.

    a. $53\frac{3}{4}$ b. $\frac{4}{215}$ c. $215\frac{215}{4}$ d. $215\frac{4}{215}$

5. Reduce: $\frac{308}{44}$

    a.   7   b. $\frac{77}{11}$ c. $\frac{28}{4}$ d. $\frac{7}{11}$

6. Reduce: $\frac{468}{91}$

    a.   36   b. $\frac{36}{13}$ c. $\frac{13}{7}$ d. $\frac{36}{7}$

7. Change $\frac{504}{77}$ to a mixed number and reduce.

    a. $6\frac{6}{77}$ b. $6\frac{6}{11}$ c. $6\frac{6}{7}$ d. $6\frac{7}{11}$

8. Change $\frac{455}{40}$ to a mixed number and reduce.

    a. $11\frac{3}{5}$ b. $11\frac{3}{40}$ c. $11\frac{3}{8}$ d. $11\frac{5}{8}$

9. The number of pounds of beef served at Jose's restaurant yesterday was $325\frac{6}{7}$ pounds. Change this number to an improper fraction.

    a.   331 pounds   b. $\frac{1950}{7}$ pounds   c.   1950 pounds   d. $\frac{2281}{7}$ pounds

10. A recipe for baking a cake requires $\frac{39}{5}$ cups of flour. Write this as a mixed number.

    a. $7\frac{4}{5}$ cups   b.   7 cups   c. $9\frac{3}{4}$ cups   d. $8\frac{3}{4}$ cups

2.4 Multiplication of Fractions and Mixed Numbers _____ *Free Response*

1. Multiply: $\dfrac{3}{7} \times \dfrac{9}{11}$

2. Multiply: $\dfrac{4}{1} \times \dfrac{2}{3} \times \dfrac{1}{11}$

3. Multiply: $3\dfrac{1}{4} \times \dfrac{8}{9}$

4. Multiply: $2\dfrac{2}{3} \times 7\dfrac{1}{2}$

5. Multiply: $4\dfrac{1}{5} \times 10\dfrac{5}{9}$

6. Solve for x: $\dfrac{3}{8} \cdot x = \dfrac{3}{10}$

7. Jennifer is building some shelves and requires 8 pieces of wood that are each $5\frac{1}{8}$ feet long. What is the total length of wood that Jennifer needs?

8. Julie is saving $\frac{3}{19}$ of her monthly income of $8550 for retirement. How much money is she setting aside each month for retirement?

9. Tom purchased a stereo for $1295. Two years later it was worth $\frac{3}{5}$ of the purchase price. What is the stereo worth after two years?

10. A bedroom measures $10\frac{1}{2}$ feet by $11\frac{1}{3}$ feet. What is the area of the bedroom? (Area is the product of the length times the width.)

2.4 Multiplication of Fractions and Mixed Numbers _____ *Multiple Choice*

1. Multiply: $\dfrac{2}{5} \times \dfrac{2}{7} \times \dfrac{2}{3}$ a. $\dfrac{14}{15}$ b. $\dfrac{8}{15}$ c. $\dfrac{4}{105}$ d. $\dfrac{8}{105}$

2. Multiply: $\dfrac{2}{5} \times \dfrac{7}{17}$ a. $\dfrac{34}{35}$ b. $\dfrac{14}{85}$ c. $\dfrac{9}{22}$ d. $\dfrac{8}{105}$

3. Multiply: $2\dfrac{2}{3} \times 7\dfrac{1}{2}$ a. $14\dfrac{5}{6}$ b. 19 c. 20 d. 21

4. Multiply: $4 \times 4\dfrac{3}{10}$ a. $17\dfrac{1}{5}$ b. $16\dfrac{3}{10}$ c. $17\dfrac{3}{5}$ d. $8\dfrac{1}{5}$

5. Multiply: $2\dfrac{4}{5} \times \dfrac{2}{7}$ a. $4\dfrac{4}{5}$ b. $2\dfrac{8}{35}$ c. $\dfrac{4}{5}$ d. $\dfrac{2}{5}$

6. Solve for x: $\dfrac{7}{20} \cdot x = \dfrac{3}{7}$.   a. $x = 46\dfrac{2}{3}$ b. $x = 1\dfrac{11}{49}$ c. $x = \dfrac{10}{27}$ d. $x = \dfrac{3}{140}$

7. Find the area of the square. Hint: The area of a square is the product of the length times the width.

     $9\dfrac{3}{5}$ ft

     $9\dfrac{3}{5}$ ft   [square] $9\dfrac{3}{5}$ ft

     $9\dfrac{3}{5}$ ft

   a. $A = 92\dfrac{4}{25}$ ft^2

   b. $A = 921\dfrac{3}{5}$ ft^2

   c. $A = 184\dfrac{8}{25}$ ft^2

   d. $A = 19\dfrac{1}{5}$ ft^2

8. Maria exercises for $1\dfrac{4}{5}$ hours every Saturday. She runs for $\dfrac{4}{5}$ of the time that she exercises. How much time does she spend running every Saturday?

   a. $\dfrac{2}{5}$ hour   b. $1\dfrac{16}{45}$ hours   c. $4\dfrac{4}{5}$ hours   d. $\dfrac{4}{5}$ hour

9. Byron rode his bicycle $9\dfrac{4}{15}$ miles on each of 9 days. What is the total distance Byron rode?

   a. $83\dfrac{4}{5}$ miles   b. $81\dfrac{4}{15}$ miles   c. $83\dfrac{2}{5}$ miles   d. $18\dfrac{2}{5}$ miles

10. A rectangular flowerbed in front of a building measures $1\dfrac{5}{9}$ feet by $5\dfrac{1}{7}$ feet. What is the total area of the flowerbed? Hint: The area of a rectangle is the product of the length times the width.

   a. 11 square feet   b. 8 square feet   c. $5\dfrac{5}{63}$ square feet   d. 9 square feet

2.5 Division of Fractions and Mixed Numbers _____ *Free Response*

1. Divide: $\dfrac{2}{9} \div \dfrac{4}{27}$

2. Divide: $0 \div \dfrac{19}{20}$

3. Divide: $\dfrac{\frac{5}{12}}{4\frac{2}{3}}$

4. Divide: $1\dfrac{1}{8} \div \dfrac{1}{8}$

5. Divide: $4\dfrac{1}{2} \div 2\dfrac{7}{9}$

6. Divide: $4\dfrac{3}{5} \div 2\dfrac{3}{5}$

7. Solve for x: $x \div \dfrac{1}{7} = \dfrac{3}{5}$

8. The perimeter of an equilateral triangle (all sides equal) is $\dfrac{25}{6}$ of a foot. How long is each side?

9. How many $\dfrac{4}{9}$ lb boxes of cereal can be made from 848 pounds of cereal?

10. Tom bought 20 yards of rope to be cut into pieces that are $1\dfrac{2}{3}$ yards long. How many pieces does he have?

2.5 Division of Fractions and Mixed Numbers _____ *Multiple Choice*

1. Divide: $\dfrac{3}{15} \div \dfrac{2}{13}$ a. $97\dfrac{1}{2}$ b. $\dfrac{13}{10}$ c. $\dfrac{5}{28}$ d. $\dfrac{2}{195}$

2. Divide: $\dfrac{\frac{7}{19}}{\frac{7}{12}}$ a. $\dfrac{11}{19}$ b. $\dfrac{10}{19}$ c. $\dfrac{12}{19}$ d. $\dfrac{12}{17}$

3. Divide: $\dfrac{1}{8} \div 0$ a. Undefined   b. $\dfrac{1}{48}$ c. $1\dfrac{1}{3}$ d. 0

4. Divide: $2\dfrac{2}{5} \div 6$ a. $\dfrac{2}{4}$ b. $\dfrac{3}{5}$ c. $\dfrac{1}{5}$ d. $\dfrac{2}{5}$

5. Divide: $4\dfrac{1}{8} \div 3\dfrac{3}{8}$ a. $1\dfrac{2}{8}$ b. $2\dfrac{2}{9}$ c. $1\dfrac{3}{9}$ d. $1\dfrac{2}{9}$

6. Divide: $3\dfrac{1}{9} \div 1\dfrac{1}{8}$ a. $2\dfrac{62}{81}$ b. $3\dfrac{62}{81}$ c. $2\dfrac{63}{81}$ d. $2\dfrac{62}{80}$

7. Solve for x: $x \div \dfrac{1}{2} = \dfrac{5}{13}$ a. $x = \dfrac{2}{5}$ b. $x = \dfrac{13}{10}$ c. $x = \dfrac{5}{26}$ d. $x = 2$

8. On a recent trip, Asher drove 202 miles on $14\frac{1}{3}$ gallons of gasoline. How many miles per gallon did she average?

   a. $14\dfrac{4}{43}$ miles per gallon   b. $\dfrac{43}{606}$ miles per gallon

   c. $2895\dfrac{1}{3}$ miles per gallon   d. 943 miles per gallon

9. Mark is filling decorative oil lamps for a reception. Each lamp can hold $\frac{1}{8}$ cup of oil. Mark has $2\frac{3}{8}$ cups of oil available. How many oil lamps can Mark fill completely?

   a. 19 oil lamps   b. 20 oil lamps   c. 18 oil lamps   d. $17\frac{1}{2}$ oil lamps

10. Ted walks around a lake on a path that is $3\frac{4}{9}$ miles long. It takes him $1\frac{1}{3}$ hours to complete his walk. What is his average speed (in miles per hour)?

   a. $3\dfrac{7}{12}$ miles per hour   b. $2\dfrac{7}{12}$ miles per hour   c. $2\dfrac{8}{12}$ miles per hour   d. $2\dfrac{7}{11}$ miles per hour

2.6 LCD and Equivalent Fractions _____ *Free Response*

1. Find the LCM of 9 and 72.

2. Find the LCM of 25 and 45.

3. Find the LCD of $\frac{1}{6}$ and $\frac{3}{5}$.

4. Find the LCD of $\frac{5}{12}$ and $\frac{11}{30}$.

5. Find the LCD of $\frac{2}{5}$, $\frac{1}{3}$, and $\frac{3}{10}$.

6. Find the LCD of $\frac{17}{18}$, $\frac{1}{12}$, and $\frac{13}{20}$.

For problems 7 and 8, build the fraction to an equivalent fraction with the denominator specified. State the numerator.

7. $\frac{2}{13} = \frac{?}{65}$

8. $\frac{2}{7} = \frac{?}{147}$

For problems 9 and 10, build up the fractions to equivalent fractions having the LCD as the denominator.

9. $\frac{7}{20}$ and $\frac{5}{16}$

10. $\frac{7}{30}$, $\frac{2}{15}$, $\frac{23}{45}$

2.6 LCD and Equivalent Fractions _____ *Multiple Choice*

1. Find the LCM of 9 and 36.

    a. 324   b. 9   c. 36   d. 45

2. Find the LCM of 32 and 28.

    a. 224   b. 896   c. 60   d. 4

3. Find the LCD of $\dfrac{3}{16}$ and $\dfrac{2}{18}$.

    a. 2   b. 288   c. 34   d. 144

4. Find the LCD for $\dfrac{7}{25}$ and $\dfrac{9}{20}$.

    a. 80   b. 200   c. 100   d. 5

5. Find the LCD of $\dfrac{1}{20}$, $\dfrac{1}{24}$, and $\dfrac{13}{30}$.

    a. 120   b. 60   c. 420   d. 210

6. Find the LCD of $\dfrac{7}{11}$, $\dfrac{1}{12}$, and $\dfrac{5}{6}$.

    a. 792   b. 72   c. 132   d. 1

For problems 7 and 8, build the fraction to an equivalent fraction with the denominator specified. State the numerator.

7. $9 = \dfrac{?}{5}$ a. 14   b. 5   c. 9   d. 45

8. $\dfrac{9}{16} = \dfrac{?}{112}$ a. 9   b. 36   c. 1008   d. 144

For problems 9 and 10, build up the fractions to equivalent fractions having the LCD as the denominator.

9. $\dfrac{2}{15}$ and $\dfrac{4}{25}$ a. $\dfrac{75}{10}$ and $\dfrac{75}{12}$ b. $\dfrac{2}{75}$ and $\dfrac{4}{75}$ c. $\dfrac{10}{75}$ and $\dfrac{12}{75}$ d. $\dfrac{12}{25}$ and $\dfrac{4}{25}$

10. $\dfrac{1}{8}$, $\dfrac{9}{14}$, $\dfrac{7}{16}$ a. $\dfrac{9}{16}$, $\dfrac{11}{16}$, $\dfrac{7}{16}$ b. $\dfrac{14}{112}$, $\dfrac{9}{14}$, $\dfrac{7}{16}$ c. $\dfrac{1}{8}$, $\dfrac{72}{112}$, $\dfrac{49}{112}$ d. $\dfrac{14}{112}$, $\dfrac{72}{112}$, $\dfrac{49}{112}$

2.7 Adding and Subtracting Fractions _____ *Free Response*

1. Subtract: $\dfrac{8}{21} - \dfrac{5}{21}$

2. Add: $\dfrac{3}{8} + \dfrac{4}{9}$

3. Subtract: $\dfrac{27}{20} - \dfrac{3}{5}$

4. Add: $\dfrac{7}{12} + \dfrac{11}{30}$

5. Subtract: $\dfrac{27}{35} - \dfrac{3}{10}$

6. Add: $\dfrac{1}{12} + \dfrac{3}{14} + \dfrac{4}{21}$

7. Find the value of x: $x + \dfrac{1}{2} = \dfrac{5}{6}$

8. Find the value of x: $x - \dfrac{1}{4} = \dfrac{1}{6}$

9. Kevin read $\frac{4}{9}$ of a book on Monday. He read $\frac{2}{13}$ of the book on Wednesday. What fractional part of the book has Kevin read so far this week?

10. David drives $\frac{3}{13}$ hour to get to his friend Tom's house. He then drives $\frac{2}{5}$ hour to get to the bowling alley. How many hours does David spend driving?

2.7 Adding and Subtracting Fractions _____ *Multiple Choice*

1. Subtract: $\dfrac{19}{46} - \dfrac{16}{46}$

   a. $\dfrac{3}{46}$ b. $\dfrac{35}{46}$ c. $6\dfrac{14}{23}$ d. $\dfrac{3}{92}$

2. Subtract: $\dfrac{5}{7} - \dfrac{1}{2}$

   a. $\dfrac{4}{7}$ b. $\dfrac{1}{7}$ c. $\dfrac{4}{9}$ d. $\dfrac{3}{14}$

3. Subtract: $\dfrac{7}{9} - \dfrac{1}{12}$

   a. $\dfrac{13}{18}$ b. $\dfrac{2}{3}$ c. $\dfrac{25}{36}$ d. $\dfrac{1}{2}$

4. Subtract: $\dfrac{8}{15} - \dfrac{1}{20}$

   a. $\dfrac{29}{60}$ b. $\dfrac{7}{15}$ c. $\dfrac{1}{2}$ d. $\dfrac{27}{60}$

5. Subtract: $\dfrac{7}{12} - \dfrac{1}{16}$

   a. $\dfrac{1}{8}$ b. $\dfrac{25}{48}$ c. $\dfrac{1}{6}$ d. $\dfrac{3}{16}$

6. Add: $\dfrac{9}{15} + \dfrac{9}{14} + \dfrac{1}{9}$

   a. $\dfrac{19}{630}$ b. $1\dfrac{223}{630}$ c. $\dfrac{1}{2}$ d. $22\dfrac{17}{38}$

7. Find the value of x: $x - \dfrac{5}{7} = -\dfrac{11}{21}$

   a. $x = \dfrac{26}{21}$ b. $x = -\dfrac{26}{21}$ c. $x = \dfrac{4}{21}$ d. $x = -\dfrac{4}{21}$

8. Find the value of x: $x - \dfrac{1}{13} = \dfrac{4}{5}$

   a. $x = \dfrac{5}{18}$ b. $x = \dfrac{57}{65}$ c. $x = \dfrac{5}{65}$ d. $x = \dfrac{57}{18}$

9. A jar is $\frac{8}{9}$ full of olives. Claudia eats $\frac{3}{5}$ of the jar of olives. What fractional part of the jar still contains olives?

   a. $\dfrac{13}{9}$ of the jar   b. $\dfrac{1}{9}$ of the jar   c. $\dfrac{5}{9}$ of the jar   d. $\dfrac{13}{45}$ of the jar

10. The distance from Ivy's house to the park is $\frac{5}{8}$ of a mile. Ivy leaves her house with her dog and walks $\frac{2}{6}$ of a mile toward the park. How much farther does she have to walk her dog to get to the park?

    a. $\dfrac{7}{24}$ of a mile   b. $\dfrac{1}{16}$ of a mile   c. $\dfrac{3}{8}$ of a mile   d. $\dfrac{7}{4}$ of a mile

2.8 Combining Mixed Numbers and Order of Operations _____ *Free Response*

For problems 1-5 express each answer as a mixed number.

1. Subtract: $7\frac{3}{4} - 6\frac{1}{4}$

2. Add: $1\frac{2}{3} + 7\frac{5}{18}$

3. Add: $\begin{array}{r} 2\frac{3}{4} \\ + \ 9\frac{7}{12} \\ \hline \end{array}$

4. Subtract: $\begin{array}{r} 27\frac{1}{10} \\ + \ 12\frac{3}{8} \\ \hline \end{array}$

5. Add: $\begin{array}{r} 2\frac{1}{8} \\ 3\frac{2}{3} \\ + \ 10\frac{1}{4} \\ \hline \end{array}$

For problems 6-8, evaluate using the correct order of operation.

6. $\frac{2}{5} + \frac{1}{3} \times \frac{4}{5}$

7. $\frac{1}{6} \times \frac{1}{2} + \frac{4}{3} \div \frac{2}{3}$

8. $\left(\frac{2}{3}\right)^2 \times \frac{1}{8}$

9. Harry cuts a board $13\frac{3}{7}$ feet long from one 20 feet long. How long is the remaining piece?

10. Chris rode her bicycle $8\frac{1}{2}$ miles on Tuesday. On Thursday, she rode $9\frac{4}{9}$ miles. What was her total biking distance for those two days?

2.8 Combining Mixed Numbers and Order of Operations _____ *Multiple Choice*

1. Add: $4\dfrac{5}{7}+4\dfrac{2}{7}$

   a. $2\dfrac{4}{7}$ b. 9 c. $9\dfrac{4}{7}$ d. 8

2. Subtract: $38\dfrac{2}{3}-25\dfrac{13}{16}$

   a. 12 b. $11\dfrac{41}{48}$ c. $13\dfrac{41}{48}$ d. $12\dfrac{41}{48}$

3. Subtract: $\begin{aligned}17\tfrac{7}{25}\\ -\ 9\tfrac{7}{20}\end{aligned}$

   a. $7\dfrac{93}{100}$ b. $8\dfrac{93}{100}$

   c. $6\dfrac{95}{100}$ d. 7

4. Subtract: $\begin{aligned}13\tfrac{2}{15}\\ -\ 7\tfrac{2}{9}\end{aligned}$

   a. $6\dfrac{43}{45}$ b. $4\dfrac{41}{45}$

   c. $5\dfrac{41}{45}$ d. 5

5. Subtract: $\begin{aligned}17\\ -\ \tfrac{5}{9}\end{aligned}$

   a. $16\dfrac{4}{9}$ b. $17\dfrac{4}{9}$

   c. $14\dfrac{4}{9}$ d. 16

For problems 6-8, evaluate using the correct order of operation.

6. $\dfrac{4}{3}+\left(\dfrac{3}{2}\right)^2-\dfrac{5}{7}$

   a. $2\dfrac{5}{42}$ b. $2\dfrac{73}{84}$ c. $1\dfrac{53}{84}$ d. $2\dfrac{71}{126}$

7. $\left(\dfrac{4}{3}+\dfrac{1}{3}\right)\times 2$

   a. $\dfrac{20}{3}$ b. $\dfrac{8}{3}$ c. $\dfrac{5}{6}$ d. $\dfrac{10}{3}$

8. $\dfrac{9}{2}\div\left(\dfrac{9}{8}+\dfrac{3}{8}\right)$

   a. $\dfrac{8}{9}$ b. $\dfrac{1}{3}$ c. 3 d. 4

9. Pat caught a fish that weight $14\dfrac{4}{9}$ pounds. Dan caught a fish that weight $9\dfrac{7}{9}$ pounds. How much more did Pat's fish weigh than Dan's fish?

   a. $23\dfrac{2}{3}$ pounds   b. $4\dfrac{2}{3}$ pounds   c. $2\dfrac{2}{3}$ pounds   d. $4\dfrac{1}{3}$ pounds

10. Angie is wrapping a present for her nephew. She has a roll of wrapping paper that has 14 feet of wrapping paper on the roll. She uses $5\dfrac{2}{5}$ feet to wrap a present. How many feet of wrapping paper are left on the roll?

    a. $9\dfrac{2}{5}$ feet   b. $9\dfrac{3}{5}$ feet   c. $13\dfrac{3}{5}$ feet   d. $8\dfrac{3}{5}$ feet

2.9 Applied Problems Involving Fractions _____ *Free Response*

1. A triangle has three sides that measure $6\frac{3}{4}$ feet, $9\frac{1}{6}$ feet, and $8\frac{7}{12}$ feet. What is the perimeter (total distance around) of the triangle?

2. A deli ordered $9\frac{1}{2}$ pounds of cheese on Friday, $12\frac{4}{5}$ pounds on Saturday, and $13\frac{9}{10}$ pounds on Sunday. How many pounds were ordered on these three days?

3. A carpenter is using an 11-foot length of wood for a frame. The carpenter needs to cut a notch in the wood that is $5\frac{3}{8}$ feet from one end and $2\frac{1}{3}$ feet from the other end. How long does the notch need to be?

4. Sam Garcia makes birdhouses as a hobby. He has a long piece of lumber that measures $20\frac{1}{4}$ feet. He needs to cut it into pieces that are $\frac{3}{4}$ foot long for the birdhouse floors. How many floors will he be able to cut from the long piece?

5. How many gallons can a tank hold that has a volume of $12\frac{1}{4}$ cubic feet? Assume that 1 cubic foot holds about $7\frac{1}{2}$ gallons.

6. Suzanne earns \$960 per week. $\frac{1}{3}$ of her income goes to rent $\frac{1}{6}$ goes to a car payment, and $\frac{1}{16}$ goes to groceries. How much money is left over after these three items are paid?

7. Lou and Sheri are building a rectangular plot for their Sebastopol Geese. The plot measures $42\frac{1}{2}$ feet by $26\frac{1}{4}$ feet. If fencing costs \$1.50 per foot, how much will it cost to put fence around the perimeter?

8. Frank bought $6\frac{1}{2}$ pounds of roast beef at \$$4\frac{3}{4}$ per pound. How much did he pay for the roast beef? Round to the nearest cent.

9. A tree is measured to be $4\frac{1}{2}$ feet tall. If it grows at a rate of $\frac{1}{8}$ foot per year, how long will it take the tree to reach a height of 10 feet?

10. Tom has a storage locker that holds 170 cubic feet of furniture. He needs a new locker that is $2\frac{1}{2}$ times as large. How many cubic feet will be in the new locker?

2.9 Applied Problems Involving Fractions _____ *Multiple Choice*

1. A square has four sides, all with an equal length of $7\frac{1}{2}$ feet. What is the perimeter (total distance around) the square.

   a. $P = 31$ ft   b. $P = 15$ ft   c. $P = 1125$ ft   d. $P = 30$ ft

2. A triangle has three sides that measure 3 ft, $10\frac{1}{6}$ ft, and $12\frac{1}{10}$ ft. What is the perimeter (total distance around) of the triangle?

   a. $25\frac{1}{8}$ feet   b. $25\frac{1}{30}$ feet   c. $25\frac{4}{15}$ feet   d. $93\frac{13}{16}$ feet

3. Jody is using a recipe that calls for $\frac{1}{2}$ cup of milk per batch. If she has $11\frac{1}{2}$ cups of milk available, how many batches can she make?

   a. 23 batches   b. 24 batches   c. 20 batches   d. 46 batches

4. Robert and Paul each took some chips from a $12\frac{1}{2}$-ounce bag of potato chips. Robert took $1\frac{1}{3}$ ounces of chips and Paul took $3\frac{5}{6}$ ounces of chips. How many ounces of chips were left in the bag?

   a. $9\frac{2}{3}$ ounces   b. $7\frac{1}{3}$ ounces   c. $8\frac{1}{3}$ ounces   d. $8\frac{2}{3}$ ounces

5. The car Colleen is driving gets $25\frac{1}{3}$ miles per gallon of gas. She used $6\frac{1}{5}$ gallons of gas going from her home to her grandparents' home. She used another $2\frac{7}{10}$ gallons traveling from her grandparents' home to her cousin's apartment. What was the total distance Colleen drove?

   a. $222\dfrac{14}{15}$ miles   b. $151\dfrac{3}{10}$ miles   c. $225\dfrac{7}{15}$ miles   d. $163\dfrac{1}{5}$ miles

6. To get credit for graduation, Brittany completed 20 hours of community service. She worked at a soup kitchen for $\frac{1}{7}$ of the time. She picked up litter along highways for $\frac{1}{2}$ of the time. The rest of the hours she spent tutoring younger children after school. How much time did Brittany spend tutoring?

   a. $7\dfrac{9}{14}$ hours   b. $8\dfrac{1}{7}$ hours   c. $9\dfrac{1}{7}$ hours   d. $7\dfrac{1}{7}$ hours

7. Matt decided to do some spring cleaning. He spent $4\frac{4}{7}$ hours cleaning his garage on Saturday. The next day he spent $5\frac{3}{7}$ hours cleaning his basement. What was the total amount of time he spent cleaning that weekend?

   a. 10 hours   b. $3\frac{5}{7}$ hours   c. $10\frac{5}{7}$ hours   d. 9 hours

8. While looking through the properties of her diskette, Amy noticed that $\frac{5}{9}$ of the space on the disk was not being used. She deleted four files that were using $\frac{1}{5}$ of the disk space. What fractional part of the disk space was free after she deleted the four files?

   a. $\dfrac{34}{7}$ of the disk   b. $\dfrac{3}{7}$ of the disk   c. $\dfrac{3}{45}$ of the disk   d. $\dfrac{34}{45}$ of the disk

9. Gary has a water ski boat that can travel $72\frac{7}{8}$ nautical miles in $5\frac{1}{2}$ hours. At how many knots is the boat traveling?

   a. 350 knots   b. $26\frac{1}{2}$ knots   c. $13\frac{1}{4}$ knots   d. 12 knots

10. A little boy is $3\frac{1}{2}$ feet tall and grows at a rate of $\frac{1}{10}$ inch per month. How many months will it take him to reach a height of 5 feet?

    a. 15 months   b. 16 months   c. 2 months   d. 10 months

3.1 Decimal Notation _____ *Free Response*

1. Write 9.671 in words.

2. Write 0.423 in words.

3. Write $823.86 in words as you would for the dollar amount on a check.

4. Write "nine hundredths" in decimal notation.

5. Write "two hundred sixty-three thousandths" in decimal notation.

6. Write "eight and two hundred ninety-four thousandths" in decimal notation.

7. Write $\frac{796}{1000}$ as a decimal.

8. Write $31\frac{52}{100}$ as a decimal.

9. Write 0.72 as a fraction in lowest terms.

10. Write 36.25 as a mixed number in lowest terms.

3.1 Decimal Notation _____ *Multiple Choice*

1. Write 7.00691 in words.

    a. Seven and six hundred ninety-one millionths

    b. Seven and six hundred ninety-one tenths

    c. Seven and six hundred ninety-one thousandths

    d. Seven and six hundred ninety-one hundred-thousandths

2. Write 9.000733 in words.

    a. Nine and seven hundred thirty-three millionths

    b. Nine and seven hundred thirty-three tenths

    c. Nine and seven hundred thirty-three hundredths

    d. Nine and seven hundred thirty-three thousandths

3. Write $25.80 in words, as you would for the dollar amount on a check.

    a. Twenty-five and 80/100 cents

    b. Twenty-five dollars and 80/100 dollars

    c. Twenty-five and 80/100 dollars

    d. Twenty-five dollars and 80 cents

4. Write "seven hundred and ninety-three millionths" in decimal notation.

    a. 0.00793   b. 0.000793   c. 0.0793   d. 0.793

5. Write "twenty-five and six hundred twenty-five ten-thousandths" in decimal notation.

    a. 25.0625   b. 25.625   c. 25.000625   d. 25.00625

6. Write $\dfrac{22}{100}$ as a decimal.

    a. 0.022   b. 0.22   c. 0.0022   d. 0.00022

7. Write $300\dfrac{301}{1000}$ as a decimal.

    a. 300.00301   b. 300.0301   c. 301.3   d. 300.301

8. Write 0.56 as a fraction.

    a. $\dfrac{1}{3136}$ b. $\dfrac{14}{250}$ c. $\dfrac{1}{56}$ d. $\dfrac{14}{25}$

9. Write 14.4 as a mixed number.

    a. $14\dfrac{1}{25}$ b. $1\dfrac{2}{5}$ c. $14\dfrac{2}{5}$ d. $1\dfrac{11}{25}$

10. Write 81.152 as a mixed number.

    a. $81\dfrac{19}{125}$ b. $16\dfrac{144}{625}$ c. $\dfrac{81.152}{1000}$ d. $\dfrac{81.152}{100}$

3.2 Compare, Order, and Round Decimals _____ *Free Response*

1. Insert <, >, or = to form a true statement: 1.409 ____ 1.490

2. Insert <, >, or = to form a true statement: $\dfrac{54}{1000}$ ____ 0.054

3. Round 1.916 to the nearest tenth.

4. Round 17.481 to the nearest hundredth.

5. Round 8.61151 to the nearest thousandth.

6. Round $17.239 to the nearest cent.

7. Arrange in order from largest to smallest: 1.853, 1.538, 1.583, 1.358

8. Arrange in order from largest to smallest: 0.0049, 0.4001, $\dfrac{4}{10}$, 0.0141, 0.0401, $\dfrac{4}{100}$, 0.00069, 0.0401

9. In a town in Texas, the average consumption of soft drinks for each elementary school student is 14.328 ounces per day. Round this value off to the nearest tenth.

10. A clothing store has a shirt on sale for $18.35. Round this value to the nearest dollar.

3.2 Compare, Order, and Round Decimals _____ *Multiple Choice*

1. Which sign fills in the blank to make 0.33600____ 0.336 a true statement?

    a. >   **b.** =   **c.** <

2. Which sign fills in the blank to make 640.401____ 640.410 a true statement?

    a. <   **b.** >   **c.** =

3. Round 1.372 to the nearest tenth.

    a. 1.37   **b.** 1.5   **c.** 1.3   **d.** 1.4

4. Round 53.123497 to the nearest ten-thousandth.

    a. 53.123497   **b.** 53.12350   **c.** 53.1235   **d.** 53.1236

5. Round 124.123487 to the nearest hundred-thousandth.

    a. 124.12348   **b.** 124.1235   **c.** 124.12349   **d.** 124.12350

6. Round $99.72 to the nearest dollar.

    a. $90   **b.** $100   **c.** $99.80   **d.** $99.70

7. Round $0.9953 to the nearest cent.

    a. $1.00   **b.** $0.10   **c.** $0.99   **d.** $1.01

8. Arrange in order from smallest to largest: 5.24, 4.69, 4.96, 5.42

    a. 4.96, 4.69, 5.42, 5.24   **b.** 5.42, 5.24, 4.96, 4.69

    c. 4.69, 5.24, 4.96, 5.42   **d.** 4.69, 4.96, 5.24, 5.42

9. Arrange in order from smallest to largest: $\frac{132}{1000}$, 0.00231, $\frac{3}{10}$, 0.0123, 0.213, $\frac{22}{100}$, 0.000321, 0.23

    a. 0.000321, 0.00231, $\frac{132}{1000}$, 0.0123, 0.213, $\frac{22}{100}$, 0.23, $\frac{3}{10}$

    b. 0.000321, 0.00231, 0.0123, $\frac{132}{1000}$, 0.213, $\frac{22}{100}$, 0.23, $\frac{3}{10}$

    c. 0.000321, 0.00231, 0.0123, $\frac{132}{1000}$, $\frac{22}{100}$, 0.213, 0.23, $\frac{3}{10}$

    d. 0.000321, 0.0123, 0.00231, $\frac{132}{1000}$, 0.213, $\frac{22}{100}$, 0.23, $\frac{3}{10}$

10. According to his ultra-precise scale, Paul gained 3.688 pounds in a three-month period. Round this weight to the nearest hundredth.

    a. 0.69 pounds   **b.** 3.7 pounds   **c.** 3.69 pounds   **d.** 3.70 pounds

3.3 Adding and Subtracting Decimals _____ *Free Response*

1. Add: 308.721
             15.253
        +   2.592

2. Add: $194.9 + 0.66 + 94.26 + 101.6$

3. Subtract: 69.521
            −15.893

4. Subtract: $19.445 − 7.718$

5. Subtract: $7 − 3.189$

6. Find the perimeter (distance around) the given figure by adding the lengths of the sides.

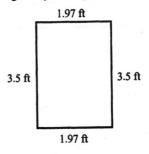

7. Find the value of x: $116.38 + x = 494$

8. Given the information below, find the total monthly cost of owning and maintaining a car.

Monthly car payment:	$274.07
Montly insurance cost:	$65.40
Average cost of gasoline per month:	$49.30
Average maintenance cost per month:	$14.50

9. Mark bought a video for $21.96. If he paid with two $20 bills, what was his charge?

10. Last year, Sabrina's average electricity bill was $109.33. Last month, her electricity bill was $145.92. How much above last year's average was last month's bill?

3.3 Adding and Subtracting Decimals _____ *Multiple Choice*

1. Add: 1.929
            19.039
       + 102.530

   a. 123.498   **b.** 123.488
   c. 123.398   **d.** 123.388

2. Add: $35.51 + 4.393 + 8.031 + 6.86$

   a. 57.894   **b.** 58.794   **c.** 57.804   **d.** 57.794

3. Subtract: 36.310
             -15.764

   a. 20.456   **b.** 20.556
   c. 20.554   **d.** 22.000

4. Subtract: $3.021 - 1.664$

   a. 3.685   **b.** 4.685
   c. 1.357   **d.** 1.457

5. Find the perimeter (distance around) of the figure below.

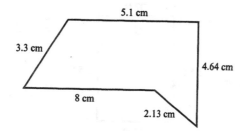

   a. 8.41 cm
   b. 23.17 cm
   c. 15.61 cm
   d. 15.97 cm

6. Find the value of x: $40.004 = 4.04 + x$

   a. 36.064   **b.** 35.934   **c.** 35.974   **d.** 36.074

7. In a practice run, a race car driver's speed is clocked at 145.151 mps at the end of her first lap, and at 165.886 at the end of the next lap. How much faster was she driving at the end of the second lap?

   a. 20.635 mph   **b.** 20.745 mph   **c.** 21.735 mph   **d.** 20.735 mph

8. Judy is planning a border for her triangular-shaped garden. One side of the garden is 8.8 feet long, another side is 15.6 feet long, and the third side is 12.1 feet long. Find the amount of border material needed.

   a. 36.4 feet   **b.** 35.5 feet   **c.** 36.5 feet   **d.** 34.5 feet

9. Jorge received a birthday check for $40 from his uncle. He immediately cashed the check and went on a shopping spree. In three different stores, he spent $11.46, $13.01, and $6.93. How much was left of the birthday money after these purchases?

   a. $8.60   **b.** $31.40   **c.** $8.90   **d.** $9.60

10. Leticia used a digitized water collection device to take daily measurements of the rain that fell on her vegetable garden. One week it rained 0.31 inches on Monday, 0.38 inches on Tuesday, and 0.26 inches on Wednesday. What was the total rainfall for those three days?

    a. 10.5 inches   **b.** 0.95 inches   **c.** 1.05 inches   **d.** 0.75 inches

3.4 Multiplying Decimals _____ *Free Response*

1. Multiply: 0.18
   $\times$ 0.03

2. Multiply: 4894
   $\times$ 0.019

3. Multiply: 0.0066×0.76

4. Multiply: 404×0.9001

5. Multiply: 3.618×100

6. Multiply: 0.01958×10^3

7. Multiply: 1.00983×10^5

8. The nutrition chart on a bag of flavored potato chips says that each serving contains 0.26 grams of cholesterol. The chart also says that there are 4 servings in the bag. How many grams of cholesterol are in the entire bag of potato chips?

9. Jose earns $13.90 per hour at his job. He worked 18 hours last week. Calculate Jose's pay before taxes.

10. A meter is a unit of measure in the metric system that is approximately equal to 39.37 inches. Gina is 1.05 meters tall. What is her approximate height in inches? Round to the nearest hundredth.

3.4 Multiplying Decimals _____ *Multiple Choice*

1. Multiply: $\begin{array}{r} 0.026 \\ \times \ \ 0.5 \\ \hline \end{array}$

    a. 0.0013
    b. 0.13
    c. 0.013
    d. 0.00013

2. Multiply: $\begin{array}{r} 9009 \\ \times \ \ 0.6006 \\ \hline \end{array}$

    a. 5945.94
    b. 5410.8054
    c. 5302.593
    d. 545.9454

3. Multiply: 0.0404×9.09

    a. 0.40996
    b. 0.377236
    c. 0.39996
    d. 0.367236

4. Multiply: 3095×0.19

    a. 588.05
    b. 5880.5
    c. 58,805
    d. 576.29

5. Multiply: 5647×0.059

    a. 333.173
    b. 331.73
    c. 33,317.3
    d. 326.51

6. Multiply: 0.4085×1000

    a. 40.85
    b. 408.5
    c. 1000.4085
    d. 0.4085000

7. Multiply: 0.000326×10^5

    a. 326
    b. 3.26
    c. 32.6
    d. 3260

8. A farmer sells 9500 bushels of tomatoes for $3.65 a bushel. How much did the farmer receive?

    a. $337,250.00
    b. $346,750.00
    c. $33.725.00
    d. $34,675.00

9. One square kilometer equals approximately 0.386 square miles. Using this conversion, how many square miles is 21 square kilometers? Round to the nearest hundredth.

    a. 8.11 sq. miles
    b. 8.21 sq. miles
    c. 9.21 sq. miles
    d. 8.51 miles

10. A share of a certain stock was selling for $18.42. How much would 1000 shares cost?

    a. $18,000
    b. $1842
    c. $184.20
    d. $18,420

3.5 Dividing Decimals _____ *Free Response*

1. Divide: $9\overline{)1.44}$

2. Divide: $3700\overline{)30.71}$

3. Divide: $11.04 \div 1.6$

4. Divide: $0.2 \div 0.001$

5. Divide: $2.6\overline{)155.76}$
   Round to the nearest tenth.

6. Divide: $0.49\overline{)10.4521}$
   Round to the nearest hundredth.

7. Find the value of n: $3.9 \times n = 159.9$

8. Find the value of n: $0.036 \times n = 0.792$

9. The staff in the main dining room on an army base has 1305 pounds of canned tapioca pudding that they want to divide into 3590 individual portions. To the nearest tenth of an ounce, approximately how many ounces will each portion contain if the tapioca pudding is all used up and is divided evenly? Hint: There are 16 ounces in a pound.

10. A packing carton used by a manufacturer of toys can hold a maximum of 32 pounds. Assuming that space is not a problem, what is the maximum number of train sets that can be packed in a single carton if each train set weighs 2.96 pounds?

3.5 Dividing Decimals _____ *Multiple Choice*

1. Divide: $56\overline{)39.2}$

   a. 17   **b.** 1.7

   c. 7   **d.** 0.7

2. Divide: $518\overline{)0.9324}$

   a. 0.0028   **b.** 0.18

   c. 0.0018   **d.** 0.19

3. Divide: $0.8 \div 0.02$

   a. 40   **b.** 0.4

   c. 0.04   **d.** 4

4. Divide: $506.29 \div 19.7$

   a. 26.7   **b.** 25.7

   c. 257   **d.** 2.57

5. Divide: $5\overline{)444.916}$ Round to the nearest thousandth.

   a. 88.993   **b.** 8898.314   **c.** 88.983   **d.** 8.8983

6. Divide: $0.39\overline{)8.4909}$ Round to the nearest thousandth.

   a. 2.177   **b.** 21.81   **c.** 21.812   **d.** 21.772

7. Find the value of n: $n \times 1.001 = 28.028$

   a. 27   **b.** 28   **c.** 29   **d.** 2.9

8. Find the value of n: $n \times 0.0052 = 52$

   a. 10,000   **b.** 1000   **c.** 100,000   **d.** 1,000,000

9. In one week, Ashok worked 34.75 hours washing windows and earned $243.74, including tips. How much did Ashok earn per hour? Round to the nearest cent if necessary.

   a. $7.03   **b.** $7.01   **c.** $6.99   **d.** $7.11

10. Some desert areas get on 8-10 inches of rainfall per year (365 days). If in one year the rainfall was 9.56 inches, what was the average daily rainfall for that year? Round to the nearest thousandth.

    a. 0.027 inch   **b.** 0.262 inch   **c.** 0.026 inch   **d.** 0.263 inch

3.6 Converting Fractions to Decimals and Order of Operations _____ *Free Response*

1. Write $1\frac{7}{16}$ as an equivalent decimal.

2. Write $\frac{4}{15}$ as an equivalent decimal. Use the appropriate notation to indicate the repeating part.

3. Write $\frac{19}{27}$ as a decimal. Round to the nearest thousandth.

4. Write $\frac{15}{32}$ as a decimal. Round to the nearest thousandth.

For problems 5-8, simplify by using the order of operations. Round your answer to the nearest hundredth.

5. $4.6^2 = 7.1 - 9.2$

6. $8.91 \div 9.75 \times 6.94$

7. $36.6 - 3.6 \times 8.5$

8. $29.1 + (2.1 + 3.01) \times 8.4$

9. A submarine model measures $19\frac{7}{8}$ inches from end to end. Write this length as a decimal.

10. A survey taken in an elementary school revealed that $\frac{31}{113}$ of the first-graders did not eat or drink a milk product at least one time every day of the week. Write this amount as a decimal, rounding to the nearest hundredth.

3.6 Converting Fractions to Decimals and Order of Operations_____ *Multiple Choice*

For problems 1 and 2, write as an equivalent decimal. If a repeating decimal is obtained, use the appropriate notation to indicate the repeating part.

1. $\dfrac{3}{16}$

   a. $0.187\overline{5}$ b. 0.1875

   c. $0.18\overline{75}$ d. $0.\overline{1875}$

2. $\dfrac{1}{11}$

   a. 0.09 b. $0.0\overline{9}$

   c. $0.\overline{09}$ d. $0.\overline{090}$

3. Write $\dfrac{215}{261}$ as a decimal. Round to the nearest thousandth.

   a. 0.824 b. 8.238 c. 0.082 d. 1.214

4. Write $\dfrac{6}{131}$ as a decimal. Round to the nearest thousandth.

   a. 0.459 b. 0.047 c. 0.458 d. 0.046

For problems 5-8, simplify by using the order of operations. Round your answer to the nearest hundredth.

5. $13+(6.9-3.8)\times12.6$

   a. 96.14 b. 202.86 c. -41.78 d. 52.06

6. $22.9-2.8\div9\times33.2$

   a. 749.95 b. 74.15 c. 12.57 d. 0.07

7. $1.5^2\div3.1+16\div4.05+5.53$

   a. 10.24 b. 0.01 c. 2.40 d. 21.71

8. $1.4+3.7\div15\times4.03+5.57$

   a. 3.26 b. 7.96 c. 6.94 d. 2.87

9. One year, Gary's height was measured with a yardstick as $62\frac{3}{8}$ inches. An advanced laser measuring device used the next year showed that his height had increased to 65.490 inches. According to these figures, how much had Gary's height increased? Round to the nearest hundredth of an inch if necessary.

   a. 3 inches   b. 3.49 inches   c. 3.02 inches   d. 3.12 inches

10. A machinist working on a car's engine mounting drilled a hold $\frac{1}{4}$ inch in diameter. She then enlarged the diameter of 0.046 inch. What was the final diameter? Round to the nearest thousandth if necessary.

   a. 0.296 inch   b. 0.03 inch   c. 0.306 inch   d. 0.003 inch

3.7 Applied Problems Using Decimals _____ *Free Response*

For problems 1-8, round the numbers so that there is only one non-zero digit, and estimate the answer. Then perform the indicated operation to find the exact answer.

1. Add: $42.63 + 38.9 + 8.2$

2. Add: $3.25 + 6.892 + 7.1952$

3. Subtract: $71.9 - 5.49$

4. Subtract: $849.6 - 7.423$

5. Multiply: 47.1×3.1

6. Multiply: 36.3×28.91

7. Divide: $738.42 \div 79.4$

8. Divide: $76.05 \div 19.5$

9. Kenan bought some deli meat to serve his friends who were coming over to his house after soccer practice. He got $1\frac{5}{16}$ pounds of turkey for \$4.85 per pound and $2\frac{7}{8}$ pounds of roast beef for \$6.75 per pound. How much did the deli meat cost him?

10. Armando and Luisa bought a rectangular building lot in a suburb of Austin, Texas. It measured 71.6 feet by 96.7 feet. What is its area in square feet?

3.7 Applied Problems Using Decimals _____ *Multiple Choice*

For problems 1-8, round the numbers so that there is only one non-zero digit, and estimate the answer. Then perform the indicated operation to find the exact answer.

1. Add: $24.77 + 42.9 + 9.2$

   a. Estimate: 69, exact: 76.87
   b. Estimate: 70; exact: 77.87
   c. Estimate: 69; exact: 66.87
   d. Estimate: 69; exact: 75.87

2. Add: $5.2 + 2.8315 + 8.5198$

   a. Estimate: 15; exact: 15.5413
   b. Estimate: 15, exact: 15.5513
   c. Estimate: 16; exact: 66.87
   d. Estimate: 17, exact 16.5513

3. Subtract: $61.8 - 5.38$

   a. Estimate: 65; exact: 65.45
   b. Estimate: 55; exact: 56.42
   c. Estimate: 55; exact: 56.52
   d. Estimate: 65; exact: 66.55

4. Subtract: $744.4 - 7.026$

   a. Estimate: 693; exact: 737.474
   b. Estimate: 793; exact: 737.374
   c. Estimate: 693; exact: 737.374
   d. Estimate: 693; exact: 737.384

5. Multiply: 29.9×2.8

   a. Estimate: 90; exact: 84.72
   b. Estimate: 90; exact: 83.72
   c. Estimate: 9; exact: 8.372
   d. Estimate: 9; exact; 8.472

6. Multiply: 59.84×29.22

   a. Estimate: 180; exact: 17,485.248
   b. Estimate: 1810; exact: 1747.5248
   c. Estimate: 180; exact: 174.85248
   d. Estimate: 1800; exact: 1748.5248

7. Divide: $669.56 \div (78.7)$

   a. Estimate: 8.75; exact: 7.6
   b. Estimate: 7.75; exact: 8.6
   c. Estimate: 8.75; exact: 8.8
   d. Estimate: 7.75; exact: 7.8

8. Divide: $96.99 \div 18.3$

   a. Estimate: 5; exact: 5.3
   b. Estimate: 5; exact: 6.3
   c. Estimate: 5.5; exact: 5.1
   d. Estimate: 5; exact: 6.1

9. Yvonne and Malena spent three weeks one summer traveling around to different national and state parks. They drove a total of 1219.04 miles and used 40.1 gallons of gas. How many miles per gallon (mpg) did they get on the trip? Round to the nearest tenth of a gallon.

   a. 29.1 mpg
   b. 31.5 mpg
   c. 30.4 mpg
   d. 30.9 mpg

10. Peter went shopping for CDs with $100 in his wallet. He bought two CDs for $8.99 each, two for $10.50 each, and one for $14.99. Sales tax was included in the prices. After paying cash for the purchases, how much did he have left from the $100?

    a. $49.23
    b. $46.03
    c. $44.23
    d. $53.97

4.1 Ratios and Rates _____ *Free Response*

1. Write $25:60$ in lowest terms.

2. Write the ratio \$21 to \$133 in lowest terms.

3. Write the ratio $9\frac{1}{3}$ to 9 in lowest terms.

4. Write the rate 192 yards in 24 seconds as a rate in lowest terms.

5. Write the rate 15 tests for 105 students as a rate in lowest terms.

6. Write the rate 531 miles on 18 gallons as a rate in lowest terms.

7. Write the rate \$500 earned in 4 weeks as a unit rate.

8. Write the rate 1320 cars in 330 households as a unit rate.

9. Natalie and Tiana wanted to compare the gas mileage they were getting. One particular week, Natalie drove 122.2 miles on 407 gallons of gas. That same week, Tiana drove 124.8 miles and used 4.8 gallons of gas. Whose car got more miles per gallon of gas?

10. Find which popcorn deal is the better buy (lower cost per ounce) by finding each unit price rounded to three decimal places if necessary.

    Popcorn Deal #1: \$1.40 for 25.5 ounces

    Popcorn Deal #2: \$0.90 for 10.0 ounces

4.1 Ratios and Rates _____ *Multiple Choice*

1. Write the ratio 136 cents to 152 cents in lowest terms.

   a. $\dfrac{136}{152}$ **b.** $\dfrac{17}{152}$ **c.** $\dfrac{19}{152}$ **d.** $\dfrac{17}{19}$

2. Write the ratio $5\dfrac{1}{3}$ to $5\dfrac{1}{2}$ in lowest terms.

   a. $\dfrac{3}{2}$ **b.** $\dfrac{32}{33}$ **c.** $\dfrac{11}{2}$ **d.** $\dfrac{16}{3}$

3. Write the rate 426 miles in 42 hours as a rate in lowest terms.

   a. $\dfrac{71 \text{ miles}}{7 \text{ hours}}$ **b.** $\dfrac{6 \text{ miles}}{42 \text{ hours}}$ **c.** $\dfrac{425 \text{ miles}}{7 \text{ hours}}$ **d.** $\dfrac{71 \text{ miles}}{42 \text{ hours}}$

4. Write the rate 117 printers for 99 computers as a rate in lowest terms.

   a. $\dfrac{99 \text{ printers}}{117 \text{ computers}}$ **b.** $\dfrac{117 \text{ printers}}{9 \text{ computers}}$ **c.** $\dfrac{13 \text{ printers}}{11 \text{ computers}}$ **d.** $\dfrac{9 \text{ printers}}{99 \text{ computers}}$

5. Write 1473 people in 30 buses as a unit rate.

   a. 0.02 person/bus   **b.** 49.1 people/bus   **c.** 1443 people/bus   **d.** 491 people/bus

Stephan kept a record on his personal expenses for one week and organized them in this table:

Eating out	CD	Bowling	Gift	Movie	Total
$22	$14	$12	$4	$8	$60

Use the table to answer problems 6–8.

6. What is the ratio of the amount for eating out to the total amount?

   a. $\dfrac{11}{60}$ **b.** $\dfrac{11}{19}$ **c.** $\dfrac{1}{3}$ **d.** $\dfrac{11}{30}$

7. What is the ratio of the amount for the gift to the total amount?

   a. $\dfrac{2}{3}$ **b.** $\dfrac{2}{11}$ **c.** $\dfrac{1}{15}$ **d.** $\dfrac{4}{1}$

8. What is the ratio of the amount for the CD to the amount for the gift?

   a. $\dfrac{7}{2}$ **b.** $\dfrac{7}{30}$ **c.** $\dfrac{2}{7}$ **d.** $\dfrac{7}{4}$

9. A 40-ounce jar of applesauce costs $4.00. A 16-ounce jar of the same brand of applesauce costs $1.92. Which size costs less per ounce and by how much?
   a. The smaller size costs $.02 less per ounce than the larger size.
   b. The larger size costs $.02 less per ounce than the smaller size.
   c. The larger size costs $.03 less per ounce than the smaller size.
   d. They both cost the same per ounce.

10. Find the better popcorn buy (lower cost per ounce) by finding each unit price rounded to three decimal places if necessary.

    Popcorn Deal #1: $4.14 for 18 ounces

    Popcorn Deal #2: $2.76 for 12 ounces

    a. Popcorn Deal #1   **b.** Popcorn Deal #2   **c.** Both cost the same per ounce

4.2 The Concept of Proportions _____ *Free Response*

For problems 104, write a proportion for each statement.

1. 6 is to 10 as 3 is to 5.

2. 6.5 is to 3 as 85.5 is to 7.

3. If 5 pounds of tuna costs $35, then 3 pounds will cost $21.

4. If 76 pounds of potatoes can feed 190 children, then 84 pounds can feed 210 children.

For problems 5-7, determine whether each of the statements is a correct proportion.

5.   a. $\dfrac{2.7}{8} \overset{?}{=} \dfrac{10}{32}$ b. $\dfrac{10}{26} \overset{?}{=} \dfrac{2}{5.6}$

6.   a. $\dfrac{310 \text{ feet}}{5 \text{ rolls}} \overset{?}{=} \dfrac{931 \text{ feet}}{15 \text{ rolls}}$ b. $\dfrac{138 \text{ points}}{48 \text{ games}} \overset{?}{=} \dfrac{23 \text{ points}}{8 \text{ games}}$

7.   a. $\dfrac{170.1 \text{ gallons}}{16 \text{ acres}} \overset{?}{=} \dfrac{510.3 \text{ gallons}}{48 \text{ acres}}$ b. $\dfrac{28 \text{ hours}}{350 \text{ pages}} \overset{?}{=} \dfrac{4 \text{ hours}}{50 \text{ pages}}$

8. In 1999, an automobile factory manufactured 50,290 sports cars and 39,000 sedans. In 2000, the output was 65,377 sports cards and 50,700 sedans. Was the ratio of sports cars to sedans the same in both years?

9. A car traveled 1023 miles in 15.5 miles. A truck traveled 396 miles in 7 hours. Did they travel at the same speed?

10. Lamar earned gross pay of $875.60 working 14 hours each week in a web design agency. Sharon's gross weekly pay was $796.00 for a 40-hour work week as a plumber. Was Lamar's pay per hour the same as Sharon's?

4.2 The Concept of Proportions _____ *Multiple Choice*

For problems 1-4, write a proportion for the statement.

1. 39 is to 54 as 6.5 is to 9.

   a. $\dfrac{39}{54} = \dfrac{9}{6.5}$ b. $\dfrac{39}{54} = \dfrac{6.5}{9}$ c. $\dfrac{39}{6.5} = \dfrac{9}{54}$ d. $\dfrac{39}{9} = \dfrac{54}{6.5}$

2. 12 is to $2\frac{1}{2}$ as 36 is to $7\frac{1}{2}$.

   a. $\dfrac{12}{36} = \dfrac{7\frac{1}{2}}{2\frac{1}{2}}$ b. $\dfrac{12}{7\frac{1}{2}} = \dfrac{2\frac{1}{2}}{36}$ c. $\dfrac{12}{2\frac{1}{2}} = \dfrac{36}{7\frac{1}{2}}$ $\dfrac{12}{2\frac{1}{2}} = \dfrac{7\frac{1}{2}}{36}$

3. If 30 acres of sorghum yields 2610 bushels, then it is reasonable to expect that 40 acres will yield 3480 bushels.

   a. $\dfrac{30 \text{ acres}}{2610 \text{ bushels}} = \dfrac{40 \text{ acres}}{3480 \text{ bushels}}$ b. $\dfrac{40 \text{ acres}}{2610 \text{ bushels}} = \dfrac{30 \text{ acres}}{3480 \text{ bushels}}$

   c. $\dfrac{30 \text{ acres}}{3480 \text{ bushels}} = \dfrac{40 \text{ acres}}{2610 \text{ bushels}}$ d. $\dfrac{3480 \text{ bushels}}{30 \text{ acres}} = \dfrac{2610 \text{ bushels}}{40 \text{ acres}}$

4. Victor knows he can type 700 words in 10 minutes, so he is sure that he can type 3500 words in 50 minutes.

   a. $\dfrac{10 \text{ minutes}}{3500 \text{ words}} = \dfrac{50 \text{ minutes}}{700 \text{ words}}$ b. $\dfrac{700 \text{ words}}{50 \text{ minutes}} = \dfrac{3500 \text{ words}}{10 \text{ minutes}}$

   c. $\dfrac{700 \text{ words}}{10 \text{ minutes}} = \dfrac{50 \text{ minutes}}{3500 \text{ words}}$ d. $\dfrac{700 \text{ words}}{10 \text{ minutes}} = \dfrac{3500 \text{ words}}{50 \text{ minutes}}$

For problems 5-7, determine if the statement is a proportion.

5. I. $\dfrac{1}{7} \overset{?}{=} \dfrac{7.4}{51.8}$ II. $\dfrac{1}{51.8} \overset{?}{=} \dfrac{5.3}{222.74}$

   a. Neither I or II are proportions.   b. I is not a proportion; II is a proportion.

   c. I and II are both proportions.   d. I is a proportion; II is not a proportion.

6. I. $\dfrac{1 \text{ meter}}{8 \text{ nails}} \overset{?}{=} \dfrac{3 \text{ meters}}{24 \text{ nails}}$ II. $\dfrac{1 \text{ truckload}}{2050 \text{ bricks}} \overset{?}{=} \dfrac{10 \text{ truckloads}}{20,500 \text{ bricks}}$

   a. I and II are both proportions.   b. I is not a proportion; II is a proportion.

   c. I is a proportion; II is not a proportion.   d. Neither I nor II are proportions.

7. I. $\dfrac{2 \text{ dogs}}{45 \text{ households}} \overset{?}{=} \dfrac{12 \text{ dogs}}{270 \text{ households}}$ II. $\dfrac{28 \text{ weeks}}{200 \text{ sq. miles}} \overset{?}{=} \dfrac{7 \text{ weeks}}{50 \text{ sq. miles}}$

   a. Neither I nor II are proportions.   b. I is not a proportion; II is a proportion.

   c. I and II are both proportions.   d. I is a proportion; II is not a proportion.

8. During one month, a local fast-food chain served 5690 hamburgers and 917 fish sandwiches. The next month, the numbers were 9144 hamburgers and 1467 fish sandwiches. Was the ratio of hamburgers to fish sandwiches the same in both months?

   a. Yes   b. No

9. In 2000, a chain of musical instrument stores sold 5987 flutes and 577 harmonicas. In 2001, the sales were 10,178 flutes and 959 harmonicas. Was the ratio of flute sales to harmonica sales the same in both years?

   a. Yes   b. No

10. Barry earned gross pay of $809.60 working 44 hours each week in an advertising agency. Chou's gross weekly pay was $774.40 for a 41-hour work week as an electrician. Was Barry's pay per hour the same as Chou's?

    a. Yes   b. No

4.3 Solving Proportions _____ *Free Response*

1. Solve for n: $n \times 7 = 84$

2. Solve for n: $n \times 6 = 17.4$

3. Solve for n: $\dfrac{5}{6} \times n = 40$

4. Find the value of n: $\dfrac{1}{2} = \dfrac{n}{15}$

5. Find the value of n: $\dfrac{1}{4\frac{1}{4}} = \dfrac{n}{34}$

6. Find the value of n: $\dfrac{n}{1.8} = \dfrac{0.05}{4}$

7. Find the value of n: $\dfrac{n \text{ ounces}}{28 \text{ quarts}} = \dfrac{5.6 \text{ ounces}}{4 \text{ quarts}}$

8. Find the value of n: $\dfrac{21 \text{ gallons}}{n \text{ cups}} = \dfrac{4 \text{ gallons}}{9.2 \text{ cups}}$

9. Find the value of n: $\dfrac{24 \text{ sq cm}}{4 \text{ sq in.}} = \dfrac{n \text{ sq cm}}{5 \text{ sq in.}}$

10. Alejandro found an old family photograph that was 7 inches wide and 5 inches high. He wanted a copy that was 1.5 inches less wide. What will the height of that reduced copy be? Round to the nearest tenth of an inch.

4.3 Solving Proportions _____ *Multiple Choice*

1. Solve for n: $320 = 8 \times n$
   - a. 30
   - b. 50
   - c. 40
   - d. 41

2. Solve for n: $42.7 = 7 \times n$
   - a. 6.1
   - b. 7
   - c. 298.9
   - d. 42.7

3. Solve for n: $\frac{4}{5} \times n = 10$
   - a. 8
   - b. 0.5
   - c. 2.5
   - d. 12.5

4. Find the value of n: $\frac{2}{n} = \frac{0.3}{1.2}$
   - a. $2\frac{2}{5}$
   - b. 8
   - c. $\frac{3}{5}$
   - d. $\frac{9}{25}$

5. Find the value of n: $\frac{7}{\frac{3}{10}} = \frac{70}{n}$
   - a. 3
   - b. 300
   - c. 21
   - d. $\frac{1}{7}$

6. Find the value of n: $\frac{1.4}{n} = \frac{1.5}{6.7}$ Round to the nearest tenth.
   - a. 1.6
   - b. 0.2
   - c. 6.3
   - d. 62.5

For problems 7-9, find the value of n. Round to the nearest hundredth if necessary.

7. $\dfrac{n \text{ people}}{40 \text{ square miles}} = \dfrac{367.85 \text{ people}}{35 \text{ square miles}}$
   - a. 14,714
   - b. 420.4
   - c. 0.26
   - d. 378.36

8. $\dfrac{1200 \text{ revolutions}}{20 \text{ minutes}} = \dfrac{n \text{ revolutions}}{23 \text{ minutes}}$
   - a. 1242
   - b. 27,600
   - c. 2.61
   - d. 1380

9. $\dfrac{n \text{ grams}}{3 \text{ ounces}} = \dfrac{141.75 \text{ grams}}{5 \text{ ounces}}$
   - a. 85.08
   - b. 80.8
   - c. 89.3
   - d. 47.25

10. The negative for an image was a 35-mm camera is 3.6 cm wide × 2.4 cm high . If a print with a width of 15.48 cm is produced from a 35-mm negative, what will the size of the print be expressed as width × height ?
    - a. 14.48 cm wide × 10.32 cm high
    - b. 10.32 cm wide × 15.48 high
    - c. 15.48 cm wide × 12.32 cm high
    - d. 15.48 cm wide × 10.32 cm high

4.4 Applications of Proportions _____ *Free Response*

1. It takes Kim 18 minutes to type and spell check 14 pages of a manuscript. Find how long it takes her to type and spell check 91 pages. Round answer to the nearest whole number if necessary.

2. It teaks Mike 40 minutes to type and spell check 6 pages. Find how many pages he can type and spell check in 3.5 hours. Round answer to the nearest tenth if necessary.

3. On an architect's blueprint, 1 inch corresponds to 3 feet. Find the length of a wall represented by a line $3\frac{1}{3}$ inches long on the blueprint. Round to the nearest tenth if necessary.

4. At a major university, 6 out of every 10 freshman are required to take Biology. If 550 freshmen are enrolled, how many will be taking Biology?

5. There are 1.61 kilometers in every mile. How many kilometers are there in a 15 mile race?

6. A new car gas gets 105 miles on 4 gallons of gas. How many gallons will it need for a trip of $376\frac{1}{2}$ miles?

7. A biologist catches 21 fish in a lake and tags and releases them. In the same lake a few days later, 50 fish are caught with 7 having tags. How many fish are in the lake?

The following chart contains the amounts of ingredients for a Parmesan omelet.

Servings	Eggs	Milk	Chopped Onions	Parmesan Cheese	Butter	Salt
2	5	1/8 cup	1/2 cup	3 tsp	3/4 tsp	1/8 tsp
4	10	1/4 cup	1 cup	6 tsp	1-1/2 tsp	1/4 tsp
6	15	3/8 cup	1-1/2 cups	9 tsp	2-1/4 tsp	3/8 tsp

Use the chart to answer problems 8 – 10.

8. How much salt would be needed to make enough omelets for 5 people?

9. How much milk would be needed to make enough omelets for 11 people?

10. If the amount of butter per serving were increased by $\frac{1}{8}$ tsp, how many teaspoons would be needed to make enough omelets for 6 people?

4.4 Applications of Proportions _____ *Multiple Choice*

1. On an architect's blueprint, 1 inch corresponds to 4 feet. If an exterior wall is 38 feet long, find how long the blueprint measurement should be. Write the answer as a mixed number if necessary.

    a. $9\frac{1}{2}$ inches   b. $12\frac{2}{3}$ inches   c. $1\frac{1}{19}$ inches   d. 38 inches

2. It is recommended that there be at least 12.1 square feet of floor space in a classroom for every student in the class. Find the minimum floor space that 26 students required. Round the answer to the nearest tenth if necessary.

    a. 112.1 sq feet   b. 214.9 sq feet   c. 46.5 sq feet   d. 314.6 sq feet

3. It is recommended that there be at least 14.35 square feet of ground space in a garden for every newly planted shrub. A garden is 25.6' by 21'. Find the maximum number of people the room can accommodate.

    a. 2 shrubs   b. 36 shrubs   c. 147 shrubs   d. 12 shrubs

4. It is recommended that there be at least 7 square feet of work space for every person in a conference room. A certain conference room is 17' by 15'. Find the maximum number of people the room can accommodate.

    a. 46 people   b. 37 people   c. 36 people   d. 56 people

5. In a random sampling from a survey concerning music listening habits, 120 out of 180 mid-level executives preferred country to heavy metal. Taking all the data from the survey, 336 mid-level executives expressed a preference for country over heavy metal. How many mid-level executives would you estimate took part in the survey?

    a. 499 executives   b. 513 executives   c. 504 executives   d. 494 executives

6. At a college in eastern Missouri, 7 out of every 10 students worked either a full- or part-time job in addition to their studies. If 5800 students were enrolled at the college, how many did not have a full-time or part-time job?

    a. 4060 students   b. 1640 students   c. 4080 students   d. 1740 students

7. Traveling in France, Alan exchanged 10 U.S. dollars for 70 Euros. A few days later, he exchanged 25 U.S. dollars for Euros and go the same exchange rate. How many Euros did Alan receive? Round the answer to the nearest tenth if necessary.

    a. 25 Euros   b. 175 Euros   c. 171.9 Euros   d. 169.3 Euros

The following chart contains the amounts of ingredients for a Parmesan omelet.

Servings	Eggs	Milk	Chopped Onions	Parmesan Cheese	Butter	Salt
2	5	1/8 cup	1/2 cup	3 tsp	3/4 tsp	1/8 tsp
4	10	1/4 cup	1 cup	6 tsp	1-1/2 tsp	1/4 tsp
6	15	3/8 cup	1-1/2 cups	9 tsp	2-1/4 tsp	3/8 tsp

Use the chart to answer problems 8 – 10.

8. How much parmesan cheese would be needed to make enough omelets for 5 people?

    a. $7\frac{1}{2}$ tsp   b. $8\frac{1}{2}$ tsp   c. $7\frac{1}{8}$ tsp   d. $9\frac{1}{2}$ tsp

9. If the amount of onions per serving were increased by $\frac{1}{8}$ cup, how much onion would be needed to prepare the omelet for 5 people?

    a. $2\frac{7}{8}$ cups   b. $1\frac{7}{16}$ cups   c. $1\frac{7}{8}$ cups   d. $2\frac{7}{32}$ cups

10. If you cut the amount of salt per serving in half, how much salt would be used for 8 servings? Express the answer as a reduced fraction.

    a. 1/2 tsp   b. 1/4 tsp   c. 3/8 tsp   d. 5/16 tsp

5.1 Understanding Percents _____ *Free Response*

1. Write $\dfrac{80}{100}$ as a percent.

2. Write $\dfrac{3.7}{100}$ as a percent.

3. Write 43% as a decimal.

4. Write 15.5% as a decimal.

5. Write 22.93% as a decimal.

6. Write 0.37 as a percent.

7. Write 0.956 as a percent.

8. A basketball player made 38 out of 100 attempted free throws. What percent of free throws was made?

9. A dart player made 33 bull's eyes out of 100 attempted throws. What percent of the throws were NOT bull's eyes?

10. The Chin family saves 0.13064 of their income. Write this decimal as a percent.

5.1 Understanding Percents _____ *Multiple Choice*

1. Write $\frac{425}{100}$ as a percent.

   a. 4.25%   b. 0.425%   c. 42.5%   d. 425%

2. Write $\frac{0.031}{100}$ as a percent.

   a. 0.31%   b. 0.031%   c. 31%   d. 3.1%

3. Write 230% as a decimal.

   a. 2.31   b. 23   c. 2.3   d. 0.23

4. Write 0.9% as a decimal.

   a. 0.009   b. 0.09   c. 0.01   d. 0.9

5. Write 0.128 as a percent.

   a. 0.128%   b. 12.8%   c. 0.0128%   d. 128%

6. Write 0.00883 as a percent.

   a. 0.4415%   b. 0.0883%   c. 0.000883%   d. 0.883%

7. Write 8 as a percent

   a. 800%   b. 0.8%   c. 0.08%   d. 400%

8. In a survey of 100 people, 29 preferred onions on their hot dogs. What percent preferred onions?

   a. 0.29%   b. $\frac{29}{100}$%   c. 29%   d. 2.9%

9. In a survey of 100 people, 37 preferred strawberry syrup on their ice cream. What percent did NOT prefer strawberry syrup?

   a. $\frac{37}{100}$%   b. 37%   c. $\frac{63}{100}$%   d. 63%

10. Last year Holly spent 0.2 of her income for insurance. Write this decimal as a percent.

   a. 2%   b. 20%   c. 0.02%   d. 0.002%

5.2 Changing Between Percents, Decimals, and Fractions _____ *Free Response*

1.   Write 62.5% as a fraction.

2.   Write 1340% as a mixed number.

3.   Write $\dfrac{29}{100}$ as a percent.

4.   Write $5\dfrac{3}{8}$ as a fraction.

5.   Express $\dfrac{11}{12}$ as a percent containing a fraction.

6.   Write $4\dfrac{3}{5}$ as a percent.

7.   Write the equivalent fraction and decimal for 35%.

8.   Write the equivalent decimal and percent for $\frac{7}{25}$.

9.   A basketball player made $\frac{8}{9}$ of the free throws she attempted. Express this fraction as a percent rounded to the nearest hundredth of a percent if necessary.

10. Last year it rained 57% of the days in a small town. Express this percent as a fraction.

5.2 Changing Between Percents, Decimals, and Fractions _____ *Multiple Choice*

1. Write 0.3% as a fraction.

   a. $\dfrac{3}{500}$ b. $\dfrac{3}{1000}$ c. $\dfrac{3}{2000}$ d. $\dfrac{3}{100}$

2. Write $166\dfrac{2}{3}\%$ as a mixed number.

   a. $\dfrac{5}{6}$ b. $3\dfrac{1}{3}$ c. $1\dfrac{2}{3}$ d. $16\dfrac{2}{3}$

3. Write $\dfrac{221}{600}$ as a percent. Round to the nearest hundredth of a percent.

   a. 36.83%   b. 3.68%   c. 2.71%   d. 27.15%

4. Write $\dfrac{8}{9}$ as a percent. Round to the nearest hundredth of a percent.

   a. 8.889%   b. 8.89%   c. 88.9%   d. 88.89%

5. Express $\dfrac{59}{60}$ as a percent containing a fraction.

   a. $1\dfrac{31}{59}\%$ b. $6\dfrac{5}{9}\%$ c. $65\dfrac{5}{9}\%$ d. $15\dfrac{15}{59}\%$

6. Express $\dfrac{187}{800}$ as a percent containing a fraction.

   a. $2\dfrac{27}{80}\%$ b. $23\dfrac{3}{8}\%$ c. $4\dfrac{52}{187}\%$ d. $42\dfrac{146}{187}\%$

7. Write the equivalent decimal and percent for $2\dfrac{3}{4}$.

   a. 2.87; 2879%   b. 2.75; 27.5%   c. 2.87; 287%   d. 2.75; 275%

8. Write the equivalent fraction and percent for 0.1.

   a. $\dfrac{1}{10}$; 10%   b. $\dfrac{1}{100}$; 1%   c. $\dfrac{1}{10}$; 1%   d. $\dfrac{1}{100}$; 10%

9. In a recent survey, a store found that $\frac{55}{67}$ of their customers were satisfied with the service they received from the store. Express this fraction as a percent rounded to the nearest hundredth of a percent if necessary.

   a. 1.22%   b. 8.21%   c. 82.09%   d. 12.28%

10. Last week $24\frac{1}{3}\%$ of all households watched a sporting event on television. Express this percent as a fraction.

   a. $\dfrac{73}{300}$ b. $24\dfrac{1}{3}$ c. $\dfrac{3}{100}$ d. $\dfrac{2}{25}$

5.3 A/B Solving Percent Problems _____ *Free Response*

1. 5% of 400 is what number?

2. 190% of 317 is what number?

3. What number is 300% of 409?

4. What number 20% of 92?

5. 97 is 20% of what number?

6. 36% of what number is 72?

7. What percent of 20 is 0.2?

8. 80 is 125% of what number?

For problems 9 and 10, translate the question into a proportion. Do not solve.

9. 78% of 64.1 is what number?

10. 10% of what number is 33.7?

5.3 A/B Solving Percent Problems _____ *Multiple Choice*

1. 190% of 317 is what number?

   a. 602.3   b. 6023   c. 60.23   d. 60,230

2. $6\frac{1}{5}\%$ of 7500 is what number?

   a. 4650   b. 46,500   c. 47   d. 465

3. What number is $5\frac{3}{4}\%$ of 118?

   a. 678.5   b. 6.785   c. 20.52   d. 67.85

4. What number is 89% of 317%?

   a. 28.21   b. 2821.3   c. 282.13   d. 28,213

5. 17 is 1% of what number?

   a. 17   b. 17,000   c. 170   d. 1700

6. $2\frac{1}{2}\%$ of what number is 58?

   a. 2320   b. 23,200   c. 232   d. 1.45

7. Find 15% of 40% of 4800.

   a. 39.22%   b. 255%   c. 2.55%   d. 3.92%

8. 224.4 is what percent of 88?

   a. 39.22%   b. 255%   c. 2.55%   d. 3.92%

For problems 9 and 10, translate the question into a proportion. Do not solve.

9. What number is 3% of 140?

   a. $\dfrac{140}{b}=\dfrac{3}{100}$ b. $\dfrac{a}{140}=\dfrac{3}{100}$ c. $\dfrac{3}{140}=\dfrac{p}{100}$ d. $\dfrac{3}{b}=\dfrac{140}{100}$

10. 15.0 is what percent of 34?

    a. $\dfrac{34}{b}=\dfrac{15.0}{100}$ b. $\dfrac{34}{15.0}=\dfrac{p}{100}$ c. $\dfrac{a}{34}=\dfrac{15.0}{100}$ d. $\dfrac{15.0}{34}=\dfrac{p}{100}$

5.4 Solving Applied Percent Problems _____ *Free Response*

Directions: Solve each problem. If necessary, round percents to the nearest tenth and all other answers to the nearest whole number.

1. 40% of the students in a school are male. If there are 90 students altogether, how many students are male?

2. Last year, Linn bought a share of stock for $19.35. She was paid a dividend of $11.61. Determine what percent of the stock prices it the dividend.

3. In a recent survey of 84 people, 42 said that their favorite color of car was black. What percent of the people surveyed liked black cars?

4. Anna has $27.60 to spend on dinner. She wants to tip the waiter 15% of the cost of her meal. How much money can she spend on the meal itself?

5. A medical research facility spent a total of $15,000,000 to develop a drug. 10% of this cost was for staff and 65% was for equipment. How much was spent to cover both the staff and the equipment?

6. Find the amount of discount when the original price is $71.00 and the discount rate is 5%.

7. Find the amount of discount when the original price is $161.40 and the discount rate if 40%.

8. Find the sale price when the original price is $36.00 and the discount rate is 41%.

9. Find the sale price when the original price is $42,800.00 and the discount rate is 12%.

10. A $650 stereo is on sale at 10% off. Find the amount of the discount.

5.4 Solving Applied Percent Problems _____ *Multiple Choice*

Directions: Solve each problem. If necessary, round percents to the nearest tenth and all other answers to the nearest whole number.

1. An inspector found 9 defective bolts during an inspection. If this is 0.015% of the total number of bolts inspected, how many bolts were inspected?
   a. 6000 bolts   b. 600 bolts   c. 60,000 bolts   d. 900 bolts

2. One day 96 office workers were sick with the flu. If this were 64% of the total number of office workers, how many office workers were there altogether?
   a. 150 office workers   b. 6144 office workers
   c. 1500 office workers   d. 61,440 office workers

3. The Powell family paid 29% of the purchase price of $108,000 home as a down payment. Determine the amount of the down payment.
   a. $3724   b. $3132   c. $313   d. $31,320

4. Lee is taking Kim out to dinner. He has $83.95 to spend. He wants to tip the server 15% of the cost of the meal. How much can be spend on the meal?
   a. $12.59   b. $73.00   c. $71.36   d. $55.97

5. Beth is building a new home. When the house is finished, it will cost $357,000. The price of building the house this year is 5% higher than it would have been last year. What would the price of the house have been last year?
   a. $340,000   b. $17,850   c. $339,150   d. $374,850

6. A $270 painting is on sale at 25% off. Find the discount.
   a. $6.75   b. $202.50   c. $67.50   d. $263.25

7. A $1900 diamond ring is on sale at 25% off. Find the discount.
   a. $1045.00   b. $855.00   c. $84.40   d. $1814.50

8. A $170 coast is on sale at 5% off. Find the sale price.
   a. $8.50   b. $1691.50   c. $0.85   d. $161.50

9. A $2500 necklace is on sale at 45% off. Find the sale price.
   a. $1375.00   b. $3287.50   c. $112.50   d. $1125.00

10. Sally and John purchased a discount card for $25. It can be used for one year at several restaurants in their area. It entitled the user to 15% off all meals purchased during the year at these restaurants. If they usually spend $280 a year at these restaurants, how many dollars would they save by purchasing this card?
    a. $255   b. $42   c. $17   d. $238

5.5 Commissions, Discount, and Interest Problems _____ *Free Response*

1. A sales representative is paid a commission rate of 5.7%. Find her commission if she sold $107,350 worth of goods last month.

2. How much commission will an agent make on the sale of a $511,300 house if she received 1.2% of the selling price?

3. A salesperson earned a commission of $5268 for selling $43,900 worth of books to various stores. Find the commission rate.

4. A house sold for $172,000 and the real estate agent earned a commission of $3096. Find the rate of commission.

5. Find the percent of increase when the original amount is 170 and the new amount is 272.

6. Find the percent of decrease when the original amount is 160 and the new amount is 128.

7. 40% of the teachers in a school are male. If there are 510 teachers altogether, how many teachers are male?

8. What is the sales tax on a scanner priced at $140 if the sales tax rate is 7.3%?

9. A calculator has a purchase price of $38. If the sales tax on this purchase is $3.61, find the sales tax rate.

10. A watch sells for $1305. If the sales tax rate is 9.4%, what is the total price?

5.5 Commissions, Discount, and Interest Problems _____ *Multiple Choice*

1. A sales representative for a medical supply company was paid $117,500 in commissions last year. If her commission rate was 5%, what was the sales total for the medical supplies she sold last year?
    a. $5875   **b.** $2,350,000   **c.** $587,500   **d.** $23,500

2. Last year a small company paid its sales staff $127,600 in commissions. If the commission rate was 4%, what was last year's sales total for the company?
    a. $5,104,000   **b.** $5104   **c.** $3,190,000   **d.** $31,900

3. A stockbroker is paid $600 per month plus 5% of the total sales of stocks that she sells. Last month Joan sold $460,000 worth of stock. What was her total income for the month?
    a. $230,000   **b.** $23,000   **c.** $230,600   **d.** $23,600

4. Keith, a real estate agent is paid $275 per month plus 0.45% of the total sales of homes that he sells. Last month Keith sold property worth $2,520,000. What was his total income for the month?
    a. $11,615   **b.** $11,340   **c.** $113,675   **d.** $113,400

5. Enrollment in a class at a local college increased from 130 to 169. What was the percent of increase?
    a. 39%   **b.** 30%   **c.** 23%   **d.** 130%

6. Shoes that regularly sell for $80 are on sale for $8. What is the percent of decrease?
    a. 10%   **b.** 72%   **c.** 900%   **d.** 90%

7. An inspector found 8 defective radios during an inspection. If this is 0.02% of the total number of radios inspected, how many radios were inspected?
    a. 40,000 radios   **b.** 400 radios   **c.** 4000 radios   **d.** 800 radios

8. A blouse costs $32 and a skirt costs $20. What is the total price for purchasing these items if the sales tax rate is 9%?
    a. $52.00   **b.** $4.68   **c.** $56.68   **d.** $98.80

9. Ted placed $2000 in a one-year CD paying simple interest of 6.5% for one year. How much interest will Ted earn in one year?
    a. $2130   **b.** $130   **c.** $1300   **d.** $3300

10. Tory borrowed $14,000 to finish college at an interest rate of 4.5% per year. How much interest will Tory need to pay next year?
    a. $630   **b.** $14,630   **c.** $6300   **d.** $20,300

6.1 American Units _____ *Free Response*

1. 21 quarts = _____ pints

2. 2 tons = _____ pounds

3. 6 feet = _____ feet

4. 6 cups = _____ fluid ounces

5. 9 pints = _____ cups

6. 0.25 pounds = _____ ounces

7. 2 days = _____ minutes

8. A recipe calls for 22 fluid ounces of water. How many cups is this?

9. For a school walk-a-thon, Rebecca got pledges totaling $9 per mile walked. If she walks 26,400 feet, how much money will she have collected for the walk-a-thon?

10. A street sign prohibits vehicles over 5.5 tons from entering a certain street. How many pounds is that?

6.1 American Units _____ *Multiple Choice*

1. 1 miles = _____ feet
   a. 2000   b. 1760   c. 5280   d. 3600

2. _____ hours = 3 days
   a. 72   b. 21   c. 180   d. 48

3. 68 quarts = _____ gallons
   a. 272   b. 34   c. 136   d. 17

4. 12 pints = _____ quarts
   a. 3   b. 6   c. 24   d. 48

5. 20 yards to _____ feet
   a. 180   b. 240   c. 720   d. 60

6. 540 seconds = _____ minutes
   a. 16   b. 4   c. 9   d. 22

7. 10 weeks = _____ days
   a. 70   b. 140   c. 240   d. 600

8. Rope sells for 3¢ per inch at the local hardware store. If Sylvia needs $7\frac{1}{2}$ feet of this rope, how much money will she spend?
   a. $2.70   b. $0.23   c. $270.00   d. $90.00

9. Keith billed a total of 26,640 minutes to one of his company's clients. How many days was this?
   a. 1110 days   b. 18.5 days   c. 144 days   d. 63.43 days

10. Dennis is hosting a dinner party. His recipe calls for 3 ounces of chicken per person. If he is expecting 19 guests, how many pounds of chicken should he buy?
    a. 7.13 pounds   b. 57 pounds   c. 912 pounds   d. 3.56 pounds

6.2 Metric Measurements: Length _____ *Free Response*

1. 54 kilometers = _____ meters

2. 88.6 meters = _____ millimeters

3. 17.3 millimeters = _____ kilometers

4. 72.4 hectometers = _____ decimeters

5. 0.21 m = _____ cm

6. 505 mm = _____ cm

7. Change 62 cm + 4 dm + 19 mm to a convenient unit of measure and add.

8. Change 71 m + 886 cm + 0.587 km to a convenient unit of measure and add.

9. A hiking trail is 16,227 meters long. What is the trail's length in kilometers?

10. A bacteria measures 131 millimeters at its widest point. What is the width of the bacteria culture in centimeters?

6.2 Metric Measurements: Length _____ *Multiple Choice*

1. 7.35 meters = _____ centimeters

   a. 0.735   **b.** 73.5   **c.** 0.0735   **d.** 735

2. 88.01 meters = _____ millimeters

   a. 8801   **b.** 88,010   **c.** 0.088   **d.** 0.88

3. 110,000 centimeters = _____ kilometers

   a. 1.1   **b.** 0.11   **c.** 11   **d.** 0.011

4. 409 cm = _____ m

   a. 4090   **b.** 40.9   **c.** 4.09   **d.** 40,900

5. 13.97 m = _____ km

   a. 13,970   **b.** 0.1397   **c.** 0.01397   **d.** 1397

6. 56.96 mm = _____ m

   a. 0.05696   **b.** 0.57   **c.** 56,960   **d.** 5696

7. Change 337 m + 9.6 km + 525 m to a convenient unit of measure and add.

   a. 871,600 m   **b.** 10,462 m   **c.** 1822 m   **d.** 871.6 m

8. Change 202 mm + 872 cm + 10.8 cm to a convenient unit of measure and add.

   a. 1084.8 cm   **b.** 903 cm   **c.** 2902.8 cm   **d.** 9030 cm

9. A race is 14 kilometers long. How long is the race in meters?

   a. 1.4 m   **b.** 1400 m   **c.** 140 m   **d.** 14,000 m

10. A special type of wire used in electronic equipment is 0.828 millimeter thick. How thick is the wire in centimeters?

   a. 8.28 cm   **b.** 0.00828 cm   **c.** 0.0828 cm   **d.** 82.8 cm

6.3 Metric Measurements: Volume and Weight _____ *Free Response*

1. 27 L = _____ mL

2. 314 mL = _____ L

3. 43 kL = _____ L

4. 20 kg = _____ mg

5. 37.3 g = _____ kg

6. 149 mg = _____ g

7. Change 831 mL + 42.5 L + 99 L to a convenient unit of measure, then add.

8. Simplify: 81.6 ml ÷ 0.5

9. A gas tank contains 40.3 L of gasoline. To top it off, 1561 ml of gasoline was added to it. Find the total number of liters in the tank.

10. In a lab experiment, 600 ml of salt water was added to 1.9 L of water. Later, 210 ml of the solution was drained off. How many milliliters of the solution still remains?

6.3 Metric Measurements: Volume and Weight _____ *Multiple Choice*

1. 18 mL = _____ L
    - **a.** 0.018
    - **b.** 0.18
    - **c.** 18,000
    - **d.** 1800

2. 0.94 L = _____ mL
    - **a.** 0.094
    - **b.** 94
    - **c.** 0.00094
    - **d.** 940

3. 760.5 mL = _____ cm³
    - **a.** 76,050
    - **b.** 760,500
    - **c.** 760.5
    - **d.** 0.7605

4. 366 g = _____ mg
    - **a.** 0.0366
    - **b.** 366,000
    - **c.** 0.366
    - **d.** 36,600

5. 735 mg = _____ kg
    - **a.** 0.0735
    - **b.** 0.000735
    - **c.** 735,000
    - **d.** 73,500

6. 25.6 g = _____ kg
    - **a.** 2560
    - **b.** 0.00256
    - **c.** 25,600
    - **d.** 0.0256

7. Change 628 mg + 8.5 kg + 75 g to a convenient unit of measure, then add.
    - **a.** 9203 g
    - **b.** 711.5 g
    - **c.** 8575.628 g
    - **d.** 84.128 g

8. Simplify: 24.2 ml + 6.2 ml
    - **a.** 30.4 ml
    - **b.** 304 ml
    - **c.** 248.2 ml
    - **d.** 86.2 ml

9. The manager of a university cafeteria needs to purchase 75 kg of mayonnaise. If his wholesaler sells mayonnaise in 3000-gram jugs for $3.75 each, how much will the manager have to spend?
    - **a.** $11.25
    - **b.** $281.25
    - **c.** $93.75
    - **d.** $9.38

10. An experimental drug costs $41,000 per liter. How much would one milliliter cost?
    - **a.** $410
    - **b.** $41
    - **c.** $4100
    - **d.** $4.10

6.4 Converting Units (Optional) _____ *Free Response*

Perform the conversion: Round to the nearest hundredth when necessary.

1. Convert 3 m to inches.

2. Convert 23.5 ft to m.

3. Convert 80 L to gal.

4. Convert 40 qt to L.

5. Convert 51 kg to lb.

6. Convert 6 oz to g.

7. Convert 100 mi/hr to ft/sec.

8. Convert 62° F to degrees Celsius.

9. Convert 330° to degrees Fahrenheit.

10. The nutrition label on a bag of candy says that a serving size is 58 grams. How many ounces are in a serving?

6.4 Converting Units (Optional) _____ *Multiple Choice*

Perform the conversion: Round to the nearest hundredth when necessary.

1. Convert 196 mi to km.
   - **a.** 121.72 km
   - **b.** 315.56 km
   - **c.** 207.76 km
   - **d.** 185.42 km

2. Convert 4.8 ft to cm.
   - **a.** 12.19 cm
   - **b.** 188.98 cm
   - **c.** 146.30 cm
   - **d.** 121.92 cm

3. Convert 92.4 m to yd.
   - **a.** 100.72 yd
   - **b.** 84.45 yd
   - **c.** 303.07 yd
   - **d.** 28.18 yd

4. Convert 61.1 gal to L.
   - **a.** 16.13 L
   - **b.** 57.80 L
   - **c.** 64.77 L
   - **d.** 231.57 L

5. Convert 68.9 lb to kg.
   - **a.** 2.43 kg
   - **b.** 151.56 kg
   - **c.** 1953 kg
   - **d.** 31.28 kg

6. Convert 59.9 g to oz
   - **a.** 131.78 oz
   - **b.** 2.11 oz
   - **c.** 1698.16 oz
   - **d.** 27.19 oz

7. Convert 90.2 km/hr to mi/hr.
   - **a.** 55.9 mi/hr
   - **b.** 145.2 mi/hr
   - **c.** 132.3 mi/hr
   - **d.** 61.5 mi/hr

8. A weather forecaster has predicted a high temperature of 18° C for tomorrow. Find this temperature in degrees Fahrenheit.
   - **a.** 90.00° F
   - **b.** 42.00° F
   - **c.** 64.60° F
   - **d.** 0.40° F

9. Riana's imported car has a gas tank that holds 68 liters of gas. She filled her tank at the beginning of a trip and used 6 gallons during the trip. How many liters of gas remained in her tank at the end of the trip?
   - **a.** 45.26 L
   - **b.** 22.74 L
   - **c.** 325.72 L
   - **d.** 66.42 L

10. On a road trip, Jackie and Meredith drove 462 miles in the United States and 115 kilometers in Canada. How many kilometers did they travel total?
    - **a.** 815.12 km
    - **b.** 577 km
    - **c.** 533.3 km
    - **d.** 858.82 km

6.5 Applied Problems _____ *Free Response*

1. Find the perimeter of a rectangle where the width is 18 in. and the length is 15 in. Express your answer in feet.

2. The maintenance crew at an amusement park has to fence in a triangular area. One side is 64 yards long, and a second side is 59 yards long. If the crew has 480 feet of fencing, how many yards of fencing will be left over for the third side?

3. A rectangular oil painting measures 91 centimeters × 148 centimeters. The painting is framed in material that costs $6 per meter. What will it cost to frame the painting?

4. Sarah bought 2.1 m of ribbon at one store and 35 cm at another store. How many centimeters of ribbon does she have altogether?

5. A beverage company received an order from the local college's cafeteria. It filled 80 bottles with a total of 62 liters of soda. How many milliliters of soda are in each bottle?

6. The local diner sells extra-long, one-pint sodas. During the lunch rush, an average of 9 sodas are sold each minute. How many gallons of soda are sold per hour?

7. A box of cereal contains 22 ounces of cereal. Of this, 17 ounces are sugar-coated puffs and the remaining ounces are miniature marshmallows. How many grams of marshmallows are in the box?

8. A recipe from a French cookbook said to preheat the oven to 200° C. Julius set his American oven to 397.4° F. What was the discrepancy in degrees Fahrenheit between the two temperatures?

9. A pole that is 132 feet long is to be cut into 8 equal pieces. How long will each piece be?

10. Sarah earned $288.75 today selling jewelry. She deposited $\frac{1}{11}$ of her earnings in the credit union. How much money did she deposit?

6.5 Applied Problems _____ *Multiple Choice*

1. Find the perimeter of a triangle with sides 48 in., $20\frac{1}{6}$ in., and $27\frac{5}{6}$ in. Express your answer in feet.

   a. 7 ft　　　　**b.** 96 ft　　　　**c.** 8 ft　　　　**d.** 91 ft

2. A hiking trail is 10.9 kilometers long. The last $\frac{1}{11}$ of the trail was washed out by a flood. How many meters of the trail were washed out? If necessary, round your answer to the nearest hundredth.

   a. 119.9 m　　　**b.** 0.99 m　　　**c.** 119,900 m　　　**d.** 990.91 m

3. Rhonda had to saw a 17.6-meter board into 5 equal pieces. How many long was each piece in centimeters?

   a. 8800 cm　　　**b.** 352 cm　　　**c.** 3.52 cm　　　**d.** 88 cm

4. Jennifer bought 17 quarts of milk for the day care center where she works. Her co-worker Henri, who is from France, says that the center only needed 12 liters of milk. If Henri is correct, how many quarts of milk will be left over?

   a. 4.28 qt　　　**b.** 4.082 qt　　　**c.** 5 qt　　　**d.** 29.72 qt

5. Hanz's scooter gets 55 kilometers per liter of gasoline. If he drives 377 kilometers to Munich, and gas costs the equivalent of $0.73 per liter, how much would the gas for the trip cost? Round to the nearest cent if necessary.

   a. $5.00　　　**b.** $275.21　　　**c.** $6.85　　　**d.** $40.15

6. One serving of yogurt contains 390 mg of potassium. If Anthony ate a serving every day for lunch, how many grams of potassium did he consume in one week? Round to the nearest tenth if necessary.

   a. 0.06 g　　　**b.** 0.39 g　　　**c.** 2.73 g　　　**d.** 2730 g

7. A ship arrived from Columbia carrying 6.7 tons of coffee beans. If the port tax on coffee beans is $0.017 per pound, what is the tax on the entire shipment of coffee beans? Round to the nearest cent if necessary.

   a. $34.00　　　**b.** $227.80　　　**c.** $13,400.00　　　**d.** $788,235.29

8. The label on a bottle of spray paint says that it should not be stored at temperatures above 90° F. A sign on the store display said that the spray paint should not be stored at temperatures above 29° C. What is the discrepancy in degrees Fahrenheit between the two suggested temperatures?

   a. The display sign is 84.2° F more than it should be.　　**b.** The display sign is 5.8° F more than it should be.
   c. The display sign is 84.2° F less than it should be.　　**d.** The display sign is 5.8° F less than it should be.

9. Karen and Ivan traveled at 100 km/hr for 4.5 hours. Their total trip will be 625 miles long. How many miles do they still need to travel? Round your answer to the nearest whole mile if necessary.

   a. 563 mi　　　**b.** 175 mi　　　**c.** 346 mi　　　**d.** 556 mi

10. Brian and Heather drove 657 miles in 9 hours. What was their average speed in kilometers per hour? Round your answer to the nearest whole number if necessary.

   a. 118 km/hr　　　**b.** 1058 km/hr　　　**c.** 73 km/hr　　　**d.** 45 km/hr

7.1 Angles _____ *Free Response*

For problems 1 and 2, identify the angle as right, acute, obtuse, or straight.

1.

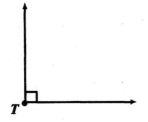

2.

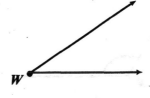

Use the figure to the right to answer problems 3-5.

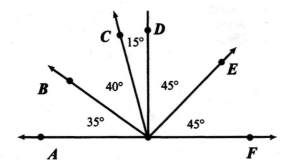

3. Find the measure of ∠DGB.

4. Find the measure of ∠DGA.

5. Find the measure of ∠FGB.

6. Find the supplement of 158°.

7. Find the complement of 13°.

8. Find the measure of ∠x.

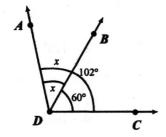

9. Find the measure of ∠z.

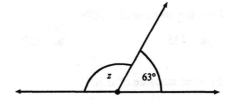

10. Find the measure of ∠x.

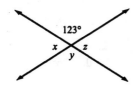

7.1 Angles _____ *Multiple Choice*

1. How would ∠R be classified?

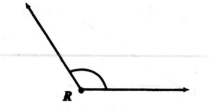

    a. Straight
    b. Acute
    c. Right
    d. Obtuse

2. How would ∠X be classified?

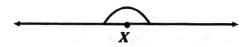

    a. Right
    b. Straight
    c. Acute
    d. Obtuse

Use the diagram below to complete problems 3-5.

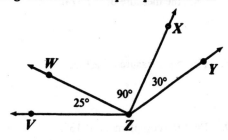

3. Find the measure of ∠WZX.

    a. 100°   b. 30°   c. 90°   d. 25°

4. Find the measure of ∠XZV.

    a. 115°   b. 120°   c. 105°   d. 125°

5. Find the measure of ∠YZV.

    a. 155°   b. 135°   c. 145°   d. 140°

6. Find the supplement of 120°.

    a. 60°   b. Not possible   c. 240°   d. 150°

7. Find the complement of 64°.

    a. 206°`   b. 116°   c. 296°   d. 26°

8. Identify the pair or pairs of complementary angles.

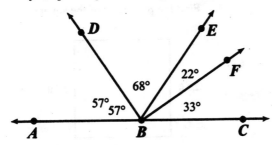

a. $\angle ABD$ and $\angle FBC$
b. $\angle ABD$ and $\angle FBC$; $\angle DBE$ and $\angle EBF$
c. $\angle DBE$ and $\angle EBF$
d. $\angle ABD$ and $\angle EBF$; $\angle DBE$ and $\angle FBC$

9. Find the measure of $\angle z$.

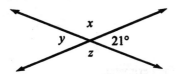

a. 111°
b. 69°
c. 159°
d. 169°

10. Find the measure of $\angle f$.

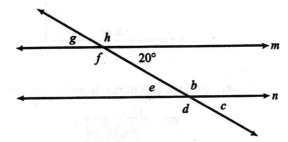

a. 160°
b. 70°
c. 110°
d. 170°

7.2 Rectangles and Squares _____ *Free Response*

1. Find the perimeter of the rectangle.

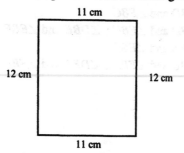

2. Find the perimeter of the square.

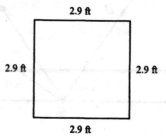

3. Find the perimeter and area of a rectangle that measures 4 in. by 7 in.

4. Find the perimeter and area of a square where each side measures 2.8 ft.

5. Find the perimeter.

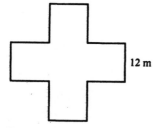

All segments are of equal length

6. Find the perimeter.

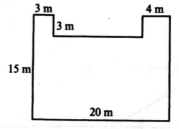

7. Find the perimeter.

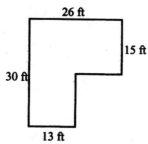

8. Find the area of the shaded region.

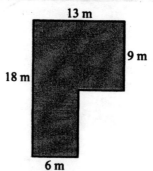

9. Find the area of the shaded region.

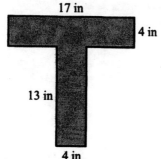

10. A hotel is building a fitness center measuring 203 ft×38 ft. The flooring to cover the space is made of a special 3-layered cushioned tile and costs $12.00 per square foot. How much will it cost for the new flooring?

7.2 Rectangles and Squares _____ *Multiple Choice*

1. Find the perimeter of the rectangle.

    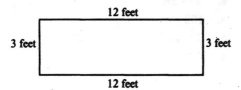

    a. 18 ft
    b. 30 ft
    c. 15 ft
    d. 12 ft

2. Find the perimeter of the square.

    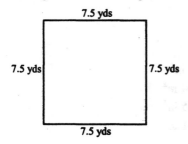

    a. 112.5 yd
    b. 15 yd
    c. 30 yd
    d. 40 yd

3. Find the perimeter and area of a rectangle with length 0.0056 cm and width 0.0049 cm.

    a. $P = 0.021$ cm, $A = 0.00002744$ cm^2
    b. $P = 0.0105$ cm, $A = 0.00002744$ cm^2
    c. $P = 0.021$ cm, $A = 0.0105$ cm^2
    d. $P = 0.021$ cm, $A = 0.00005488$ cm^2

4. Find the perimeter and area of a rectangle with length 180 m and width 69 m.

    a. $P = 498$ m, $A = 24,840$ m^2
    b. $P = 249$ m, $A = 12,420$ m^2
    c. $P = 498$ m, $A = 249$ m^2
    d. $P = 498$ m, $A = 12,420$ m^2

For problems 5 and 6, find the perimeter of the shapes made up of rectangles and squares.

5.

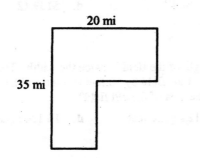

   a. 55 mi
   b. 110 mi
   c. 75 mi
   d. Not enough information given

6.

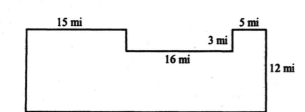

   a. 99 mi
   b. 51 mi
   c. 102 mi
   d. Not enough information given

For problems 7 and 8, find the area of the shaded figures.

7.

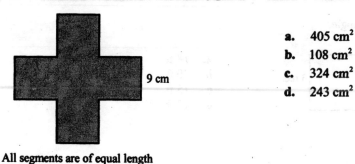

9 cm

All segments are of equal length

   a. 405 cm²
   b. 108 cm²
   c. 324 cm²
   d. 243 cm²

8.

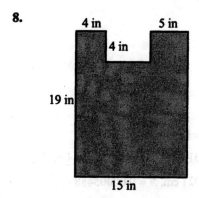

4 in   5 in
4 in
19 in
15 in

   a. 61 in²
   b. 269 in²
   c. 265 in²
   d. 261 in²

9. Julia made a quilt that took first place at the county fair. The quilt measured 18.3 ft by 2.1 ft. She sewed a unique fringed border on each side of it. If the border material costs $3.62 per foot, how much did the border cost?

   a. $73.85   b. $147.70   c. $556.47   d. $139.12

10. The perimeter of a school's rectangular field is 492 feet. The length of the field is twice the width. The principal decides to cut down some trees and increase the length of the field by 60 feet and the width by 50 feet. How much larger will the area of the new field be compared to the area of the old field?

   a. 13,448 square feet   b. 29,568 square feet   c. 712 square feet   d. 16,120 square feet

7.3 Parallelograms, Trapezoids, and Rhombuses _____ *Free Response*

1. Find the perimeter of the parallelogram.

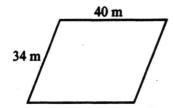

2. Find the perimeter of the parallelogram.

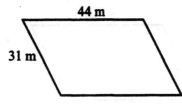

3. A parallelogram has base 15 yd and height 31 yd. Find the area.

4. A parallelogram has base 34 ft and height 13 ft. Find the area.

5. Find the area of a rhombus with height 7 meters and base 18 meters.

6. Find the perimeter of the figure below.

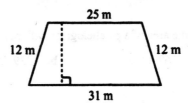

7. Find the area of the trapezoid with height 8 m and bases that are 6 m and 10 m.

8. Find the area of the figure below.

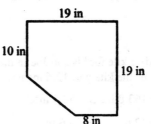

9. Find the area of the figure below.

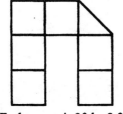

Each square is 9ft by 9 ft

10. Find the area of the figure below.

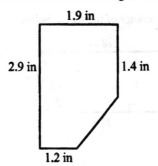

7.3 Parallelograms, Trapezoids, and Rhombuses _____ *Multiple Choice*

1. Find the perimeter of the parallelogram.

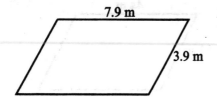

     a. 19.7 m
     b. 11.8 m
     c. 23.6 m
     d. 15.7 m

2. Find the perimeter of the parallelogram.

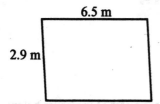

     a. 12.3 m
     b. 9.4 m
     c. 15.9 m
     d. 18.8 m

3. Find the area of a parallelogram with base 15.1 m and height 22.5 m.

     a. 169.875 m^2 b. 339.75 m^2 c. 37.6 m^2 d. 75.2 m^2

4. A courtyard is shaped like a parallelogram. Its base is 174 yd and its height is 62 yd. Find its area.

     a. $10,788 \text{ yd}^2$ b. 5394 yd^2 c. 236 yd^2 d. 472 yd^2

5. Walter made a kite for his son Joe in the shape of a rhombus. The height of the kite was 13 inches. The length of the base of the kite was 12.6 inches. Find the perimeter and area of the kite.

     a. $P = 163.8 \text{ in.}, A = 50.4 \text{ in}^2$ b. $P = 50.4 \text{ in.}, A = 163.8 \text{ in}^2$

     c. $P = 12.6 \text{ in.}, A = 25.6 \text{ in}^2$ d. $P = 25.2 \text{ in.}, A = 81.9 \text{ in}^2$

6. Find the perimeter of the figure below.

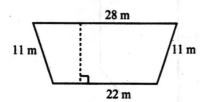

     a. 283 m
     b. 242 m
     c. 39 m
     d. 72 m

7. A park in Canada is laid out in the shape of a trapezoid. The trapezoid has a height of 210 m. The bases are 459 m and 486 m. Find the area of the park.

     a. $198,450 \text{ m}^2$ **b.** $99,225 \text{ m}^2$ **c.** $23,422,770 \text{ m}^2$ **d.** 577.5 m^2

For problems 8 – 10, find the area of each figure.

8.

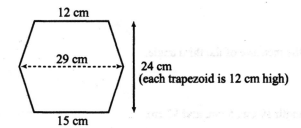

     a. 1020 cm^2

     b. 612 cm^2

     c. 510 cm^2

     d. 324 cm^2

9.

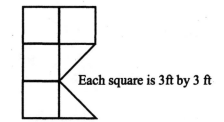

Each square is 3ft by 3 ft

     a. 45 ft^2

     b. 22.5 ft^2

     c. 72 ft^2

     d. 36 ft^2

10.

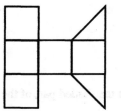

Each square is 9 ft by 9 ft

     a. 972 ft^2

     b. 405 ft^2

     c. 648 ft^2

     d. 486 ft^2

1. The sum of the measures of the angles in a triangle is 90°. True or false?

2. A right triangle has one angle of 90°. True or false?

3. Two angles of a triangle are 30° and 20°. Find the measure of the third angle.

4. Two angles of a triangle are 47° and 5°. Find the measure of the third angle.

5. Find the perimeter of a triangle with sides of length 10 cm, 5 cm, and 11 cm.

6. Find the perimeter of a triangle with sides that measure 10 cm.

7. Find the area of the triangle.

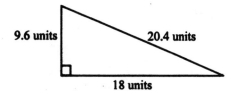

8. Find the area of a triangle that has a base of 15.7 cm and a height 15.2 cm.

9. Find the area of the shaded part of the figure.

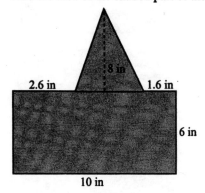

10. Find the area of the shaded part of the figure.

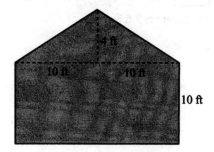

7.4 Triangles _____ *Multiple Choice*

1. An isosceles triangle has two sides of equal length.   **a.** True   **b.** False

2. All angles in an equilateral triangle are less than 90°.   **a.** True   **b.** False

3. Two angles of a triangle are both 31°. Find the measure of the third angle.
      a. 28°   **b.** 62°   **c.** 298°   **d.** 118°

4. An isosceles triangle has sides that are 8 yd, 12 yd, and 12 yd. Find the perimeter.
      a. 24 yd   **b.** 48 yd   **c.** 32 yd   **d.** 30 yd

5. A triangle has sides that are 9.9 ft, 7.9 ft, and 11.6 ft. Find the perimeter.
      a. 30.4 ft   **b.** 57.42 ft   **c.** 28.4 ft   **d.** 29.4 ft

6. Find the area of the triangle

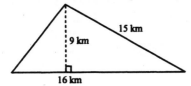

   a. 72 km^2
   b. 144 km^2
   c. 67.5 km^2
   d. 120 km^2

7. Find the area of the triangle.

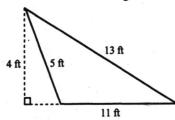

   a. 10 ft^2
   b. 44 ft^2
   c. 22 ft^2
   d. 26 ft^2

8. A triangle has base 15.7 cm and height 15.2 cm. Find the area of the triangle.
      a. 238.64 cm^2 **b.** 119.32 cm^2 **c.** 15.45 cm^2 **d.** 477.28 cm^2

9. Find the area of the shaded region in the figure below.

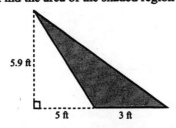

   a. 17.7 ft^2
   b. 23.6 ft^2
   c. 8.85 ft^2
   d. 14.75 ft^2

10. Find the total area of all of the vertical sides of the building, including the sides not shown here.

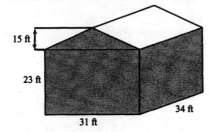

   a. 3455 ft^2
   b. 1727.5 ft^2
   c. 3920 ft^2
   d. 1891 ft^2

Basic College Mathematics
Chapter 7: Geometry
7.5 Square Roots _____ *Free Response*

Additional Exercises

For problems 1-6, do not use a calculator.

1. Evaluate: $\sqrt{64}$

2. Evaluate: $\sqrt{169}$

3. Evaluate and subtract: $\sqrt{121} - \sqrt{36}$

4. Evaluate and combine: $\sqrt{81} + \sqrt{9} - \sqrt{100}$

5. Evaluate and multiply: $\sqrt{5^2} \times \sqrt{12^2}$

6. Evaluate and multiply: $\sqrt{7^2} \times \sqrt{8^2}$

7. Approximate $\sqrt{6}$. Round to the nearest thousandth.

8. Approximate $\sqrt{147}$. Round to the nearest thousandth.

9. A square has an area of 81 m². Find the length of a side of this square.

10. Find the square root of 1.44 without using a calculator.

7.5 Square Roots _____ *Multiple Choice*

For problems 1-6, do not use a calculator.

1. Evaluate: $\sqrt{49}$

   a. 2401   **b.** 7   **c.** 49   **d.** $\dfrac{1}{49}$

2. Evaluate: $\sqrt{225}$

   a. 225   **b.** 325   **c.** 15   **d.** $\dfrac{1}{225}$

3. Evaluate and combine: $\sqrt{100} + \sqrt{225}$

   a. 25   **b.** 325   **c.** −5   **d.** 150

4. Evaluate and subtract: $\sqrt{144} - \sqrt{16}$

   a. −48   **b.** 128   **c.** 16   **d.** 8

5. Evaluate and multiply: $\sqrt{3^2} \times \sqrt{13^2}$

   a. 16   **b.** 1521   **c.** 39   **d.** 117

6. Evaluate and multiply: $\sqrt{4^2} \times \sqrt{9^2}$

   a. 1296   **b.** 36   **c.** 13   **d.** 144

For problems 7 and 8, approximate the square roots to the nearest thousandth.

7. $\sqrt{15}$ **a.** 3.873   **b.** 3.878   **c.** 3.870   **d.** 15.000

8. $\sqrt{118}$ **a.** 118.000   **b.** 10.868   **c.** 10.860   **d.** 10.863

9. Find the length of the side of a square with area 63 m². If the area is not a perfect square, approximate and round your answer to the nearest hundredth.

   a. 3639 m   **b.** 7.94 m   **c.** 15.75 m   **d.** 63 m

10. Find the square root of 0.0049 without using a calculator.

    a. 0.49   **b.** 7   **c.** 0.07   **d.** 0.007

7.6 The Pythagorean Theorem _____ *Free Response*

For problems 1-4, find the unknown side of the right triangle. Use a calculator or a square root table when necessary and round your answer to the nearest thousandth.

1.
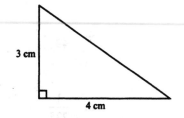
3 cm
4 cm

2.
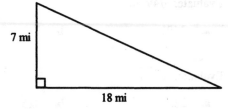
7 mi
18 mi

3.
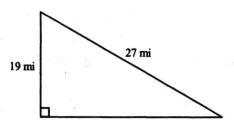
27 mi
19 mi

4.
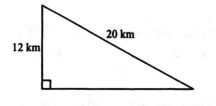
20 km
12 km

5. A right triangle has hypotenuse 13 yd and another side that measures 5 yd. Find the third side.

6. A right triangle has sides with lengths 8 ft and 4 ft. Find the third side.

7. Shane is flying his kite on 32 yd of string. The kite is directly above the edge of a pond. The edge of the pond is 27 yd from where the kite is tied to the ground. How far is the kite above the pond? Round your answer to the nearest tenth.

8. Tom walks 10 miles east and then rides a bike 12 miles south. How far is he from the original starting point? Round your answer to the nearest tenth.

9. Using your knowledge of special right triangles, find the lengths of both sides. Round your answer to the nearest tenth.

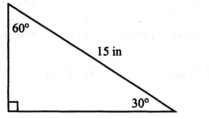
60°
15 in
30°

10. Using your knowledge of special right triangles, find the lengths of both sides. Round your answer to the nearest tenth.

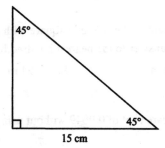
45°
45°
15 cm

7.6 The Pythagorean Theorem _____ *Multiple Choice*

For problems 1–4, find the unknown side of the right triangle. When necessary, approximate and round your answer to the nearest thousandth.

1.

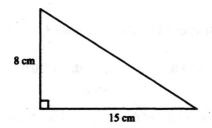

   a. 144.5 cm
   b. 289 cm
   c. 17 cm
   d. 11.5 cm

2.

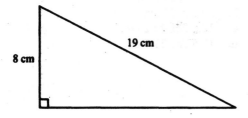

   a. 13.5 cm
   b. 297 cm
   c. 148.5 cm
   d. 17.234 cm

3.

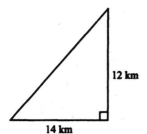

   a. 340 km
   b. 18.439 km
   c. 170 km
   d. 13 km

4.

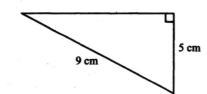

   a. 7.483 cm
   b. 56 cm
   c. 28 cm
   d. 7 cm

5. A right triangle has hypotenuse 20 yd and a side that measures 16 yd. Find the length of the third side.

   a. 25.612 yd   **b.** 12 yd   **c.** 2 yd   **d.** 6 yd

6. A right triangle has sides that measure 16 ft and 12 ft. Find the missing side.

   a. 2 ft   **b.** 10.583 ft   **c.** 5.292 ft   **d.** 20 ft

7. Juliet runs out of gas in Barnhaven, South Carolina. She walks 7 mi west and then 4 mi south looking for a gas station. How far is she from her starting point? Round your answer to the nearest tenth.

    a. 8.1 mi   **b.** 5.7 mi   **c.** 3.3 mi   **d.** 6.5 mi

8. A 29-ft ladder is placed against a college classroom building at a point 17 ft above the ground. What is the distance form the base of the ladder to the building?

    a. 552 ft   **b.** 33.6 ft   **c.** 23.5 ft   **d.** 1130 ft

9. Using your knowledge of special triangles, find the lengths of both sides of the triangle below. Round your answer to the nearest tenth.

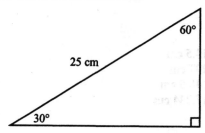

    a. 25 cm, 24.5 cm
    b. 50 cm, 24 cm
    c. 12.5 cm, 25.2 cm
    d. 12.5 cm, 21.7 cm

10. Using your knowledge of special triangles, find the lengths of both sides of the triangle below. Round your answer to the nearest tenth.

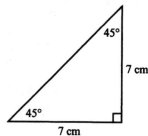

    a. 9.9 cm
    b. 15 cm
    c. 3.5 cm
    d. 4.9 cm

7.7 Circles _____ *Free Response*

For problems 1-10, use $\pi \approx 3.14$ *to approximate the value of* π.

1. Find the length of the radius of a circle if the diameter is 78 yd.

2. Find the length of the diameter of a circle if the radius is 6.2 m.

3. Find the circumference of the circle if the diameter is 41 in. Round your answer to the nearest hundredth.

4. A bicycle wheel makes 5 revolutions. Determine how far the bicycle travels, in inches, if the diameter of the wheel is 15 in. Round your answer to the nearest tenth.

5. Find the area of the circle if the diameter is 25 cm. Round your answer to the nearest tenth.

6. Find the area of the semicircle. Round your answer to the nearest tenth.

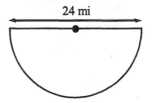

7. Find the area of the shaded region. Round your answer to the nearest tenth.

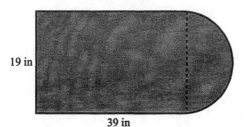

8. A water sprinkler sends water out in a circular pattern. Determine how large an area is watered if the radius of watering is 13 ft. Round your answer to the nearest hundredth.

9. A radio station sends out waves in all directions from a tower at the center of the circle of broadcast range. Determine how large an area is reached if the broadcast range has a diameter of 192 mi. Round your answer to the nearest hundredth.

10. The rectangular part of the field shown below is 138 yd long and the diameter of each semicircle is 16 yd. Find the cost of fertilizing the field at $0.25 per square yard. Round your answer to the nearest hundredth.

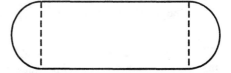

7.7 Circles _____ *Multiple Choice*

For problems 1-10, use $\pi \approx 3.14$ ***to approximate the value of*** π.

1. Find the length of the radius of a circle if the diameter is 2.6 in.

   a. 5.31 in.   **b.** 0.65 in.   **c.** 4.082 in.   **d.** 1.3 in.

2. Find the length of the diameter of a circle if the radius is 43.9 cm.

   a. 87.8 cm   **b.** 21.95 cm   **c.** 137.885 cm   **d.** 6051.44 cm

3. A bicycle wheel makes 5 revolutions. Determine how far the bicycle travels, in feet, if the diameter of the wheel is 24 in. Round your answer to the nearest tenth.

   a. 10 ft   **b.** 376.8 ft   **c.** 31.4 ft   **d.** 62.8 ft

4. Find the circumference of a circle if the radius is 87 m. Round your answer to the nearest hundredth.

   a. 273.18 m   **b.** 546.36 m   **c.** 23,766.66 m   **d.** 136.59 m

5. Find the area of a circle if the radius is 27 in. Round your answer to the nearest tenth.

   a. 2289.1 in.^{2} **b.** 84.8 in.^{2} **c.** 572.3 in.^{2} **d.** 169.6 in.^{2}

6. Find the area of the semicircle. Round your answer to the nearest tenth.

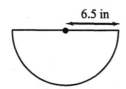

                                      a. 132.7 in.^{2}

                                      b. 40.8 in.^{2}

                                      c. 66.3 in.^{2}

                                      d. 81.6 in.^{2}

7. Find the area of the shaded region. Round your answer to the nearest tenth.

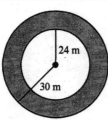

                                      a. 1017.4 in.^{2}

                                      b. 2826 m^2

                                      c. 1808.6 m^2

                                      d. 37.7 m^2

8. Bob's truck has tires with a radius of 12 inches. How many feet does his truck travel if a wheel makes 9 revolutions? Round your answer to the nearest hundredth.

   a. 4069.44 ft   **b.** 28.26 ft   **c.** 6.28 ft   **d.** 56.52 ft

9. Find the area of a circular flower bed with a diameter of 22 ft. Round your answer to the nearest hundredth.

   a. 69.08 ft^2 **b.** 1519.76 ft^2 **c.** 379.94 ft^2 **d.** 34.54 ft^2

10. Ellis bought a circular etched-glass table top to use as her dining room table. The glass is 6 ft in diameter. Find the cost of the table top at $57 per square yard of glass.

   a. $1610.82   **b.** $178.98   **c.** $715.92   **d.** $2863.68

7.8 Volume _____ *Free Response*

For problems 1- 10, use $\pi \approx 3.14$ *and round results to the nearest tenth if necessary.*

1. Find the volume of a rectangular solid with width 9 in., length 2 in., and height 5 in.

2. Find the volume of a rectangular solid with width 11 cm, length 0.6 m, and height 3 cm.

3. Find the volume of a cylinder with radius 7 m and height 12 m.

4. Find the volume of a cylinder with radius 12 cm and height 5 cm.

5. Find the volume of a sphere with radius 9 cm.

6. Find the volume of a cone with height 18 in. and radius 7 in.

7. Find the volume of a pyramid with height 9 ft and a square base with 10 ft on each side.

8. The Smiths want to put down a rectangular crushed-stone driveway to their house. The driveway is 10 yd wide and 186 yd long. The crushed stone is to be 6 in. thick. How many cubic yards of stone will they need?

9. A new pyramid has been found in South America. The pyramid has a rectangular base that measures 74 yd by 120 yd, and has a height of 60 yd. The pyramid is not hollow like the Egyptian pyramids and is composed of layer after layer of cut stone. The stone weights 456 lb per cubic yard. How many pounds does the pyramid weigh?

10. The Jones have ordered new plants for a rectangular garden, which is 17 ft by 48 in. The company charges $5.20 per square foot for the new plants. How much will it cost to plant the garden?

7.8 Volume _____ *Multiple Choice*

For problems 1- 10, use $\pi \approx 3.14$ *and round results to the nearest tenth if necessary.*

1. Find the volume of a rectangular solid with width 9 cm, length 18 cm, and height 19 cm.
    - **a.** 2916 cm^3
    - **b.** 3078 cm^3
    - **c.** 6498 cm^3
    - **d.** 1539 cm^3

2. Find the volume of a rectangular solid with width 8.4 cm, length 2 cm, and height 3 cm.
    - **a.** 211.7 cm^3
    - **b.** 33.6 cm^3
    - **c.** 18 cm^3
    - **d.** 50.4 cm^3

3. Find the volume of a cylinder with radius 8.5 yd and height 14 yd.
    - **a.** 3176.1 yd^3
    - **b.** 12,704.4 yd^3
    - **c.** 747.3 yd^3
    - **d.** 373.7 yd^3

4. Find the volume of a cylinder with radius 6.5 m and height 19 m.
    - **a.** 775.6 m^3
    - **b.** 10,082.5 m^3
    - **c.** 2520.6 m^3
    - **d.** 387.8 m^3

5. Find the volume of a hemisphere with radius 2 yd.
    - **a.** 9.4 yd^3
    - **b.** 33.5 yd^3
    - **c.** 18.8 yd^3
    - **d.** 16.7 yd^3

6. Find the volume of a cone with height 14 cm and diameter 6 cm.
    - **a.** 131.9 cm^3
    - **b.** 527.5cm^3
    - **c.** 175.8 cm^3
    - **d.** 791.3 cm^3

7. Find the volume of a pyramid with height 16 m and a rectangular base measuring 8 m by 20 m.
    - **a.** 2679.5 m^3
    - **b.** 853.3 m^3
    - **c.** 2560 m^3
    - **d.** 136,533.3 m^3

8. A special stainless-steel cone sits on top of a cable television antenna. The cost of the stainless steel is $3.00 per cm^3. The cone has radius 8 cm and height 6 cm. What is the cost of the stainless steel needed to make this *solid* steel cone? Round your answer to the nearest cent.
    - **a.** $150.72
    - **b.** $1205.76
    - **c.** $384.00
    - **d.** $301.44

9. A fragile glass box in the shape of a rectangular solid has width 9 in., length 19 in., and height 12 in. It is being shipped in a larger box of width 10 in., length 29 in., and height 24 in. All of the space between the glass box and shipping box will be packed with styrofoam "peanuts." How many cubic inches of the shipping box will be styrofoam peanuts?
    - **a.** 120 in.^{3}
    - **b.** 6960 in.^{3}
    - **c.** 2051 in.^{3}
    - **d.** 4908 in.^{3}

10. A storage garage rents space for people who need to store items on a monthly basis. The rooms measure 6 ft by 5 ft by 10 ft and rent for $45 per month. If you rented a storage space for one month, how much would you pay per cubic foot? Round your answer to the nearest cent.
    - **a.** $3.00 per cubic foot
    - **b.** $6.67 per cubic foot
    - **c.** $0.15 per cubic foot
    - **d.** $13.50 per cubic foot

7.9 Similar Geometric Figures _____ *Free Response*

For problems 1-3, each pair of triangles is similar. Find the missing side n. Round your answer to the nearest tenth when necessary.

1.

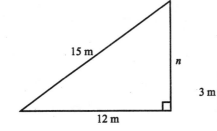

2.

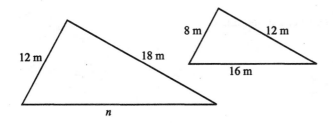

3.

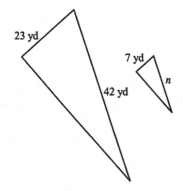

For problems 4 and 5, the pair of triangles is similar. Determine the three pairs of corresponding sides.

4.

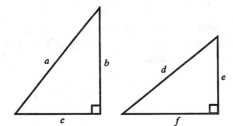

5.

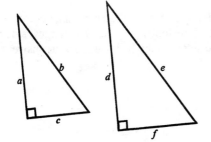

For problems 6 and 7, round your answer to the nearest tenth if necessary.

6.   The rectangles are similar. Find the perimeter of the second rectangle.

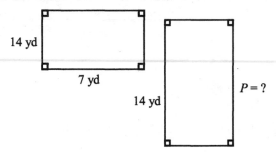

7.   The parallelograms are similar. Find the perimeter of the smaller parallelogram.

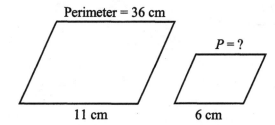

8.   Hillary is standing outside of the shopping mall. She is 5.1 feet tall and her shadow measures 7.1 feet long. The outside of the department store casts a shadow of 89 feet. How tall is the store? Round your answer to the nearest tenth, if necessary.

9.   Barbara took a great photo of the entire family at this year's reunion. She brought it to a professional photography studio and asked that the 4-in. by 6-in. photo be blown up to poster size, which is 3.5 ft tall. How wide will the poster be? Round your answer to the nearest tenth if necessary.

10. The zoo has hired a landscape architect to design the triangular lobby of the children's petting zoo. In his scale drawing, the longest side of the lobby is 9 cm. The shortest side of the lobby is 5 cm. The longest side of the actual lobby will be 60 m. How long will the shortest side of the actual lobby be? Round your answer to the nearest tenth if necessary.

7.9 Similar Geometric Figures _____ *Multiple Choice*

For problems 1-3, each pair of triangles is similar. Find the missing side n. Round your answer to the nearest tenth when necessary.

1.

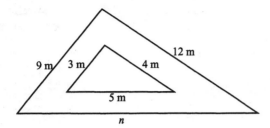

a. $n = 15$ m
b. $n = 5$ m
c. $n = 20$ m
d. $n = 16$ m

2.

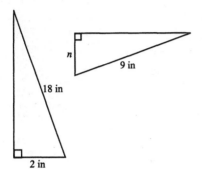

a. 81 in.
b. 4 in.
c. 1 in.
d. 324 in.

3.

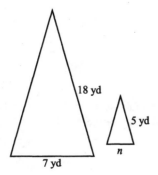

a. 1.94 yd
b. 1.9 yd
c. 7.5 yd
d. 12.6 yd

For problems 4 and 5, the pair of triangles is similar. Determine the three pairs of corresponding sides.

4.

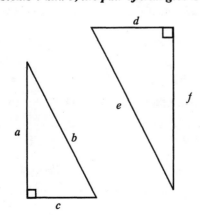

a. *a* corresponds to *f*
   b corresponds to *d*
   c corresponds to *e*

b. *a* corresponds to *e*
   b corresponds to *d*
   c corresponds to *f*

c. *a* corresponds to *d*
   b corresponds to *f*
   c corresponds to *e*

d. *a* corresponds to *f*
   b corresponds to *e*
   c corresponds to *d*

5.

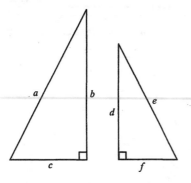

a. *a* corresponds to *d*
    b corresponds to *f*
    c corresponds to *e*

b. *a* corresponds to *f*
    b corresponds to *e*
    c corresponds to *d*

c. *a* corresponds to *e*
    b corresponds to *d*
    c corresponds to *f*

d. *a* corresponds to *f*
    b corresponds to *d*
    c corresponds to *e*

6. The pair of trapezoids is similar. Find the measure of side *n*.

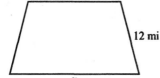
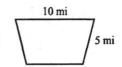

a. $n = 6$ mi
b. $n = 24$ mi
c. $n = 4.2$ mi
d. $n = 600$ mi

7. The pair of parallelograms is similar. Find the perimeter of the larger parallelogram.

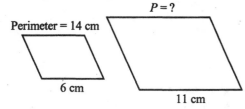

a. $P = 25.7$ cm
b. $P = 4.7$ cm
c. $P = 7.6$ cm
d. $P = 924$ cm

8. The zoo has hired a landscape architect to design the triangular lobby of the children's petting zoo. In his scale drawing, the longest side of the lobby is 17 cm. The shortest side of the lobby is 5 cm. The longest side of the actual lobby will be 44 m. How long will the shortest side of the actual lobby be? Round your answer to the nearest tenth if necessary.

    a. 149.6 m   **b.** 0.1 m   **c.** 12.9 m   **d.** 1.5 m

9. Jack and Jill are planning a new kitchen. The old kitchen measured 6 ft by 14 ft. The new kitchen is similar in shape, but the longest dimension is 21 ft. What is the smaller dimension of the new kitchen? Round your answer to the nearest tenth if necessary.

    a. 49 ft   **b.** 9 ft   **c.** 4 ft   **d.** 1764 ft

10. A flagpole casts a shadow of 39 ft. Nearby, a 7-ft tree casts a shadow of 6 ft. What is the height of the flagpole? Round your answer to the nearest tenth if necessary.

    a. 45.5 ft   **b.** 33.4 ft   **c.** 1.1 ft   **d.** 1638 ft

7.10 Applications of Geometry _____ *Free Response*

Use $\pi \approx 3.14$ and round your answers to the nearest tenth.

1. The Minkner family started a flower garden. The rectangular garden measures 15 ft long and 17 ft wide. To keep out animals, they had to surround it with fencing, which costs $1.15 per foot. How much did the garden fencing cost?

2. A professional painter can pain 184 ft² in 30 minutes. She will be painting three walls in a house. They measure 3 ft×13 ft, 7 ft ×11 ft, and 8 ft× 20 ft. How many minutes will it take her to paint all three walls?

3. The Nguyens want to put siding on the front of their home in Dallas. The house dimensions are 17 ft by 33 ft. There is one door that measures 6 ft by 4 ft. There are also 10 windows, each measuring 5 ft by 4 ft. Excluding windows and doors, how many square feet of siding will be needed?

4. A conical pile of grain is 8 ft in diameter and 14 ft high. How many bushels of grain are in a pile if 1 cubic foot = 0.8 bushel?

5. A dentist places a silver filling in the shape of a cylinder with a hemispherical top. The radius of the filling is 6 mm. The height of the cylindrical portion is 4 mm. If dental silver costs $16 per cubic millimeter, how much did the silver for the filling cost?

6. A communications satellite orbits the Earth in a circular pattern. Assume that the radius of orbit is 7200 km. If the satellite goes through one orbit around the Earth in 2 hours, what is its speed in kilometers per hour?

7. For Christmas, a company makes decorative cylinder-shaped canisters and fills them with green candy. They want to make 120 canisters and need to determine how much candy to buy. If each canister is 16 inches in diameter and 9 inches tall, what is the total cubic inches of candy needed to fill all the canisters?

8. Bob is making cone-shaped candles. The mold he pours the wax into is 8 inches in diameter and 9 inches high. Bob needs to know how much wax to buy. How many cubic inches of wax total will he need to make 43 candles?

Barbara has planned a trip from Suffolk to Palermo going through Bridgetown. Use the figure to answer the following questions.

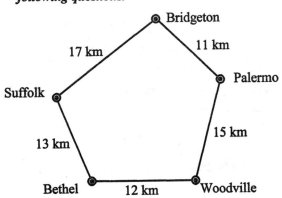

9. What is the total distance she drives?

10. How fast does she travel if the trip takes 0.7 hr?

7.10 Applications of Geometry _____ *Multiple Choice*

Use $\pi \approx 3.14$ and round your answers to the nearest tenth.

1. The Hanson family started a flower garden. The rectangular garden measures 13 ft long and 17 ft wide. To keep out animals, they had to surround it with fencing, which costs $0.65 per foot. How much did the garden fencing cost?

   a. $19.50   b. $143.65   c. $39.00   d. 92.31

2. A professional painter can paint 192 ft² in 56 minutes. She will be painting four walls in a house. They measure $2\,\text{ft} \times 15\,\text{ft}$, $3\,\text{ft} \times 13\,\text{ft}$, $4\,\text{ft} \times 11\,\text{ft}$, and $2\,\text{ft} \times 20\,\text{ft}$. How many minutes will it take her to paint all four walls?

   a. 524.6 minutes   b. 44.6 minutes   c. 600,600 minutes   d. 204 minutes

3. The Carpenters want to put siding on the front of their home in Chicago. The house dimensions are 17 ft by 33 ft. There is one door that measures 5 ft by 3 ft. There are also 9 windows, each measuring 3 ft by 2 ft. Excluding windows and doors, how many square feet of siding will be needed?

   a. 540 ft²   b. 561 ft²   c. 69 ft²   d. 492 ft²

4. A conical pile of grain is 12 ft in diameter and 12 ft high. How many bushels of grain are in a pile if 1 cubic foot = 0.8 bushel?

   a. 361.7 bushels   b. 452.2 bushels   c. 115.2 bushels   d. 60.3 bushels

5. A dentis places a gold filling in the shape of a cylinder with a hemispherical top. The radius of the filling is 5 mm. The height of the cylindrical portion is 8 mm. If dental gold costs $20 per cubic millimeter, how much did the gold for the filling cost? Round your answer to the nearest cent.

   a. $13,606.67   b. $17,793.33   c. $9210.67   d. $800.00

6. A Landstar satellite orbits the Earth in a circular pattern. Assume that the radius of orbit is 6800 km. If the satellite goes through one orbit around the Earth in 2 hours, what is its speed in kilometers per hour?

   a. 541.4 km/hr   b. 10,676 km/hr   c. 72,596,800 km/hr   d. 21,352 km/hr

7. For Valentine's Day, a company makes decorative cylinder-shaped canisters and fills them with red-hot candies. They want to make 330 canisters and need to determine how much candy to buy. If each canister is 16 inches in diameter and 7 inches tall, what is the total cubic inches of candy needed to fill all the canisters?

   a. 1406.7 in³   b. 1,856,870.4 in³   c. 464,217.6 in³   d. 66,3168 in³

8. Jack is making cone-shaped candles. The mold he pours the wax into is 10 inches in diameter and 15 inches high. Jack needs to know how much wax to buy. How many cubic inches of wax will he need to make 79 candles?

   a. 31,007.5 in³   b. 12,403 in³   c. 6201.5 in³   d. 93,022.5 in³

Tom drives from work to home to change his clothes. He then drives to the supermarket. Use the figure below to answer the following questions.

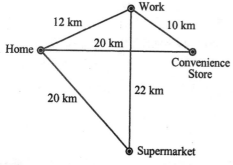

9. What is the total distance he drives?

   a. 20 km   b. 32 km
   c. 52 km   d. 12 km

10. How fast does he travel if the trip takes 0.4 hr?

   a. 90 km/hr   b. 30 km/hr
   c. 12.8 km/hr   d. 80 km/hr

8.1 Circle Graphs _____ *Free Response*

The circle graphs for problems 1-10, show results of some recent college elections. The complete circular area represents 100% of the votes and the sections show what percent of the vote each person received.

Student Council President
400 Total Votes

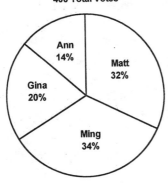

1. Who got the most votes?

2. How many votes did Ann get?

3. How many more votes did Matt get than Gina?

4. How many votes did Ming and Matt get together?

5. If Matt had received 7 of Ming's votes, would he have won the election?

Student Council Vice-President
700 Total Votes

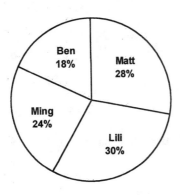

6. Who got the least votes?

7. How many votes did Ben get?

8. How many more votes did Lili get than Ming?

9. How many votes did Matt and Ming get together?

10. If Ben had received 42 of Matt's votes, would he have won the election?

8.1 Circle Graphs _____ *Multiple Choice*

The circle graphs show results of some recent college elections. The complete circular area represents 100% of the votes and the sections show what percent of the vote each person received.

Head Cheerleader
600 Total Votes

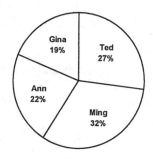

1. Who got the most votes?
      a. Ann   b. Gina   c. Ted   d. Ming

2. How many votes did Ann get?
      a. 120   b. 132   c. 22   d. 130

3. How many more votes did Ming get than Ted?
      a. 300   b. 3   c. 30   d. 33

4. How many votes did Gina and Ming get together?
      a. 306   b. 30.6   c. 300   d. 360

5. If Ann had received 54 of Ted's votes, would she have won the election?
      a. No   b. Yes   c. Don't Know

Chess Club President
800 Total Votes

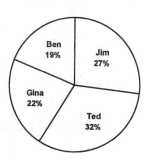

6. Who got the least votes?
      a. Ted   b. Ben   c. Gina   d. Jim

7. How many votes did Jim get?
      a. 21.6   b. 162   c. 216   d. 116

8. How many more votes did Ted get than Gina?
      a. 88   b. 8   c. 18   d. 80

9. How many votes did Ben and Gina get together?
      a. 300   b. 318   c. 32.8   d. 328

10. Find the ratio of Ted's votes to Jim's votes.
      a. $\dfrac{32}{59}$ b. $\dfrac{27}{32}$ c. $\dfrac{32}{27}$ d. $\dfrac{59}{32}$

8.2 Bar Graphs and Line Graphs _____ *Free Response*

The bar graph shows the number of tickets sold each week by the garden club for their annual flower show. Use the graph to answer questions 1-3.

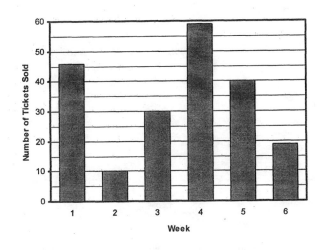

1. During which week were the most tickets sold?

2. How many tickets were sold in weeks 2, 4, and 5?

3. During which week were 19 tickets sold?

The following double-bar graph illustrates the revenue for a company for the four quarters of the year for two different years. Use the graph to answer questions 4-6.

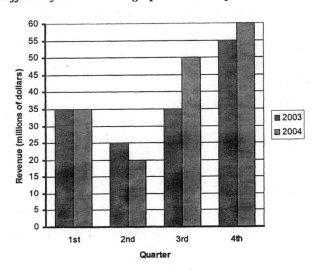

4. Which quarter in 2003 had the most revenue?

5. What was the difference in revenue between the third quarter of 2003 and the third quarter of 2004?

6. What was the total revenue for all of 2004?

The line graph shows the recorded hourly temperatures in degrees Fahrenheit at an airport. Use the graph to answer questions 7 and 8.

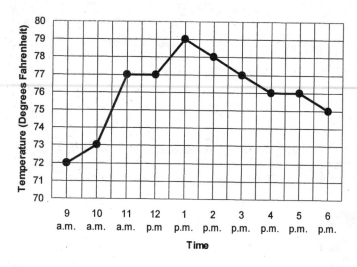

7. What temperature was recorded at 2 P.M.?

8. How much did the temperature change between 10 A.M. and 1 P.M.?

The following comparison line graph indicates the number of vehicles sold for a seven-week period by two different salespeople. Use the graph to answer questions 9 and 10.

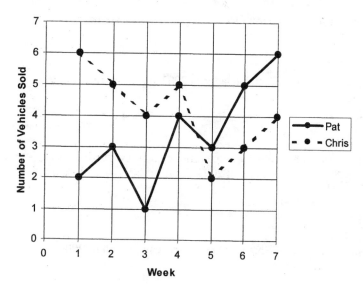

9. During which weeks did Pat sell more vehicles than Chris?

10. What total number of vehicles did Pat sell during the seven weeks?

8.2 Bar Graphs and Line Graphs _____ *Multiple Choice*

The bar graph shows the number of tickets sold each week by the garden club for their annual flower show. Use the graph to answer questions 1-3.

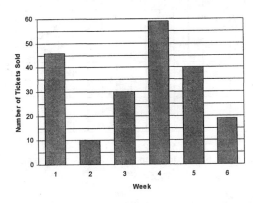

1. How many tickets were sold during week 6?

   a. 11   **b.** 46   **c.** 19   **d.** 30

2. How many more tickets were sold during week 5 than week 3?

   a. 10   **b.** 20   **c.** 70   **d.** 15

3. How many tickets were sold in all?

   a. 215   **b.** 195   **c.** 105   **d.** 205

The following double-bar graph illustrates the revenue for a company for the four quarters of the year for two different years. Use the graph to answer questions 4-6.

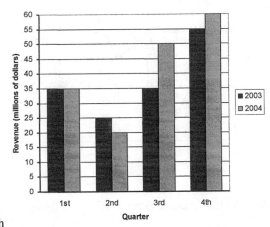

4. In what quarter was th

   a. First   **b.** Second   **c.** Fourth   **d.** Third

5. Which quarter in 2004 had the greatest decrease in revenue compared to the same quarter for 2003?

   a. Third   **b.** First   **c.** Second   **d.** Fourth

6. Which quarter has the same revenue for 2003 and 2004?

   a. Fourth   **b.** Second   **c.** Third   **d.** First

The line graph shows the recorded hourly temperatures in degrees Fahrenheit at an airport. Use the graph to answer questions 7 and 8.

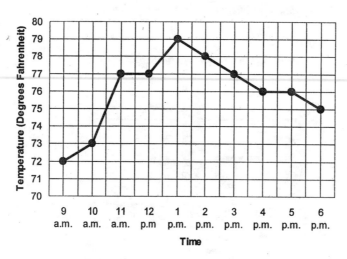

7. During which hour did the temperature increase the most?

    a. 10 – 11 A.M.   **b.** 1 – 2 P.M.   **c.** 12 – 1 P.M.   **d.** 9 – 10 A.M.

8. At what time was the temperature 79°?

    a. 2 P.M.   **b.** 1 P.M.   **c.** 12 P.M.   **d.** 6 P.M.

The following comparison line graph indicates the number of vehicles sold for a seven-week period by two different salespeople. Use the graph to answer questions 9 and 10.

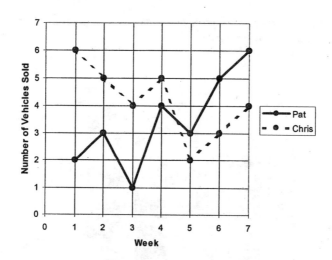

9. During what weeks did Pat sell more vehicles than Chris?

    a. Weeks 1, 3, 4   **b.** Weeks 5, 6, 7   **c.** Weeks 1, 2, 3, 4   **d.** Weeks 1, 2, 3

10. How many more vehicles did Pat sell than Chris in Week 6?

    a. 2 vehicles   **b.** 5 vehicles   **c.** 3 vehicles   **d.** 4 vehicles

8.3 Histograms _____ *Free Response*

A new car dealership has taken an inventory of the vehicles it has in stock. Below is a histogram indicating the number of vehicles in stock in certain price ranges. Use the histogram to answer questions 1-6.

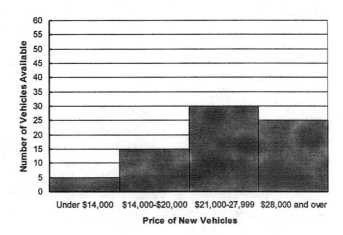

1. How many vehicles does the dealership have in stock that are priced $21,000 - $27,999?

2. How many vehicles does the dealership have in stock that are priced at $28,000 or over?

3. How many more vehicles are in stock that are priced $28,000 or over than are priced at $14,000 - $20,999?

4. How many vehicles does the dealership have in stock that are priced under $21,000?

5. If 6 vehicles are sold in the price range $14,000 - $20,999, how many vehicles are left over?

6. What is the total number of vehicles in stock at the dealership?

Each number below is the number of miles the Hoover family has driven during each week. Determine the frequency of the class intervals for this data.

142	284	557	354	315
265	239	157	379	294
425	498	198	297	414
210	342	171	416	305

7.

Class Interval	Tally	Frequency
140-240	_____	_____

8.

Class Interval	Tally	Frequency
200-350	_____	_____

9.

Class Interval	Tally	Frequency
315-400	_____	_____

10.

Class Interval	Tally	Frequency
360-590	_____	_____

8.3 Histograms _____ *Multiple Choice*

A new car dealership has taken an inventory of the vehicles it has in stock. Below is a histogram indicating the number of vehicles in stock in certain price ranges. Use the histogram to answer questions 1-6.

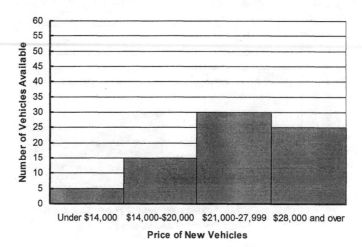

1. How many vehicles does the dealership have in stock that are priced under $14,000?

   a. 1 vehicle   **b.** 5 vehicles   **c.** 10 vehicles   **d.** 2 vehicles

2. Which price category of vehicles does the dealership have the most of?

   a. Vehicles costing $14,000 – $20,999   **b.** Vehicles costing under $14,000

   c. Vehicles costing $21,000 – $27,999   **d.** Vehicles costing $28,000 or over

3. Which price category of vehicles does the dealership have the least of?

   a. Vehicles costing under $14,000   **b.** Vehicles costing $21,000 – $27,999

   c. Vehicles costing $14,000 – $20,999   **d.** Vehicles costing $28,000 or over

4. How many vehicles does the dealership have in stock that are priced at less than $28,000?

   a. 6 vehicles   **b.** 10 vehicles   **c.** 30 vehicles   **d.** 50 vehicles

5. How many vehicles does the dealership have in stock that are priced at $28,000 or more?

   a. 5 vehicles   **b.** 25 vehicles   **c.** 20 vehicles   **d.** 4 vehicles

6. How many vehicles does the dealership have in stock that are priced between $14,000 and $27,999?

   a. 45 vehicles   **b.** 9 vehicles   **c.** 15 vehicles   **d.** 50 vehicles

Each number below is the number of miles the Hoover family has driven during each week. Determine the frequency of the class intervals for this data.

142	284	557	354	315
265	239	157	379	294
425	498	198	297	414
210	342	171	416	305

7.

Class Interval	Tally	Frequency
220-334	_____	_____

a. 4
b. 6
c. 5
d. 7

8.

Class Interval	Tally	Frequency
320-394	_____	_____

a. 6
b. 5
c. 4
d. 7

9.

Class Interval	Tally	Frequency
390-454	_____	_____

a. 3
b. 4
c. 2
d. 5

10.

Class Interval	Tally	Frequency
455-564	_____	_____

a. 4
b. 3
c. 1
d. 2

8.4 Mean, Median, and Mode _____ *Free Response*

1. The numbers of points Dee scored playing basketball over the last four games were 20, 2, 24, and 20. Find the mean of Dee's points scored.

2. The numbers of tickets sold in the five days preceding the play were 70, 50, 70, 95, and 50. Find the mean number of tickets sold.

3. The numbers of miles driven in one week were 85, 62, 93, 24, 89, 116, and 135. Find the mean number of miles driven in one week.

4. Find the median: 16, 30, 39, 44, 65, 75, 82

5. Find the median: 1,1, 22, 24, 47, 50

6. The numbers of minutes Maria spent looking on the internet for gifts for her family during the last six days are as follows: 2, 11, 29, 28, 35, 45. Find the median.

7. Find the mode: 20, 36, 46, 36, 49, 39, 36

8. Find the mode: 92, 16, 39, 54, 92, 83, 79, 81, 116, 54

9. Find the mode: 46, 83, 93, 27, 76, 63, 83, 92

10. Find the mode: 59, 63, 58, 69, 57, 42, 63, 91, 57, 48

8.4 Mean, Median, and Mode _____ *Multiple Choice*

1. The numbers of miles John ran over the last six days were 5, 6, 10, 4, 11, and 10. Find the mean number of miles John ran, and round your answer to the nearest tenth if necessary.

   a. 7.7 miles   b. 8.2 miles   c. 9.2 miles   d. 6.2 miles

2. The numbers of calls from telemarketers Lori received over the last seven weeks were 16, 13, 4, 11, 7, 2, and 4. Find the mean number of calls received per week, and round your answer to the nearest tenth if necessary.

   a. 7.6 calls   b. 9.6 calls   c. 9.5 calls   d. 8.1 calls

3. The weights in pounds of the five books in Lynn's backpack are 2.7, 3, 1.7, 1.1, and 3. Find the mean weight of her books, and round your answer to the nearest tenth if necessary.

   a. 2.8 pounds   b. 2.3 pounds   c. 1.8 pounds   d. 1.9 pounds

4. Find the median: 9, 9, 22, 16, 28, 48, 33, 33

   a. 28   b. 22   c. 25   d. 24.5

5. The numbers of vehicles passing through a toll booth in one hour for five consecutive hours are 2, 20, 29, 34, and 36. Find the median value, and round your answer to the nearest tenth if necessary.

   a. 24.8 vehicles   b. 29 vehicles   c. 20 vehicles   d. 34 vehicles

6. The numbers of vehicles passing through a toll booth in one hour for seven consecutive hours are 8, 9, 15, 23, 30, 39, and 46. Find the median value, and round your answer to the nearest tenth if necessary.

   a. 23 vehicles   b. 24.8 vehicles   c. 15 vehicles   d. 30 vehicles

7. Find the mode: 77, 74, 32, 74, 29, 77

   a. The mode is 77.   b. The mode is 74.

   c. The two modes are 77 and 74.   d. The mode is 60.5.

8. Find the mode: 382, 376, 332, 376, 329, 382

   a. The mode is 362.8.   b. The mode is 376.

   c. The mode is 382.   d. The two modes are 382 and 376.

9. Find the mode: 78, 25, 78, 13, 25, 29, 56, 78

   a. The mode is 47.8.   b. The mode is 25.

   c. The mode is 78.   d. The mode is 42.5.

10. Find the mode: $20, $38, $46, $38, $49, $38, $49

    a. The mode is $38.   b. The mode is $49.

    c. The mode is $39.70.   d. The mode is $46.

9.1 Addition of Signed Numbers _____ *Free Response*

1. Add: $-23+(-31)$

2. Add: $7.4+(-5.6)$

3. Add: $\dfrac{5}{6}+(-6)$

4. Add: $-9+(-4)+20$

5. Add: $-7+13+8+(-19)$

6. Add: $\dfrac{1}{9}+\left(-\dfrac{1}{2}\right)+\dfrac{4}{5}$

7. A bicycle manufacturer records a profit of $28,000 in April, followed by a loss of $21,000 in May, and a profit of $25,000 in June. What is the net effect of these three results? Show a positive or negative sign in your answer.

8. A picture frame manufacturer records a loss of $25,000 in September, followed by a loss of $22,000 in October, and a profit of $34,000 in November. What is the net effect of these three results? Show a positive or negative sign in your answer.

9. On the morning of December 19 the temperature was $-4°$ F. The next morning the temperature had risen $11°$F. What was the temperature on the morning of December 20?

10. Lupe made a New Year's resolution to lose weight. He started off weighing 166 pounds. In January he lost 9.5 pounds, in February he gained back 5.2 pounds, in March he lost 5.2 pounds, and in April he put on 3.5 pounds. What was Lupe's weight at the end of April?

9.1 Addition of Signed Numbers _____ *Multiple Choice*

1. Add: $-43+(55)$

   a. -12 **b.** 12 **c.** -98 **d.** 98

2. Add: $7.4+(-2.7)$

   a. 4.7 **b.** 10.1 **c.** -4.7 **d.** -10.1

3. Add: $-3+\dfrac{5}{7}$

   a. $-3\dfrac{5}{7}$ **b.** $3\dfrac{5}{7}$ **c.** $-2\dfrac{2}{7}$ **d.** $2\dfrac{2}{7}$

4. Add: $-1+(-2)+2+(-4)+(-2)$

   a. -3 **b.** -11 **c.** -7 **d.** 7

5. Add: $2+(-6)+(-3)+12+(-19)+3$

   a. -5 **b.** 1 **c.** -35 **d.** -11

6. Add: $-\dfrac{7}{15}+\left(-\dfrac{2}{5}\right)+\dfrac{1}{11}$

   a. $-\dfrac{128}{165}$ **b.** $\dfrac{4}{165}$ **c.** $\dfrac{158}{165}$ **d.** $-\dfrac{4}{165}$

7. Tyrone added $114 to his bank account on Wednesday and withdrew $248 two days later on Friday. What was the effect on the amount in the account from these two transactions? Show a positive or negative sign in your answer.

   a. +$114   **b.** +$134   **c.** −$134   **d.** −$248

8. On the morning of February 2 the temperature was 9° F. The next morning the temperature had dropped 18° F. What was the temperature on the morning of February 3?

   a. −18° F   **b.** −9° F   **c.** 27° F   **d.** −27° F

9. Meredith got a monthly cable bill for a base rate of $18.30, an additional $5.40 for a package of movie channels, a charge of $2.37 for taxes, and a credit of $11.20 to make up for a billing error the previous month. How much was the cable bill?

   a. $40.27   **b.** $37.27   **c.** $12.87   **d.** $14.87

10. Herbert, an African elephant living in a zoo, had been sick and lost a lot of weight. He was down to 9455 pounds. The zoo made a special effort to get food into him. The first month of this effort, he gained 142 pounds, the second month he gained another 89 pounds, the third month he had a setback and lost 27 pounds, and the fourth month he gained 117 pounds. What was Herbert's total weight gain or loss in those four months?

   a. A gain of 375 pounds   **b.** A gain of 321 pounds

   c. He weighs 9776 pounds   **d.** A gain of 390 pounds

9.2 Subtraction of Signed Numbers _____ *Free Response*

1. Subtract: $-6+(-10)$

2. Subtract: $-17-(-31)$

3. Subtract: $4.4-(-5.7)$

4. Subtract: $-\dfrac{1}{12}+\left(-\dfrac{1}{6}\right)$

5. Subtract: $\dfrac{5}{7}-(-7)$

6. Subtract: $-3+16-27$

7. Subtract: $9-(-2)+6$

8. Subtract: $-5.2+1.6-0.8-(-2.9)$

9. Kerry owed $200, borrowed an additional $190, and paid back $55. How much did she still owe?

10. On March of 2001, the value of a share of a certain company was $38.93. Over the course of the month, the price decreased by $4.52, rose $2.43, decreased again by $3.71, then gained $3.52 on the last day of the month. What was the value of the stock at the end of the month?

9.2 Subtraction of Signed Numbers _____ *Multiple Choice*

1. Subtract: $220 - 280$

    a. -500 b. 500 c. 60 d. -60

2. Subtract: $-145 - (-38)$

    a. 107 b. -183 c. -107 d. 183

3. Subtract: $-14.52 - 48.17$

    a. -62.69 b. 33.65 c. 62.69 d. -33.65

4. Subtract: $-\dfrac{3}{7} - \left(-\dfrac{3}{8}\right)$

    a. $\dfrac{45}{36}$ b. $-\dfrac{3}{56}$ c. $\dfrac{3}{56}$ d. $-\dfrac{45}{56}$

5. Subtract: $-\dfrac{1}{9} - \dfrac{1}{7}$

    a. $\dfrac{16}{63}$ b. $-\dfrac{2}{63}$ c. $-\dfrac{16}{63}$ d. $\dfrac{2}{63}$

6. Subtract: $-15 + 9 - 8 - (-3)$

    a. -17 b. -1 c. -19 d. -11

7. Subtract: $-9 + 7 - 18 - (-8) + 15$

    a. 3 b. 23 c. -21 d. -13

8. Subtract: $1.787 - (-0.533) + 0.415$

    a. 1.669 b. 2.735 c. 0.839 d. -0.839

9. On April 1 of 2001, the value of a share of a certain company was $13.34. Over the course of the month, the price decreased by $0.98, rose $2.40, decreased again $1.34, then gained $4.88 on April 30. What was the total gain or loss in the price of the stock between the beginning and end of the month?

    a. Gain of $4.96   b. Gain of $18.30

    c. Loss of $4.96   d. Loss of $20.98

10. Mohamed had a credit of $127.50 on his debit card. He went to a department store and returned a set of napkins for a credit of $13.87, then charged a pair of shoes for $52.65, and a pair of sunglasses for $12.08, sales tax included. After the return and two purchases, what was the balance on his card?

    a. $206.10   b. $11.91   c. $-$76.64   d. $76.64

9.3 Multiplication and Division of Signed Numbers _____ *Free Response*

1. Multiply: $(-8)(15)$

2. Multiply: $(3.2)(-5.34)$

3. Multiply: $\left(-\dfrac{2}{5}\right)\left(\dfrac{3}{4}\right)$

4. Divide: $-60 \div (-4)$

5. Divide: $\dfrac{\frac{21}{19}}{-\frac{7}{4}}$

6. Multiply: $(-4)(-5)(5)$

7. Multiply: $(-3)(-6)(-2)$

8. Multiply: $5(-1)(6)(2)(-7)$

9. Ben lost $429 on each of 4 consecutive days in the stock market. If he had $15,638 before his loss, how much does he have after his loss?

10. A weather forecaster predicts that the temperature will drop 2 degrees each hour for the next 9 hours. If the temperature is 6 degrees before the temperature starts falling, what is the temperature after the drop?

9.3 Multiplication and Division of Signed Numbers _____ *Multiple Choice*

1. Multiply: $(-7)(10)$

   a. 63   b. -63 c. -70 d. -80

2. Multiply: $(2.29)(-8.0)$

   a. -10.29 b. -5.71 c. 10.29 d. 18.32

3. Multiply: $\left(-\dfrac{1}{3}\right)\left(-\dfrac{10}{11}\right)$

   a. $-\dfrac{10}{33}$ b. $\dfrac{10}{33}$ c. $-\dfrac{13}{99}$ d. $\dfrac{41}{33}$

4. Divide: $\dfrac{-570}{19}$

   a. -30 b. $-\dfrac{1}{30}$ c. 30   d. -40

5. Divide: $\dfrac{-\frac{3}{2}}{\frac{7}{8}}$

   a. $-\dfrac{80}{63}$ b. $-\dfrac{12}{7}$ c. $\dfrac{8}{7}$ d. 40

6. Multiply: $(-8)(-6)(-9)$

   a. -442 b. -332 c. -432 d. 432

7. Multiply: $(-5)(-5)(-5)$

   a. -115 b. 125   c. -135 d. -125

8. Multiply: $(-23)(0)(5)$

   a. 0   b. -23 c. 23   d. 1

9. The formula for converting a temperature from Fahrenheit to Celsius is $F = \dfrac{9}{5}C + 32$. When $C = -485°$, what does F equal?

   a. $-841°$ b. $-905°$ c. $905°$ d. $841°$

10. A checking account had a beginning balance of $1322. A deposit was made in the amount of $1447. Every month for 15 months, $45 was withdrawn. How much money was left in the account at the end of the 15 months?

    a. $772   b. $2724   c. $675   d. $2094

9.4 Order of Operations with Signed Numbers _____ *Free Response*

For problems 1-6, perform the operations in the proper order.

1. $30 \div 10(3) + (-10)$

2. $7^2 - 3(2) + 50 \div 5$

3. $\dfrac{-9 - (-7)}{50 - 50 \div 5}$

4. $-\dfrac{2}{3} + \dfrac{1}{4} - \dfrac{1}{3}\left(-\dfrac{3}{4}\right)$

5. $3.9(-8) + (4.1 - 2.1)^2$

6. $2.8(-8) + 5(3.5)$

A football team had control of the ball of the first nine plays in a game. The chart shows the yards gained or lost in each of those plays. Use the chart to answer questions 7 and 8.

Play #	1	2	3	4	5	6	7	8	9
Yards gained (+) or lost (−)	+2	+15	−2	−3	+20	−5	−12	−13	+7

7. What was the net gain or loss considering all nine plays? Label your answer with "yards gained" or "yards lost."

8. If the team had lost four times as many yards in the third play as it did, what would the total loss have been for the third and fourth plays combined? Begin your answer with "A loss of..."

9. After one week of dieting, Manuel lost 1.9 pounds. The second week he lost twice as many pounds as the first week, and at the end of the third week he had lost a total of 7.1 pounds. How many pounds did Manuel lose during the third week?

10. In Fagersta, Sweden, the temperature one day was −12° C. The next day the temperature rose 7 degrees. What was the new temperature?

9.4 Order of Operations with Signed Numbers _____ *Multiple Choice*

For problems 1-6, perform the operations in the proper order.

1. $6(-2)+(9-7)^2$

   a. -8 **b.** 20 **c.** 16 **d.** 100

2. $\dfrac{8(-3)-4+7}{-105 \div 5}$

   a. $\dfrac{1}{5}$ **b.** 1 **c.** 5 **d.** -1

3. $\left(\dfrac{1}{5}\right)^2 + \dfrac{3}{7}\left(\dfrac{3}{5}\right)$

   a. $\dfrac{2}{7}$ **b.** $\dfrac{246}{875}$ **c.** $\dfrac{16}{35}$ **d.** $\dfrac{52}{175}$

4. $\dfrac{1}{2} \div \left(-\dfrac{2}{7}\right)\left(-\dfrac{1}{2}\right) + \left(-\dfrac{1}{12}\right)$

   a. $-\dfrac{1}{21}$ **b.** $\dfrac{43}{12}$ **c.** $\dfrac{41}{12}$ **d.** $-\dfrac{2}{63}$

5. $(2.3)^2 - 4.1(5) + 10.8 \div 4$

   a. -12.51 **b.** -1.1 **c.** 8.65 **d.** 333.94

6. $-18 - (-5.7)(-4) + (-12.8) \div (-4)$

   a. -37.6 **b.** 8 **c.** -44 **d.** -13.4

A football team had control of the ball of the first nine plays in a game. The chart shows the yards gained or lost in each of those plays. Use the chart to answer questions 7 and 8.

Play #	1	2	3	4	5	6	7	8	9
Yards gained (+) or lost (−)	+2	+15	−2	−3	+20	−5	−12	−13	+7

7. What was the average gain or loss in one play considering all nine plays? Round to the nearest tenth if necessary.

   a. Average gain of 13.7 yards   **b.** Average gain of 1 yard
   c. Average loss of 3.9 yards   **d.** Average loss of 4.9 yards

8. How many total yards were lost in those plays that resulted in a loss?

   a. 22 yards lost   **b.** 9 yards lost   **c.** 35 yards lost   **d.** 14 yards lost

9. In Fairbanks, Alaska, the temperature one day was 2° F. The next day the temperature fell 3 degrees, and on the third day the temperature fell another 4 degrees. What was the temperature on the third day?

   a. $-2°$ F   **b.** $-5°$ F   **c.** $-1°$ F   **d.** $-7°$ F

10. Mara received a phone bill with a base charge of $17.15, an extra-minutes charge of $3.74, and a combination of surcharges and taxes totaling $3.88. There was also a credit for $4.66. Mara could see that the credit was twice as large as it should have been, so she reduced it accordingly. How much was the check she sent to the phone company?

    a. $27.10   **b.** $20.11   **c.** $15.45   **d.** $10.06

9.5 Scientific Notation _____ *Free Response*

1. Write 1740 in scientific notation.

2. Write 716,000 in scientific notation.

3. Write 0.0001463 in scientific notation.

4. Write 0.0093 in scientific notation.

5. Write 1.39×10^4 in standard notation.

6. Write 7.148×10^8 in standard notation.

7. Write 6.951×10^{-3} in standard notation.

8. Add: 3.63×10^7 dollars + 5.4×10^7 dollars

9. Subtract: 8.18×10^9 atoms − 5.6×10^9 atoms

10. During the eruption of a volcano, approximately 1.4×10^{10} tons of ash were carried up into the air. What is the amount in standard notation?

9.5 Scientific Notation _____ *Multiple Choice*

1. Write 410,000 in scientific notation.

    a. 4.1×10^{-5} **b.** 4.1×10^{5} **c.** 4.1×10^{6} **d.** 4.1×10^{-6}

2. Write 0.000791 in scientific notation.

    a. 7.91×10^{-3} **b.** 7.91×10^{4} **c.** 7.91×10^{-5} **d.** 7.91×10^{-4}

3. Write 0.000097717 in scientific notation.

    a. 9.7717×10^{-5} **b.** 9.7717×10^{5} **c.** 9.7717×10^{-4} **d.** 9.7717×10^{4}

4. Write 7.256×10^{7} in standard notation

    a. 7,256,000   **b.** 725,600,000   **c.** 72,560,000   **d.** 507.92

5. Write 2.9918×10^{4} in standard notation.

    a. 299,180   **b.** 29,918   **c.** 2991.8   **d.** 119.672

6. Write 6.113×10^{-6} in standard notation.

    a. −6,113,000   **b.** 0.00006113   **c.** 0.0000006113   **d.** 0.000006113

7. Write 3.0605×10^{-7} in standard notation.

    a. 0.00000030605   **b.** 0.0000030605   **c.** 0.000000030605   **d.** −306,050,000

8. A particle of dust gathered by a space probe is found to have a mass of 7.05×10^{-13} grams. Express this amount in standard notation.

    a. 0.0000000000000705   **b.** 0.00000000000705

    c. 0.000000000000705   **d.** 705×10^{-11}

9. The land area of China is 3.692×10^{6} square miles, and that of India is 1.18×10^{6} square miles. What is the total land area of China and India expressed in standard notation?

    a. 4,852,000 square miles   **b.** 3,810,000 square miles

    c. 4,872,000 square miles   **d.** 4,685,000 square miles

10. The land surface of the Earth is 57,900,000 square miles. Of this, 19, 200, 000 square miles are forested. Using scientific notation, express the number of square miles that is not forested.

    a. 3.87×10^{7} square miles   **b.** 38.7×10^{6} square miles

    c. 3.87×10^{6} square miles   **d.** 3.87×10^{8} square miles

10.1 Variables and Like Terms _____ *Free Response*

1. Identify all variables in the equation $P = 4s$.

2. Identify all variables in the equation $A = \dfrac{bh}{2}$.

3. Write the equation $C = 2 \times \pi \times r$ without a multiplication sign.

4. Write the equation $V = \dfrac{\pi \times r^2 \times h}{3}$ without a multiplication sign.

5. Combine like terms: $-9x + 7x - 5x$

6. Combine like terms: $-3.1x - 9 + 7x + 21$

7. Combine like terms:
   $-2a + 9b + 2c + 5b + 4a - 12c$

8. Find the perimeter.

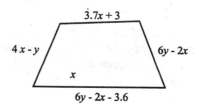

9. Combine like terms: $\dfrac{2}{7}x + \dfrac{3}{8}x + \left(-\dfrac{5}{8}\right)x$

10. Combine like terms: $-\dfrac{2}{5}x + \dfrac{7}{6} + \dfrac{5}{6}x - 8$

10.1 Variables and Like Terms _____ *Multiple Choice*

1. Identify all variable in the equation $V = \pi r^2 h$.

   a. V, π, r, h **b.** V, r, h **c.** V, π, h **d.** r, h

2. Identify all variable in the equation $A = \frac{1}{2}b(h_1 - h_2)$

   a. A, b, h_1, h_2 **b.** $A, 2, b, h_1, h_2$ **c.** b, h_1, h_2 **d.** A, b

3. Write the equation $V = \frac{4 \times \pi \times r^3}{3}$ without a multiplication sign.

   a. $V = \frac{4}{3} \times \pi r^3$ **b.** $V = \frac{\pi r^{12}}{3}$ **c.** $V = 4\pi r^3$ **d.** $V = \frac{4\pi r^3}{3}$

4. Write the equation $T = 4 \times b - 5 \times v$ without a multiplication sign.

   a. $T = 4 + b - 5 + v$ **b.** $T = 4b - 5 \times v$ **c.** $T = 4b - 5v$ **d.** $T = 4b5v$

5. Combine like terms: $-5x - 7.3y + 11.3x - 2.8y - 6.3x + 10.1y$

   a. $-8.3x + 7.1y$ **b.** $8.3x - 7.1y$ **c.** $8.3x - 7.1y$ **d.** 0

6. Combine like terms: $-2x - 4y + 7x - 8y$

   a. $-7xy$ **b.** $5x - 12y$ **c.** $-12x + 5y$ **d.** $-2x + 7x - 4y - 8y$

7. Combine like terms: $-7x + 2.8y - 1.9x - 3y$

   a. $-1.2x - 8.9y$ **b.** $-9.1xy$ **c.** $-8.9x - 0.2y$ **d.** $-7x - 1.9x + 2.8y - 3y$

8. Combine like terms: $4a - 1.4 + 2.2c + 3a + 3 + 6c - 7a$

   a. $8.2c + 1.6$ **b.** $14a + 8.2c + 1.6$ **c.** $6.8c + 3$ **d.** $7a - 3.8c + 1.6$

9. Combine like terms: $-\frac{1}{4}x + \frac{3}{5} + \frac{3}{5}x + \frac{1}{6}$

   a. $\frac{7}{20}x + \frac{23}{30}$ **b.** $\frac{7}{20}x + \frac{1}{10}$ **c.** $-\frac{2}{5}x + \frac{1}{10}$ **d.** $-\frac{17}{20}x + \frac{23}{30}$

10. Combine like terms: $-\frac{1}{2}x - \frac{11}{12}y + \frac{19}{12}x - \frac{1}{6}y - \frac{13}{12}x + \frac{13}{12}y$

    a. $\frac{2}{3}x + \frac{3}{4}y$ **b.** $\frac{5}{6}x + \frac{11}{12}y$ **c.** $\frac{2}{3}x + \frac{11}{12}y$ **d.** 0

10.2 The Distributive Property _____ *Free Response*

1. Simplify: $8(4x-3)$

2. Simplify: $7(9x+6y-11z)$

3. Simplify: $6(1.2x-2.3y+9.5)$

4. Simplify: $5\left(\dfrac{1}{3}x-\dfrac{1}{7}\right)$

5. Simplify: $2\left(\dfrac{1}{3}x+\dfrac{1}{6}y\right)$

6. Simplify: $3(4x+y)+5(x+y)$

7. Simplify: $3(2x-y)-4(x-y)$

8. Simplify: $4(3x+2)+2(x+1)$

9. Simplify: $3(3.8x+4)-7(x+2.8)$

10. Simplify: $7(6x-3)-8(x-4)$

10.2 The Distributive Property _____ *Multiple Choice*

1. Simplify: $3(-6x - 5y - 7z - 6)$
   - **a.** $18x - 15y + 21z - 18$
   - **b.** $-3x - 2y - 4z - 3$
   - **c.** $-18x - 15y - 21z - 18$
   - **d.** $-18x + 15y - 21z + 18$

2. Simplify: $6(-3.7 - 3y - 2.3z)$
   - **a.** $-22.2x + 18y + 13.8z$
   - **b.** $2.3x + 3y + 3.7z$
   - **c.** $22.2x - 18y - 13.8z$
   - **d.** $-22.2x - 18y - 13.8z$

3. Simplify: $3(6x + 0.6y - 6z - 0.6)$
   - **a.** $18x + 1.8y - 18z - 1.8$
   - **b.** $9x + 3.6y - 3x + 2.4$
   - **c.** $-18x + 1.8y + 18z - 1.8$
   - **d.** $18x - 1.8y - 18z + 1.8$

4. Simplify: $2\left(\dfrac{1}{6}x - \dfrac{4}{9}y + \dfrac{1}{9}\right)$
   - **a.** $\dfrac{1}{3}x - \dfrac{4}{9}y + \dfrac{1}{9}$
   - **b.** $\dfrac{1}{3}x - \dfrac{8}{9}y + \dfrac{2}{9}$
   - **c.** $3x - \dfrac{9}{8}y + \dfrac{9}{2}$
   - **d.** $\dfrac{1}{4}x - \dfrac{5}{9}y + \dfrac{2}{9}$

5. Simplify: $\dfrac{1}{6}\left(2x - 11y + 10z + \dfrac{1}{3}\right)$
   - **a.** $\dfrac{2x - 11y + 10z + 1}{18}$
   - **b.** $\dfrac{1}{2}x - \dfrac{5}{3}y + \dfrac{11}{6}z + \dfrac{1}{9}$
   - **c.** $\dfrac{1}{3}x - \dfrac{5}{3}y + \dfrac{11}{6}z + \dfrac{1}{18}$
   - **d.** $\dfrac{1}{3}x - \dfrac{11}{6}y + \dfrac{5}{3}z + \dfrac{1}{18}$

6. Simplify: $3(5x - 1.7y) + 2.6(x + 2y)$
   - **a.** $17.6x + 3.7y$
   - **b.** $17.6x + 10.3y$
   - **c.** $22.8x + 10.3y$
   - **d.** $1.6x + 3.7y|3$

7. Simplify: $-3(2x - 2.9y) - 1.2(-x + 3y)$
   - **a.** $-4.8x + 5.1y$
   - **b.** $-4.8x - 0.1y$
   - **c.** $-2.4x + 5.1y$
   - **d.** $3.2x + 5.9y + 3$

8. Simplify: $3(x + 2y - z) - 3(2x - y + 3z)$
   - **a.** $-3x + 3y - 12z$
   - **b.** $9x + 9y - 12z$
   - **c.** $-3x + 9y - 12z$
   - **d.** $-3x + 9y + 12z$

9. The area of the vertical faces of a rectangular solid with height h and base edges 1 and b can be expressed as $A = h \times 2(1 + b)$. Write this formula without parentheses and without multiplication signs.
   - **a.** $A = 2hl + b$
   - **b.** $A = 2hl + 2hb$
   - **c.** $A = 2h + 1b$
   - **d.** $A = 2hl\,b$

10. The volume of a spherical shell with outer radius R and inner radius r is $V = \frac{4\pi}{3}\left(R^3 - r^3\right)$. Write this formula without parentheses and without multiplication signs.
   - **a.** $V = \dfrac{4\pi R^3 - 4\pi r^3}{3}$
   - **b.** $V = 4\pi R^3 - 4\pi r^3$
   - **c.** $V = \dfrac{4\pi R^3}{3} - r^3$
   - **d.** $V = \dfrac{4\pi R^3 r^3}{3}$

10.3 Solve Equations Using the Addition Property _____ *Free Response*

1. Solve: $a - 7 = 3$

2. Solve: $-10 = f - 9$

3. Solve: $14 = b - 1$

4. Solve: $\dfrac{1}{2} + x = 8$

5. Solve: $c - \dfrac{2}{13} = \dfrac{5}{13}$

6. Solve: $-5.1 + x = 22$

7. Solve: $8.8 = 19.2 - x$

8. Solve: $6p + 12 = 5p + 2$

9. Solve: $4m - 24 = 3m - 15$

10. Solve: $10y = 2y - 9 + 7y$

10.3 Solve Equations Using the Addition Property _____ *Multiple Choice*

1. Solve: $t - 2 = 13$

   a. -11 **b.** -15 **c.** 11 **d.** 15

2. Solve: $16 = -25 + n$

   a. 9 **b.** 41 **c.** -41 **d.** -9

3. Solve: $t - (-8) = 18$

   a. 26 **b.** -10 **c.** 10 **d.** -26

4. Solve: $-2.2 + x = 20.4$

   a. 22.6 **b.** 18.2 **c.** 22.1 **d.** 17.7

5. Solve: $3.5 = 23 - x$

   a. 19 **b.** 26.5 **c.** 19.5 **d.** 26

6. Solve: $x + \dfrac{1}{12} = \dfrac{11}{12}$

   a. $\dfrac{5}{6}$ **b.** 1 **c.** $\dfrac{3}{4}$ **d.** $\dfrac{10}{11}$

7. Solve: $x - \dfrac{14}{25} = -\dfrac{13}{25}$

   a. $-\dfrac{1}{25}$ **b.** $-1\dfrac{2}{25}$ **c.** $1\dfrac{2}{25}$ **d.** $\dfrac{1}{25}$

8. Solve: $-2a + 2 + 3a = 14 - 24$

   a. 40 **b.** 12 **c.** -40 **d.** -12

9. Solve: $-8b + 1 + 6b = -3b + 6$

   a. 6 **b.** -1 **c.** 5 **d.** -6

10. Solve: $3.6p - 12 = 2.6p - 13$

    a. -2 **b.** -1 **c.** 0 **d.** -7

10.4 Solve Equations Using the Division of Multiplication Property _____ *Free Response*

1. Solve: $5a = -30$

2. Solve: $-18 = -2c$

3. Solve: $-6b = -42$

4. Solve: $-8n = 128$

5. Solve: $23t = -115$

6. Solve: $\dfrac{n}{7} = 3$

7. Solve: $-\dfrac{1}{4}b = 8$

8. Solve: $\dfrac{3}{7}x = -\dfrac{6}{35}$

9. Solve: $-\dfrac{3}{4}t = \dfrac{2}{7}$

10. Solve: $-\dfrac{1}{12}c = -2.3$

10.4 Solve Equations Using the Division of Multiplication Property _____ *Multiple Choice*

1. Solve: $32 = -2z$

    a. -16 b. 34 c. -34 d. 1

2. Solve: $-108 = 6t$

    a. 114 b. -114 c. -18 d. 2

3. Solve: $-104 = -8n$

    a. -96 b. 13 c. 96 d. 2

4. Solve: $-4s = -72$

    a. 2 b. -68 c. 68 d. 18

5. Solve: $4t = -18.8$

    a. -0.21 b. -4.7 c. -22.8 d. -75.2

6. Solve: $9 = \dfrac{1}{2}a$

    a. 4 b. 11 c. 18 d. 10

7. Solve: $\dfrac{1}{14}b = -2.39$

    a. 11.61 b. -33.46 c. -6.00 d. 10.61

8. Solve: $-\dfrac{1}{8}a = 0$

    a. 0 b. -8 c. 8 d. 1

9. Solve: $\dfrac{n}{3} = 7$

    a. 9 b. 10 c. 2 d. 21

10. Solve: $\dfrac{1}{7}d = -\dfrac{1}{9}$

    a. $\dfrac{7}{9}$ b. $-\dfrac{9}{7}$ c. $-\dfrac{7}{9}$ d. $\dfrac{9}{7}$

10.5 Solve Equations Using Two Properties _____ *Free Response*

1. Solve: $10 = 3x - 2$

2. Solve: $-17 = 3x + 7$

3. Solve: $176 = 12x + 20$

4. Solve: $\frac{1}{4}x - 4 = -9$

5. Solve: $\frac{1}{2}x - 6 = 4$

6. Solve: $3(4x - 1) = 12$

7. Solve: $9p = 8(7p + 9)$

8. Solve: $12(6c - 2) = 8c - 9$

9. Solve: $2(y + 4) = 3(y - 7)$

10. Solve: $2(2z - 5) = 3(z + 5)$

10.5 Solve Equations Using Two Properties _____ *Multiple Choice*

1. Solve: $10y - 2 = -8 - 5y$

   a. $\dfrac{5}{2}$

   b. $-\dfrac{5}{2}$

   c. $-\dfrac{2}{5}$

   d. $-\dfrac{1}{2}$

2. Solve: $-7p + 9 = 2 - 10p$

   a. $-\dfrac{17}{11}$

   b. $-\dfrac{3}{7}$

   c. $\dfrac{3}{7}$

   d. $-\dfrac{7}{3}$

3. Solve: $6t - 10 = 7 + 3t + 2t$

   a. 17

   b. $\dfrac{1}{17}$

   c. $-\dfrac{1}{17}$

   d. -9

4. Solve: $-\dfrac{5}{6}x - 3 = -38$

   a. 49.2

   b. 42

   c. 45.6

   d. 5.4

5. Solve: $-\dfrac{1}{2}x - 8 = 6$

   a. 2

   b. 4

   c. -12

   d. -28

6. Solve: $4(2z - 5) = 7(z + 3)$

   a. 1

   b. -1

   c. 41

   d. 5

7. Solve: $2x - 4(x - 1) = -3x + 4$

   a. 0

   b. -4

   c. -16

   d. 1

8. Solve: $0.2(-1.5x - 6) = -1.3x - 6$

   a. 0

   b. -4.8

   c. 3

   d. 1.6

9. Solve: $-0.3(x - 4) - 6(0.2x - 0.26) = 0.8(x + 4) - 5.04$

   a. 1.3

   b. 4

   c. 2

   d. 2.83

10. Solve: $2(x - 1) + 2(3x - 3) = 4(x - 6) + 4.4$

    a. -2.9

    b. 0

    c. -5.3

    d. -0.9

10.6 Translating English to Algebra _____ *Free Response*

For problems 1-7, translate the problem into an equation using the variable indicated.

1. The Brown house has 12 more rooms than the Nguyen house. Use *b* for the number of rooms in the Brown house and *n* for the number of rooms in the Nguyen house.

2. The temperature on Monday decreased by 26° on Tuesday. Use *m* for the number of degrees on Monday and *t* for the number of degrees on Tuesday.

3. The length of a rectangle is 5 m longer than triple the width. Use *L* for the length and *W* for the width of the rectangle.

4. When a number is added to another, the total is five times the first number. Use *f* for the first number and *s* for the second number.

5. The number of degrees in the second angle is 7 times the number of degrees in the first angle. Use *f* for the first angle and *s* for the second angle.

6. Robert and James together spent $325 for a used stereo. Let *r* be the amount spent by Robert and *j* be the amount spent by James.

7. The ratio of boys to girls in a school is 4 to 5. Let *b* be the number of boys and *g* be the number of girls.

8. The second angle of a triangle is 8° smaller than the first. The third angle is triple the size of the first angle. Express the second and third angles as separate algebraic expressions, using the variable *x* to represent the first angle.

9. Barbara's hourly salary is $5.40 more than Richard's salary. Express Barbara's salary as an algebraic expression, using *r* to represent Richard's salary.

10. Lake Huron has 23,000 more gallons of water than Lake Superior. Express the amount of water in Lake Huron, using *s* to represent the mount of water in Lake Superior.

10.6 Translating English to Algebra _____ *Multiple Choice*

For problems 1-7, translate the problem into an equation using the variables indicated.

1. The Kellog Building has 19 more floors than the Transcontinental Towers. Use k for the number of floors in the Kellog Building and t for the number of floors in the Transcontinental Towers.

   a. $t = k + 19$ **b.** $k = t + 19$ **c.** $k = 19 - t$ **d.** $k = 19t$

2. The temperature on Friday showed a decrease of 8 degrees compared to the temperature two days before on Wednesday. Use f for the number of degrees on Friday and w for the number of degrees on Wednesday.

   a. $f = w - 8$ **b.** $f = w + 8$ **c.** $f = 2w - 8$ **d.** $f = 8w$

3. Then length of a rectangle is 9 cm greater than twice the width. Use L for the length and W for the width of the rectangle.

   a. $L = 92W$ **b.** $L = 9W + 2$ **c.** $L = 2W + 9$ **d.** $L + W = 92$

4. When a number is added to another number, the total is two times the first number. Use f for the first number and s for the second number.

   a. $f + 2 = s$ **b.** $f + s = 2$ **c.** $s = 2f$ **d.** $f + s = 2f$

5. The length of the second side of a triangle is 5 inches shorter than three times the first side of the triangle. Use f to represent the length of the first side of the triangle and s to represent the length of the second side of the triangle.

   a. $s = 3f + 5$ **b.** $s = 3f - 5$ **c.** $f = 3f - s$ **d.** $f + s = 3f$

6. Raquel and Jeremy both had summer jobs. At the end of the season, they had worked a combined total of 731 hours. Use r for the number of hours Raquel worked and j for the number of hours that Jeremy worked.

   a. $r + j = 731$ **b.** $j = r - 731$ **c.** $r - j = 731$ **d.** $j = 731r$

7. The ratio of brick houses to wooden houses in a particular city is 3 to 8. Let b = the number of brick houses and w = the number of wooden houses.

   a. $\dfrac{b}{b+w} = \dfrac{3}{8}$ or $8b = 3(b + w)$ **b.** $\dfrac{b}{w} = \dfrac{8}{3}$ or $3b = 8w$

   c. $\dfrac{b}{w} = \dfrac{3}{8}$ or $8b = 3w$ **d.** $\dfrac{b}{3} = \dfrac{8}{w}$ or $bw = 24$

For problems 8-10, write an algebraic expression using the given variable.

8. Rashid's monthly salary is $10 more than Fred's monthly salary. Express Rashid's monthly salary as an algebraic expression, using the variable f to represent Fred's salary.

   a. Rashid $= f + 100$ **b.** Rashid $= f - 100$ **c.** Rashid $+ f = 100$ **d.** Rashid $= 100 - f$

9. Lake Regina has 140,000 fewer square feet of surface area than Lake Montrose. Express the square feet of surface area of Lake Regina, R, in an algebraic expression, using the variable M to represent the square feet of surface area of Lake Montrose.

   a. $R = 140,000 - M$ **b.** $R = M = 140,000$

   c. $R = M + 140,000$ **d.** $R = M - 140,000$

10. An Excalibur entertainment console costs $90 less than five times the cost of a Radix radio. Express the cost of an Excalibur entertainment console, E, in an algebraic expression, using the variable r to represent the cost of a Radix radio.

    a. $E = 5r + 90$ **b.** $E = 5r - 90$

    c. $E = 90 - 5r$ **d.** $E + r = 5(90)$

10.6 Applications _____ *Free Response*

1. Together, Jodi and Bob lost 46 pounds on a new diet program. If Bob lost 16 pounds more than Jodi, how many pounds did Jodi lose?

2. Minh needs to cut a 40-foot plank into two pieces such that the longer piece is 18 feet longer than the shorter piece. What is the length of the shorter piece?

3. The perimeter of a square is 48 cm. If each side is doubled, what will be the perimeter of the larger square?

4. The perimeter of a rectangle is 94 m. The length is 7 m longer than triple the width. What are the dimensions of the rectangle?

5. A triangle has three angles: *A*, *B*, and *C*. Angle *B* is double Angle *A*. Angle *C* is 5° larger than Angle *B*. Find the measure of each angle.

6. Sheri Minkner has a triangular plot for crested ducks. The perimeter is 177 feet. The length of the second side is 17 feet more than the length of the first side, and the length of the third side is double the length of the first side. Find the length of each side.

7. Bruce and Ted sell used cars. Since Ted is the better salesperson, he can sell twice cars as Bruce. If they sold a combined total of 63 cars in one week, how many cars did each person sell?

8. The city airport had a total of 84 departures on Monday, Tuesday, and Wednesday. There were 9 more departures on Tuesday than on Monday. There were 6 fewer departures on Wednesday than on Monday. How many departures occurred on each day?

9. A salesperson in an exclusive clothing store earns $2100 per month base pay plus a 5.5% commission on sales. One month he earned $3931.50. What were his sales for that month?

10. A salesperson in a leather store earns $2100 per month base pay plus a commission on sales. One month she earned $5324 on sales of $49,600. What percent is her commission?

10.6 Applications _____ *Multiple Choice*

1. A 15-ft length of pipe is cut into two pieces. The shorter piece is 5 ft shorter than the longer piece. What is the length of the longer piece?

   a. 11 ft   **b.** 12.5 ft   **c.** 10.5 ft   **d.** 10 ft

2. Lisbeth and Rudy went shopping. Together they spent $68. Rudy spent three times as much as Lisbeth. How much did Lisbeth spend?

   a. $51.00   **b.** $17.00   **c.** $4.00   **d.** $34.00

3. For three days in a row, volunteers picked up trash on a particular beach. They picked up a total of 684 pounds. On the second day they collected 12 pounds more than on the first day. On the third day, the picked up 30 pounds less than on the first day. How many pounds of trash did they pick up on the first day?

   a. 618 pounds   **b.** 234 pounds   **c.** 22 pounds   **d.** 242 pounds

4. A hardware store took an inventory of its paint. They had two times as many gallons of red paint than blue paint. They had 16 more gallons of yellow paint than red paint. Taken together, the red, yellow, and blue paint came to 276 gallons. How many gallons of blue paint were there? Round to the nearest tenth of a gallon.

   a. 84.0 gallons   **b.** 78.0 gallons   **c.** 52.0 gallons   **d.** 18.0 gallons

5. To top trim the edges of a rectangular table cloth, 54 feet of lace are needed. The length of the tablecloth is exactly one-half its width. What are the dimensions of the tablecloth?

   a. Length: 9 feet; width: 18 feet   **b.** Length: 18 feet; width: 9 feet

   c. Length: 18 feet; width: 36 feet   **d.** Length: $4\frac{1}{2}$ feet; width: 9 feet

6. A poster in the shape of a triangle has one side that is five inches more than the length of the shortest side, and another side that is three inches less than twice the shortest side. Find the dimensions of the posters if its perimeter is 26 inches.

   a. 6 inches, 11 inches, 10 inches   **b.** 7 inches, 11 inches, 9 inches

   c. 6 inches, 12 inches, 9 inches   **d.** 6 inches, 11 inches, 9 inches

7. A triangle has three angles: R, S, and T. Angle T is 36° greater than angle S. Angle R is 2 times angle S. What is the measurement of each angle?

   a. $S = 38°$, $T = 70°$, $R = 72°$ **b.** $S = 36°$, $T = 72°$, $R = 72°$

   c. $S = 38°$, $T = 72°$, $R = 70°$ **d.** $S = 36°$, $T = 70°$, $R = 74°$

8. A four-sided garden plot has an irregular shape. The second side is 13 feet longer than the first. The third side is 26 feet longer than the second. The fourth side is 39 feet longer than the third. If the perimeter of the plot measures 146 feet, what is the length of the longest side?

   a. 56 feet   **b.** 30 feet   **c.** 82 feet   **d.** 78 feet

9. A rental agent for vacation houses in southern Spain earns a flat amount of base pay per month plus a 5.5% commission on rentals sold during that month. One month he earns $4455 on rental sales of $41,000. What is his base monthly pay?

   a. $2200   **b.** $2300   **c.** $245.03   **d.** $2000

10. The number of dogs licensed in a particular city this year is 1222. This is a 5% increase over last year. How many dog licenses were on record last year? Round to the nearest whole number.

    a. 1217 licenses   **b.** 244 licenses   **c.** 815 licenses   **d.** 1164 licenses

Chapter 1 Whole Numbers

Section 1.1 (FR)

1. $300 + 50 + 2$

2. $80,000 + 5000 + 200 + 60 + 4$

3.   87,306

4.   134,689

5.   6; 5

6.   7;3

7.   100

8.   Two hundred thirty-five thousand, sixty

9.   Sixty-four million, five hundred sixty-eight thousand, nine

10. Seven thousand, ninety-two and $\frac{00}{100}$

Section 1.2 (FR)

1.   26

2.   195

3.   14,265

4.   14,015,625

5.   136,150

6.   18,681

7.   7262

8.   186,737

9.   352

10. 81

Section 1.3 (FR)

1.   476

2.   6212

3.   688

4.   43,185

5.   487,607

6.   28

7.   79

8. $2074

9. $17,027

10. 380,501

Section 1.1 (MC)

1.   a

2.   d

3.   c

4.   b

5.   d

6.   b

7.   a

8.   c

9.   b

10. c

Section 1.2 (MC)

1.   d

2.   b

3.   c

4.   b

5.   c

6.   a

7.   d

8.   b

9.   c

10. d

Section 1.3 (MC)

1.   c

2.   a

3.   d

4.   c

5.   b

6.   b

7.   a

8.   d

9.   d

10. c

Section 1.4 (FR)

1. 13,244
2. 281,560
3. 649,200
4. 333,753
5. 2,752,320
6. 420
7. 3
8. $1449
9. 153
10. 224

Section 1.5 (FR)

1. 9
2. 900
3. 967
4. 324 R2
5. 958 R13
6. 227 R15
7. 13
8. 28
9. $322,000
10. 154 pounds

Section 1.6 (FR)

1. 6^4
2. 9^3
3. 64
4. 243
5. 38
6. 60
7. 159
8. 50
9. 63
10. 161

Section 1.4 (MC)

1. d
2. a
3. c
4. c
5. b
6. d
7. a
8. b
9. b
10. d

Section 1.5 (MC)

1. b
2. d
3. a
4. c
5. c
6. d
7. b
8. a
9. c
10. a

Section 1.6 (MC)

1. a
2. c
3. d
4. b
5. d
6. a
7. b
8. c
9. a
10. d

Section 1.7 (FR)

1. 8870
2. 5000
3. 84,000
4. 30,000,000
5. 600,000
6. 1,800,000
7. Correct. Estimate 4000
8. 2700 miles
9. 36,000
10. 60

Section 1.8 (FR)

1. 899 miles
2. $0.11 per orange
3. 2700 feet
4. $138.36
5. 260 magazines
6. $314
7. 12,280 words
8. $48 per share
9. $775
10. 700,000 people

Section 1.7 (MC)

1. c
2. a
3. d
4. b
5. b
6. a
7. d
8. c
9. b
10. c

Section 1.8 (MC)

1. d
2. b
3. c
4. a
5. c
6. b
7. a
8. d
9. a
10. c

Chapter 2 Fractions

Section 2.1 (FR)

1. N: 7; D: 11

2. N: 13; D: 5

3. $\frac{5}{6}$

4. $\frac{3}{8}$

5.

6.

7. $\frac{48}{177}$

8. $\frac{220}{248}$

9. $\frac{88}{96}$

10. $\frac{27}{96}$

Section 2.2 (FR)

1. $3 \times 3 \times 7$

2. $2 \times 7 \times 11$

3. $\frac{3}{7}$

4. $\frac{11}{18}$

5. $\frac{4}{9}$

6. $\frac{7}{11}$

7. $\frac{2}{7}$

8. No

9. $\frac{1}{44}$

10. $\frac{7}{75}$

Section 2.3 (FR)

1. $\frac{37}{7}$

2. $\frac{53}{6}$

3. $8\frac{1}{5}$

4. 9

5. $\frac{21}{10}$

6. 3

7. $6\frac{1}{9}$

8. $14\frac{1}{7}$

9. $\frac{53}{8}$

10. $\frac{495}{23}$

Section 2.1 (MC)

1. a

2. d

3. c

4. c

5. b

6. a

7. d

8. b

9. a

10. c

Section 2.2 (MC)

1. b

2. a

3. d

4. c

5. d

6. a

7. c

8. b

9. b

10. d

Section 2.3 (MC)

1. c

2. d

3. b

4. a

5. a

6. d

7. b

8. c

9. d

10. a

Section 2.4 (FR)

1. $\frac{27}{77}$

2. $\frac{8}{33}$

3. $2\frac{8}{9}$

4. 20

5. $44\frac{1}{3}$

6. $\frac{4}{5}$

7. 41 feet

8. $1350

9. $777

10. 119 square feet

Section 2.5 (FR)

1. $\frac{3}{2} = 1\frac{1}{2}$

2. 0

3. $\frac{5}{56}$

4. 9

5. $\frac{81}{50} = 1\frac{31}{50}$

6. $\frac{23}{13} = 1\frac{10}{13}$

7. $\frac{21}{5} = 4\frac{1}{5}$

8. $\frac{28}{18} = 1\frac{7}{18}$ feet

9. 1908 boxes

10. 12 pieces

Section 2.6 (FR)

1. 72

2. 225

3. 30

4. 60

5. 30

6. 180

7. 10

8. 42

9. $\frac{7}{20} = \frac{28}{80}$; $\frac{5}{16} = \frac{25}{80}$

10. $\frac{7}{30} = \frac{21}{90}$; $\frac{2}{15} = \frac{12}{90}$; $\frac{23}{45} = \frac{46}{90}$

Section 2.4 (MC)

1. d

2. b

3. c

4. a

5. c

6. b

7. a

8. d

9. c

10. b

Section 2.5 (MC)

1. b

2. c

3. a

4. d

5. d

6. b

7. c

8. a

9. a

10. b

Section 2.6 (MC)

1. c

2. a

3. d

4. b

5. a

6. c

7. d

8. b

9. c

10. d

Basic College Mathematics
Answers to Additional Exercises

Section 2.7 (FR)

1. $\frac{1}{7}$

2. $\frac{59}{72}$

3. $\frac{3}{4}$

4. $\frac{19}{20}$

5. $\frac{33}{70}$

6. $\frac{41}{84}$

7. $\frac{1}{3}$

8. $\frac{5}{12}$

9. $\frac{70}{117}$

10. $\frac{41}{65}$

Section 2.8 (FR)

1. $1\frac{1}{2}$

2. $8\frac{17}{18}$

3. $12\frac{1}{3}$

4. $14\frac{29}{40}$

5. $16\frac{1}{24}$

6. $\frac{2}{3}$

7. $2\frac{1}{12}$

8. $\frac{1}{18}$

9. $6\frac{4}{7}$ feet

10. $17\frac{17}{18}$ miles

Section 2.9 (FR)

1. $24\frac{1}{2}$ feet

2. $36\frac{1}{5}$ pounds

3. $3\frac{7}{24}$ feet

4. 27 floors

5. $91\frac{7}{8}$ gallons

6. $420

7. $206.25

8. $30.88

9. 44 years

10. 425 cubic feet

Section 2.7 (MC)

1. a

2. d

3. c

4. a

5. b

6. b

7. c

8. b

9. d

10. a

Section 2.8 (MC)

1. b

2. d

3. a

4. c

5. a

6. b

7. d

8. c

9. b

10. d

Section 2.9 (MC)

1. d

2. c

3. a

4. b

5. c

6. d

7. a

8. d

9. c

10. a

Chapter 3 Decimals

Section 3.1 (FR)

1. Nine and six hundred seventy-one thousandths

2. Four hundred twenty-three thousandths

3. Eight hundred twenty-three and $\frac{86}{100}$ dollars

4. 0.09

5. 0.263

6. 8.294

7. 0.796

8. 31.52

9. $\frac{18}{25}$

10. $36\frac{1}{4}$

Section 3.2 (FR)

1. <

2. =

3. 1.9

4. 17.48

5. 8.612

6. $17.24

7. Order is 1.853, 1.583, 1.538, 1.358

8. Order is 0.4001, $\frac{4}{10}$, 0.041, 0.0401, $\frac{4}{100}$, 0.0141, 0.0049, 0.00069

9. 14.3 ounces

10. $18.00

Section 3.3 (FR)

1. 326.596

2. 391.42

3. 53.628

4. 11.727

5. 3.811

6. 10.94 feet

7. 377.62

8. $403.27

9. $18.04

10. $36.58

Section 3.1 (MC)

1. d
2. a
3. c
4. b
5. a
6. b
7. d
8. d
9. c
10. a

Section 3.2 (MC)

1. b
2. a
3. d
4. c
5. c
6. b
7. a
8. d
9. b
10. c

Section 3.3 (MC)

1. a
2. d
3. a
4. c
5. b
6. b
7. d
8. c
9. a
10. b

Answers to Additional Exercises

Section 3.4 (FR)

1. 0.0054
2. 92.986
3. 0.005016
4. 363.6404
5. 361.8
6. 19.58
7. 100,983
8. 1.04 grams
9. $250.20
10. 41.34 inches

Section 3.5 (FR)

1. 0.16
2. 0.0083
3. 6.9
4. 0.005
5. 59.9
6. 21.33
7. 41
8. 22
9. 5.8 ounces
10. 10 trains

Section 3.6 (FR)

1. 1.4375
2. $0.2\overline{6}$
3. 0.704
4. 0.469
5. 19.06
6. 6.34
7. 8.55
8. 72.02
9. 19.875 inches
10. 0.27

Section 3.4 (MC)

1. c
2. b
3. d
4. a
5. a
6. b
7. c
8. d
9. a
10. d

Section 3.5 (MC)

1. d
2. c
3. a
4. b
5. c
6. d
7. b
8. a
9. b
10. c

Section 3.6 (MC)

1. b
2. c
3. a
4. d
5. d
6. c
7. a
8. b
9. d
10. a

Answers to Additional Exercises

Section 3.7 (FR)

1. 88; 89.73

2. 17; 17.3372

3. 65; 66.44

4. 793; 842.177

5. 150; 146.01

6. 1200; 1046.542

7. 8.75; 9.3

8. 4; 3.9

9. $25.77

10. 6933.72 square feet

Section 3.7 (MC)

1. a

2. d

3. b

4. c

5. b

6. d

7. c

8. a

9. c

10. b

Chapter 4 Ratio and Proportion

Section 4.1 (FR)

1. $\frac{5}{12}$

2. $\frac{3}{19}$

3. $\frac{28}{27}$

4. $\frac{8 \text{ yards}}{1 \text{ second}}$

5. $\frac{1 \text{ test}}{7 \text{ students}}$

6. $\frac{59 \text{ miles}}{2 \text{ gallons}}$

7. $125/week

8. 4 cars/household

9. Same

10. Popcorn Deal #1

Section 4.2 (FR)

1. $\frac{6}{10} = \frac{3}{5}$

2. $\frac{6.5}{3} = \frac{85.5}{7}$

3. $\frac{5 \text{ pounds}}{\$35} = \frac{3 \text{ pounds}}{\$21}$

4. $\frac{76 \text{ pounds}}{190 \text{ children}}$

5. a. No   b. No

6. a. No   b. Yes

7. a. Yes   b. Yes

8. Yes

9. No

10. Yes

Section 4.3 (FR)

1. 12

2. 2.9

3. 48

4. $\frac{15}{2} = 7\frac{1}{2}$

5. 8

6. 0.0225

7. 39.2

8. 48.3

9. 30

10. 3.9 inches

Section 4.1 (MC)

1. d
2. b
3. a
4. c
5. b
6. d
7. c
8. a
9. b
10. b

Section 4.2 (MC)

1. b
2. c
3. a
4. d
5. d
6. a
7. c
8. a
9. b
10. a

Section 4.3 (MC)

1. c
2. a
3. d
4. b
5. a
6. c
7. b
8. d
9. a
10. d

Section 4.4 (FR)

1.   117 minutes

2.   31.5 pages

3.   10 feet

4.   330 students

5.   24.15 kilometers

6.   14 gallons

7.   150 fish

8. $\frac{5}{16}$ tsp

9. $\frac{11}{16}$ cup

10. 3 tsp

Section 4.4 (MC)

1.   a

2.   d

3.   b

4.   c

5.   c

6.   d

7.   b

8.   a

9.   c

10. b

Chapter 5 Percent

Section 5.1 (FR)

1. 80%

2. 3.7%

3. 0.43

4. 0.155

5. 0.2293

6. 37%

7. 95.6%

8. 38%

9. 67%

10. 13.064%

Section 5.2 (FR)

1. $\frac{5}{8}$

2. $13\frac{2}{5}$

3. 29%

4. 537.5%

5. $91\frac{2}{3}\%$

6. 460%

7. $0.35 = \frac{7}{20}$

8. $0.28 = 28\%$

9. 88.89%

10. $\frac{57}{100}$

Section 5.3 (FR)

1. 20

2. 602.3

3. 1227

4. 18.4

5. 485

6. 200

7. 1%

8. 64

9. $\frac{a}{64.1} = \frac{78}{100}$

10. $\frac{33.7}{b} = \frac{10}{100}$

Section 5.1 (MC)

1. d

2. b

3. c

4. a

5. b

6. d

7. a

8. c

9. d

10. b

Section 5.2 (MC)

1. b

2. c

3. a

4. d

5. c

6. b

7. d

8. a

9. c

10. a

Section 5.3 (MC)

1. a

2. d

3. b

4. c

5. d

6. a

7. c

8. b

9. b

10. d

Section 5.4 (FR)

1. 36
2. 60%
3. 50%
4. $24
5. $11,250,000
6. $3.55
7. $64.56
8. $21.24
9. $37,664.00
10. $65.00

Section 5.5 (FC)

1. $6118.95
2. $6135.60
3. 12%
4. 1.8%
5. 60%
6. 20%
7. 204
8. $10.22
9. 9.5%
10. $1427.67

Section 5.4 (MC)

1. c
2. a
3. d
4. b
5. a
6. c
7. b
8. d
9. a
10. c

Section 5.5 (MC)

1. b
2. c
3. d
4. a
5. b
6. d
7. a
8. c
9. b
10. a

Chapter 6 Measurement

Section 6.1 (FR)

1. 42
2. 4000
3. 72
4. 48
5. 18
6. 4
7. 2880
8. 2.75 cups
9. $45.00
10. 11,000 pounds

Section 6.2 (FR)

1. 54,000
2. 88,600
3. 0.0000173
4. 72,400
5. 21
6. 50.5
7. 103.9 cm
8. 66,686 cm
9. 16.227
10. 13.1

Section 6.3 (FR)

1. 27,000
2. 0.314
3. 43,000
4. 20,000,000
5. 0.0373
6. 0.149
7. 142.331 L
8. 163.2 mL
9. 41.861 L
10. 2.29 ml

Section 6.1 (MC)

1. c
2. a
3. d
4. b
5. d
6. c
7. a
8. a
9. b
10. d

Section 6.2 (MC)

1. d
2. b
3. a
4. c
5. c
6. a
7. b
8. b
9. d
10. c

Section 6.3 (MC)

1. a
2. d
3. c
4. b
5. b
6. d
7. c
8. a
9. c
10. d

Section 6.4 (FR)

1. 118.08 in.
2. 7.17 m
3. 21.12 gal
4. 37.84 L
5. 112.2 lb
6. 170.1 g
7. 146.67 ft/sec
8. 16.7° C
9. 626° F
10. 2.05 g

Section 6.5 (FR)

1. 5.5 ft
2. 37 yd
3. $28.68
4. 245 cm
5. 775 mL
6. 67.5 gal
7. 141.75 g
8. The oven is set 5.4° F more than it should be
9. 16.5 feet
10. $26.25

Section 6.4 (MC)

1. b
2. c
3. a
4. d
5. d
6. b
7. a
8. c
9. a
10. d

Section 6.5 (MC)

1. c
2. d
3. b
4. a
5. a
6. c
7. b
8. d
9. c
10. a

Chapter 7 Geometry

Section 7.1 (FR)

1. Right angle
2. Acute angle
3. 55°
4. 90°
5. 145°
6. 22°
7. 77°
8. 42°
9. 117°
10. 57°

Section 7.2 (FR)

1. 46 cm
2. 11.6 ft
3. $P = 22$ in. $A = 28$ ft^2
4. $P = 11.2$ ft $A = 7.84$ ft^2
5. 144 m
6. 76 m
7. 112 ft
8. 171 m^2
9. 120 in.^{2}
10. $92,568

Section 7.3 (FR)

1. 148 m
2. 150 m
3. 465 yd^2
4. 442 ft^2
5. 126 ft^2
6. 80 m
7. 64 m^2
8. 311.5 in.^{2}
9. 526.5 ft^2
10. 4.985 in^2

Section 7.1 (MC)

1. d
2. b
3. c
4. a
5. c
6. a
7. d
8. b
9. c
10. a

Section 7.2 (MC)

1. b
2. c
3. a
4. d
5. b
6. c
7. a
8. d
9. b
10. d

Section 7.3 (MC)

1. c
2. d
3. b
4. a
5. b
6. d
7. b
8. c
9. a
10. d

Section 7.4 (FR)

1. False
2. True
3. 130°
4. 128°
5. 26 cm
6. 30 cm
7. 86.4 units^2
8. 119.32 cm^2
9. 83.2 in.^{2}
10. 240 ft^2

Section 7.5 (FR)

1. 8
2. 13
3. 5
4. 2
5. 60
6. 56
7. 2.449
8. 12.124
9. 9 m
10. 1.2

Section 7.6 (FR)

1. 5 cm
2. 19.183 mi
3. 19.313 mi
4. 16 km
5. Leg = 12 yd
6. Hypotenuse = 8.944 ft
7. 17.2 yd
8. 15.6 mi
9. 7.5 in.;
   13.0 in.
10. 21.2 cm

Section 7.4 (MC)

1. a
2. a
3. d
4. c
5. d
6. a
7. c
8. b
9. c
10. a

Section 7.5 (MC)

1. b
2. c
3. a
4. d
5. c
6. b
7. a
8. d
9. b
10. c

Section 7.6 (MC)

1. c
2. d
3. b
4. a
5. b
6. d
7. a
8. c
9. d
10. a

Basic College Mathematics
Answers to Additional Exercises

Section 7.7 (FR)

1. 39 yd
2. 12.4 m
3. 128.74 in.
4. 235.5 in.
5. 490.6 cm^2
6. 226.1 mi^2
7. 882.7 in.^{2}
8. 530.66 ft^2
9. 28,938.24 mi^2
10. $602.24

Section 7.8 (FR)

1. 90 in.^{3}
2. 1980 cm^3
3. 1846.3 m^3
4. 565.2 cm^3
5. 3052.1 cm^3
6. 923.2 in^3
7. 300 ft^3
8. 310 yd^3
9. 80,965,600 lb
10. $353.60

Section 7.9 (FC)

1. 9 m
2. 24 m
3. 12.8 yd
4. *a* corresponds to *d*
   c corresponds to *e*
   b corresponds to *f*
5. *a* corresponds to *d*
   b corresponds to *e*
   c corresponds to *f*
6. 48 yd
7. 19.6 cm
8. 63.9 ft
9. 2.3 ft
10. 33.3 m

Section 7.7 (MC)

1. d
2. a
3. c
4. b
5. a
6. c
7. a
8. d
9. c
10. b

Section 7.8 (MC)

1. b
2. d
3. a
4. c
5. d
6. a
7. b
8. b
9. d
10. c

Section 7.9 (MC)

1. a
2. c
3. b
4. d
5. c
6. b
7. a
8. c
9. b
10. a

Section 7.10 (FR)

1. $73.60

2. 45 minutes

3. 337 ft^2

4. 187.6 bushels

5. $14,469.12

6. 22,608 km/hr

7. 217,036.8 in.^{3}

8. 8641.3 in.^{3}

9. 28 km

10. 40 km/hr

Section 7.10 (MC)

1. c

2. b

3. d

4. a

5. b

6. d

7. c

8. a

9. b

10. d

Chapter 8 Statistics

Section 8.1 (FR)	Section 8.2 (FR)	Section 8.3 (FR)
1. Ming	1. Week 4	1. 30
2. 56	2. 110	2. 25
3. 48	3. Week 6	3. 10
4. 264	4. 4th quarter	4. 20
5. Yes	5. $15 million	5. 9
6. Ben	6. $165 million	6. 75
7. 126	7. 78° F	7. 5
8. 42	8. 6° F	8. 9
9. 364	9. Weeks 5-7	9. 5
10. Yes	10. 24 vehicles	10. 6

Section 8.1 (MC)	Section 8.2 (MC)	Section 8.3 (MC)
1. d	1. c	1. b
2. b	2. a	2. c
3. c	3. d	3. a
4. a	4. b	4. d
5. a	5. c	5. b
6. b	6. d	6. a
7. c	7. a	7. d
8. d	8. b	8. c
9. d	9. b	9. a
10. c	10. a	10. d

Section 8.4 (FR)

1. 16.5 points

2. 67 tickets

3. 86.3 miles

4. 44

5. 23

6. 28.5

7. 36

8. 54 and 92

9. 83

10. 57 and 63

Section 8.4 (MC)

1. a

2. d

3. b

4. c

5. b

6. a

7. c

8. d

9. c

10. a

Chapter 9 Signed Numbers

Section 9.1 (FR)

1. -54
2. 1.8
3. $-5\frac{1}{6}$
4. 7
5. -5
6. $\frac{37}{90}$
7. $+\$32,000$
8. $-\$13,000$
9. $7°$ F
10. 160 pounds

Section 9.2 (FR)

1. -16
2. 14
3. 10.1
4. $-\frac{1}{4}$
5. $7\frac{5}{7}$
6. -14
7. 17
8. -1.5
9. $\$335$
10. $\$36.65$

Section 9.3 (FR)

1. -120
2. -17.088
3. $-\frac{3}{10}$
4. 15
5. $-\frac{12}{19}$
6. 100
7. -36
8. 420
9. $\$13,922$
10. $-12°$

Section 9.1 (MC)

1. b
2. a
3. d
4. c
5. d
6. a
7. c
8. b
9. d
10. b

Section 9.2 (MC)

1. d
2. c
3. a
4. b
5. c
6. d
7. a
8. b
9. a
10. d

Section 9.3 (MC)

1. c
2. d
3. b
4. a
5. b
6. c
7. d
8. a
9. a
10. d

Basic College Mathematics
Answers to Additional Exercises

Section 9.4 (FR)

1. -1

2. 53

3. $-\frac{1}{20}$

4. $-\frac{1}{6}$

5. -27.2

6. -4.9

7. 9 yards gained

8. A loss of 11 yards

9. 1.4 pounds

10. $-5°$ C

Section 9.5 (FR)

1. 1.74×10^3

2. 7.16×10^5

3. 1.463×10^{-4}

4. 9.3×10^{-3}

5. 13,900

6. 714,800,000

7. 0.006951

8. 9.03×10^7 dollars

9. 2.58×10^9 atoms

10. 14,000,000,000 tons

Section 9.4 (MC)

1. a

2. b

3. d

4. c

5. a

6. a

7. b

8. c

9. b

10. d

Section 9.5 (MC)

1. b

2. d

3. a

4. c

5. b

6. d

7. a

8. c

9. c

10. a

Chapter 10 Introduction to Algebra

Section 10.1 (FR)

1. P, s
2. A, b, h
3. $C = 2\pi r$
4. $V = \frac{\pi r^2 h}{3}$
5. $-7x$
6. $3.9x + 12$
7. $2a + 14b - 10c$
8. $3.7x + 11y - 0.6$
9. $\frac{1}{28}x$
10. $\frac{13}{30}x - 6\frac{5}{6}$

Section 10.2 (FR)

1. $32x - 24$
2. $63x + 42y - 77z$
3. $7.2x - 13.8y + 57$
4. $\frac{5}{3}x - \frac{5}{7}$
5. $\frac{2}{3}x + \frac{1}{3}y$
6. $17x + 8y$
7. $2x + y$
8. $14x + 10$
9. $4.4x - 7.6$
10. $34x + 11$

Section 10.3 (FR)

1. 10
2. -1
3. 15
4. $7\frac{1}{2}$
5. $\frac{7}{13}$
6. 27.1
7. 10.4
8. -10
9. 9
10. -9

Section 10.1 (MC)

1. b
2. a
3. d
4. c
5. d
6. b
7. c
8. a
9. a
10. d

Section 10.2 (MC)

1. c
2. d
3. a
4. b
5. d
6. b
7. a
8. c
9. b
10. a

Section 10.3 (MC)

1. d
2. b
3. c
4. a
5. c
6. a
7. d
8. d
9. c
10. b

Section 10.4 (FR)

1. -6
2. 9
3. 7
4. -16
5. -5
6. 21
7. -32
8. $-\frac{2}{5}$
9. $-\frac{8}{21}$
10. 27.6

Section 10.5 (FR)

1. 4
2. -8
3. 13
4. -20
5. 20
6. $\frac{5}{4}$
7. $-\frac{72}{47}$
8. $\frac{15}{64}$
9. 29
10. 25

Section 10.6 (FR)

1. $b = 12 + n$
2. $m = t + 26$
3. $L = 3W + 5$
4. $f + s = 5f$
5. $s = 7f$
6. $r + j = 325$
7. $\frac{b}{g} = \frac{4}{5}$ or 5b=4g
8. Second angle $= x - 8$
   Third angle $= 3x$
9. Barbara's salary
   $= r + 5.40$
10. Lake Huron
    $= s + 23,000$

Section 10.4 (MC)

1. a
2. c
3. b
4. d
5. b
6. c
7. b
8. a
9. d
10. c

Section 10.5 (MC)

1. c
2. d
3. a
4. b
5. d
6. c
7. a
8. b
9. c
10. a

Section 10.6 (MC)

1. b
2. a
3. c
4. d
5. b
6. a
7. c
8. a
9. d
10. b

Section 10.7

1. 15 lb

2. 11 ft

3. 96 cm

4. Width = 10 m
   Length = 37 m

5. Angle A = 35°
   Angle B = 70°
   Angle C = 75°

6. 40 ft, 57 ft, 80 ft

7. Bruce = 21 cars
   Ted = 42 cars

8. Monday = 27
   Tuesday = 36
   Wednesday = 21

9. $33,300

10. 6.5%

Section 10.7 (MC)

1. d

2. b

3. b

4. c

5. a

6. d

7. b

8. c

9. a

10. d

If you are familiar with the topics in this chapter, take this test now. If you can't answer a question, study the appropriate section of the chapter. If you are not familiar with the topics in this chapter, don't take this test now. Instead, study the examples, work the practice problems, and then take the test. This test will help you identify which concepts you have mastered, and which you need to study further.

1. Write in words: 352,416

2. Write in expanded notation: 43,289

3. Write in standard notation: Eight million, seventy-four thousand, six hundred twenty-five

Use the following table to answer questions 4 and 5:

Year	Public H.S. Graduates (in thousands)
1980	2747
1995	2273
2000	2583

4. How many public school graduates were there in 1995?

5. How many public school graduates were there in 2000?

6. Add:
$$\begin{array}{r} 15 \\ 26 \\ 82 \\ +\ 41 \\ \hline \end{array}$$

7. Add:
$$\begin{array}{r} 32{,}162 \\ 5{,}029 \\ +\ 19{,}756 \\ \hline \end{array}$$

8. Add:
$$\begin{array}{r} 6251 \\ 400 \\ 18 \\ +\ 8093 \\ \hline \end{array}$$

9. Subtract:
$$\begin{array}{r} 8953 \\ -\ 6812 \\ \hline \end{array}$$

10. Subtract:
$$\begin{array}{r} 200{,}680 \\ -\ 23{,}129 \\ \hline \end{array}$$

11. Subtract:
$$\begin{array}{r} 68{,}819{,}236 \\ -\ 24{,}857{,}792 \\ \hline \end{array}$$

12. Multiply: $8 \times 3 \times 1 \times 4$

13. Multiply: $\begin{array}{r} 3462 \\ \times\ \ \ 7 \\ \hline \end{array}$

14. Multiply: $\begin{array}{r} 84 \\ \times 63 \\ \hline \end{array}$

15. Multiply: $\begin{array}{r} 491 \\ \times 803 \\ \hline \end{array}$

16. Divide: $0 \div 2$

17. Divide and indicate the remainder: $7\overline{)32,076}$

18. Divide: $43\overline{)7998}$

19. Write in exponential form: $5 \times 5 \times 5 \times 5 \times 5 \times 5$

20. Evaluate: 4^3

21. Perform the operations in the proper order:
$$3 \times 2^4 - (5+1)^2$$

22. Perform the operations in the proper order:
$$3^3 + (5^2 + 10) \div 7$$

23. Perform the operations in the proper order:
$$4 \times 8 - 2 \times 5 - 2^3 + 19 \div 19$$

24. Round to the nearest thousand: 582,794

25. Round to the nearest hundred: 83,432

26. Round to the nearest million: 19,517,000

27. Use the principle of estimation to find an estimate:
$296 + 112 + 672 + 201$

28. Use the principle of estimation to find an estimate:
$58,192 \times 488,321$

29. Sam planned a trip of 1692 miles to Atlanta. He traveled 718 miles on the first day. How many miles must he travel on the second day to reach his destination?

30. Sally bought 93 CDs at a total cost of $1395. How much did each CD cost?

31. Tom bought four chairs at $37 each, two lamps at $19 each, and three end tables at $26 each. How much did the total purchase cost?

31. Using the table below, how much did the population of Alaska increase from 1970 to 1990?

Population for the State of Alaska, U.S. Census Report

Year	1970	1980	1990	2000
Population	302,853	401,851	550,043	653,000

If you <u>are</u> familiar with the topics in this chapter, take this test now. If you can't answer a question, study the appropriate section of the chapter. If you are <u>not</u> familiar with the topics in this chapter, don't take this test now. Instead, study the examples, work the practice problems, and then take the test. This test will help you identify which concepts you have mastered, and which you need to study further.

_____ **1.** Write in words: 853,926

    a. Eight hundred fifty-three thousand, nine hundred twenty-six

    b. Eight hundred fifty-three, nine twenty-six

    c. Eight five three, nine two six

    d. Eight hundred fifty-three million, nine hundred thousand, twenty-six

_____ **2.** Write in expanded notation: 721,859

    a. $700+20+1+800+50+9$ **b.** $700,000+20+1+859$

    c. $700,000+20,000+100+800+500+9$ **d.** $700,000+20,000+1000+800+50+9$

_____ **3.** Write in standard notation: Seven million, twenty-four thousand, six hundred eighty-five

    a. 724,685   **b.** 7,024,685   **c.** 7,240,685   **d.** 7,240,600,085

Use the following table to answer questions 4 and 5:

Year	Public H.S. Graduates (in thousands)
1980	2747
1995	2273
2000	2583

_____ **4.** How many public school graduates were there in 1980?

    a. 1995   **b.** 2747   **c.** 2273   **d.** 2000

_____ **5.** How many public school graduates were there in 1995?

    a. 2273   **b.** 2000   **c.** 1980   **d.** 2747

_____ **6.** Add: 25
          37
          82
      + 59

    a. 183   **b.** 1823   **c.** 203   **d.** 218

_____ **7.** Add: 31,472
        5,528
     + 26,783

    a. 52,783   **b.** 52,763   **c.** 63,783   **d.** 63,673

____ **8.** Add: 7261
        300
         92
  + 5048

  a. 12,701   **b.** 12,501

  c. 12,791   **d.** 12,591

____ **9.** Subtract: 8764
       − 2513

  a. 6277   **b.** 6251

  c. 6257   **d.** 6351

____ **10.** Subtract: 500,280
       − 24,237

  a. 476,057   **b.** 476,050

  c. 476,053   **d.** 476,043

____ **11.** Subtract: 76,517,225
       − 34,563,894

  a. 43,954,671   **b.** 43,964,444

  c. 42,054,444   **d.** 42,054,671

____ **12.** Multiply: $9 \times 2 \times 1 \times 3$

  a. 54   **b.** 27   **c.** 48   **d.** 63

____ **13.** Multiply: 7451
       × 8

  a. 56,208   **b.** 59,608

  c. 592,408   **d.** 58,808

____ **14.** Multiply: 93
       ×54

  a. 5022   **b.** 144

  c. 8127   **d.** 48,762

____ **15.** Multiply: 392
       × 704

  a. 22,044   **b.** 4704

  c. 2108   **d.** 275,968

____ **16.** Divide: $28 \div 7$

  a. 14   **b.** 5   **c.** 3   **d.** 4

____ **17.** Divide. If there is a remainder, be sure to state it as part of the answer:

$7\overline{)32,078}$

   a. 4582 R3   **b.** 31,582 R3

   c. 4582 R4   **d.** 4582

____ **18.** Divide. If there is a remainder, be sure to state it as part of the answer:

$42\overline{)7392}$

   a. 176 R25   **b.** 176

   c. 1052 R25   **d.** 1052

____ **19.** Write in exponential form: $5 \times 5 \times 5 \times 5$

   a. 5^3 **b.** 5^4 **c.** 5^5 **d.** 5^2

____ **20.** Evaluate: 2^5

   a. 32   **b.** 16   **c.** 48   **d.** 24

____ **21.** Perform the operations in their proper order: $4 \times 2^3 - (3+1)^2$

   a. 21   **b.** 22   **c.** 900   **d.** 16

____ **22.** Perform the operations in their proper order: $2^4 + (4^2 + 26) \div 7$

   a. 8   **b.** 22   **c.** 6   **d.** 24

____ **23.** Perform the operations in their proper order: $5 \times 7 - 3 \times 6 - 3^2 + 21 \div 21$

   a. 236   **b.** 183   **c.** 9   **d.** 35,721

____ **24.** Round to the nearest thousand: 683,884

   a. 684,000   **b.** 683,900   **c.** 680,000   **d.** 700,000

____ **25.** Round to the nearest hundred: 53,649

   a. 53,700   **b.** 53,650   **c.** 54,000   **d.** 53,600

____ **26.** Round to the nearest million: 29,546,000

   a. 30,000,000   **b.** 29,500,000   **c.** 29,550,000   **d.** 29,000,000

____ **27.** Use the principle of estimation to find an estimate for the calculation: $486 + 274 + 521 + 309$

    a. 1600   **b.** 1700   **c.** 1400   **d.** 1500

____ **28.** Use the principle of estimation to find an estimate for the calculation: $78,283 \times 218,974$

    a. 17,000,000,000   **b.** 16,500,000,000   **c.** 16,000,000,000   **d.** 18,500,000,000

____ **29.** Sam planned a trip of 1482 miles to Atlanta. He traveled 637 miles on the first day. How many miles must he travel on the second day to reach his destination?

    a. 2119 miles   **b.** 845 miles   **c.** 1255 miles   **d.** 855 miles

____ **30.** Sally purchased 87 CDs at a cost of $1218. How much did each CD cost?

    a. $13   **b.** $15   **c.** $10   **d.** $14

____ **31.** Tom bought four chairs at $34 each, two lamps at $26 each, and three end tables at $18 each. How much did the total purchase cost?

    a. $78   **b.** $242   **c.** $156   **d.** $224

____ **32.** How much did the population of Alaska increase from 1970 to 2000?

Population for the State of Alaska, U.S. Census Report

Year	1970	1980	1990	2000
Population	302,853	401,851	550,043	653,000

    a. 251,149   **b.** 248,000   **c.** 350,417   **d.** 247,460

1. Write in standard notation: Four million, three hundred five thousand, six hundred and five

2. Add: 292
          81
           3
        + 255

3. Add: $429 + 205 + 28$

4. Subtract: 232,062
             - 15,235

5. Multiply: $6 \times 11 \times 2 \times 4$

6. Multiply: 29
             $\times$ 54

7. Multiply: 691×7

8. Divide: $6\overline{)3702}$

9. Write in exponential form: $7 \times 7 \times 7 \times 7$

10. Round to the nearest hundred: 37,596

11. Perform each operation in the proper order:
$$3^3 + 3 \times 4 \div 2 - 2^2 \times (8 - 6)$$

12. Perform each operation in the proper order:
$$3 \times 3 \times 2 + 3 - 10 \div 2 + 2^4$$

13. Estimate the answer using the principle of estimation:
$$2005 + 4798 + 7816$$

14. A club purchased five boxes of paper at $15 per box, nine boxes of envelopes at $4 per box, and fourteen pens at $2 each. The six members agreed to divide the cost equally. Assuming no sales tax, how much did each member have to pay?

15. Jennifer had $191 when she started shopping. She bought two belts at $29 each, a blouse for $57, and a pair of shoes for $49. Assuming no sales tax, how much money did she have left after paying her bill?

1. Write in standard notation: Eight million, eight hundred forty-four thousand, one hundred and three

2. Add: $34 + 721 + 561$

3. Add: 423
         927
       $+\ 848$

4. Subtract: 9732
             $-\ 4417$

5. Multiply: $10 \times 2 \times 5 \times 7$

6. Multiply: 36
             $\times\ 42$

7. Multiply: 462×8

8. Divide: $3\overline{)2705}$

9. Write in exponential form: $3 \times 3 \times 3 \times 3 \times 3 \times 3$

10. Round to the nearest ten thousand: 2,547,423

11. Perform each operation in the proper order:
$$2^3 \times 3 \div 8 + 10 \times 6 - 2$$

12. Perform each operation in the proper order:
$$4^3 - 10 \div 2 + 5 \times 3 + 2^2$$

13. Estimate the answer using the principle of estimation:
$$219 + 299 + 5129$$

14. Mary owns 112 acres of farmland. She rents it to a farmer for $750 per acre per year. Her property taxes are $290 per acre per year. How much profit does she make on land each year?

15. Randy drove his car 6300 miles and used 252 gallons of gas. How many miles per gallon did his car get?

1. Write in standard notation: Ninety-five million, six hundred thirty-four thousand, seven hundred and eighty three

2. Add: $524 + 19 + 376$

3. Add: $\begin{array}{r} 23{,}691 \\ + \ 28{,}444 \\ \hline \end{array}$

4. Subtract: $\begin{array}{r} 3989 \\ - \ 1728 \\ \hline \end{array}$

5. Multiply: $6 \times 9 \times 0 \times 15$

6. Multiply: 392×100

7. Multiply: $\begin{array}{r} 518 \\ \times \ 470 \\ \hline \end{array}$

8. Divide: $22\overline{)11{,}924}$

9. Write in exponential form: $8 \times 8 \times 8 \times 8$

10. Round to the nearest thousand: 652,907

11. Perform each operation in the proper order:
$$2^3 + 4 \times 10 + 3^2 \div 3 - 2$$

12. Perform each operation in the proper order:
$$10 \times 3^2 - 2 \times 4^2 + 5 - 1$$

13. Estimate the answer using the principle of estimation:
$$325 + 649 + 688$$

14. Mr. Moore owns 29 townhouses. He rents each one for $779 per month. His mortgage payments are $575 per month per townhouse. How much profit does he make on townhouses per month?

15. Lisa received $500 for her birthday. She bought a dress for $95 and two pairs of shoes at $49 each. Assuming no sales tax, how much money did she have left?

_____ **1.** Write in standard notation: Four million, three hundred sixty-five thousand, two hundred and five

     a. 4,365,250   **b.** 4,365,205   **c.** 4,365,205,000   **d.** 4,000,365,205

_____ **2.** Add: 300,605
              2,115
       + 32,007

     a. 334,717   **b.** 640,727

     c. 334,727   **d.** 304,717

_____ **3.** Subtract: 29,328
              − 2,473

     a. 26,855   **b.** 31,801

     c. 26,755   **d.** 26,955

_____ **4.** Subtract: $18,313,702 - 4,560,778$

     a. 14,752,924   **b.** 13,752,934   **c.** 13,752,914   **d.** 13,752,924

_____ **5.** Multiply: $2 \times 10 \times 6 \times 12$

     a. 1440   **b.** 144   **c.** 32   **d.** 14,400

_____ **6.** Multiply: 521
             × 630

     a. 328,230   **b.** 3,282,300

     c. 32,823   **d.** 328,751

_____ **7.** Multiply: $13,284 \times 3$

     a. 39,842   **b.** 38,582   **c.** 39,852   **d.** 39,752

_____ **8.** Divide: $7\overline{)10,669}$

     a. 1524   **b.** 1524 R1   **c.** 1525 R1   **d.** 1528

_____ **9.** Write in exponent form: $10 \times 10 \times 10 \times 10$

     a. 1000^4 **b.** 100^2 **c.** 10^4 **d.** 10^3

_____ **10.** Round to the nearest hundred: 246,515,619

     a. 247,000,000   **b.** 246,514,000   **c.** 246,516,000   **d.** 246,515,000

_____ **11.** Perform the operations in the proper order: $2^3 + 5 \times 10 \div 2 - 3^3 + (11 - 8)$

     a. 10   **b.** 9   **c.** 55   **d.** 41

_____ **12.** Perform the operations in the proper order: $3 + 10^2 - 4 \times (12 - 5)$

     a. 2072   **b.** 75   **c.** 693   **d.** 65

_____ **13.** Estimate the answer using the principle of estimation: $5,002,319 \times 24,625$

     a. 125,000   **b.** 100,000,000,000   **c.** 120,000,000   **d.** 12,000,000

_____ **14.** A rental car cost a total of $282 for a week. Six students shared the car. How much should each pay?

     a. $48   **b.** $35   **c.** $50   **d.** $47

_____ **15.** Vanita began her trip to Washington D.C. on a full tank of gas. Her odometer read 54,250. When she arrived in Washington, her odometer read 54,538. She filled her car's gas tank and it tool exactly 9 gallons. How many miles per gallon did she get?

     a. 32   **b.** 30   **c.** 22   **d.** 36

Name: _____

____ **1.** Write in standard notation: Three million, two hundred sixty-four thousand, seven hundred and two

    a. 3,264,720   **b.** 3,000,264,702   **c.** 3,264,702   **d.** 3,264,702,000

____ **2.** Add: $143 + 59 + 1172$

    a. 1364   **b.** 2508

    c. 1384   **d.** 1374

____ **3.** Subtract: $\begin{array}{r} 12,360,512 \\ -\ 6,519,207 \end{array}$

    a. 5,841,205   **b.** 5,841,305

    c. 5,841,315   **d.** 20,649,139

____ **4.** Subtract: $158,445 - 9568$

    a. 148,887   **b.** 163,763   **c.** 148,877   **d.** 148,867

____ **5.** Multiply: $3 \times 2 \times 9 \times 5$

    a. 360   **b.** 2700   **c.** 270   **d.** 180

____ **6.** Multiply: $\begin{array}{r} 382 \\ \times\ 119 \end{array}$

    a. 45,458   **b.** 45,448

    c. 7258   **d.** 41,638

____ **7.** Multiply: $12,547 \times 6$

    a. 75,262   **b.** 75,282   **c.** 75,582   **d.** 65,282

____ **8.** Divide: $5\overline{)261,034}$

    a. 50,206 R4   **b.** 52,216 R4   **c.** 52,206 R4   **d.** 52,206

____ **9.** Write in exponent form: $9 \times 9 \times 9$

    a. 9^2 **b.** 9^3 **c.** 81^3 **d.** 9^4

_____ **10.** Round to the nearest ten thousand: 508,247,936

    a. 508,250,000   **b.** 508,246,000   **c.** 508,240,000   **d.** 510,000,000

_____ **11.** Perform the operations in the proper order: $3 \times 5 + 2^2 \times 3 + 7 \div 7$

    a. 96   **b.** 106   **c.** 28   **d.** $4\dfrac{3}{8}$

_____ **12.** Perform the operations in the proper order: $4 + 5^2 \times 2 + (9 - 6) \times 2^3$

    a. 244   **b.** 82   **c.** 488   **d.** 78

_____ **13.** Estimate the answer using the principle of estimation: $3,017,000 \times 239$

    a. 6000   **b.** 60,000,000   **c.** 6,000,000   **d.** 600,000,000

_____ **14.** Mrs. McMahan had $380 when she started shopping. She bought two blouses at $31 each, a pair of shoes at $59, and a necklace at $39. Assuming no sales tax, how much money did she have left after her purchases?

    a. $220   **b.** $251   **c.** $215   **d.** $120

_____ **15.** A club purchases six books of stamps at $8 each, seven pads of paper at $2 each, and three boxes of envelopes at $3 each. The six members agreed to divide the cost equally. Assuming no sales tax, how much did each member have to pay?

    a. $10   **b.** $15   **c.** $9   **d.** $12

____ **1.** Write in standard notation: Five million, four hundred eighty-two thousand, and fifteen

    a. 5,482,050   **b.** 5,482,150   **c.** 5,482,015   **d.** 5,482,105

____ **2.** Add: 301,116
                2,100
         + 15,115

    a. 318,331   **b.** 318,321

    c. 453,331   **d.** 318,431

____ **3.** Subtract: 38,256
              − 10,829

    a. 27,437   **b.** 27,427

    c. 27,447   **d.** 38,981

____ **4.** Subtract: $210,768 - 12,487$

    a. 204,729   **b.** 198,181   **c.** 198,381   **d.** 198,281

____ **5.** Multiply: $3 \times 10 \times 5 \times 6 \times 2$

    a. 1000   **b.** 18,000   **c.** 1500   **d.** 1800

____ **6.** Multiply: 387
             × 78

    a. 30,176   **b.** 30,086

    c. 30,186   **d.** 3176

____ **7.** Multiply: 4282×5

    a. 21,410   **b.** 21,400   **c.** 20,410   **d.** 20,400

____ **8.** Divide: $8 \overline{)32,039}$

    a. 4004   **b.** 4004 R7   **c.** 404 R7   **d.** 4005

____ **9.** Write in exponent form: $8 \times 8 \times 8 \times 8$

    a. 64^4 **b.** 64^3 **c.** 8^3 **d.** 8^4

____ **10.** Round to the nearest hundred: 2,418,593

     a. 2,418,600   **b.** 2,418,500   **c.** 2,418,560   **d.** 2,418,000

____ **11.** Perform the operations in the proper order: $2\times2\times2+3^2\times5+11\div11$

     a. 86   **b.** 76   **c.** $10\dfrac{4}{9}$ **d.** 54

____ **12.** Perform the operations in the proper order: $4+10^2-2\times5-(7-4)$

     a. 195   **b.** 91   **c.** 85   **d.** 189

____ **13.** Estimate the answer using the principle of estimation: 2891×6157

     a. 18,000,000   **b.** 18,000   **c.** 1800   **d.** 180,000,000

____ **14.** Bill had $185 when he started shopping. He bought two hats at $17 each, a pair of shoes at $43, and a belt at $22. He had a coupon for $15 off the total purchase. Assuming no sales tax, how much money did he have left after paying his bill?

     a. $69   **b.** $54   **c.** $91   **d.** $84

____ **15.** Seventeen friends agreed to equally divide a $2533 bill for renting a hotel ballroom. How much did each of them pay?

     a. $362   **b.** $149   **c.** $209   **d.** $119

If you <u>are</u> familiar with the topics in this chapter, take this test now. If you can't answer a question, study the appropriate section of the chapter. If you are <u>not</u> familiar with the topics in this chapter, don't take this test now. Instead, study the examples, work the practice problems, and then take the test. This test will help you identify which concepts you have mastered, and which you need to study further

1. Use a fraction to represent the shaded portion of this object:

2. Draw a sketch to show $\frac{2}{5}$ of the object:

3. Tom bought 47 apples. Of these, six were rotten. Write a fraction that describes the proportion of apples that were rotten.

4. Reduce: $\frac{4}{24}$

5. Reduce: $\frac{15}{45}$

6. Reduce: $\frac{17}{119}$

7. Reduce: $\frac{125}{200}$

8. Reduce: $\frac{55}{121}$

9. Change $4\frac{1}{3}$ to an improper fraction.

10. Change $7\frac{2}{9}$ to an improper fraction.

11. Change $\frac{79}{4}$ to a mixed number.

12. Change $\frac{37}{5}$ to a mixed number.

13. Change $\frac{41}{17}$ to a mixed number.

14. Multiply: $\frac{3}{7} \times \frac{1}{8}$

15. Multiply: $\frac{4}{11} \times \frac{33}{28}$

16. Multiply: $8\frac{1}{3} \times 6\frac{1}{2}$

17. Divide: $\dfrac{4}{7} \div \dfrac{4}{7}$

18. Divide: $\dfrac{3}{17} \div \dfrac{3}{34}$

19. Divide: $3\dfrac{3}{7} \div 2\dfrac{2}{21}$

20. Divide: $12 \div \dfrac{8}{7}$

21. Find the least common denominator: $\dfrac{1}{6}, \dfrac{3}{4}, \dfrac{1}{2}$

22. Find the least common denominator: $\dfrac{2}{5}, \dfrac{7}{45}$

23. Find the least common denominator: $\dfrac{2}{11}, \dfrac{9}{77}$

24. Find the least common denominator: $\dfrac{9}{25}, \dfrac{11}{15}$

25. Subtract: $\dfrac{8}{15} - \dfrac{1}{20}$

26. Simplify: $\dfrac{7}{9} - \dfrac{1}{12} + \dfrac{5}{18}$

27. Subtract: $9 - 2\dfrac{1}{3}$

28. Add: $2\dfrac{1}{6} + 3\dfrac{5}{7}$

29. Simplify: $\dfrac{2}{7} \times \dfrac{7}{9} \div \dfrac{5}{3}$

30. Tuan and Frank set out to walk $17\frac{1}{2}$ miles from Alexandria to Manassas. During the first 5 hours, they covered $9\frac{1}{3}$ miles going from Alexandria to Bedford. How many miles are left to be covered from Bedford to Manassas.

31. Barbara picked $7\frac{1}{4}$ bushels of peppers. Her son picked $2\frac{1}{18}$ bushels of peppers. How much did they pick together?

32. The students on the fifth floor of Thompson Hall contributed money to make a stock purchase of one share of stock each. The paid $422 in all to buy the shares of stock. The cost of one share was $23\frac{4}{9}$. How many students shared in the purchase?

If you <u>are</u> familiar with the topics in this chapter, take this test now. If you can't answer a question, study the appropriate section of the chapter. If you are <u>not</u> familiar with the topics in this chapter, don't take this test now. Instead, study the examples, work the practice problems, and then take the test. This test will help you identify which concepts you have mastered, and which you need to study further.

____ 1. What fraction best represents the shaded portions of this object:

    a. $\dfrac{2}{8}$ **b.** $\dfrac{6}{8}$

    c. $\dfrac{5}{8}$ **d.** $\dfrac{6}{7}$

____ 2. Which of the following objects best depicts the fraction: $\dfrac{3}{5}$

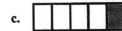

  a.   **b.**   **c.**   **d.**

____ 3. Tom bought 43 apples. Of these, 8 were rotten. Write a fraction that bests describe to portion of apples that were rotten.

    a. $\dfrac{43}{8}$ **b.** $\dfrac{8}{43}$ **c.** $\dfrac{1}{8}$ **d.** $\dfrac{1}{4}$

____ 4. Reduce: $\dfrac{5}{35}$

    a. $\dfrac{1}{35}$ **b.** $\dfrac{5}{7}$

    c. $\dfrac{1}{5}$ **d.** $\dfrac{1}{7}$

____ 5. Reduce: $\dfrac{15}{75}$

    a. $\dfrac{1}{5}$ **b.** $\dfrac{1}{3}$

    c. $\dfrac{3}{25}$ **d.** $\dfrac{5}{25}$

____ 6. Reduce: $\dfrac{9}{207}$

    a. $\dfrac{1}{90}$ **b.** $\dfrac{1}{23}$

    c. $\dfrac{3}{19}$ **d.** $\dfrac{1}{19}$

____ 7. Reduce: $\dfrac{150}{200}$

    a. $\dfrac{1}{3}$ **b.** $\dfrac{3}{4}$

    c. $\dfrac{1}{2}$ **d.** $\dfrac{3}{5}$

____ 8. Reduce: $\dfrac{77}{121}$

    a. $\dfrac{7}{13}$ **b.** $\dfrac{8}{9}$

    c. $\dfrac{9}{13}$ **d.** $\dfrac{7}{11}$

____ 9. Change $5\dfrac{2}{3}$ to an improper fraction.

    a. $\dfrac{10}{3}$ **b.** $\dfrac{30}{3}$

    c. $\dfrac{16}{3}$ **d.** $\dfrac{17}{3}$

_____ **10.** Change $8\dfrac{2}{7}$ to an improper fraction.

    a. $\dfrac{58}{7}$ **b.** $\dfrac{23}{7}$

    c. $\dfrac{17}{7}$ **d.** $\dfrac{112}{7}$

_____ **11.** Change $\dfrac{85}{4}$ to a mixed number.

    a. $21\dfrac{1}{2}$ **b.** $21\dfrac{3}{4}$

    c. $21\dfrac{1}{4}$ **d.** $22\dfrac{1}{4}$

_____ **12.** Change $\dfrac{39}{5}$ to a mixed number.

    a. $6\dfrac{5}{9}$ **b.** $8\dfrac{1}{5}$

    c. $5\dfrac{3}{5}$ **d.** $7\dfrac{4}{5}$

_____ **13.** Change $\dfrac{43}{17}$ to a mixed number.

    a. $2\dfrac{10}{17}$ **b.** $3\dfrac{1}{17}$

    c. $2\dfrac{9}{17}$ **d.** $2\dfrac{11}{17}$

_____ **14.** Multiply: $\dfrac{5}{7}\times\dfrac{1}{6}$

    a. $\dfrac{5}{42}$ **b.** $\dfrac{5}{13}$

    c. $\dfrac{30}{7}$ **d.** $\dfrac{7}{30}$

_____ **15.** Multiply: $\dfrac{5}{8}\times\dfrac{32}{35}$

    a. $\dfrac{4}{7}$ **b.** $\dfrac{7}{4}$

    c. $\dfrac{175}{256}$ **d.** $1\dfrac{4}{7}$

_____ **16.** Multiply: $11\dfrac{1}{3}\times4\dfrac{1}{2}$

    a. $44\dfrac{1}{6}$ **b.** 51

    c. $44\dfrac{1}{5}$ **d.** $1\dfrac{7}{27}$

_____ **17.** Divide: $\dfrac{5}{7}\div\dfrac{5}{7}$

    a. 1 **b.** 0

    c. $\dfrac{25}{49}$ **d.** $\dfrac{5}{7}$

_____ **18.** Divide: $\dfrac{4}{34}\div\dfrac{4}{17}$

    a. $1\dfrac{1}{2}$ **b.** 2

    c. $\dfrac{8}{289}$ **d.** $\dfrac{1}{2}$

____ **19.** Divide: $4\frac{5}{7} \div 2\frac{2}{21}$ **a.** $2\frac{1}{4}$ **b.** $2\frac{1}{8}$

                                               c. $\frac{175}{336}$ **d.** $1\frac{49}{50}$

____ **20.** Divide: $9 \div \frac{18}{7}$ **a.** $3\frac{1}{7}$ **b.** $3\frac{1}{2}$

                                   c. $\frac{2}{7}$ **d.** $1\frac{2}{7}$

____ **21.** Find the least common denominator: $\frac{1}{10}, \frac{3}{2}, \frac{1}{5}$

   a. 20   **b.** 10   **c.** 15   **d.** 100

____ **22.** Find the least common denominator: $\frac{2}{14}, \frac{6}{49}$

   a. 7   **b.** 28   **c.** 98   **d.** 49

____ **23.** Find the least common denominator: $\frac{2}{11}, \frac{5}{66}$

   a. 11   **b.** 122   **c.** 66   **d.** 22

____ **24.** Find the least common denominator: $\frac{9}{39}, \frac{11}{26}$

   a. 6   **b.** 78   **c.** 117   **d.** 3

____ **25.** Subtract: $\frac{8}{15} - \frac{3}{20}$ **a.** $\frac{7}{20}$ **b.** $\frac{23}{60}$

                                       c. 1   **d.** $\frac{5}{60}$

____ **26.** Simplify: $\frac{2}{9} - \frac{5}{12} + \frac{7}{18}$ **a.** $\frac{7}{39}$ **b.** $\frac{5}{9}$

                                           c. $\frac{5}{39}$ **d.** $\frac{7}{36}$

____ **27.** Subtract: $7 - 2\frac{2}{3}$ **a.** $4\frac{1}{3}$ **b.** $5\frac{2}{3}$

                                   c. $5\frac{1}{3}$ **d.** $4\frac{2}{3}$

____ **28.** Add: $3\frac{1}{6} + 2\frac{4}{7}$

    a. $5\frac{5}{13}$ **b.** $5\frac{31}{42}$

    c. $\frac{9}{14}$ **d.** $2\frac{1}{13}$

____ **29.** Simplify: $\frac{2}{9} \times \frac{9}{7} \div \frac{5}{3}$

    a. $\frac{10}{21}$ **b.** $\frac{12}{35}$

    c. $\frac{6}{35}$ **d.** $\frac{2}{105}$

____ **30.** Tuan and Frank set out to walk the $26\frac{1}{2}$ miles from Alexandria to Lorton, During the first 5 hours they covered $14\frac{2}{3}$ miles going from Alexandria to Bedford. How many miles are left to be covered from Bedford to Lorton?

    a. $11\frac{5}{6}$ miles   **b.** $9\frac{2}{3}$ miles   **c.** $11\frac{1}{3}$ miles   **d.** $19\frac{1}{2}$ miles

____ **31.** Barbara picked $9\frac{3}{4}$ bushels of peppers. Her son picked $2\frac{1}{18}$ bushels of peppers. How much did they pick together?

    a. $11\frac{1}{24}$ bushels   **b.** $11\frac{2}{11}$ bushels   **c.** $7\frac{25}{36}$ bushels   **d.** $11\frac{29}{36}$ bushels

____ **32.** The students on the fifth floor of Thompson Hall contributed money to make a stock purchase of one share of stock each. They paid $476 in all to buy the shares of stock. The cost of buying one share was $$26\frac{4}{9}$$. How many students shared in the purchase?

    a. $18\frac{1}{9}$ **b.** 18   **c.** 17   **d.** $17\frac{8}{9}$

1. Express the number 150 as a product of prime factors.

2. Is 95 a prime number? If not, then express it as a product of prime numbers.

3. Reduce $\dfrac{15}{65}$ to lowest terms.

4. Reduce $\dfrac{54}{81}$ to lowest terms.

5. Change $6\dfrac{2}{5}$ to an improper fraction.

6. Change $\dfrac{71}{33}$ to a mixed number.

7. Change $\dfrac{142}{60}$ to a mixed number, then reduce.

8. Multiply: $\dfrac{4}{7} \times \dfrac{11}{15}$

9. Divide: $\dfrac{9}{10} \div \dfrac{12}{5}$

10. What is the LCD for $\dfrac{7}{16}$ and $\dfrac{5}{36}$?

11. Change this fraction to an equivalent fraction with the specified denominator:
$$\dfrac{13}{24} = \dfrac{?}{120}$$

12. Add: $7\dfrac{1}{3} + 8\dfrac{5}{6}$

13. Subtract: $9 - 3\dfrac{3}{4}$

14. Add: $\dfrac{1}{8} + \dfrac{1}{4} + \dfrac{1}{2}$

15. Add, then reduce to lowest terms: $7\dfrac{3}{4} + 13\dfrac{1}{4}$

16. Subtract, then reduce to lowest terms: $\dfrac{71}{30} - \dfrac{9}{5}$

17. Mary Ann had $\frac{5}{8}$ pound of candy. She gave $\frac{2}{3}$ of it to a friend. How much candy did she have left?

18. A butcher has $50\frac{3}{4}$ pounds of ground beef. He wishes to prepare it in $1\frac{1}{4}$ pound packages. How many packages can he prepare?

19. Jeremy bought a bolt of fabric. He sold $\frac{3}{4}$ of it to a dressmaker, gave $\frac{1}{8}$ of it to friend, and put the rest in his store. What portion of the bolt did he put in his store?

20. David and Michael bought an brought home two large pizzas. David ate $\frac{3}{4}$ of a pizza, while Michael ate $\frac{3}{8}$ of a pizza. How much pizza was left for their father when he came home?

1. Express the number 56 as a product of prime factors.

2. Is 65 a prime number? If not, then express it as a product of prime numbers.

3. Reduce $\dfrac{18}{60}$ to lowest terms.

4. Reduce $\dfrac{77}{330}$ to lowest terms.

5. Change $3\dfrac{2}{7}$ to an improper fraction.

6. Change $\dfrac{57}{13}$ to a mixed number.

7. Change $\dfrac{158}{50}$ to a mixed number, then reduce.

8. Multiply: $\dfrac{7}{12} \times \dfrac{5}{4}$

9. Divide: $\dfrac{5}{13} \div \dfrac{70}{26}$

10. What is the LCD for $\dfrac{19}{34}$ and $\dfrac{11}{24}$?

11. Change this fraction to an equivalent fraction with the specified denominator:
$$\dfrac{12}{25} = \dfrac{?}{125}$$

12. Add: $9\dfrac{2}{5} + 1\dfrac{1}{4}$

13. Add: $\dfrac{4}{9} + \dfrac{12}{15}$

14. Subtract: $13 - 7\dfrac{5}{8}$

15. Add: $\dfrac{2}{5} + \dfrac{2}{7} + \dfrac{1}{35}$

16. Subtract: $\dfrac{49}{20} - 1\dfrac{9}{20}$

17. A rectangular flowerbed measures $9\dfrac{1}{2}$ feet by $4\dfrac{1}{4}$ feet. Find the area of the bed in square feet.

18. How many $\dfrac{3}{4}$ ounce seed packets can be prepared from $88\dfrac{1}{2}$ ounces of marigold seeds?

19. Jeff bought two cords of firewood. He gave $\dfrac{1}{2}$ to his minister, and $\dfrac{7}{8}$ cord to his brother. How much firewood was left?

20. Katie is making chocolate chip cookies. Her recipe calls for $\dfrac{5}{8}$ cup sugar, but Katie wants to multiply the recipe so that she will get $1\dfrac{1}{2}$ times as many cookies. How much sugar should she use?

1. Express the number 62 as a product of prime factors.

2. Is 110 a prime number? If not, then express it as a product of prime numbers.

3. Reduce $\dfrac{30}{96}$ to lowest terms.

4. Reduce $\dfrac{110}{280}$ to lowest terms.

5. Change $4\dfrac{3}{8}$ to an improper fraction.

6. Change $\dfrac{77}{17}$ to a mixed number.

7. Change $\dfrac{315}{50}$ to a mixed number, then reduce.

8. Multiply: $\dfrac{1}{11} \times \dfrac{5}{13}$

9. Divide: $\dfrac{5}{19} \div \dfrac{10}{3}$

10. What is the LCD for $\dfrac{19}{35}$ and $\dfrac{7}{60}$?

11. Change this fraction to an equivalent fraction with the specified denominator:
$$\frac{8}{35} = \frac{?}{315}$$

12. Add: $4\dfrac{1}{5} + 1\dfrac{3}{10}$

13. Add: $\dfrac{1}{8} + \dfrac{1}{2} + \dfrac{1}{5}$

14. Subtract: $11\dfrac{1}{8} - 5\dfrac{5}{8}$

15. Add: $4\dfrac{1}{5} + 11\dfrac{3}{8}$

16. Subtract: $\dfrac{15}{8} - \dfrac{6}{5}$

17. A hallway measures $8\dfrac{2}{5}$ feet by $16\dfrac{3}{8}$ feet. Find the area of the hallway in square feet.

18. Tim wants to parcel out 60 pounds of dry dog food into $\dfrac{1}{3}$ pound packages. How many packages can he make?

19. Victoria purchased a crate of strawberries. She gave $\dfrac{1}{3}$ of them to friends at work and $\dfrac{3}{8}$ of them to her sister. She froze the rest. What part of the crate did she freeze?

20. A carpenter has a board that is $10\dfrac{3}{16}$ inches long. He needs a piece of wood that is $7\dfrac{5}{8}$ inches long. How much of the board should be cut off?

_____ 1. Express the number 52 as a product of prime factors.

    a. $4 \times 4 \times 13$ **b.** 4×13 **c.** $2 \times 2 \times 13$ **d.** $2 \times 2 \times 2 \times 6$

_____ 2. Is 39 a prime number? If not, then express it as a product of prime factors.

    a. No; 3×19 **b.** Yes   **c.** No; 3×31 **d.** No; 3×13

_____ 3. Reduce $\dfrac{42}{98}$ to lowest terms.

    a. $\dfrac{4}{7}$ **b.** $\dfrac{3}{7}$ **c.** $\dfrac{3}{8}$ **d.** $\dfrac{7}{9}$

_____ 4. Reduce $\dfrac{16}{38}$ to lowest terms.

    a. $\dfrac{8}{9}$ **b.** $\dfrac{16}{38}$ **c.** $\dfrac{4}{9}$ **d.** $\dfrac{8}{19}$

_____ 5. Change $2\dfrac{5}{7}$ to an improper fraction.

    a. $\dfrac{14}{7}$ **b.** $\dfrac{37}{7}$ **c.** $\dfrac{19}{7}$ **d.** $\dfrac{19}{5}$

_____ 6. Change $\dfrac{65}{18}$ to a mixed number.

    a. $3\dfrac{11}{18}$ **b.** $3\dfrac{1}{18}$ **c.** $3\dfrac{10}{18}$ **d.** $4\dfrac{1}{18}$

_____ 7. Change $\dfrac{570}{200}$ to a mixed number, then reduce.

    a. $2\dfrac{85}{100}$ **b.** $2\dfrac{17}{20}$ **c.** $3\dfrac{17}{20}$ **d.** $2\dfrac{19}{20}$

_____ 8. Multiply: $\dfrac{4}{7} \times \dfrac{3}{11}$

    a. $\dfrac{12}{77}$ **b.** $\dfrac{33}{28}$ **c.** $\dfrac{7}{77}$ **d.** $\dfrac{12}{18}$

_____ 9. Divide: $\dfrac{6}{10} \div \dfrac{12}{7}$

    a. $\dfrac{36}{35}$ **b.** $\dfrac{20}{7}$ **c.** $\dfrac{15}{35}$ **d.** $\dfrac{7}{20}$

_____ 10. What is the LCD for $\dfrac{11}{21}$ and $\dfrac{31}{45}$?

    a. 945   **b.** 315   **c.** 66   **d.** 105

_____ 11. Change this fraction to an equivalent fraction with the specified denominator: $\dfrac{7}{8} = \dfrac{?}{56}$

    a. $\dfrac{55}{56}$ **b.** $\dfrac{42}{56}$ **c.** $\dfrac{48}{56}$ **d.** $\dfrac{49}{56}$

_____ **12.** Add: $\dfrac{3}{7}+\dfrac{5}{14}$　　　**a.** $\dfrac{8}{14}$　　　　　**b.** $\dfrac{11}{14}$

　　　　　　　　　　　　　　c. $\dfrac{8}{7}$　　　　　**d.** $\dfrac{8}{21}$

_____ **13.** Add: $5+4\dfrac{2}{7}$　　　**a.** $9\dfrac{2}{7}$　　　　**b.** $20\dfrac{2}{7}$

　　　　　　　　　　　　c. $1\dfrac{2}{7}$　　　　**d.** $9\dfrac{5}{7}$

_____ **14.** Subtract: $12\dfrac{2}{5}-5\dfrac{1}{10}$　　**a.** $7\dfrac{1}{5}$　　　　**b.** $7\dfrac{1}{10}$

　　　　　　　　　　　　　　　　　c. $7\dfrac{3}{10}$　　　**d.** $7\dfrac{4}{10}$

_____ **15.** Add: $2\dfrac{2}{5}+3\dfrac{1}{4}$　　**a.** $5\dfrac{1}{3}$　　　　**b.** $\dfrac{25}{9}$

　　　　　　　　　　　　　c. $\dfrac{113}{20}$　　　**d.** $\dfrac{113}{9}$

_____ **16.** Subtract: $7\dfrac{5}{9}-3\dfrac{7}{9}$　　**a.** $4\dfrac{2}{9}$　　　**b.** $\dfrac{34}{9}$

　　　　　　　　　　　　　　c. $\dfrac{25}{9}$　　　　**d.** $\dfrac{41}{9}$

_____ **17.** A rectangular garden measures $6\dfrac{1}{5}$ yards by $9\dfrac{1}{2}$ yards. What is the area of the garden?

　　a. $62\dfrac{15}{19}$ sq. yd.　　　**b.** $32\dfrac{1}{4}$ sq. yd.　　　**c.** $54\dfrac{5}{16}$ sq. yd.　　　**d.** $58\dfrac{9}{10}$ sq. yd.

_____ **18.** A landscape designer had $50\dfrac{2}{3}$ pounds of seeds that she wishes to parcel into packages of $\dfrac{2}{3}$ pound each. How many packages can she make?

　　a. 76 packages　　　**b.** $33\dfrac{7}{9}$ packages　　　**c.** 50 packages　　　**d.** 60 packages

_____ **19.** Maggie bought a crate of oranges. She gave $\dfrac{1}{3}$ of the crate to friends, and $\dfrac{1}{2}$ of the crate to family. What portion of the crate did she have left?

　　a. $\dfrac{3}{5}$ crate　　　**b.** $\dfrac{5}{6}$ crate　　　**c.** $\dfrac{1}{6}$ crate　　　**d.** $\dfrac{2}{5}$ crate

_____ **20.** Dave jogged $6\dfrac{1}{2}$ miles on Monday, $3\dfrac{1}{4}$ miles on Tuesday, and $3\dfrac{3}{4}$ miles on Wednesday. What is his total mileage for these three days?

　　a. $14\dfrac{1}{4}$ miles　　　**b.** $12\dfrac{1}{2}$ miles　　　**c.** 13 miles　　　**d.** $13\dfrac{1}{2}$ miles

_____ **1.** Express the number 56 as a product of prime factors.

   a. 7×8 **b.** $4 \times 4 \times 7$ **c.** $2 \times 2 \times 2 \times 7$ **d.** $2 \times 2 \times 7$

_____ **2.** Is 51 a prime number? If not, then express it as a product of prime factors.

   a. No; 3×19 **b.** No; 3×17 **c.** No; 3×27 **d.** Yes

_____ **3.** Reduce $\dfrac{26}{130}$ to lowest terms.

   a. $\dfrac{1}{7}$ **b.** $\dfrac{1}{5}$ **c.** $\dfrac{1}{13}$ **d.** $\dfrac{1}{4}$

_____ **4.** Reduce $\dfrac{68}{140}$ to lowest terms.

   a. $\dfrac{1}{2}$ **b.** $\dfrac{2}{35}$ **c.** $\dfrac{17}{25}$ **d.** $\dfrac{17}{35}$

_____ **5.** Change $2\dfrac{5}{14}$ to an improper fraction.

   a. $\dfrac{33}{14}$ **b.** $\dfrac{33}{28}$ **c.** $\dfrac{30}{14}$ **d.** $\dfrac{35}{14}$

_____ **6.** Change $\dfrac{35}{11}$ to a mixed number.

   a. $3\dfrac{1}{11}$ **b.** $2\dfrac{13}{11}$ **c.** $3\dfrac{2}{11}$ **d.** $3\dfrac{3}{11}$

_____ **7.** Change $\dfrac{132}{55}$ to a mixed number, then reduce.

   a. $2\dfrac{4}{10}$ **b.** $2\dfrac{44}{110}$ **c.** $2\dfrac{4}{11}$ **d.** $2\dfrac{2}{5}$

_____ **8.** Multiply: $\dfrac{3}{5} \times \dfrac{9}{10}$

   a. $\dfrac{27}{25}$ **b.** $\dfrac{12}{50}$ **c.** $\dfrac{12}{15}$ **d.** $\dfrac{27}{50}$

_____ **9.** Divide: $2\dfrac{1}{5} \div \dfrac{31}{5}$

   a. $\dfrac{52}{5}$ **b.** $\dfrac{11}{31}$ **c.** $\dfrac{31}{11}$ **d.** $\dfrac{341}{25}$

_____ **10.** What is the LCD for this set of fractions: $\dfrac{11}{28}$ and $\dfrac{17}{49}$?

   a. 945   **b.** 1372   **c.** 196   **d.** 98

____ 11. Change this fraction to an equivalent fraction with the specified denominator: $\frac{7}{16} = \frac{?}{256}$

a. $\frac{112}{256}$ b. $\frac{49}{256}$ c. $\frac{247}{256}$ d. $\frac{98}{256}$

____ 12. Add: $8\frac{5}{6} + 3\frac{7}{9}$

a. $\frac{227}{18}$ b. $\frac{87}{15}$

c. $\frac{176}{9}$ d. $\frac{87}{9}$

____ 13. Add: $\frac{1}{3} + \frac{1}{5} + \frac{1}{6}$

a. $\frac{11}{30}$ b. $\frac{3}{14}$

c. $\frac{21}{30}$ d. $\frac{3}{30}$

____ 14. Subtract: $\frac{7}{8} - \frac{2}{5}$

a. $\frac{5}{40}$ b. $\frac{5}{8}$

c. $\frac{19}{40}$ d. $\frac{5}{3}$

____ 15. Add: $4\frac{5}{16} + 13\frac{2}{3}$

a. $18\frac{5}{6}$ b. $18\frac{1}{2}$

c. $18\frac{1}{6}$ d. $17\frac{1}{2}$

____ 16. Subtract: $\frac{11}{15} - \frac{2}{9}$

a. $\frac{13}{45}$ b. $\frac{3}{2}$

c. $\frac{5}{9}$ d. $\frac{23}{45}$

____ 17. Monica had $\frac{3}{4}$ pound of candy. She gave $\frac{2}{3}$ of it to Leann. How much candy did she give to Leann?

a. $\frac{15}{8}$ pound   b. $\frac{1}{2}$ pound   c. $\frac{7}{20}$ pound   d. $\frac{8}{15}$ pound

____ 18. How many $\frac{1}{2}$ pound packages of peanuts can be prepared from $12\frac{1}{2}$ pounds of peanuts?

a. $6\frac{1}{4}$ packages   b. 12 packages   c. 25 packages   d. 6 packages

____ 19. Jared bought a bushel of apples. He gave $\frac{1}{4}$ to his brothers and $\frac{1}{5}$ to the mailman. What portion of the bushel did he have left?

a. $\frac{11}{20}$ bushel   b. $\frac{9}{9}$ bushel   c. $\frac{9}{29}$ bushel   d. $\frac{2}{9}$ bushel

____ 20. Midway High School has a track for runners that is one-quarter mile in length. Sheila ran a total of 11 times around the track. Her sister Nancy ran 25 laps around the track. How much further did Nancy run than Sheila?

a. $3\frac{1}{4}$ miles   b. $3\frac{1}{2}$ miles   c. $2\frac{1}{2}$ miles   d. 4 miles

_____ 1. Express the number 150 as a product of prime factors.

    a. $2 \times 3 \times 3 \times 5$ **b.** 6×25 **c.** $2 \times 3 \times 5 \times 5$ **d.** $2 \times 3 \times 5$

_____ 2. Is 38 a prime number? If not, then express it as a product of prime factors.

    a. No; 4×19 **b.** No; 2×19 **c.** Yes   **d.** No; $2 \times 3 \times 19$

_____ 3. Reduce $\dfrac{18}{48}$ to lowest terms.

    a. $\dfrac{3}{6}$ **b.** $\dfrac{3}{8}$ **c.** $\dfrac{1}{3}$ **d.** $\dfrac{1}{7}$

_____ 4. Reduce $\dfrac{51}{210}$ to lowest terms.

    a. $\dfrac{17}{70}$ **b.** $\dfrac{17}{30}$ **c.** $\dfrac{3}{70}$ **d.** $\dfrac{7}{70}$

_____ 5. Change $4\dfrac{3}{7}$ to an improper fraction.

    a. $\dfrac{43}{7}$ **b.** $\dfrac{12}{7}$ **c.** $\dfrac{31}{3}$ **d.** $\dfrac{31}{7}$

_____ 6. Change $\dfrac{71}{12}$ to a mixed number.

    a. $5\dfrac{7}{12}$ **b.** $5\dfrac{11}{12}$ **c.** $4\dfrac{7}{12}$ **d.** $5\dfrac{5}{12}$

_____ 7. Change $\dfrac{385}{120}$ to a mixed number, then reduce.

    a. $3\dfrac{5}{24}$ **b.** $3\dfrac{3}{24}$ **c.** $3\dfrac{25}{120}$ **d.** $3\dfrac{5}{12}$

_____ 8. Multiply: $\dfrac{2}{5} \times \dfrac{7}{23}$

    a. $\dfrac{14}{115}$ **b.** $\dfrac{14}{28}$ **c.** $\dfrac{9}{115}$ **d.** $\dfrac{24}{115}$

_____ 9. Divide: $\dfrac{9}{11} \div \dfrac{13}{7}$

    a. $\dfrac{117}{77}$ **b.** $\dfrac{63}{143}$ **c.** $\dfrac{53}{117}$ **d.** $\dfrac{63}{133}$

_____ 10. What is the LCD for this set of fractions: $\dfrac{9}{49}$ and $\dfrac{11}{48}$?

    a. 98   **b.** 144   **c.** 336   **d.** 2352

_____ 11. Change this fraction to an equivalent fraction with the specified denominator: $\dfrac{11}{12} = \dfrac{?}{156}$

     a. $\dfrac{132}{156}$ **b.** $\dfrac{155}{156}$ **c.** $\dfrac{143}{156}$ **d.** $\dfrac{154}{156}$

_____ 12. Add: $6\dfrac{12}{13} + \dfrac{1}{2}$

     a. $7\dfrac{5}{26}$ **b.** $7\dfrac{11}{26}$

     c. $3\dfrac{12}{13}$ **d.** $10\dfrac{5}{13}$

_____ 13. Subtract: $18 - 7\dfrac{1}{4}$

     a. $10\dfrac{1}{2}$ **b.** $10\dfrac{1}{4}$

     c. $11\dfrac{3}{4}$ **d.** $10\dfrac{3}{4}$

_____ 14. Add: $\dfrac{3}{8} + \dfrac{1}{4} + \dfrac{5}{12}$

     a. $\dfrac{14}{12}$ **b.** $\dfrac{9}{24}$

     c. $2\dfrac{1}{24}$ **d.** $1\dfrac{1}{24}$

_____ 15. Subtract: $11\dfrac{1}{4} - 6\dfrac{3}{4}$

     a. $5\dfrac{1}{4}$ **b.** $4\dfrac{3}{4}$

     c. $5\dfrac{1}{4}$ **d.** $4\dfrac{1}{2}$

_____ 16. Add: $3\dfrac{1}{4} + 4\dfrac{1}{3}$

     a. $7\dfrac{7}{12}$ **b.** $7\dfrac{5}{12}$

     c. $7\dfrac{2}{7}$ **d.** $8\dfrac{7}{12}$

_____ 17. Janie had a large bag of candy. She gave $\dfrac{1}{3}$ of it to her coworkers, $\dfrac{1}{2}$ of it to her mother, and took the rest home. What portion of the bag did she take home?

     a. $\dfrac{5}{6}$ bag   **b.** $\dfrac{2}{5}$ bag   **c.** $\dfrac{3}{5}$ bag   **d.** $\dfrac{1}{6}$ bag

_____ 18. How many $\dfrac{2}{3}$ ounce packages of spices can be prepared from 100 ounces of spices?

     a. $66\dfrac{2}{3}$ packages   **b.** 100 packages   **c.** 300 packages   **d.** 150 packages

_____ 19. Tom built a rectangular kennel measuring $20\dfrac{1}{2}$ feet by 25 feet. What is the area of the kennel?

     a. 91 sq. ft.   **b.** $512\dfrac{1}{2}$ sq. ft.   **c.** $587\dfrac{1}{2}$ sq. ft.   **d.** 510 sq. ft.

_____ 20. One share of Alpine Computer Company stock sold for $\$25\dfrac{5}{8}$ on Monday. By Wednesday, it had gone up $\$2\dfrac{1}{2}$. What was the price per share on Wednesday?

     a. $\$27\dfrac{1}{8}$ **b.** $\$27\dfrac{6}{8}$ **c.** $\$28\dfrac{1}{8}$ **d.** $\$29\dfrac{1}{8}$

1. Add: 2953
      467
    + 381

2. Subtract: 49,108
       −2,559

3. Multiply: $3 \times 10 \times 4 \times 8$

4. Divide: $6 \overline{)9408}$

5. Write in exponent form: $7 \times 7 \times 7 \times 7 \times 7$

6. Round to the nearest hundred: 25,738

7. Perform the operations the proper order:
$$3^2 + 4 \times 7 \div 4 + 5^2 - 15 \div 3$$

8. Amy drove from Chicago to Washington, a distance of 450 miles. She started with a full tank of gas. In Washington, she filled her tank again, and it needed 12 gallons. How many miles per gallon did her car get?

9. Thirty-five fraternity brothers rented a bus for a ski trip for a total cost of $539. How much did each one pay?

10. A biology class consists of 8 freshman, 12 sophomores, and 5 juniors. What fractional part of the class are not freshmen?

11. Reduce: $\dfrac{12}{420}$

12. Add: $\dfrac{1}{5} + \dfrac{1}{3} + \dfrac{1}{10}$

13. Subtract: $12\dfrac{1}{9} - 3\dfrac{5}{9}$

14. Multiply: $1\dfrac{3}{8} \times 2\dfrac{3}{5}$

15. Divide: $\dfrac{5}{7} \div 2\dfrac{3}{4}$

16. What is the LCD of $\dfrac{9}{14}$ and $\dfrac{5}{21}$?

17. A rectangular kennel measures $26\frac{1}{2}$ feet by $20\frac{1}{4}$ feet. Find the area of the kennel in square feet.

18. How many $\frac{3}{5}$ ounce packages of spices can be prepared from 75 ounces of spices?

19. Christy bought a large bag of candy. She gave $\frac{1}{5}$ of it to her brother, $\frac{2}{3}$ to her mother, and took the rest home. What part of the bag did she take home?

20. A frame that is 18 inches by 24 inches has a mat in it that is $2\frac{1}{4}$ inches all around. What are the dimensions of the picture within the mat?

____ 1. Add: 4216
              3191
            + 578

  a. 7915   **b.** 7985

  c. 7965   **d.** 7875

____ 2. Subtract: 2318
                 − 1499

  a. 819   **b.** 1181

  c. 881   **d.** 829

____ 3. Multiply: $2 \times 3 \times 5 \times 9$

  a. 275   **b.** 225   **c.** 360   **d.** 270

____ 4. Divide: $8\overline{)60,328}$

  a. 52,541   **b.** 7541

  c. 8893   **d.** 8041

____ 5. Write in exponent form: $8 \times 8 \times 8$

  a. 8^2 **b.** 8×3 **c.** 8^3 **d.** 3^8

____ 6. Round to the nearest thousand: 35,709

  a. 35,700   **b.** 35,000   **c.** 36,000   **d.** 35,710

____ 7. Perform each operation in the proper order: $5^2 - 2 \times 10 + 3^2 \times 2 - 20 \div 4$

  a. 87   **b.** 18   **c.** 114   **d.** 529

____ 8. Professor Ranjan corrected some final exams, and it took him $5\frac{1}{4}$ hours. His teaching assistant corrected the rest of the exams, and it took her $8\frac{5}{6}$ hours. How many hours total did it take to correct all the exams?

  a. $14\frac{1}{2}$ hours   **b.** $14\frac{3}{5}$ hours   **c.** $13\frac{3}{5}$ hours   **d.** $13\frac{3}{10}$ hours

____ 9. David ran the Boston Marathon, 26 miles, in $3\frac{1}{2}$ hours. What was his average rate of speed?

  a. $7\frac{1}{2}$ miles per hour   **b.** $7\frac{4}{7}$ miles per hour   **c.** $7\frac{3}{8}$ miles per hour   **d.** $7\frac{3}{7}$ miles per hour

____ 10. Michael is a math tutor who charges $25 per hour. Last month he made $1075 tutoring. How many total hours did he work as a tutor?

  a. 53 hours   **b.** 403 hours   **c.** 45 hours   **d.** 43 hours

____ 11. Reduce: $\frac{822}{56}$

  a. $\frac{28}{56}$ **b.** $\frac{411}{28}$

  c. $\frac{411}{56}$ **d.** $\frac{411}{14}$

____ **12.** Add: $\dfrac{1}{3}+\dfrac{2}{7}$

  a. $\dfrac{3}{10}$ **b.** $\dfrac{6}{8}$

  c. $\dfrac{13}{21}$ **d.** $\dfrac{2}{21}$

____ **13.** Subtract: $16\dfrac{1}{8}-5\dfrac{3}{4}$

  a. $10\dfrac{3}{8}$ **b.** $11\dfrac{1}{2}$

  c. $3\dfrac{1}{4}$ **d.** $12\dfrac{1}{8}$

____ **14.** Multiply: $\dfrac{5}{12}\times2\dfrac{2}{3}$

  a. $1\dfrac{1}{9}$ **b.** $2\dfrac{5}{9}$

  c. $\dfrac{5}{9}$ **d.** $2\dfrac{1}{9}$

____ **15.** Divide: $2\dfrac{1}{7}\div3\dfrac{1}{4}$

  a. $6\dfrac{27}{28}$ **b.** $\dfrac{60}{91}$

  c. $1\dfrac{2}{5}$ **d.** $\dfrac{2}{3}$

____ **16.** What is the least common denominator of $\dfrac{9}{70}$ and $\dfrac{5}{14}$?

  a. 980   **b.** 28   **c.** 70   **d.** 7

____ **17.** A rectangular garden measures $4\dfrac{7}{8}$ yards by $9\dfrac{1}{4}$ yards. Find the area of the garden in square yards.

  a. $5\dfrac{7}{8}$ sq. yds.   **b.** $36\dfrac{7}{32}$ sq. yds.   **c.** $45\dfrac{3}{32}$ sq. yds.   **d.** $8\dfrac{5}{8}$ sq. yds.

____ **18.** How many $\dfrac{3}{4}$-pound packages of meat can be prepared from 60 pounds of meat?

  a. 80 packages   **b.** 45 packages   **c.** 60 packages   **d.** 50 packages

____ **19.** Martha bought a bolt of fabric. She gave $\dfrac{1}{3}$ of it to her daughter and $\dfrac{2}{5}$ of it to her neighbor. What portion of the bolt did she have left?

  a. $\dfrac{13}{15}$ bolt   **b.** $\dfrac{2}{5}$ bolt   **c.** $\dfrac{12}{15}$ bolt   **d.** $\dfrac{4}{15}$ bolt

____ **20.** A picture frame is 15 inches by 20 inches. A mat that is $2\dfrac{3}{4}$ inches wide all around is used to enclose a painting. What are the dimensions of the painting within the mat?

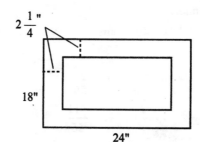

  a. $12\dfrac{1}{4}''$ by $17\dfrac{1}{4}''$

  b. $9\dfrac{1}{2}''$ by $14\dfrac{1}{2}''$

  c. $17\dfrac{3}{4}''$ by $22\dfrac{3}{4}''$

  d. $11\dfrac{1}{4}''$ by $15\dfrac{1}{4}''$

If you <u>are</u> familiar with the topics in this chapter, take this test now. If you can't answer a question, study the appropriate section of the chapter. If you are <u>not</u> familiar with the topics in this chapter, don't take this test now. Instead, study the examples, work the practice problems, and then take the test. This test will help you identify which concepts you have mastered, and which you need to study further.

1. Write a name for the decimal: 32.925

2. Express as a decimal: $\dfrac{391}{10,000}$

3. Write 8.13 as a mixed number in reduced form.

4. Write 0.625 as a fraction in reduced form.

5. Place the set of numbers in the proper order from smallest to largest: 3.5, 3.49, 3.51, 3.501

6. Round 689.59162 to the nearest tenth.

7. Round 3.062489 to the nearest thousandth.

8. Add:
$$\begin{array}{r} 6.31 \\ 5.9 \\ 9.04 \\ +\ 7.4 \\ \hline \end{array}$$

9. Add: $32.724 + 0.214 + 4.318$

10. Subtract:
$$\begin{array}{r} 39.17 \\ -12.69 \\ \hline \end{array}$$

11. Subtract: $89 - 23.417$

12. Multiply:
$$\begin{array}{r} 22.13 \\ \times\ 0.004 \\ \hline \end{array}$$

13. Multiply: 5.8703×1000

14. Multiply: 0.0004981×10^5

15. Divide: $0.03 \overline{) 0.04167}$

16. Divide: $1.1776 \div 3.2$

17. Write $\dfrac{13}{16}$ as a decimal.

18. Write $\dfrac{7}{22}$ as a repeating decimal.

19. Perform the operations in the correct order:
$(0.3)^2 + 9.2 \times 0.4 - 2.74$

20. Megan made her weekly trip to the fish market. This time she bought 2.7 pounds of cod for $2.99 per pound and 2.7 pounds of halibut for $8.75 per pound. How much did she spend altogether for fish? Round to the nearest cent if necessary.

21. Yvonne and Malena spent three weeks one summer traveling around to different national and state parks. They drove a total of 1219.04 miles and used 40.1 gallons of gas. How man miles per gallon did they get on the trip? Round to the nearest tenth of a gallon.

22. Fran worked 36 hours last week. She was paid $342.72. How much was she paid per hour?

If you __are__ familiar with the topics in this chapter, take this test now. If you can't answer a question, study the appropriate section of the chapter. If you are __not__ familiar with the topics in this chapter, don't take this test now. Instead, study the examples, work the practice problems, and then take the test. This test will help you identify which concepts you have mastered, and which you need to study further

____ 1. Write a name for the decimal: 43.815

    a. Forty-three and eight hundred fifteen tenths
    b. Forty-three and eight hundred fifteen thousandths
    c. Forty-three and eight hundred fifteen ten-thousandths
    d. Forty-three and eight hundred fifteen hundredths

____ 2. Express as a decimal: $\dfrac{659}{10,000}$

    a. 0.0659   **b.** 0.00659   **c.** 6.59   **d.** 0.659

____ 3. Write 9.17 as a mixed number, reduce if possible.

    a. $9\dfrac{17}{1000}$ **b.** $9\dfrac{17}{10}$ **c.** $9\dfrac{17}{100}$ **d.** $9\dfrac{17}{10,000}$

____ 4. Write 0.125 as a fraction, reduce if possible.

    a. $\dfrac{1}{8}$ **b.** $\dfrac{1}{4}$ **c.** $\dfrac{1}{16}$ **d.** $\dfrac{1}{7}$

____ 5. Place the set of numbers in the proper order from smallest to largest: 6.5, 6.49, 6.53, 6.504

    a. 6.53, 6.504, 6.5, 6.49   **b.** 6.49, 6.53, 6.504, 6.5
    c. 6.49, 6.5, 6.53, 6.504   **d.** 6.49, 6.5, 6.504, 6.53

____ 6. Round to the nearest tenth: 719.58273

    a. 719.58   **b.** 719.6   **c.** 719.59   **d.** 719.5

____ 7. Round to the nearest thousandth: 4.072381

    a. 4.07   **b.** 4.073   **c.** 4.072   **d.** 4.0723

____ 8. Add: 7.21
              6.9
              9.05
        + 8.3

    a. 31.146   **b.** 30.38
    c. 31.46   **d.** 30.146

____ **9.** Add: $34.914 + 0.364 + 4.257$

     a. 39.535   **b.** 38.141215   **c.** 38.1535   **d.** 38.425

____ **10.** Subtract: $\begin{array}{r} 58.29 \\ -13.57 \\ \hline \end{array}$

     a. 45.32   **b.** 44.72

     c. 44.32   **d.** 45.72

____ **11.** Subtract: $97 - 21.627$

     a. 76.373   **b.** 75.373   **c.** 76.627   **d.** 75.627

____ **12.** Multiply: $\begin{array}{r} 23.17 \\ \times 0.006 \\ \hline \end{array}$

     a. 0.013902   **b.** 139.02

     c. 1.3902   **d.** 0.13902

____ **13.** Multiply: 6.9403×1000

     a. 6940.3   **b.** 0.69403   **c.** 694.03   **d.** 69,403

____ **14.** Multiply: 0.0005972×10^5

     a. 59,720   **b.** 597.2   **c.** 59.72   **d.** 0.05972

____ **15.** Divide: $0.09\overline{)0.06417}$

     a. 0.0713   **b.** 1.403   **c.** 7.13   **d.** 0.713

____ **16.** Divide: $1.1776 \div 6.4$

     a. 1.84   **b.** 0.2775   **c.** 0.195   **d.** 0.184

_____ 17. Write $\dfrac{9}{16}$ as a decimal.

     a. 0.05625   **b.** 0.5625   **c.** 5.625   **d.** 0.005625

_____ 18. Write $\dfrac{3}{22}$ as a decimal.

     a. $0.13\overline{6}$ **b.** $0.13\overline{6}$ **c.** $0.\overline{136}$ **d.** $1.\overline{36}$

_____ 19. Perform the operations in the correct order: $(0.4)^2 + 9.6 \times 0.4 - 2.43$

     a. −19.8128   **b.** 1.57   **c.** 17.41   **d.** 1.474

_____ 20. Megan made her weekly trip to the fish market. This time she bought 2.3 pounds of cod for $3.19 per pound and 3.4 pounds of halibut for $8.75 per pound. How much did she spend altogether for fish? Round to the nearest cent if necessary.

     a. $37.09   **b.** $11.94   **c.** $30.97   **d.** $17.64

_____ 21. Yvonne and Malena spent three weeks one summer traveling around to different national and state parks. They drove a total of 1209.78 miles and used 28.6 gallons of gas. How man miles per gallon did they get on the trip? Round to the nearest tenth.

     a. 34,599.71   **b.** 40   **c.** 42.3   **d.** 40.3

_____ 22. Fran worked 38 hours last week. She was paid $324.52. How much was she paid per hour?

     a. $8.53   **b.** $286.52   **c.** $8.54   **d.** $12,331.76

1. Write a word name for 3.279.

2. Write 0.164 in fractional form and reduce, if possible.

3. Place the set of numbers in the proper order from smallest to largest:

    9.9, 9.91, 9.903, 9.09

4. Round 6547.2837 to the nearest thousandth.

5. Fill in the blank with one of the symbols: $<, =, or >$

    $\dfrac{7}{9}$ ____ 0.79

6. Find the value of x: $x + 0.025 = 7.775$

7. Add: $16 + 2.3 + 1.138$

8. Subtract: $11.0095 - 0.1$

9. Add: $8.94 + 1.244 + 17$

10. Multiply: $\begin{array}{r} 15.314 \\ \times\, 0.26 \\ \hline \end{array}$

11. Divide and round your answer to the nearest hundredth:

$$14.2\overline{)16.235}$$

12. Write $\dfrac{17}{12}$ as a decimal.

13. Perform the operations in the proper order:

$$(0.26)^2 \div 1.3 + 2.7 \times 0.01$$

14. A beef roast weighing 8.2 pounds costs $5.25 per pound. How much does the roast cost?

15. Perform the operations in the proper order:

$$(0.02 - 0.015) \times 0.3 + (0.5)^2 \times 0.2$$

16. Write $\dfrac{11}{14}$ as a decimal. Round to the nearest thousandth.

17. Ron traveled 169.6 miles on 7.6 gallons of gasoline. How many miles per gallon did the car get? Round to the nearest tenth.

18. On a given day, a charity received donations of $125,000, $67.50, and $25.00, and paid utility bills of $49.65 and $38.99. After paying the utility bills, how much money was left from the day's donations?

19. Emma and Jesse are waitresses who earn $3.85 per hour, plus tips. Emma worked 30 hours last week and received $68.35 in tips. Jesse worked 33 hours and received $73.40 in tips. Who earned more?

20. A group of college students rented five condominiums at a ski resort. Each condo's rent is $115 for the week. The group totals 35 students. How much will each one pay?

1. Write a word name for 0.0943 .

2. Write 0.105 in fractional form and reduce, if possible.

3. Place the set of numbers in the proper order from smallest to largest:

   8.801, 8.81, 8.8, 8.08

4. Round 0.698 to the nearest hundredth.

5. Fill in the blank with one of the symbols: $<, =, or >$

   $$\frac{5}{32} \underline{\qquad} 0.17$$

6. Find the value of x: $x - 7.63 = 19.02$

7. Add: $18 + 3.2 + 0.617$

8. Subtract: $15.0089 - 0.1$

9. Simplify: $13.96 - 0.8012 + 3$

10. Multiply: $\begin{array}{r} 14.382 \\ \times\, 0.17 \\ \hline \end{array}$

11. Divide and round your answer to the nearest tenth:

$$1.01 \overline{)17.95}$$

12. Write $\frac{3}{8}$ as a decimal.

13. Perform the operations in the proper order:
$$(0.15)^2 \div 0.09 + 0.06 \times 0.1$$

14. Beef roast costs \$6.98 per pound. How much does a 6.5 pound roast cost?

15. Perform the operations in the proper order:
$$(0.4)^3 + 3.18 \div 0.05 - 1.02$$

16. Write $\frac{5}{13}$ as a decimal. Round the answer to the nearest thousandth.

17. At the beginning of Amy's vacation, her odometer read 25,982.7 miles, and it read 28,111.1 miles at the end. She used 86.8 gallons of gas. How many miles per gallon did the car get? Round to the nearest tenth.

18. This year the rainfall for March, April, and May in Hastings Hamlet was 5.25, 1.99, and 8.08 inches, respectively. The all-time high total rainfall for those three months in Hastings Hamlet was 17.02 inches. How much below the all-time high was this year's three-month total?

19. Rick bought his lunch in the college cafeteria. His salad costs \$0.45 per ounce, while his submarine sandwich costs \$0.55 per inch. He ordered 6 ounces of salad, 10 inches of sandwich, and apple pie for \$1.75. How much did he pay?

20. A car salesman receives a monthly base salary of \$550. He also earns 0.15 of his total sales as a commission. Also, he receives a \$200 bonus if he makes his monthly quota. One month he sold \$15,800 worth of cars, and also made his quota. How much did he earn for the month?

1. Write a word name for 8.0025.

2. Write 0.505 in fractional form and reduce, if possible.

3. Place the set of number in the proper order from smallest to largest:

    6.995, 6.199, 6.9991, 6.9919

4. Round 793.0039 to the nearest thousandth.

5. Fill in the blank with one of the symbols: $<, =, or >$

    $2.17 \underline{\quad} 2\dfrac{1}{6}$

6. Find the value of x: $x + 9.72 = 21.5$

7. Add: $18 + 0.036 + 5.4$

8. Subtract: $12.0029 - 0.29$

9. Simplify: $6 - 0.015 + 0.2$

10. Multiply: $\begin{array}{r} 13.489 \\ \times\, 0.12 \\ \hline \end{array}$

11. Divide and round your answer to the nearest whole number:

$$1.2 \overline{)16.295}$$

12. Write $\dfrac{7}{15}$ as a decimal.

13. Perform the operations in the proper order:

$$(0.18)^2 \div (0.04) + (0.05) \times (0.1)$$

14. A 40-gallon tank of gasoline is being used at the rate of 0.4 gallons per day. How many days will it last?

15. Perform the operations in the proper order:

$$(0.05)^2 \div 5 + (0.3)^3 \times 2 + 0.04$$

16. Write $\dfrac{3}{19}$ as a decimal and round to the nearest ten thousandth.

17. At the beginning of the month, Tom had $723.99 in his checking account. What was his balance after deductions of $189.92, $65.45, $18.99, and $12.44, and deposits of $76.88, and $25.25?

18. Stock in Research, Inc. is selling for $75.25 per share. Beth bought 140 shares. How much did she pay for the stock?

19. Amy and Vanessa ran in a 23.5-kilometer race. If one mile equals 1.6 kilometers, how many miles did they run? Round to the nearest hundredth.

20. Nancy earns $4.85 per hour selling TV's and VCR's in a large department store. She also earns $15.50 commission for each TV she sells, and $12.75 for each VCR she sells. One day she sold 3 TV's and 4 VCR's while working $7\frac{1}{2}$ hours. How much did she earn that day?

_____ **1.** What decimal is indicated by the word name "forty-six and seven thousandths"?

    a. 46,007   **b.** 46.7000   **c.** 46.007   **d.** 46.0007

_____ **2.** Write 0.008 in fractional form and reduce, if possible.

    a. $\dfrac{1}{25}$ **b.** $\dfrac{1}{125}$ **c.** $\dfrac{2}{5}$ **d.** $\dfrac{2}{25}$

_____ **3.** Place the set of numbers 1.08, 1.8, 1.081, and 1.801 in the proper order from smallest to largest.

    a. 1.08, 1.8, 1.081, 1.801   **b.** 1.8, 1.08, 1.081, 1.801

    c. 1.801, 1.8, 1.081, 1.08   **d.** 1.08, 1.081, 1.8, 1.801

_____ **4.** Round 8.9613 to the nearest tenth

    a. 10.0   **b.** 8.9   **c.** 9.0   **d.** 8.95

_____ **5.** Fill in the blank with one of these symbols: <, =, *or* >

    $1.07 \underline{\quad} 1\dfrac{7}{10}$

    a. <   **b.** =   **c.** >   **d.** none of these

_____ **6.** Find the value of x: $x + 3.35 = 11.78$

    a. 8.43   **b.** 8.53   **c.** 13.13   **d.** 4.587

_____ **7.** Add: $1.27 + 0.5 + 3.329$

    a. 1.661   **b.** 2.156   **c.** 4.604   **d.** 5.099

_____ **8.** Subtract: $5.002 - 4.1$

    a. 0.902   **b.** 1.001   **c.** 0.002   **d.** 1.102

_____ **9.** Simplify: $7 - 0.993 + 1.5$

    a. 7.507   **b.** 7.491   **c.** 7.707   **d.** 7.293

_____ **10.** Multiply: $\begin{array}{r} 2.634 \\ \times\, 0.005 \\ \hline \end{array}$

    a. 0.001317   **b.** 13.17

    c. 0.01317   **d.** 0.1317

_____ 11. Divide and round your answer to the nearest whole number: $0.23 \overline{)25.24}$

    a. 1   **b.** 109   **c.** 11   **d.** 110

_____ 12. Write $\dfrac{15}{11}$ as a decimal.

    a. $1.\overline{36}$ **b.** $0.7\overline{3}$ **c.** 1.4   **d.** $1.2\overline{6}$

_____ 13. Perform the operations in the proper order: $(0.21)^2 \div 0.09 + 0.4 \times 0.01$

    a. 0.0089   **b.** 0.494   **c.** 0.0009   **d.** 9

_____ 14. A 50-gallon drum of liquid fertilizer is being used at a rate of 0.5 gallons per day. How many days will it last?

    a. 25 days   **b.** 250 days   **c.** 100 days   **d.** 10 days

_____ 15. Perform the operations in the proper order: $(0.01)^2 \times 0.5 + 2.3 \times (0.3)^2$

    a. 0.20705   **b.** 0.00275   **c.** 0.02075   **d.** 0.2075

_____ 16. Write $\dfrac{2}{3}$ as a repeating decimal.

    a. $0.222\overline{2}$ **b.** $0.666\overline{6}$ **c.** $0.333\overline{3}$ **d.** $0.677\overline{7}$

_____ 17. At the beginning of the month, Joanna had $585.87 in her checking account. She deposited an additional $89.93 and wrote checks of $39.32, $25.00, and $112.29. The bank deducted $57.76 for her monthly life insurance premium, and the bank also charged her an $8.80 service charge. What was her new balance?

    a. $657.21   **b.** $548.15   **c.** $252.77   **d.** $432.63

_____ 18. Ground beef sells for $1.89 per pound. How much will 6.77 pounds cost? Round to the nearest cent.

    a. $12.80   **b.** $12.79   **c.** $12.69   **d.** $12.70

_____ 19. Five brothers pooled their money to buy their mother a gold chain for her birthday. The jeweler said that the type of gold chain they wanted cost $5.65 per inch, plus state tax, which was 0.05 of the purchase price. They want to buy an 18-inch necklace. How much money will they need?

    a. $101.70   **b.** $106.79   **c.** $96.62   **d.** $101.75

_____ 20. Mike opened a savings account with $20.00 cash. Over the next few weeks, he made five deposits of: $28.00, $17.50, $20.25, $15.00, and $115.38. The teller, at his latest deposit, also added 11 cents interest to his account. What is his new balance?

    a. $216.13   **b.** $201.24   **c.** $216.24   **d.** $196.24

____ 1. What decimal is indicated by the word name "five and four hundred sixty-seven ten thousandths"?

    a. 5.467   **b.** 5.0467   **c.** 5,647,000   **d.** 0.5467

____ 2. Write 0.0155 in fractional form and reduce, if possible.

    a. $\dfrac{3}{2000}$ **b.** $\dfrac{31}{200}$ **c.** $\dfrac{31}{2000}$ **d.** $\dfrac{3}{20}$

____ 3. Place the set of numbers 0.709, 0.710, 0.79, and 0.079 in the proper order from smallest to largest.

    a. 0.079, 0.709, 0.710, 0.79   **b.** 0.079, 0.79, 0.709, 0.710

    c. 0.79, 0.709, 0.710, 0.079   **d.** 0.79, 0.079, 0.709, 0.710

____ 4. Round 11.4596 to the nearest thousandth.

    a. 11.500   **b.** 11.460   **c.** 11.459   **d.** 11.4595

____ 5. Fill in the blank with one of these symbols: <, =, *or* >

    $1\dfrac{2}{7}$____1.27

    a. <   **b.** =

    c. >   **d.** none of these

____ 6. Find the value of x: $0.15 \times x = 8.25$

    a. 55   **b.** 0..55   **c.** 0.1375   **d.** 75

____ 7. Add: $9 + 6.9 + 0.223$

    a. 0.292   **b.** 0.382   **c.** 16.123   **d.** 7.123

____ 8. Subtract: $6.004 - 0.4$

    a. 2.004   **b.** 6   **c.** 5.604   **d.** 5.964

____ 9. Simplify: $6 - 0.881 + 4.3$

    a. 7.78   **b.** 2.381   **c.** 2.219   **d.** 9.419

____ 10. Multiply: $\begin{array}{r} 5.636 \\ \times\, 0.105 \\ \hline \end{array}$

    a. 0.059178   **b.** 5.9178

    c. 5.741   **d.** 0.59178

Chapter 3: Test Form E (cont.)   Name: _____

Page 2 of 2

____ 11. Divide and round your answer to the nearest tenth: $0.19\overline{)1.89}$

     a. 10.0   **b.** 9.9   **c.** 1.0   **d.** 0.9

____ 12. Write $\dfrac{3}{8}$ as a decimal.

     a. $0.\overline{4}$ **b.** $2.\overline{6}$ **c.** 0.375   **d.** 0.4375

____ 13. Perform the operations in the proper order: $(0.24)^2 \div 0.16 + 0.32 \times 0.1$

     a. 0.068   **b.** 0.012   **c.** 0.3   **d.** 0.392

____ 14. A butcher has 66 pounds of meat. He wants to pack the meat into packages weighing 0.75 pounds each. How many packages can he make?

     a. 49.5 packages   **b.** 80 packages   **c.** 86 packages   **d.** 88 packages

____ 15. Perform the operations in the proper order: $1.55 \div 0.05 + (0.03)^2 \div 10$

     a. 3.10009   **b.** 3.1009   **c.** 0.31009   **d.** 31.00009

____ 16. Write $\dfrac{15}{16}$ as a decimal.

     a. 0.9375   **b.** 0.8375   **c.** 0.3125   **d.** $1.06\overline{66}$

____ 17. Mary Ann follows her investments in the stock market daily. Over a five-day period she gained $98.87, gained $14.24, lost $88.18, gained $23.44, and lost $49.00. How much did she lose overall?

     a. $22.01   **b.** $100.37   **c.** $0.63   **d.** $50.49

____ 18. Harold purchased 18.7 gallons of gasoline at a price of $1.13 per gallon. How much did he pay? Round to the nearest cent.

     a. $16.55   **b.** $21.13   **c.** $20.94   **d.** $20.00

____ 19. Boston had five snowstorms in one month, whose snowfall amounts were: 16.3 inches, 10.2 inches, 4.25 inches, 22.3 inches, and 8.9 inches. The normal amount of snow for the month was 22.35 inches. How many more inches of snow than normal fell that month?

     a. 29.6 inches   **b.** 39.6 inches   **c.** 49.6 inches   **d.** 61.95 inches

____ 20. Dennis and Rob rented a van and drove from Boulder, Colorado to Palo Alto, California. The cost was $300 for the first two weeks and the $50 per day after that. Also, they were not charged a mileage fee for the first 2000 miles, but had to pay 12 cents a mile for every mile after that. They took their trip, and it took two weeks and five days. Also, they drove 2350 miles total. What was the total cost of the van rental?

     a. $592   **b.** $832   **c.** $550   **d.** $342

_____ **1.** What decimal is indicated by the word name "seven hundred forty-three thousandths"?

     a. 0.743   **b.** 0.000743   **c.** 743,000   **d.** 700.043

_____ **2.** Write 0.264 in fractional form and reduce, if possible.

     a. $\dfrac{33}{125}$ **b.** $\dfrac{53}{200}$ **c.** $\dfrac{13}{50}$ **d.** $\dfrac{13}{125}$

_____ **3.** Place the set of numbers 0.98, 9.8, 9.08, and 9.081 in the proper order from smallest to largest.

     a. 0.98, 9.8, 9.08, 9.081   **b.** 0.98, 9.08, 9.081, 9.8

     c. 9.8, 0.98, 9.08, 9.081   **d.** 0.98, 9.081, 9.08, 9.8

_____ **4.** Round 76.5972 to the nearest hundredth.

     a. 100   **b.** 76.59   **c.** 76.597   **d.** 76.60

_____ **5.** Fill in the blank with one of these symbols: <, =, *or* >

     $0.625 \underline{} \dfrac{5}{8}$

     a. <   **b.** =

     c. >   **d.** none of these

_____ **6.** Find the value of x : $x \times 0.04 = 0.1008$

     a. 2.52   **b.** 0.252   **c.** 0.0252   **d.** 0.001008

_____ **7.** Add: $1 + 2.4 + 0.536$

     a. 3.936   **b.** 0.561   **c.** 3.036   **d.** 2.937

_____ **8.** Subtract: $7.774 - 2.4$

     a. 5.77   **b.** 5.734   **c.** 1.774   **d.** 5.374

_____ **9.** Simplify: $4 - 1.95 + 3.3$

     a. 5.8   **b.** 5.35   **c.** 2.2   **d.** 0.4

_____ **10.** Multiply: $\begin{array}{r} 6.25 \\ \times\, 0.012 \\ \hline \end{array}$

     a. 0.00075   **b.** 0.075

     c. 0.0075   **d.** 6.37

____ 11. Divide and round your answer to the nearest tenth: $0.23\overline{)25.2}$

     a. 109.6   **b.** 110   **c.** 109.5   **d.** 1.1

____ 12. Write $\dfrac{9}{200}$ as a decimal.

     a. 4.5   **b.** 0.45   **c.** $22.\overline{2}$ **d.** 0.045

____ 13. Perform the operations in the proper order: $(0.15)^2 \div 0.09 + 0.16 \times 0.01$

     a. 0.0009   **b.** 156.25   **c.** 0.2516   **d.** 0.0041

____ 14. A 250-gallon tank of gasoline is being used at a rate of 0.75 gallon per day. How many days will it last?

     a. 187.5 days   **b.** $333.\overline{3}$ days   **c.** 30 days   **d.** 500 days

____ 15. Perform the operations in the proper order: $(0.2)^3 + (0.3)^2 \div 0.01 + 0.5 \times 2.1$

     a. 1.0589   **b.** 10.13   **c.** 1.18   **d.** 10.058

____ 16. Write $1\dfrac{1}{6}$ as a decimal.

     a. $1.67\overline{7}$ **b.** 1.06   **c.** $1.66\overline{6}$ **d.** $1.1666\overline{6}$

____ 17. Gasoline is sold at $1.13 per gallon. How much will 19.9 gallons cost? Round to the nearest cent.

     a. $22.49   **b.** $22.29   **c.** $22.28   **d.** $22.48

____ 18. At the beginning of the month, Andy had $289.79 in his checking account. During the month he made deposits of $94.68, $25.05, and $9.98. He wrote checks of $55.10, $29.19, and $75.76. The bank deducted $7.95 in service charges. What was his new balance?

     a. $267.40   **b.** $328.08   **c.** $251.50   **d.** $461.40

____ 19. David and Kris biked across Ireland, from Dublin to Galway City, in 5 days. On the first day, they rode 76.2 kilometers; on the second day, 43.5 kilometers; on the third day, 52.8 kilometers; on the fourth day, 32 kilometers; and on the fifth day, 92.5 kilometers. They knew that 1 mile equals 1.6 kilometers. How many miles did they bike?

     a. 185.625 miles   **b.** 293 miles   **c.** 468.8 miles   **d.** 18.3125 miles

____ 20. Mukul and Claire want to buy a home that costs $155,000. The need an amount equal to 0.15 of the purchase price for the down payment. They also need an amount equal to 0.01 of the purchase price to cover closing costs. If they have saved $24,500, how much more money do they need?

     a. 0   **b.** $300   **c.** $3300   **d.** $500

If you <u>are</u> familiar with the topics in this chapter, take this test now. If you can't answer a question, study the appropriate section of the chapter. If you are <u>not</u> familiar with the topics in this chapter, don't take this test now. Instead, study the examples, work the practice problems, and then take the test. This test will help you identify which concepts you have mastered, and which you need to study further.

1. Write this ratio in simplest form: 15 to 29

2. Write this ratio in simplest form: 66 to 220

3. Write this ratio in simplest form: $98 to $28

4. Write this ratio in simplest form: 77 meters to 132 meters

5. Bob's salary is $230 per week. $80 per week is withheld for taxes. Find the ratio of withheld taxes to salary.

6. Write this rate in simplest form:
   18 aspirin for 300 athletes

7. Write in this rate simplest form:
   120 lbs of fertilizer for each 800 square feet of lawn

8. 146 miles are traveled in 4 hours. What is the unit rate in miles per hour? Round to the nearest tenth if necessary.

9. 18 CD players are purchased for $486. What is the unit cost per CD player?

10. Write as a proportion: 23 is to 49 as 37 is to 101

11. Write as a proportion: 126 is to 148 as 52 is to 88

12. Is $\frac{16}{41} = \frac{48}{123}$ a proportion?

13. Is $\dfrac{15}{34} = \dfrac{26}{61}$ a proportion?

14. Solve for n: $8 \times n = 152$

15. Solve for n: $336 = 21 \times n$

16. Solve for n: $\dfrac{42}{182} = \dfrac{6}{n}$

17. Solve for n: $\dfrac{4}{164} = \dfrac{n}{246}$

18. Solve for n: $\dfrac{n}{600} = \dfrac{300}{22.5}$

19. Solve for n: $\dfrac{\frac{1}{3}}{n} = \dfrac{\frac{1}{2}}{9}$

20. A recipe for six portions calls for 1.5 cups of flour. How many cups of flour are needed to make 11 portions?

21. Maria's car can travel 72 miles on 2 gallons of gas. How far can she travel on 9 gallons of gas?

22. Two cities are 5 inches apart on a map, but the actual distance between them is 365 miles. What is the actual distance between two other cities that are 7 inches apart on the map?

23. A shipment of 121 light bulbs had 8 defective bulbs. How many defective bulbs would we expect, at the same rate, in a shipment of 1089 light bulbs?

24. Last year one of the Red Sox pitchers gave up 67 runs in 235 innings. If he normally gives up runs at this rate, how many runs would you expect him to give up if he pitched a nine-inning game? Round your answer to the nearest tenth.

25. A recent survey showed that 3 out of every 10 people in Massachusetts read the *Boston Globe*. In a Massachusetts town of 35,600 people, how many people would you expect to read the *Boston Globe*?

If you are familiar with the topics in this chapter, take this test now. If you can't answer a question, study the appropriate section of the chapter. If you are not familiar with the topics in this chapter, don't take this test now. Instead, study the examples, work the practice problems, and then take the test. This test will help you identify which concepts you have mastered, and which you need to study further

_____ 1. Write the ratio 13 to 37 in simplest form.

    a. $\dfrac{1}{3}$ b. $\dfrac{13}{37}$ c. $\dfrac{37}{13}$ d. $\dfrac{3}{1}$

_____ 2. Write the ratio 55 to 220 in simplest form.

    a. $\dfrac{55}{220}$ b. $\dfrac{1}{4}$ c. $\dfrac{11}{44}$ d. $\dfrac{220}{55}$

_____ 3. Write the ratio "$98 to $35" in simplest form

    a. $\dfrac{14}{5}$ b. $\dfrac{49}{17}$ c. $\dfrac{98}{35}$ d. $\dfrac{3}{1}$

_____ 4. Write the ratio " 88 meters to 132 meters" in simplest form.

    a. $\dfrac{88}{132}$ b. $\dfrac{44}{66}$ c. $\dfrac{66}{44}$ d. $\dfrac{2}{3}$

_____ 5. Bob's salary is $210 per week. $60 is withheld for taxes. Find the ratio, in simplest form, of withheld taxes to salary.

    a. $\dfrac{30}{105}$ b. $\dfrac{2}{7}$ c. $\dfrac{6}{21}$ d. $\dfrac{60}{210}$

_____ 6. Write "18 aspirin for 246 athletes" as a rate in simplest form.

    a. $\dfrac{9 \text{ aspirin}}{82 \text{ athletes}}$ b. $\dfrac{82 \text{ athletes}}{9 \text{ aspirin}}$ c. $\dfrac{3 \text{ aspirin}}{41 \text{ athletes}}$ d. $\dfrac{18 \text{ aspirin}}{246 \text{ athletes}}$

_____ 7. Write "140 pounds of fertilizer for each 700 square feet of lawn" as rate in simplest form.

    a. $\dfrac{70 \text{ pounds}}{350 \text{ sq. ft.}}$ b. $\dfrac{7 \text{ pounds}}{35 \text{ sq. ft.}}$ c. $\dfrac{1 \text{ pounds}}{5 \text{ sq. ft.}}$ d. $\dfrac{35 \text{ pounds}}{175 \text{ sq. ft.}}$

_____ 8. 219 miles are traveled in 6 hours. What is the unit rate in miles per hours? Round to the nearest tenth if necessary.

    a. 36.5 miles per hour   b. 73 miles per hour   c. .027 miles per hour   d. 54.75 miles per hour

_____ 9. 17 CD players are purchased for $578. What is the cost per CD player? Round to the nearest tenth if necessary.

    a. $68 per CD player   b. $34 per CD player   c. $17 per CD player   d. $578 per CD player

_____ 10. Write "27 is to 46 as 21 is to 34" as a proportion.

    a. $\dfrac{46}{27}=\dfrac{21}{34}$ b. $\dfrac{46}{21}=\dfrac{27}{34}$ c. $\dfrac{21}{27}=\dfrac{46}{34}$ d. $\dfrac{27}{46}=\dfrac{21}{34}$

_____ 11. Write "136 is to 158 as 47 is to 81" as a proportion.

    a. $\dfrac{158}{81}=\dfrac{136}{47}$ b. $\dfrac{136}{47}=\dfrac{81}{158}$ c. $\dfrac{136}{158}=\dfrac{47}{81}$ d. $\dfrac{158}{136}=\dfrac{47}{81}$

_____ **12.** Which of the following is a true proportion?

    a. $\dfrac{16}{51} = \dfrac{48}{153}$
    b. $\dfrac{16}{51} = \dfrac{116}{151}$
    c. $\dfrac{16}{51} = \dfrac{49}{123}$
    d. $\dfrac{16}{51} = \dfrac{102}{32}$

_____ **13.** Which of the following is a true proportion?

    a. $\dfrac{14}{35} = \dfrac{22}{55}$
    b. $\dfrac{14}{35} = \dfrac{30}{70}$
    c. $\dfrac{14}{35} = \dfrac{7}{15}$
    d. $\dfrac{14}{35} = \dfrac{12}{60}$

_____ **14.** Solve for n: $7 \times n = 133$

    a. 140
    b. 19
    c. .053
    d. 931

_____ **15.** Solve for n: $364 = 26 \times n$

    a. 14
    b. 9464
    c. 390
    d. .765

_____ **16.** Solve for n: $\dfrac{42}{198} = \dfrac{7}{n}$

    a. 1188
    b. 42
    c. 33
    d. 6

_____ **17.** Solve for n: $\dfrac{4}{164} = \dfrac{n}{246}$

    a. 2
    b. 6
    c. 16
    d. 8

_____ **18.** Solve for n: $\dfrac{n}{300} = \dfrac{60}{22.5}$

    a. 18,000
    b. 800
    c. 112.5
    d. 80

_____ **19.** Solve for n: $\dfrac{\frac{1}{3}}{n} = \dfrac{\frac{1}{2}}{15}$

    a. 7.5
    b. 9
    c. 10
    d. 6

_____ **20.** A recipe for six portions calls for 1.5 cups of flour. How many cups of flour are needed to make 8 portions?

    a. 6 cups
    b. 4 cups
    c. 12 cups
    d. 2 cups

_____ **21.** Maria's car can travel 68 miles on 2 gallons of gas. How far can she travel on 9 gallons of gas?

    a. 1224 miles
    b. 272 miles
    c. 612 miles
    d. 306 miles

_____ **22.** Two cities are 5 inches apart on a map, but the actual distance between them is 365 miles. What is the actual distance between two other cities that are 12 inches apart on the map?

    a. 175.2 miles
    b. 876 miles
    c. 4380 miles
    d. 60 miles

_____ **23.** A shipment of 121 light bulbs had 5 defective bulbs. How many defective bulbs would we expect, at the same rate, in a shipment of 1089 light bulbs?

    a. 45 defective bulbs
    b. 9 defective bulbs
    c. 218 defective bulbs
    d. 50 defective bulbs

_____ **24.** Last year one of the Red Sox pitchers gave up 64 runs in 235 innings. If he normally gives up runs at this rate, how many runs would you expect him to give up if he pitched a nine-inning game? Round your answer to the nearest tenth.

    a. 2.5 runs
    b. 7.1 runs
    c. 26.1 runs
    d. 3.7 runs

_____ **25.** A recent survey showed that 6 out of every 10 people in Massachusetts read the *Boston Globe*. In a Massachusetts town of 12,400 people, how many would you expect to read the *Boston Globe*?

    a. 1240 people
    b. 60 people
    c. 7440 people
    d. 2067 people

1. Write $27:28$ as a ratio in its simplest form.

2. Write "784 miles per 40 gallons" as a rate in simplest form.

3. Write "50 pounds in 28 weeks" as a unit rate. Round to the nearest hundredth, if necessary.

4. Write "$6248 for 83 shares of stock" as a unit rate. Round to the nearest hundredth, if necessary.

5. Angelique knows she should keep her fat intake to less than 65 grams per day if on a 2000 calorie diet. She is on a 1600 calorie per day diet. How many grams of fat should she limit herself to everyday?

6. If a pitcher strikes out 6 hitters in 5 innings, how many hitters is it likely he will strike out in 9 innings? Round to the nearest whole number.

7. Which of the following proportions is true:

   a. $\dfrac{6.7}{3.4} = \dfrac{10.05}{4.76}$

   b. $\dfrac{11}{23} = \dfrac{33}{68}$

   c. $\dfrac{2.6}{8.1}$

   d. $\dfrac{5.2}{11} = \dfrac{1.56}{3.3}$

8. Which of the following proportions is true:

   a. $\dfrac{\$3.85}{6 \text{ ounces}} = \dfrac{\$5.39}{8.1 \text{ ounces}}$

   b. $\dfrac{\$4.10}{5 \text{ ounces}} = \dfrac{\$9.10}{10 \text{ ounces}}$

   c. $\dfrac{\$6.20}{10 \text{ ounces}} = \dfrac{\$12.20}{20 \text{ ounces}}$

   d. $\dfrac{\$2.99}{4 \text{ ounces}} = \dfrac{\$59.80}{80 \text{ ounces}}$

9. Solve for n. Round to the nearest tenth if necessary.
$$\frac{25}{45} = \frac{n}{99}$$

10. Solve for n. Round to the nearest tenth if necessary.
$$\frac{1.5}{n} = \frac{3.3}{2.8}$$

11. Solve for n. Round to the nearest tenth if necessary.
$$\frac{3 \text{ cups of flour}}{n} = \frac{16 \text{ cups of flour}}{28 \text{ tablespoons of butter}}$$

12. Solve for n. Round to the nearest tenth if necessary.
$$\frac{\$6.95}{n} = \frac{\$12.95}{15 \text{ ounces}}$$

*For problems 13-20, solve each problem by using a proportion. **Round your answer to the nearest hundredth, if necessary.***

13. Josh typed 88 words in 100 seconds. At this rate, how many words did he type in a minute?

14. If 4 inches on a map represents 96 miles, what does 5 inches represent?

15. If it costs $310 to fertilize 3600 square feet, what does it cost to fertilize a lawn of 5900 square feet?

16. In the 2000-2001 winter, there were a total of 62 polar bears in the Barrow, Alaska region, as reported by an extensive helicopter-aided count. There were also 12 polar bear sightings within the town limits of Barrow. This year, the town cannot afford the helicopter research, but there were 19 polar bear sightings within the town limits of Barrow. Estimate, to the nearest whole number, the number of polar bears in the whole region.

17. Medway High School has 2150 students and 86 teachers. Next year, there will be 2475 students. In order to keep the same student-teacher ratio, how many teachers should Medway High have?

18. The town of Morrisville has 3550 registered voters, of which 2025 are Democrats, 1330 are Republicans, and 195 are independent. What is the ratio of Democrats to independents (in lowest terms)

19. One Saturday, the Wheeling Along bicycle shop had 255 customers and sold 23 bikes. The next Saturday they sold 32 bikes. Estimate how many customers they had that day. Round to the nearest whole number.

20. State Senator Magnani's campaign manager conducted a telephone survey and discovered that 13 out of every 20 voters said they would vote for the Senator. If there are 185,500 voters who voted on election day, and this trend holds, how many votes will Senator Magnani receive?

1. Write $52:65$ as a ratio in its simplest form. Express your answer as a fraction.

2. Write "582 miles per 20 gallons" as a rate in simplest form. Express your answer as a fraction.

3. Write "342 words in 3 minutes" as a unit rate. Round to the nearest hundredth, if necessary.

4. Write "$2993 for 180 shares of stock" as a unit rate. Round to the nearest hundredth, if necessary.

5. Tuan was on sale. A can that contained $6\frac{1}{8}$ ounces cost $1.69. What is the cost per ounce? Round to the nearest hundredth.

6. Mike had 18 foul shots in his latest basketball game. He made 12 of them. At this rate, if he had 100 foul shots, estimate how many baskets he would make. Round to the nearest whole number.

7. Is the following proportion true or false?
$$\frac{33}{41} = \frac{149}{168}$$

8. Is the following proportion true or false?
$$\frac{17}{19} = \frac{153}{171}$$

9. Solve for n. Round to the nearest tenth if necessary.
$$\frac{n}{14} = \frac{10.5}{49}$$

10. Solve for n. Round to the nearest tenth if necessary.
$$\frac{0.3}{0.5} = \frac{7}{n}$$

11. Solve for n. Round to the nearest tenth if necessary.
$$\frac{75 \text{ cups}}{21 \text{ people}} = \frac{n}{14 \text{ people}}$$

12. Solve for n. Round to the nearest tenth if necessary.
$$\frac{\$6.48}{n} = \frac{\$10.00}{12 \text{ ounces}}$$

For problems 13-20, solve each problem by using a proportion. Round your answer to the nearest hundredth, if necessary.

13. Maria hiked 50 miles in 3 days. At this rate, how far could she hike in 36 days?

14. If 2.5 centimeters on a map represents 48 miles, what distance does 12 centimeters represent?

15. In a manufacturing process, for every 128 items assembled, 2 are defective. At this rate, if 6400 are assembled, how many will be defective?

16. A biologist catches 52 lake trout, tags them, and then releases them into the lake. A few days later, she catches 110 trout. 13 of them have the original tag. Estimate the number of trout in the lake.

17. Kris and David biked the west coast of Ireland. In 5 days they biked 165 miles. If they can continue this rate, how long will it take them to bike 561 miles? Round to the nearest tenth.

18. In the Medway High School Class of 1994, there were 58 boys and 61 girls. 21 of the boys were left-handed and 13 of the girls were left-handed. What is the ratio of left-handed students to right-handed students? Reduce to lowest terms.

19. Mrs. Bench started a tutoring business. She spent $210 on newspaper advertising and obtained 42 students. Next year she plans to spend $500 on newspaper advertising. Estimate, to the nearest whole number, the number of students she can expect to sign up for her tutoring.

20. In ancient Greece, architects used the "golden rectangle," a ratio of length to height that is 1.618 to 1. They felt that this was the most "pleasing to the eye." If this golden rectangle is to be used, and the building is 25 feet high, how long should it be?

1. Write $28:126$ as a ratio in its simplest form. Express your answer as a fraction.

2. Write "484 words in 8 minutes" as a rate in simplest form. Express your answer as a fraction.

3. Write "923 miles per 26 gallons" as a unit rate. Round to the nearest hundredth, if necessary.

4. Write "$982 for 8 shares of stock" as a unit rate. Round to the nearest hundredth, if necessary.

5. Kelly received $300 form her aunt to use on her trip to England. She exchanged the money for English pounds, and received 215 pounds for 300 American dollars. What is the exchange rate, or, how much does it cost in American dollars for one English pound? Round to the nearest hundredth?

6. Driving from Boston to South Bend, Indiana, a distance of 960 miles, Joe and Eileen saw that their car used 30 gallons of gas. Now they need to drive 585 miles to Washington D.C. How many gallons of gas will their car use? Round to the nearest whole number.

7. Is the following proportion true or false?
$$\frac{0.4}{0.9} = \frac{2}{4.5}$$

8. Is the following proportion true or false?
$$\frac{136}{11} = \frac{148}{12}$$

9. Solve for n. Round to the nearest tenth if necessary.
$$\frac{15}{n} = \frac{120}{56}$$

10. Solve for n. Round to the nearest tenth if necessary.
$$\frac{2\frac{1}{2}}{6} = \frac{n}{24}$$

11. Solve for n. Round to the nearest tenth if necessary.
$$\frac{18 \text{ words}}{0.3 \text{ minute}} = \frac{70 \text{ words}}{n}$$

12. Solve for n. Round to the nearest tenth if necessary.
$$\frac{n}{8.8 \text{ cups of flour}} = \frac{12 \text{ cakes}}{21 \text{ cups of flour}}$$

For problems 13-20, solve each problem by using a proportion. Round your answer to the nearest hundredth, if necessary.

13. Amy hiked 160 miles in 3 days. At this rate, how far could she hike in 36 days?

14. If 210 miles is represented on a map by 7 centimeters, how many centimeters are needed to represent 360 miles?

15. In a manufacturing process, for every 340 items assembled, 5 are defective. At this rate, if 5100 items are assembled, how many of them will be defective?

16. On a certain day, a 6-foot tall man cast a shadow $4\frac{1}{2}$ feet long. At the same time, a building cast a shadow 90 feet long. How tall is the building?

17. A math professor is writing a textbook. In 5 weeks, he wrote $1\frac{1}{2}$ chapters. At this rate, how long will it take her to write the whole text, if she plans to have 14 chapters? Round to the nearest whole number.

18. On a set of blueprints for a new house, one inch equals 4 feet. One room is shown as $3\frac{1}{2}$ inches wide by $5\frac{3}{8}$ inches long. What are the real dimensions of the room?

19. A photocopying business discovers that it needs 200 boxes of regular size white paper every 7 business days. How many boxes of paper should they order to cover 280 business days?

20. Over the years, a college has learned that for every 100 applicants accepted for admission, a total of 74 actually attend their college. This years, 703 students are coming in September. How many students were accepted by the College?

_____ **1.** Write $30:84$ as a ratio in simplest form.

     a. $\dfrac{1}{27}$ **b.** $\dfrac{3}{7}$ **c.** $\dfrac{5}{14}$ **d.** $\dfrac{1}{3}$

_____ **2.** Write "252 miles per 8 gallons" as a rate in simplest form.

     a. $\dfrac{28 \text{ miles}}{1 \text{ gallon}}$ **b.** $\dfrac{63 \text{ miles}}{2 \text{ gallon}}$ **c.** $\dfrac{125 \text{ miles}}{4 \text{ gallon}}$ **d.** $\dfrac{64 \text{ miles}}{3 \text{ gallon}}$

_____ **3.** Write "48 gallons in 14 days" as a unit rate. Round to the nearest hundredth, if necessary.

     a. 3.43 gallons/day   **b.** 4 gallons/day   **c.** 3.14 gallons/day   **d.** 292 gallons/day

_____ **4.** Write "$6188 for 82 shares of stock" as a unit rate. Round to the nearest hundredth if necessary.

     a. $13.25/share   **b.** $69.24/share   **c.** $80.92 per share   **d.** $75.46/share

_____ **5.** Kim knows she should keep her fat intake to less than 130 grams per day if on a 4000 calorie diet. She is on a 1500 calorie per day diet. How many grams of fat should she limit herself to each day?

     a. 48   **b.** 50   **c.** 48.75   **d.** 86.67

_____ **6.** If a pitcher strikes out 5 hitters in 4 innings, how many hitters is it likely he will strike out in 9 innings? Round to the nearest whole number.

     a. 12   **b.** 11   **c.** 10   **d.** 9

_____ **7.** Which of the following proportions is true?

     a. $\dfrac{12}{42}=\dfrac{10}{35}$ **b.** $\dfrac{1}{2}=\dfrac{3}{4}$ **c.** $\dfrac{10}{9}=\dfrac{11}{10}$ **d.** $\dfrac{48}{56}=\dfrac{40}{48}$

_____ **8.** Which of the following proportions is true?

     a. $\dfrac{15}{8}=\dfrac{22}{12}$ **b.** $\dfrac{11}{12}=\dfrac{13\frac{3}{4}}{15}$ **c.** $\dfrac{7}{8}=\dfrac{15\frac{1}{2}}{18}$ **d.** $\dfrac{2.5}{6}=\dfrac{1.6}{4}$

_____ **9.** Solve for n: $\dfrac{8}{n}=\dfrac{33}{45}$ Round to the nearest tenth, if necessary.

     a. $n=12$ **b.** $n\approx 9.5$ **c.** $n=11$ **d.** $n\approx 10.9$

_____ **10.** Solve for n: $\dfrac{14}{21.2}=\dfrac{n}{15}$ Round to the nearest tenth, if necessary.

     a. $n\approx 7.8$ **b.** $n\approx 20.2$ **c.** $n\approx 9.9$ **d.** $n\approx 19.8$

___ 11. Solve for n: $\dfrac{14.2 \text{ cups of flour}}{6 \text{ loaves of bread}} = \dfrac{20 \text{ cups of flour}}{n}$ Round to the nearest tenth, if necessary.

   a. $n = 47.3$ loaves   **b.** $n = 11.8$ loaves   **c.** $n = 8.5$ loaves   **d.** $n = 10.7$ loaves

___ 12. Solve for n: $\dfrac{\$9.75}{24 \text{ ounces}} = \dfrac{\$5.85}{n}$ Round to the nearest tenth, if necessary.

   a. $n = 10.6$ ounces   **b.** $n = 14.4$ ounces   **c.** $n = 9.8$ ounces   **d.** $n = 15.2$ ounces

___ 13. Mark traveled 455 miles in 5 hours. At this rate, how far could he travel in $7\frac{1}{2}$ hours?

   a. 682.5 miles   **b.** 728 miles   **c.** 1137.5 miles   **d.** 650 miles

___ 14. If 2 centimeters on a map represents 86 miles, what distance does 5 centimeters represent?

   a. 92 miles   **b.** 34.4 miles   **c.** 258 miles   **d.** 215 miles

___ 15. At a bakery, for every 55 cakes baked, 3 have unacceptable texture. If the bakery makes 935 cakes per month, how many have unacceptable texture?

   a. 48 cakes   **b.** 51 cakes   **c.** 156 cakes   **d.** 85 cakes

___ 16. A biologist catches 43 lake trout, tags them, and then releases them into the lake. A few days later she catches 100 trout. 15 of them have the original tag. Estimate the number of trout in the lake.

   a. 285   **b.** 645   **c.** 286   **d.** 287

___ 17. Medway High School has 1350 students and 55 teachers. Next year, there will be 125 more students. How many teachers should be on the faculty to keep the same student-teacher ratio?

   a. 60   **b.** 61   **c.** 65   **d.** 55

___ 18. A calculus class contains 9 sophomore men, 8 sophomore women, 11 male graduate students, and 5 female graduate students. What is the ratio of men to women in the class?

   a. $\dfrac{13}{20}$ **b.** $\dfrac{20}{13}$ **c.** $\dfrac{20}{33}$ **d.** $\dfrac{8}{10}$

___ 19. The Bagel Express Shop sold 585 bagels one Sunday when 110 customers were served. Next Sunday they expect 250 customers. How many bagels can they expect to sell? Round to the nearest whole number.

   a. 1329   **b.** 1170   **c.** 1330   **d.** 1250

___ 20. In one small town in Massachusetts, all 600 voters voted early in the day, and 438 voted for the Democratic candidate for U.S. Senator. If this trend continues throughout the state, and there are 500,000 voters, how many will likely vote for the Democratic candidate?

   a. 3,650,000   **b.** 684,932   **c.** 365,000   **d.** 36,500

____ **1.** Write $9:33$ as a ratio in simplest form.

     a. $\dfrac{3}{11}$ **b.** $\dfrac{1}{48}$ **c.** $\dfrac{2}{7}$ **d.** $\dfrac{1}{4}$

____ **2.** Write "400 pounds per 340 square feet" as a rate in simplest form.

     a. $\dfrac{12 \text{ pounds}}{1 \text{ sq. ft.}}$ **b.** $\dfrac{5 \text{ pounds}}{4 \text{ sq. ft.}}$ **c.** $\dfrac{9 \text{ pounds}}{7 \text{ sq. ft.}}$ **d.** $\dfrac{20 \text{ pounds}}{17 \text{ sq. ft.}}$

____ **3.** Write "108 gallons in 14 hours" as a unit rate. Round to the nearest hundredth, if necessary.

     a. 8 gallons / hr.   **b.** 7.71 gallons / hr.   **c.** 6.92 gallons / hr.   **d.** 7.43 gallons / hr.

____ **4.** Write "$4915 for 72 shares of stock" as a unit rate. Round to the nearest hundredth if necessary.

     a. $14.65 / share   **b.** $72.57 / share   **c.** $68.26 / share   **d.** $77.60 / share

____ **5.** To stay healthy, Vin knows that it is recommended that a person on a 2000 calorie per day diet consume no more that 65 grams of fat. Vin is in training for football and consumes 2800 calories per day. How many grams of fat should he limit himself to?

     a. 90   **b.** 91   **c.** 26   **d.** 93

____ **6.** Roger Clemens struck out 11 batters in the first 5 innings of a game. At this rate, how many total batters will he strike out in a nine-inning game?

     a. 55   **b.** 19   **c.** 20   **d.** 22

____ **7.** Which of the following proportions is true?

     a. $\dfrac{6.8}{2.1}=\dfrac{17}{5.3}$ **b.** $\dfrac{3}{5}=\dfrac{5}{7}$ **c.** $\dfrac{2\frac{1}{2}}{7}=\dfrac{1\frac{1}{4}}{3\frac{1}{2}}$ **d.** $\dfrac{1.1}{1.2}=\dfrac{2.1}{2.2}$

____ **8.** Which of the following proportions is true?

     a. $\dfrac{\$0.92}{8 \text{ ounces}}=\dfrac{\$1.92}{24 \text{ ounces}}$ **b.** $\dfrac{\$1.93}{10 \text{ ounces}}=\dfrac{\$1.53}{8 \text{ ounces}}$ **c.** $\dfrac{\$1.24}{5 \text{ ounces}}=\dfrac{\$1.86}{7.5 \text{ ounces}}$ **d.** $\dfrac{\$0.51}{4 \text{ ounces}}=\dfrac{\$0.65}{5 \text{ ounces}}$

____ **9.** Solve for n: $\dfrac{25}{39}=\dfrac{n}{351}$ Round to the nearest tenth, if necessary.

     a. $n=225$ **b.** $n=337$ **c.** $n=200$ **d.** $n=230$

____ **10.** Solve for n: $\dfrac{15}{16.7}=\dfrac{17}{n}$ Round to the nearest tenth, if necessary.

     a. $n\approx17.9$ **b.** $n\approx18.9$ **c.** $n\approx57.1$ **d.** $n\approx16.8$

____ **11.** Solve for n: $\dfrac{7 \text{ sticks of butter}}{n}=\dfrac{24 \text{ sticks of butter}}{40 \text{ cakes}}$ Round to the nearest tenth, if necessary.

     a. $n=14$ cakes   **b.** $n=15$ cakes   **c.** $n=9$ cakes   **d.** $n\approx11.7$ cakes

____ 12. Solve for n: $\dfrac{\$3.25}{n} = \dfrac{\$4.29}{15 \text{ ounces}}$ Round to the nearest tenth, if necessary.

     a. $n = 11.4$ ounces   **b.** $n = 12.1$ ounce   **c.** $n = 9.8$ ounces   **d.** $n = 9.5$ ounces

____ 13. Lisa traveled 710 miles in 12 hours. At this rate, how far could she travel in 8 hours?

     a. 480 miles   **b.** 266.25 miles   **c.** 473.33 miles   **d.** 458 miles

____ 14. If 5 centimeters on a map represents 35 miles, what distance does 26 centimeters represent?

     a. 120 miles   **b.** 182 miles   **c.** 260 miles   **d.** 156 miles

____ 15. The Rolf's found it would cost $290 to fertilize their back lawn of 3500 square feet. How much would it cost to fertilize 5100 square feet?

     a. $422.57   **b.** $1890   **c.** $437.14   **d.** $394.92

____ 16. A game warden captures 35 deer, tags them, and then releases them into the forest. A few days later she captures 40 deer, and 8 of them have her tag. Estimate the number of deer in the forest.

     a. 165   **b.** 280   **c.** 175   **d.** 170

____ 17. Dave pedals his new racing bike at 70 revolutions per minute in a certain gear. He finds he is going 10 miles per hour. If he stays in the same gear, how many revolutions per minute does he need to pedal to go 13 miles per hour?

     a. 90   **b.** 75   **c.** 81   **d.** 91

____ 18. A quality control engineer tested 300 calculators at the end of the assembly line and found 17 were defective. If the factory manufactures 5500 calculators every day, how many are likely to be defective? Round to the nearest whole number.

     a. 310   **b.** 312   **c.** 300   **d.** 28

____ 19. Steve and Nick run a moped rental shop on Block Island, Rhode Island. On Saturdays and Sundays, when approximately 5500 people are on the island, they rent 215 mopeds a day. On weekdays, there are only 2500 people on the island. How many moped can they expect to rent?

     a. 90   **b.** 98   **c.** 110   **d.** 260

____ 20. In a survey of 500 voters in Rhode Island, 235 said they would vote for a certain candidate. If there are 685,500 voters in the whole state, how many votes will this candidate likely receive?

     a. 32,218   **b.** 322,000   **c.** 322,185   **d.** 2917

____ 1. Write $64:108$ as a ratio in simplest form.

    a. $\dfrac{4}{7}$ **b.** $\dfrac{16}{27}$ **c.** $\dfrac{2}{3}$ **d.** $\dfrac{5}{9}$

____ 2. Write "870 pounds per 30 square feet" as a rate in simplest form.

    a. $\dfrac{29 \text{ pounds}}{1 \text{ sq. ft.}}$ **b.** $\dfrac{88 \text{ pounds}}{3 \text{ sq. ft.}}$ **c.** $\dfrac{144 \text{ pounds}}{5 \text{ sq. ft.}}$ **d.** $\dfrac{48 \text{ pounds}}{9 \text{ sq. ft.}}$

____ 3. Write "54 gallons in 7 hours" as a unit rate. Round to the nearest hundredth, if necessary.

    a. 22 gallons/ hr.   **b.** 14.3 gallons / hr.   **c.** 7.71 gallons / hr.   **d.** 22.25 gallons / hr.

____ 4. Write "$5015 for 72 shares of stock" as a unit rate. Round to the nearest hundredth, if necessary.

    a. \$77.47 / share   **b.** \$69.65 / share   **c.** \$59.55 / share   **d.** \$77.36 / share

____ 5. A 5.5 ounce can of tuna costs $2.33. What is the cost per ounce? Round to the nearest hundredth.

    a. \$0.45   **b.** \$0.50   **c.** \$0.42   **d.** \$0.24

____ 6. Keith got a total of 67 hits when he was up to bat 214 times. At this rate, what would be his number of hits if he has 1000 "at bats?" (This number is his "batting average.")

    a. 214   **b.** 367   **c.** 319   **d.** 313

____ 7. Which of the following proportions is true?

    a. $\dfrac{2.7}{5.5}=\dfrac{3.6}{7.2}$ **b.** $\dfrac{11}{13}=\dfrac{132}{156}$ **c.** $\dfrac{2\frac{1}{2}}{5}=\dfrac{5}{9}$ **d.** $\dfrac{9}{11}=\dfrac{9\frac{1}{2}}{11\frac{1}{2}}$

____ 8. Which of the following proportions is true?

    a. $\dfrac{3\frac{1}{2}}{11}=\dfrac{10\frac{1}{2}}{33}$ **b.** $\dfrac{7.5}{12}=\dfrac{22.5}{48}$ **c.** $\dfrac{6.3}{8}=\dfrac{9.3}{11}$ **d.** $\dfrac{6\frac{3}{4}}{12}=\dfrac{13}{25}$

____ 9. Solve for n: $\dfrac{16}{29}=\dfrac{n}{43.5}$ Round to the nearest tenth, if necessary.

    a. $n=30.5$ **b.** $n\approx 23.5$ **c.** $n=24$ **d.** $n\approx 78.8$

____ 10. Solve for n: $\dfrac{17}{29}=\dfrac{24}{n}$ Round to the nearest tenth, if necessary.

    a. $n=48$ **b.** $n\approx 42.4$ **c.** $n=58$ **d.** $n\approx 40.9$

____ 11. Solve for n: $\dfrac{4.5 \text{ cups of flour}}{n}=\dfrac{30 \text{ cups of flour}}{20 \text{ loaves of bread}}$ Round to the nearest tenth, if necessary.

    a. $n=3$ loaves   **b.** $n=6.8$ loaves   **c.** $n=2$ loaves   **d.** $n=4.7$ loaves

___ 12. Solve for n: $\dfrac{\$4.45}{9\ \text{ounces}} = \dfrac{\$40.05}{n}$ Round to the nearest tenth, if necessary.

   a. $n = 35.5$ ounces   b. $n = 19.8$ ounces   c. $n = 63$ ounces   d. $n = 81$ ounces

___ 13. Allison worked 27 problems in 45 minutes. At this rate, how many problems could she work in an hour?

   a. 42 problems   b. 36 problems   c. 100 problems   d. 33.33 problems

___ 14. If 11 centimeters on a map represents 47 miles, what distance does 19 centimeters represent?

   a. 4.45 miles   b. 55 miles   c. 81.18 miles   d. 27.21 miles

___ 15. A metal cable 46 feet long weighs 147.2 pounds. How much would 60 feet of this cable weigh?

   a. 161.2 pounds   b. 112.85 pounds   c. 192 pounds   d. 195.65 pounds

___ 16. During the winter of 1990-1991, there was an extensive helicopter aided count of all the polar bears in the Barrow, Alaska area. The number counted was 58. During that same time, a total of 15 polar bear sightings were made within the town limits of Barrow. In 1992-1994, there were 28 total bear sightings within the town limits of Barrow. Estimate the total number of polar bears in the region. Round to the nearest whole number.

   a. 108   b. 116   c. 100   d. 31

___ 17. Medway High School has 2850 students and 97 teachers. Next year's enrollment will be down by 520 students. In order to keep the same student-teacher ratio, how many teachers should Medway High School have?

   a. 79   b. 97   c. 78   d. 793

___ 18. A quality control engineer randomly selected 55 light bulbs off the assembly line. She found that 2 were defective. If the factory manufactures 30,000 light bulbs a day, how many are likely to be defective? Round to the nearest whole number.

   a. 109   b. 1091   c. 1090   d. 1909

___ 19. A baseball pitcher gave up 51 earned runs in 275 innings of pitching. At this rate, how many runs would he give up in a nine-inning game? (This is his "earned run average" or ERA) Round to the nearest tenth.

   a. 2.7   b. 1.8   c. 1.7   d. 5.4

___ 20. In ancient Greece, architects used what is called the "golden rectangle." They felt that the most pleasing-to-the-eye rectangle was one in which the length and height were in the ratio of 1.618 to 1. In other words, if a building's front side is 16.18 feet long, then the height should be 10 feet. Using this golden rectangle, if a building is to be 22 feet high, how long should it be? Round to the nearest tenth.

   a. 36 feet   b. 32.4 feet   c. 13.6 feet   d. 35.6 feet

1. Write "$1.15 per 2.5 ounces" as a unit rate. Round to the nearest hundredth, if necessary.

2. Write "34.56 miles per 1.8 gallon" as a unit rate. Round to the nearest hundredth, if necessary.

3. Determine if this proportion is true or false:
$$\frac{\frac{3}{4}}{7} = \frac{15}{140}$$

4. Solve for n. Round to the nearest tenth, if necessary.
$$\frac{n}{66} = \frac{32.5}{130}$$

5. Solve for n. Round to the nearest tenth, if necessary.
$$\frac{6}{13} = \frac{15}{n}$$

6. Solve for n. Round to the nearest tenth, if necessary.
$$\frac{50 \text{ milligrams}}{n} = \frac{35 \text{ milligrams}}{14.2 \text{ pounds}}$$

7. Solve for n. Round to the nearest tenth, if necessary.
$$\frac{25 \text{ gallons}}{0.8 \text{ miles}} = \frac{n}{14 \text{ miles}}$$

8. Larkin drove 140 miles on 3.6 gallons of gasoline. At that rate, how far could she drive on 20 gallons of gasoline?

9. A recipe calls for 0.5 stick of butter for 1.75 cups of flour. How much butter would be required for 4 cups of flour?

10. If 250 miles is represented on a map by 1.4 inches, how many inches are needed to represent 325 miles?

11. Multiply: $2\dfrac{1}{4} \times \dfrac{3}{8}$

12. Add: $5\dfrac{1}{8} + 4\dfrac{1}{2}$

13. Evaluate: $5^2 + 12\dfrac{1}{2} \div 8 - 3 \times 2$

14. A room that measures 20 feet by $13\dfrac{1}{2}$ feet needs to be carpeted. If carpet costs $3 per square foot, how much will the total cost be?

15. Add: $13.68 + 3.012$

16. Divide: $0.03\overline{)158.58}$

17. Round to the nearest hundredth: 185.365732

18. A wooden plance 24 feet long needs to be cut into pieces that are $\frac{3}{4}$-foot in length. How many pieces can be cut?

19. Nancy bought a bike that was marked $279.95. She got a 0.05 discount. What did she pay?

20. Evaluate: $(0.03)^2 + 0.5 \div 2 + (0.9)^2$

_____ 1. Write "$684 for 13 shares of stock" as a unit rate. Round to the nearest hundredth, if necessary.

   a. $52 per share   b. $88.72 per share   c. $52.62 per share   d. $53 per share

_____ 2. Write "345 ants per 23 square inches" as a unit rate. Round to the nearest hundredth, if necessary.

   a. 15 ants per square inch   b. 345 ants per square inch

   c. 17.25 ants per square inch   d. 7935 ants per square inch

_____ 3. Which if the following proportions is true?

   a. $\dfrac{18}{42}=\dfrac{12}{28}$ b. $\dfrac{18}{42}=\dfrac{9}{24}$ c. $\dfrac{18}{42}=\dfrac{21}{48}$ d. $\dfrac{18}{42}=\dfrac{118}{142}$

_____ 4. Solve for n: $\dfrac{47}{n}=\dfrac{36}{54}$ Round to the nearest tenth, if necessary.

   a. $n=1.3$ b. $n=70.5$ c. $n=0.7$ d. $n=2538$

_____ 5. Solve for n: $\dfrac{6}{25}=\dfrac{11}{n}$ Round to the nearest tenth, if necessary.

   a. $n=1.8$ b. $n=45.8$ c. $n=0.2$ d. $n=2.3$

_____ 6. Solve for n: $\dfrac{40 \text{ milligrams}}{n}=\dfrac{28 \text{ milligrams}}{15 \text{ pounds}}$ Round to the nearest tenth, if necessary.

   a. $n=420$ pounds   b. $n=1120$ pounds   c. $n=1.9$ pounds   d. $n=21.4$ pounds

_____ 7. Solve for n: $\dfrac{12 \text{ people}}{23 \text{ cups}}=\dfrac{n}{34.5 \text{ cups}}$ Round to the nearest tenth, if necessary.

   a. $n=9$ people   b. $n=2.9$ people   c. $n=18$ people   d. $n=793.5$ people

_____ 8. If 190 miles is represented on a map by 3 centimeters, what distance does 10 centimeters represent?

   a. 57 miles   b. 633.33 miles   c. 63.33 miles   d. 19 miles

_____ 9. A recipe calls for 0.5 stick of butter for 1.2 cups of flour. How much butter would be required for 6 cups of flour?

   a. 12 sticks   b. 6 sticks   c. 2.5 sticks   d. 3 sticks

_____ 10. In a manufacturing process, for every 465 items assembled, 4 are defective. At this rate, if 5115 items are assembled, how many will be defective?

   a. 116.25 defective   b. 1279 defective   c. 44 defective   d. 1860 defective

____ **11.** Multiply: $5\frac{1}{3} \times \frac{3}{4}$

    a. 4   **b.** $5\frac{3}{12}$

    c. $2\frac{3}{12}$ **d.** $7\frac{1}{4}$

____ **12.** Add: $8\frac{1}{2} + 5\frac{1}{8}$

    a. $13\frac{1}{4}$ **b.** $13\frac{5}{8}$

    c. $13\frac{1}{16}$ **d.** $13\frac{1}{5}$

____ **13.** Evaluate: $10^2 \div 2 + 3^2 \div 4 - 10 \times \frac{1}{3}$

    a. $51\frac{1}{6}$ **b.** $\frac{2}{3}$ **c.** $6\frac{1}{12}$ **d.** $48\frac{11}{12}$

____ **14.** A picture that measures $16\frac{1}{2}$ inches by $20\frac{3}{4}$ inches is matted with a mat that is $2\frac{1}{4}$ inches wide all around. What are the new dimensions of the picture and mat together?

    a. $14\frac{1}{4}''$ by $18\frac{1}{2}''$ **b.** $18\frac{3}{4}''$ by $23''$ **c.** $20\frac{3}{4}''$ by $24''$ **d.** $21''$ by $25\frac{1}{4}''$

____ **15.** Add: $23.43 + 2.003$

    a. 25.403   **b.** 21.433   **c.** 25.433   **d.** 25.46

____ **16.** Divide: $0.05\overline{)58.32}$

    a. 116.64   **b.** 1166.4   **c.** 11.664   **d.** 11,664

____ **17.** Round to the nearest hundredth: 2.5685168

    a. 2.57   **b.** 2.569   **c.** 2.56   **d.** 2.6

____ **18.** For and Indian "sari" (a woman's garb), $3\frac{1}{4}$ yard of material are needed (one yard wide). If Preti had 182 yards of material, one yard wide, how many saris can she make?

    a. 591.5 saris   **b.** 91 saris   **c.** 61 saris   **d.** 56 saris

____ **19.** A new car marked $6900 is offered for sale with a 0.07 discount. What is the price of the car now?

    a. $7183   **b.** $6417   **c.** $4830   **d.** $483

____ **20.** Evaluate: $(0.04)^2 + 0.3 \div 2 + (0.7)^3$

    a. 0.4946   **b.** .43   **c.** 4.946   **d.** 4.3

If you are <u>are</u> familiar with the topics in this chapter, take this test now. If you can't answer a question, study the appropriate section of the chapter. If you are <u>not</u> familiar with the topics in this chapter, don't take this test now. Instead, study the examples, work the practice problems, and then take the test. This test will help you identify which concepts you have mastered, and which you need to study further.

For problems 1-12, write each number as a percent.

1. 0.23

2. 0.391

3. 6.59

4. 1.57

5. 0.003

6. 0.009

7. $\dfrac{19}{100}$

8. $\dfrac{31}{100}$

9. $\dfrac{24.9}{100}$

10. $\dfrac{29.1}{100}$

11. $\dfrac{7\frac{1}{2}}{100}$

12. $\dfrac{2\frac{3}{8}}{100}$

For problems 13-24, change to a percent. Round to the nearest hundredth if necessary.

13. $\dfrac{7}{10}$

14. $\dfrac{3}{40}$

15. $\dfrac{62}{20}$

16. $\dfrac{19}{16}$

17. $\dfrac{4}{7}$

18. $\dfrac{3}{17}$

19. $\dfrac{21}{23}$

20. $\dfrac{17}{19}$

21. $8\dfrac{2}{5}$

22. $2\dfrac{1}{4}$

23. $\dfrac{1}{600}$

24. $\dfrac{3}{400}$

For problems 25-32, write each percent as a fraction in simplified form.

25. 32%

26. 59%

27. 120%

28. 180%

29. $7\dfrac{1}{3}\%$

30. $5\dfrac{2}{3}\%$

31. $61\dfrac{1}{4}\%$

32. $41\dfrac{3}{4}\%$

33. Find 26% of 280.

34. What is 32% of 94?

35. 68 is what percent of 76?

36. What percent of 42 is 31?

37. 12% of what number is 360?

38. 409.2 is 60% of what number?

39. The home team won 24 of 42 basketball games. What percent of the basketball games did the home team win?

40. Robert paid sales tax of $0.72 on his dinner. The sales tax rate is 4%. What was the cost of his dinner without the tax?

41. A television set that sold originally for $480 was sold for $300. What was the percent of decrease in the selling price?

42. A salesperson earns a commission rate of 22 %. How much commission would be paid if the salesperson sold $32,600 worth of goods?

43. Find the simple interest on a loan of $1400 that is borrowed at 12% annual interest for a period of three years.

If you <u>are</u> familiar with the topics in this chapter, take this test now. If you can't answer a question, study the appropriate section of the chapter. If you are <u>not</u> familiar with the topics in this chapter, don't take this test now. Instead, study the examples, work the practice problems, and then take the test. This test will help you identify which concepts you have mastered, and which you need to study further.

_____ 1. Write 0.29 as a percent.

    a. 0.29%   **b.** 29%   **c.** 290%   **d.** 2.9%

_____ 2. Write 0.461 as a percent.

    a. 46.1%   **b.** 461%   **c.** 4.61%   **d.** .0461%

_____ 3. Write 7.39 as a percent.

    a. 7.39%   **b.** 73.9%   **c.** .0739%   **d.** 739%

_____ 4. Write 2.43 as a percent.

    a. 243%   **b.** 24.3%   **c.** .00243%   **d.** 2.43%

_____ 5. Change 0.0007 to a percent.

    a. 7%   **b.** 0.7%   **c.** 0.07%   **d.** 0.007%

_____ 6. Change 0.008 to a percent.

    a. 0.008%   **b.** 0.08%   **c.** 0.8%   **d.** 8%

_____ 7. Write $\dfrac{16}{100}$ as a percent.

    a. 0.16%   **b.** 160%   **c.** 16%   **d.** 1.6%

_____ 8. Write $\dfrac{57}{100}$ as a percent.

    a. 5.7%   **b.** 57%   **c.** 0.57%   **d.** 0.057%

_____ 9. Write $\dfrac{36.9}{100}$ as a percent.

    a. 0.369%   **b.** 3.69%   **c.** 36.9%   **d.** 369%

_____ 10. Write $\dfrac{42.9}{100}$ as a percent.

    a. 42.9%   **b.** 4.29%   **c.** 429%   **d.** 0.429%

_____ 11. Write $\dfrac{3\frac{1}{2}}{100}$ as a percent.

    a. 350%   **b.** 0.035%   **c.** 3.2%   **d.** 3.5%

_____ 12. Write $\dfrac{5\frac{3}{8}}{100}$ as a percent.

    a. 5.38%   **b.** 53.75%   **c.** 537.5%   **d.** 5.375%

_____ 13. Change $\dfrac{9}{10}$ to a percent.

    a. 0.9%   **b.** 0.09%   **c.** 90%   **d.** 9%

____ 14. Change $\frac{7}{40}$ to a percent.

    a. 17.5%   **b.** 175%   **c.** 0.175%   **d.** 1.75%

____ 15. Change $\frac{72}{20}$ to a percent.

    a. 360%   **b.** 3.6%   **c.** 36%   **d.** 3600%

____ 16. Change $\frac{21}{16}$ to a percent.

    a. 13.125%   **b.** 1312.5%   **c.** 1.3125%   **d.** 131.25%

____ 17. Change $\frac{3}{7}$ to a percent.

    a. 428.6%   **b.** 42.86%   **c.** .04286%   **d.** 4.286%

____ 18. 0Change $\frac{15}{19}$ to a percent.

    a. 78.95%   **b.** 1.27%   **c.** 7.90%   **d.** 126.67%

____ 19. Change $6\frac{2}{5}$ to a percent.

    a. 640%   **b.** 1200%   **c.** 260%   **d.** 440%

____ 20. Change $3\frac{1}{4}$ to a percent.

    a. 175%   **b.** 200%   **c.** 300%   **d.** 325%

____ 21. Change $\frac{7}{300}$ to a percent.

    a. 420.86%   **b.** 42.86%   **c.** 23.33%   **d.** 2.33%

____ 22. Change $\frac{3}{800}$ to a percent.

    a. 3.8%   **b.** 266.67%   **c.** 0.38%   **d.** 2660.67%

____ 23. Write 26% as a fraction in simplified form.

    a. $\frac{8}{25}$ **b.** $\frac{13}{500}$ **c.** $\frac{13}{50}$ **d.** $\frac{26}{50}$

____ 24. Write 57% as a fraction in simplified form.

    a. $\frac{57}{100}$ **b.** $\frac{57}{10}$ **c.** 57   **d.** $\frac{57}{1000}$

____ 25. Write 130% as a fraction in simplified form.

    a. $1\frac{13}{10}$ **b.** $1\frac{3}{10}$ **c.** $1\frac{13}{100}$ **d.** $1\frac{3}{100}$

_____ 26. Write $8\frac{1}{3}\%$ as a fraction in simplified form.

     a. $\dfrac{2}{75}$ b. $\dfrac{1}{12}$ c. $\dfrac{83}{100}$ d. $\dfrac{83}{1000}$

_____ 27. Write $3\frac{2}{3}\%$ as a fraction in simplified form.

     a. $\dfrac{11}{300}$ b. $\dfrac{32}{300}$ c. $\dfrac{36}{1000}$ d. $\dfrac{2}{75}$

_____ 28. Write $41\frac{1}{4}\%$ as a fraction in simplified form.

     a. $\dfrac{165}{4}$ b. $\dfrac{23}{200}$ c. $\dfrac{33}{100}$ d. $\dfrac{33}{80}$

_____ 29. Find 26% of 210.

     a. 546   b. 5468   c. 5.46   d. 54.6

_____ 30. What is 76% of 74?

     a. 562.4   b. 56.24   c. 9.737   d. 97.37

_____ 31. 64 is what percent of 76?

     a. 48.64%   b. 118.75%   c. 84.21%   d. 119%

_____ 32. What percent of 72 is 31?

     a. 43.06%   b. 4.31%   c. 2.32%   d. 232.25%

_____ 33. 12% of what number is 180?

     a. 2160   b. 1500   c. 21.6   d. 15

_____ 34. 205.2 is 30% of what number?

     a. 684   b. 6.84   c. 6156   d. 61.56

_____ 35. The home team won 24 of 35 basketball games. What percent of the basketball games did the home team win?

     a. 6.86%   b. 31.43%   c. 68.57%   d. 146%

_____ 36. Robert paid sales tax of $0.84 on his dinner. The sales tax rate is 4%. What was the cost of his dinner without the tax?

     a. $33.60   b. $21.00   c. $3.36   d. $2.10

_____ 37. A television set that sold originally for $360 was sold for $300. What was the percent of decrease in the selling price?

     a. 30%   b. 60%   c. $60   d. 16.67%

_____ 38. A salesperson earns a commission rate of 26%. How much commission would be paid of the salesperson sold $32,600 worth of goods?

     a. $8476   b. $1253.85   c. $84,760   d. $847.60

_____ 39. Find the simple interest on a loan of $1600 that is borrowed at 12% annual interest for a period of four years.

     a. $1333.33   b. $19,200   c. $133.33   d. $768

1. Write $\dfrac{5.29}{100}$ as a percent.

2. Write 2.61 as a percent.

3. Write 0.79 as a percent.

4. Write $\dfrac{0.81}{100}$ as a percent.

5. Change $\dfrac{27}{80}$ to a percent.

6. Change $6\dfrac{5}{8}$ to a percent.

7. Write 3.2614 as a percent.

8. Write $9\dfrac{1}{8}\%$ as a fraction in simplified form.

9. Find 1.6% of 60.

10. What percent of 60 is 180?

11. 32% of what number is 44.8?

12. 19 is 135% of what number?

13. Mary Ann's annual income is $32,000. She spends $7680 per year on housing. What percent of her annual income is spent on housing?

14. 160 out of 200 student passed a competency exam. What percent passed?

15. Tim bought a sweater originally priced at $49.95. He received a 15% discount. Assuming no sales tax, how much did he pay for the sweater?

16. The town of Milford's population grew from 25,500 to 27,540 in 3 years. What percent increase was this?

17. The Massachusetts State Police issued 2780 speeding tickets on the Massachusetts turnpike in 1999, but 2919 tickets in 2001. What percent increase is this?

18. Jerome needs a car loan of $6200. He can get a bank loan, at a simple interest rate of 12%, if he pays it in one year. How much interest will he have to pay?

19. Of 680 new freshman, 589 passed the math placement test. What percent passed the test? Round to the nearest hundredth.

20. The Consumer Price Index (CPI) for 2000 was 13.5; in other words, it costs 13.5% more to keep the same standard of living as in 1999. If Mr. And Mrs. Wilson earned $65,300 in 1999, what do they need to earn in 2000 to keep their same standard of living?

1. Write 0.013 as a percent.

2. Write $\dfrac{59}{100}$ as a percent.

3. Write 6.29 as a percent.

4. Write $\dfrac{7\frac{1}{2}}{100}$ as a percent.

5. Change $\dfrac{17}{40}$ to a percent.

6. Change $3\dfrac{1}{8}$ to a percent.

7. Write 1.8923 as a percent.

8. Write $6\dfrac{1}{3}\%$ as a fraction in simplified form.

9. Find 6.5 % of 60.

10. What percent of 80 is 30?

11. 47% of what number is 2961?

12. 12 is 0.25% of what number?

13. Elaine purchased a couch at a 25% discount. The list price was $680. How much did she pay?

14. 21 out of 35 students failed a true / false test. What percent of the students passed?

15. A total of 1575 students voted in the Student Government elections. This was 60% of the student enrolled. How many students were enrolled?

16. Eulalia earns 7.2% commission on all her real estate sales. This month, she sold one home at $68,000. What was her commission?

17. The brain of an average person has a weight that is approximately 2.5% of the body's whole weight. If an average man weighs 200 pounds, what is the approximate weight of his brain?

18. If 3.1% of the population of the U.S. has AB positive blood, how many one-pint donors will the Red Cross need to find in order to obtain 240 pints of AB positive? Round to the nearest whole number.

19. Bobby Orr scored 14 times out of 55 shots at the goal. What percent is this? Round to the nearest hundredth.

20. On a loan of $8600, Jorge had to pay $1118 interest for one years. What percent interest rate is this?

1. Write 0.861 as a percent.

2. Write $\dfrac{1.69}{100}$ as a percent.

3. Write 13.64 as a percent.

4. Write 0.0007 as a percent.

5. Change $\dfrac{31}{80}$ to a percent.

6. Change $9\dfrac{1}{4}$ to a percent.

7. Write 0.0198 as a percent.

8. Write $6\dfrac{7}{8}\%$ as a fraction in simplified form.

9. 16.5 is 22% of what number?

10. What percent of 24 is 9?

11. 125% of what number is 525?

12. Find 13.5% of 48.

13. Matt borrowed $1300 at a 12% simple rate of interest. How much interest did he pay in six months?

14. There were 60 people in algebra class last semester. There are 78 in the class this semester. What is the percent of increase?

15. Monica's salary is $34,500. This is 75% of her last year's salary. What was her salary last year?

16. 2330 law graduates took the Alaska Bar Exam over the last ten years. 1780 passed the exam. What percent passed the exam?

17. The population of Anchorage, Alaska, in 1990 was 234,300. This was a 3% increase over 1985. What was the population in 1985?

18. How much sales tax would you pay to purchase a new bicycle that costs $429 if the sales tax rate is 5.2%?

19. Coach Hanlon won 65 games and lost 38 games in his ten years of coaching football. What percent of his games did he win? Round to the nearest percent.

20. A real estate agent sold a total of $1,450,000 in property one year and earned $79,750 in commission. What commission rate did she earn?

____ 1. Write $\frac{19}{100}$ as a percent.

     a. 0.19%   **b.** 19%   **c.** 1900%   **d.** 0.0019%

____ 2. Write 0.615 as a percent.

     a. 61.5%   **b.** 0.615%   **c.** 615%   **d.** .00615%

____ 3. Write 0.009 as a percent.

     a. 9%   **b.** 90%   **c.** 0.9%   **d.** 0.009%

____ 4. Write $\frac{5.9}{100}$ as a percent.

     a. 0.059%   **b.** 0.59%   **c.** 59%   **d.** 5.9%

____ 5. Change $\frac{17}{80}$ to a percent.

     a. 34%   **b.** 17.80%   **c.** 21.25%   **d.** 42.5%

____ 6. Change $5\frac{1}{10}$ to a percent.

     a. 510%   **b.** 5.1%   **c.** 51%   **d.** 0.51%

____ 7. Write 2.467 as a percent

     a. 0.02467%   **b.** 246.7%   **c.** 24.67%   **d.** 2467%

____ 8. Write 135% as a fraction in simplified form.

     a. $\frac{13.5}{100}$ **b.** $\frac{29}{20}$ **c.** $\frac{5}{4}$ **d.** $\frac{27}{20}$

____ 9. What is 18% of 318?

     a. 57.24   **b.** 5.72   **c.** 31.8   **d.** 10.44

____ 10. What percent of 85 is 72?

     a. 1.18%   **b.** 84.71%   **c.** 118%   **d.** 91.46%

_____ 11. 15% of what number is 45?

    a. 450   **b.** 6.75   **c.** 300   **d.** 200

_____ 12. 17.4 is 25% of what number?

    a. 4.35   **b.** 52.2   **c.** 69.6   **d.** 34.8

_____ 13. A real estate agent sells a house for $87,000. She gets a commission of 6% on the sale. What is her commission?

    a. $1458.33   **b.** $5220.00   **c.** $4395.00   **d.** $14,583.33

_____ 14. An inspector found that 4 out of 116 parts were defective. What percent of the parts were defective?

    a. 3.45%   **b.** 29%   **c.** 26.1%   **d.** 3.03%

_____ 15. A total of 2480 students voted in the Student Government elections. This was 32% of the students enrolled. How many students were enrolled?

    a. 794   **b.** 7440   **c.** 6200   **d.** 7750

_____ 16. In Massachusetts, 0.0461 of the state is covered by water. What percent is covered by water?

    a. 4.61%   **b.** 0.0461%   **c.** 46.1%   **d.** 0.461%

_____ 17. The brain represents $\frac{3}{40}$ of an average person's weight. What percent is this?

    a. 75%   **b.** 7.5%   **c.** 0.075%   **d.** 3.4%

_____ 18. Bill and Ellen have $65.00 total to go out to dinner. Knowing they need to leave 15% of their bill as a tip for the waiter, what is the maximum amount they can spend on dinner?

    a. $55.25   **b.** $65.00   **c.** $56.52   **d.** $74.75

_____ 19. Larry Bird scored a basket 123 times out of 150 shots. What percent of his shots did he score?

    a. 59%   **b.** 83%   **c.** 82%   **d.** 80%

_____ 20. A hotel charges an 8% tax, as required by law to pay the city. If Mr. and Mrs. Lafferty paid $167.40, what was their bill before the tax was added to it?

    a. $155.00   **b.** $154.00   **c.** $93.00   **d.** $133.92

____ 1. Write 1.93 as a percent.

       a. 0.193%   b. 19.3%   c. 1.93%   d. 193%

____ 2. Write 0.004 as a percent.

       a. 4%   b. 0.04%   c. 0.4%   d. 40%

____ 3. Write $\frac{5.4}{100}$ as a percent.

       a. 5.4%   b. 0.054%   c. 540%   d. 54%

____ 4. Write $\frac{178}{100}$ as a percent.

       a. 0.178%   b. 178%   c. 1.78%   d. 17.8%

____ 5. Change $\frac{23}{80}$ to a percent.

       a. 57.5%   b. 28.75%   c. 25%   d. 23.8%

____ 6. Change $2\frac{4}{5}$ to a percent.

       a. 14%   b. 140%   c. 280%   d. 160%

____ 7. Write 0.3591 as a percent

       a. 0.3591%   b. 3.591%   c. 359.1%   d. 35.91%

____ 8. Write $8\frac{3}{4}$% as a fraction in simplified form.

       a. $\frac{7}{80}$ b. $\frac{35}{4}$ c. $\frac{5}{7}$ d. $\frac{2}{25}$

____ 9. Find 0.2% of 35,000.

       a. 700   b. 7000   c. 70   d. 2850

____ 10. What percent of 125 is 75?

       a. 166.67%   b. 56%   c. 53.85%   d. 60%

____ **11.** 18% of what number of 99?

     a. 550   **b.** 17.82   **c.** 1782   **d.** 495

____ **12.** 16.4 is 40% of what number?

     a. 6.56   **b.** 41   **c.** 0.41   **d.** 656

____ **13.** Lorraine bought a sweater on sale. The original price was $62.99, but she received a 20% discount. Assuming no sales tax, how much did she pay for the sweater?

     a. $50.39   **b.** $12.60   **c.** $37.79   **d.** $42.99

____ **14.** An inspector found that 5 out of 87 parts were defective. What percent of the parts were defective?

     a. 5.75%   **b.** 94.25%   **c.** 0.0575%   **d.** 0.575%

____ **15.** A real estate agent received a commission of $10,800 for selling a house at $120,000. What percent of the selling price was the commission?

     a. 44.44%   **b.** 9%   **c.** 12%   **d.** 25%

____ **16.** David had to take an exam with 285 questions. He got 208 questions correct. What percent is this? Round to the nearest percent.

     a. 37%   **b.** 75%   **c.** 73%   **d.** 81%

____ **17.** Potassium represents $\frac{9}{2000}$ of an average person's weight. Express this fraction as a percent.

     a. 45%   **b.** 0.45%   **c.** 0.045%   **d.** 4.5%

____ **18.** Find the simple interest on a $2000 loan that is borrowed for 3 years at an annual interest rate of $7\frac{1}{2}$%.

     a. $45   **b.** $300   **c.** $150   **d.** $450

____ **19.** Mary now weighs 135 pounds. She said that she had just lost 17% of her weight. How much did she weigh before her diet. Round to the nearest whole number.

     a. 163 lbs.   **b.** 165 lbs.   **c.** 158 lbs.   **d.** 152 lbs.

____ **20.** The Consumer Price Index (CPI) for 1985 was 3.6. In other words, the cost of living went up 3.6% from 1984 to 1985. If someone earned $15,000 in 1984, how much should they heave earned in 1985 to keep up with the increase?

     a. $14,478   **b.** $15,500   **c.** $15,540   **d.** $20,400

____ 1. Write $\dfrac{7.9}{100}$ as a percent.

     a. 0.079%   b. 790%   c. 7.9%   d. 79%

____ 2. Write 0.0007 as a percent.

     a. 7%   b. 0.07%   c. 0.000007%   d. 70%

____ 3. Write 0.39 as a percent.

     a. 0.39%   b. 0.0039%   c. 3.9%   d. 39%

____ 4. Write $\dfrac{259}{100}$ as a percent.

     a. 259%   b. 2.59%   c. 0.259%   d. 25.9%

____ 5. Change $\dfrac{43}{80}$ to a percent.

     a. 43.8%   b. 537.5%   c. 0.54%   d. 53.75%

____ 6. Change $7\dfrac{1}{5}$ to a percent.

     a. $\dfrac{36}{5}$%   b. 720%   c. 7.2%   d. 131%

____ 7. Write 0.8736 as a percent

     a. 87.36%   b. 8.736%   c. 873.6%   d. 0.008736%

____ 8. Write $9\dfrac{1}{4}$% as a fraction in simplified form.

     a. $\dfrac{37}{4}$ b. $\dfrac{37}{25}$ c. $\dfrac{37}{400}$ d. $\dfrac{3700}{4}$

____ 9. Find 0.3% of 512.

     a. 153.6   b. 1706.67   c. 15.36   d. 1.54

____ 10. What percent of 150 is 80?

     a. 120%   b. 1.875%   c. 53.33%   d. 187.5%

____ **11.** 28% of what number is 140?

    a. 39.2   **b.** 500   **c.** 80   **d.** 800

____ **12.** 14 is 65% of what number?

    a. 21.54   **b.** 9.1   **c.** 4.64   **d.** 91

____ **13.** A real estate agent sells a house for $99,500. He gets a commission of 6% on the sale. What is his commission?

    a. $4975.00   **b.** $1990.00   **c.** $5970.00   **d.** $2487.50

____ **14.** Harry now earns $27,630 per year. This is 118% of what he earned last year. What was his salary last year?

    a. $32,604.40   **b.** $4973.40   **c.** $22,656.60   **d.** $23,415.25

____ **15.** An inspector found that 114 of 124 parts were not defective. What percent of the parts were defective?

    a. 6.45%   **b.** 91.94%   **c.** 93.55%   **d.** 8.06%

____ **16.** Jose correctly answered 165 questions out of 235 questions on an exam. What percent did he answer correctly? Round to the nearest percent.

    a. 75%   **b.** 42%   **c.** 70%   **d.** 71%

____ **17.** The monthly interest rate on a certain charge card is 1.525% per month. Anna owes $1500 on her account. How much interest does she have to pay this month?

    a. $228.75   **b.** $23.00   **c.** $22.88   **d.** $22.50

____ **18.** Mary and Ralph spent a total of $62.10 on dinner, but this included the 15% tip for the waiter. What was the bill before the tip?

    a. $54.00   **b.** $55.00   **c.** $52.78   **d.** $52.79

____ **19.** Roger Clemens struck out 83 batters out of 332 batters he faced. What percent of batters did he strike out?

    a. 250%   **b.** 75%   **c.** 2.5%   **d.** 25%

____ **20.** In 1981, the Consumers Price Index, or CPI, was 10.3. In other words, the cost of living went up 10.3% from 1980 to 1981. If a couple earned $45,000 in 1980, what should they have earned in 1981 to keep up with the CPI increase?

    a. $50,000.00   **b.** $49,635.00   **c.** $46,865.00   **d.** $51,415.00

If you <u>are</u> familiar with the topics in this chapter, take this test now. If you can't answer a question, study the appropriate section of the chapter. If you are <u>not</u> familiar with the topics in this chapter, don't take this test now. Instead, study the examples, work the practice problems, and then take the test. This test will help you identify which concepts you have mastered, and which you need to study further.

1. Convert: 17 ft = _____ in

2. Convert: 9 gal = _____ pt

3. Convert: 4 mi = _____ yd

4. Convert: 1.6 tons = _____ lb

5. Convert: 48 min = _____ sec

6. Convert: 13 gal = _____ qt

7. Convert: 7.36 km = _____ m

8. Convert: 68.1 m = _____ cm

9. Convert: 823 mm = _____ cm

10. Convert: 23 mm = _____ m

11. Convert: 6951 mm = _____ cm

12. Convert: 597 m = _____ km

13. Convert to meters and add:
    1.6 km + 281 m + 916 m

14. Convert to meters and add:
    4823 cm + 6714 mm + 31.5 m

15. Convert: 6.29 L = _____ mL

16. Convert: 1939 g = _____ kg

17. Convert: 41.8 kg = _____ t

18. Convert: 5.7 kL = _____ L

19. Convert: 832 mg = _____ g

20. Convert: 12.5 L = _____ cm^3

21. Convert: 16 cm = _____ in

22. Convert: 6.8 ft = _____ m

23. Convert: 82 km = _____ mi

24. Convert: 284 gal = _____ L

25. Convert: 3.4 oz = _____ g

26. Convert: 62 kg = _____ lb

27. A triangle has sides that measure $8\frac{4}{5}$ yd, $6\frac{3}{5}$ yd, and $4\frac{1}{5}$ yd. Find the perimeter of the triangle and express your answer in feet.

28. The radio reported the temperature today as 30° C. The record high temperature for this day is 98° F. What was the Fahrenheit temperature today, and did it set a new record?

29. Juanita traveled in Mexico for two hours at 85 kilometers per hour. She had to travel a distance of 130 miles. How far does she still need to travel? Express your answer in miles.

30. A pump is running at 4.5 quarts per minute. What is this rate in gallons per hour?

If you <u>are</u> familiar with the topics in this chapter, take this test now. If you can't answer a question, study the appropriate section of the chapter. If you are <u>not</u> familiar with the topics in this chapter, don't take this test now. Instead, study the examples, work the practice problems, and then take the test. This test will help you identify which concepts you have mastered, and which you need to study further.

____ **1.** Convert: 13 ft = _____ in

    a. 130   **b.** 156   **c.** 208   **d.** 1.08

____ **2.** Convert: 7 gal = _____ pt

    a. 14   **b.** 28   **c.** 56   **d.** 112

____ **3.** Convert: 6 mi = _____ yd

    a. 5280   **b.** 10,560   **c.** 3520   **d.** 31,680

____ **4.** Convert: 2.8 tons = _____ lb

    a. 280   **b.** 2800   **c.** 560   **d.** 5600

____ **5.** Convert: 35 min = _____ sec

    a. 2150   **b.** 3500   **c.** 2100   **d.** 3150

____ **6.** Convert: 26 gal = _____ qt

    a. 104   **b.** 208   **c.** 52   **d.** 78

____ **7.** Convert: 8.47 km = _____ m

    a. 0.847   **b.** 8470   **c.** 847   **d.** 84.7

____ **8.** Convert: 73.4 m = _____ cm

    a. 7340   **b.** 73,400   **c.** 7.34   **d.** 734

____ **9.** Convert: 925 mm = _____ cm

    a. 92.5   **b.** 925   **c.** 9250   **d.** 9.25

____ **10.** Convert: 46 mm = _____ m

    a. 0.46   **b.** 4.6   **c.** 460   **d.** 0.046

___ **11.** Convert: 7915 mm = _____ cm

    a. 79.15   **b.** 0.7915   **c.** 791.5   **d.** 7.915

___ **12.** Convert: 467 m = _____ km

    a. 0.467   **b.** 46.7   **c.** 4670   **d.** 4.67

___ **13.** Convert to meters and add: 1.6 km + 351 m + 692 m

    a. 17,043 m   **b.** 2643 m   **c.** 2.643 m   **d.** 1203 m

___ **14.** Convert to meters and add: 5962 cm + 7614 mm + 91.4 m

    a. 104.98 m   **b.** 695.21 m   **c.** 227.16 m   **d.** 158.634 m

___ **15.** Convert: 7.31 L = _____ mL

    a. 731   **b.** 0.731   **c.** 73.1   **d.** 7310

___ **16.** Convert: 1836 g = _____ kg

    a. 18.36   **b.** 183.6   **c.** 1.836   **d.** 0.1836

___ **17.** Convert: 52.9 kg = _____ t

    a. 0.0529   **b.** 0.529   **c.** 5.29   **d.** 529

___ **18.** Convert: 8.4 kL = _____ L

    a. 8400   **b.** 840   **c.** 0.084   **d.** 0.84

___ **19.** Convert: 517 mg = _____ g

    a. 51.7   **b.** 0.517   **c.** 5.17   **d.** 0.0517

___ **20.** Convert: 28.9 L = _____ cm^3

    a. 289,000   **b.** 2.89   **c.** 28,900   **d.** 2890

____ **21.** Convert: 18 cm = _____ in

     a. 216   **b.** 45.63   **c.** 7.10   **d.** 10.90

____ **22.** Convert: 7.8 ft = _____ m

     a. 2.38   **b.** 23.4   **c.** 25.58   **d.** 2.6

____ **23.** Convert: 72 km = _____ mi

     a. 27.73   **b.** 116.13   **c.** 0.72   **d.** 44.64

____ **24.** Convert: 152 gal = _____ L

     a. 608   **b.** 40.11   **c.** 576.08   **d.** 38

____ **25.** Convert: 2.8 oz = _____ g

     a. 44.8   **b.** 79.38   **c.** 0.10   **d.** 280

____ **26.** Convert: 58 kg = _____ lb

     a. 57.42   **b.** 127.6   **c.** 128.88   **d.** 26.36

____ **27.** Find the perimeter of a triangle whose sides are $7\frac{4}{5}$ yd, $5\frac{3}{5}$ yd, and $6\frac{3}{5}$ yd in length. Express the answer in feet.

     a. $6\frac{3}{5}$ ft   **b.** 20 ft   **c.** $6\frac{2}{3}$ ft   **d.** 60 ft

____ **28.** The radio reported the temperature today as $40°C$. What was the Fahrenheit temperature today?

     a. $34°$ **b.** $58°$ **c.** $138°$ **d.** $104°$

____ **29.** Juanita traveled in Mexico for two hours at 90 kilometers per hour. She had to travel a distance of 130 miles. How far did she still need to travel, in miles?

     a. 40 miles   **b.** 160 miles   **c.** 18.4 miles   **d.** 50 miles

____ **30.** A pump is running at 7.5 quarts per minute. What is this rate in gallons per hour?

     a. 112.5 gal / hr   **b.** 225 gal / hr   **c.** 30 gal / hr   **d.** 450 gal / hr

1. Convert: 4.6 mi = _____ ft

2. Convert: 7200 sec = _____ hr

3. Convert: 42 gal = _____ qt

4. Convert: 292.3 m = _____ km

5. Convert: 61.3 cm = _____ mm

6. Convert: 0.213 km = _____ mm

7. Convert: 51.2 L = _____ mL

8. Convert: 123 mg = _____ kg

9. Convert: 531.7 mm = _____ cm

10. Convert: 10.3 yd = _____ m

11. Convert: 35.2 km = _____ mi

12. Convert: 75 qt = _____ L

13. A tank is being emptied at the rate of 7.5 quarts per minute. How many gallons per hour is this?

14. A rectangular garden measures 75 feet by 60 feet. Find the perimeter in yards.

15. The high temperature one summer day was 94° F. What was the Celsius reading of the high temperature?

16. The distance around the earth is 41,000 km. What is this distance in miles?

17. Convert: 6.42 kg = _____ lb

18. Convert: 125 cm = _____ in

19. Laura's baby, Conor, weighed 3.75 kg at birth. What is this in pounds and ounces? Round to the nearest ounce.

20. On the coldest day this past winter in Barrow, Alaska, the temperature was 49 degrees below zero on the Celsius scale. What is this temperature on the Fahrenheit scale? Round to the nearest tenth.

1. Convert: 208 oz = _____ lb

2. Convert: 1.8 mi = _____ ft

3. Convert: 50 qt = _____ gal

4. Convert: 1.7 km = _____ cm

5. Convert: 35.9 mm = _____ m

6. Convert: 12.4 m = _____ km

7. Convert: 6951 mL = _____ kL

8. Convert: 45.2 g = _____ mg

9. Convert: 319 mg = _____ kg

10. Convert: 28 L = _____ gal

11. Convert: 48 L = _____ gal

12. Convert: 140 km = _____ mi

13. A triangle has sides of length 123 cm, 1.4 m, and 403 mm. Find the perimeter of the triangle in centimeters.

14. A tank is being filled at the rate of 20 gallons per hour. How many quarts per minute is this?

15. The temperature at noon was 22°C. Find the Fahrenheit reading of the temperature.

16. Joyce is putting up a wallpaper border along four walls of her dining room, which measures 14 ft by $6\frac{1}{2}$ ft. If each roll of border is 4 meters in length, how many rolls does she need to buy?

17. Convert: 158 pounds = _____ kg

18. Convert: 29.3 m = _____ yards

19. Rhonda's baby, Jerome, weighed 3.95 kg at birth. What is this in pounds and ounces? Round to the nearest ounce.

20. The worst wind chill recorded at Barrow, Alaska, last winter was 68 degrees below zero on the Celsius scale. What is this on the Fahrenheit scale? Round to the nearest tenth of a degree.

1. Convert: 4500 lb = _____ tons

2. Convert: 1.6 hr = _____ sec

3. Convert: 1.2 mi = _____ ft

4. Convert: 91.3 cm = _____ km

5. Convert: 652 m = _____ mm

6. Convert: 123.24 mm = _____ cm

7. Convert: 712 mL = _____ L

8. Convert: 68.9 kg = _____ g

9. Convert: 2945 mg = _____ g

10. Convert: 24 mi = _____ km

11. Convert: 22 L = _____ qts

12. Convert: 860 miles = _____ km

13. A faucet was leaking at the rate of 4.5 quarts per minute. How many gallons per hour is this?

14. The temperature at midnight was 41° F. Find the Celsius reading of this temperature.

15. A rectangular kennel measures 46 feet by 35 feet. Find the perimeter of the kennel in yards.

16. Convert: 82°F = _____ °C

17. Pat is putting up a wallpaper border along all 4 walls in her living room, which measures 14 ft by $20\frac{1}{2}$ ft. If each roll of border is 4 meters in length, how many rolls does she need to buy?

18. Stephanie and Andrew's new baby, Emily, weighed 3.69 kg at birth. How much did she weigh in pounds and ounces? Round to the nearest ounce.

19. The speed limit on a highway in Canada says 88. This is in kilometers per hour. What is the speed limit in miles per hour? Round to the nearest whole number.

20. Grant is 6 ft, 8 in tall. He bought skis that are 210 cm long. How much longer, in inches, are his skis than his height? Round to the nearest tenth.

_____ 1. Convert: 2.6 tons = _____ lb

      a. 5200   **b.** 2600   **c.** 4150   **d.** 52

_____ 2. Convert: 13,200 ft = _____ mi

      a. 2   **b.** 3.2   **c.** 2.5   **d.** 4

_____ 3. Convert: 12 cups = _____ qt

      a. 6   **b.** 4   **c.** 8   **d.** 3

_____ 4. Convert: 79 mm = _____ m

      a. 790   **b.** 7900   **c.** 0.79   **d.** 0.079

_____ 5. Convert: 0.68 km = _____ cm

      a. 680   **b.** 68,000   **c.** 6800   **d.** 0.00068

_____ 6. Convert: 2.7 mm = _____ cm

      a. 0.27   **b.** 27   **c.** 0.027   **d.** 270

_____ 7. Convert: 19 L = _____ mL

      a. 0.019   **b.** 1900   **c.** 19,000   **d.** 0.190

_____ 8. Convert: 453 g = _____ kg

      a. 0.453   **b.** 453,000   **c.** 4530   **d.** 4.53

_____ 9. Convert: 14.2 mL = _____ kL

      a. 1,420,000   **b.** 14,200   **c.** 0.0142   **d.** 0.0000142

_____ 10. Convert: 106 mi = _____ km

      a. 65.72   **b.** 170.66   **c.** 106.66   **d.** 85.33

____ 11. Convert: 360 km = _____ mi

     a. 180   **b.** 583.2   **c.** 580.5   **d.** 223.2

____ 12. Convert: 32 L = _____ qt

     a. 8.45   **b.** 33.92   **c.** 52.8   **d.** 36

____ 13. A pump is running at a rate of 6.4 quarts per minute. How many gallons per hour is this?

     a. 192 gal / hr   **b.** 48 gal / hr   **c.** 96 gal / hr   **d.** 1536 gal /hr

____ 14. A rectangular picture frame measures 50 cm by 75 cm. What is the perimeter of the picture frame in meters?

     a. 37.5 m   **b.** 1.25 m   **c.** 2.5 m   **d.** 375 m

____ 15. A recipe calls for an oven temperature of $400°F$. The cook set the oven for $220°C$. By how many degrees Fahrenheit was the temperature off?

     a. $16°$ to cool   **b.** $28°$ too hot   **c.** $8°$ too cool   **d.** $3°$ too hot

____ 16. Convert: $76.8°F$ = _____ $°C$

     a. 21.5   **b.** 25   **c.** 170.24   **d.** 24.89

____ 17. Convert: 17 kg = _____ lb

     a. 37.4   **b.** 7.73   **c.** 385   **d.** 374

____ 18. Convert: 175 cm = _____ in

     a. 70   **b.** 68.95   **c.** 69.85   **d.** 444.16

____ 19. Nancy drove 110 km using 13.5 liters of gas. What was her gas mileage in miles per gallon?

     a. 3.47   **b.** 68.2   **c.** 19.14   **d.** 20

____ 20. The record ski jump for women is 110 meters. What is this length in feet?

     a. 360.8   **b.** 33.54   **c.** 119.9   **d.** 350

_____ 1. Convert: 162 sec = _____ min

   a. 13   b. 2.7   c. 7.5   d. 5.4

_____ 2. Convert: 27 ft = _____ in

   a. 115   b. 2.7   c. 2.25   d. 324

_____ 3. Convert: 6400 lb = _____ tons

   a. 3.2   b. 5.33   c. 12,800,000   d. 64,000

_____ 4. Convert: 361 mm = _____ m

   a. 0.361   b. 3.61   c. 361,000   d. 0.0361

_____ 5. Convert: 5.7 km = _____ cm

   a. 0.000057   b. 5700   c. 570,000   d. 57,000

_____ 6. Convert: 0.81 cm = _____ mm

   a. 81   b. 8.1   c. 0.081   d. 0.0081

_____ 7. Convert: 0.34 kL = _____ L

   a. 34   b. 340   c. 0.00034   d. 0.034

_____ 8. Convert: 2.91 mg = _____ kg

   a. 2910   b. 2,910,000   c. 0.00291   d. 0.00000291

_____ 9. Convert: 23.27 g = _____ mg

   a. 23,270   b. 0.02327   c. 2327   d. 0.2327

_____ 10. Convert: 30 cm = _____ in

   a. 101.52   b. 60   c. 11.82   d. 20.31

_____ 11. Convert: 350 km = _____ mi

    a. 567   **b.** 217   **c.** 564.52   **d.** 210

_____ 12. Convert: 23 qt = _____ L

    a. 217   **b.** 24.38   **c.** 21.76   **d.** 36.8

_____ 13. An engine is using 223.4 quarts of gasoline per minute. How many gallons per hour is this?

    a. 14.89 gal / hr   **b.** 53,616 gal / hr   **c.** 6702 gal / hr   **d.** 3351 gal / hr

_____ 14. Find the perimeter, in yards, of a triangle with sides of 9 feet, 72 inches, and 1.5 yards.

    a. 6.5 yd   **b.** 5 yd   **c.** 27 yd   **d.** 5.5 yd

_____ 15. The temperature is 98°F today. What is today's temperature on the Celsius scale?

    a. 36.67°C   **b.** 66°C   **c.** 208.4°C   **d.** 29.26°C

_____ 16. Convert: 34°C = _____ °F

    a. 1.11°   **b.** 118.8°   **c.** 66°   **d.** 93.2°

_____ 17. Convert: 185 lb = _____ kg

    a. 407   **b.** 83.99   **c.** 84.09   **d.** 84.1

_____ 18. Convert: 182 cm = _____ ft

    a. 38.49   **b.** 5.97   **c.** 6   **d.** 71.71

_____ 19. Sean drove 255 km using 27.2 liters of gasoline. What was his gas mileage in miles per gallon?

    a. 23   **b.** 9.37   **c.** 22.02   **d.** 11.53

_____ 20. Kathleen bought skis that are 175 cm long. She is 5 ft, 3 in tall. How much longer, in inches, are her skis than her height?

    a. 5.95 in   **b.** 6 in   **c.** 6.89 in   **d.** 3 in

____ 1. Convert: 6.4 min = _____ sec

    a. 192   **b.** 0.11   **c.** 320   **d.** 384

____ 2. Convert: 45 qt = _____ gal

    a. 11.25   **b.** 180   **c.** 90   **d.** 22.5

____ 3. Convert: 12,672 ft = _____ mi

    a. 6   **b.** 2.4   **c.** 6691   **d.** 4.7

____ 4. Convert: 6.51 cm = _____ km

    a. 651,000   **b.** 6510   **c.** 0.0000651   **d.** 0.00651

____ 5. Convert: 0.249 mm = _____ cm

    a. 2.49   **b.** 24.9   **c.** 0.0049   **d.** 0.0249

____ 6. Convert: 71 km = _____ m

    a. 0.071   **b.** 7100   **c.** 71,000   **d.** 0.0071

____ 7. Convert: 14.2 kg = _____ mg

    a. 14,200,000   **b.** 14,200   **c.** 0.000142   **d.** 142,000

____ 8. Convert: 387 L = _____ kL

    a. 3.87   **b.** 387,000   **c.** 0.387   **d.** 0.0387

____ 9. Convert: 0.15 mL = _____ L

    a. 0.015   **b.** 0.00015   **c.** 150   **d.** 1500

____ 10. Convert: 24 L = _____ gal

    a. 25.44   **b.** 22.70   **c.** 8.92   **d.** 6.34

____ **11.** Convert: 365 km = _____ mi

     a. 225   **b.** 588.71   **c.** 226.3   **d.** 228.12

____ **12.** Convert: 118 qt = _____ L

     a. 110   **b.** 111.63   **c.** 124.74   **d.** 447.22

____ **13.** A swimming pool is being filled at the rate of 18 pints per minute. How many gallons per hour is this?

     a. 60 gal / hr   **b.** 30 gal / hr   **c.** 45 gal / hr   **d.** 32 gal / hr

____ **14.** A rectangular picture measures 12 cm by 14 cm. What is the perimeter of the picture frame in meters?

     a. 0.28 m   **b.** 0.52 m   **c.** 1.68 m   **d.** 0.0168 m

____ **15.** The temperature is 24°C today. What is today's temperature on the Fahrenheit scale?

     a. 4.44°F   **b.** 56°F   **c.** 75.2°F   **d.** 68.6°F

____ **16.** Eleanor is putting up a wallpaper border along all 4 walls of her living room. Her border comes in rolls of 4 meters. How many rolls should she buy if her living room is $22\frac{1}{2}$ feet by 12 feet

     a. 4 rolls   **b.** 3 rolls   **c.** 6 rolls   **d.** 7 rolls

____ **17.** Convert: 205 lb = _____ kg

     a. 93.07   **b.** 298.07   **c.** 451.51   **d.** 930.7

____ **18.** Convert: 125 cm = _____ in

     a. 50   **b.** 48   **c.** 317.26   **d.** 49.25

____ **19.** Katie's baby, Evan, weighed 4.23 kg at birth. What was the baby' weight in pounds and ounces? Round to the nearest ounce.

     a. 10 lb, 5 oz   **b.** 9 lb, 5 oz   **c.** 9 lb, 1 oz   **d.** 7 lb, 2 oz

____ **20.** Mike is 6 ft, 2 in tall. He bought new skis that are 200 cm long. How much longer, in inches, are his skis than his height? Round to the nearest tenth.

     a. 6.8 in   **b.** 7 in   **c.** 6 in   **d.** 4.8 in

1. A man was running at the rate of nine miles per hour. Find his rate in feet per second.

2. The temperature yesterday was 20°C. Find the Fahrenheit reading of this temperature.

3. A rectangular picture frame measures 60 cm by 35 cm. Find the perimeter of the frame in meters.

4. Convert: 8.75 kg = _____ lb

5. Convert: 38 quarts = _____ gallons

6. Convert: 320 cm = _____ inches

7. Convert: 61 m = _____ cm

8. Add: $5\frac{1}{2} + 7\frac{1}{8}$

9. Divide: $\frac{11}{16} \div \frac{3}{8}$

10. Simplify using the order of operations:
$5^2 + 2(3+5) \div 4 + 2^3$

11. Gasoline is sold at \$1.88 per gallon. How much will 20.5 gallons cost?

12. Simplify: $2.03 + 14.5 - 1.7$

13. A racecar driver traveled 455 miles in 5 hours. At this rate, how far could he travel in 8.5 hours?

14. Solve for n: $\frac{16}{25} = \frac{n}{175}$

15. My car traveled 975 miles on 25 gallons of gasoline. What is my car's mileage in miles per gallon?

16. What is 13% of \$780?

17. Write $\frac{19}{152}$ as a percent.

18. Write $4\frac{2}{15}$ as a decimal. Round to 2 decimal places.

19. Write 65% as a fraction.

20. Janet borrowed \$2500 at an 8.5% simple rate of interest for one year. How much interest did she pay?

____ 1. A triangle has sides that measure 30 in, 19 ft, and 7 yd. Find the perimeter of the triangle in feet.

    a. 23.83 ft   **b.** 42.5 ft   **c.** 28.5 ft   **d.** 56 ft

____ 2. Convert 167°F to a reading on the Celsius scale.

    a. 135°C   **b.** 3.33°C   **c.** 75°C   **d.** 23.89°C

____ 3. A cyclist was traveling at a rate of 15 miles per hour. Find the rate in feet per minute.

    a. 1320 ft / min   **b.** 21,120 ft / min   **c.** 88 ft / min   **d.** 352 ft / min

____ 4. Convert: 98 lb = _____ kg

    a. 215.6   **b.** 6.125   **c.** 215.86   **d.** 44.9

____ 5. Convert: 14 gallons = _____ quarts

    a. 56   **b.** 7   **c.** 28   **d.** 3.5

____ 6. Convert: 55 inches = _____ cm

    a. 165   **b.** 139.7   **c.** 21.67   **d.** 660

____ 7. Convert: 1658 cm = _____ m

    a. 16.58   **b.** 165.8   **c.** 1.658   **d.** 0.1658

____ 8. Add: $2\frac{1}{3} + 5\frac{2}{7}$

    a. $4\frac{2}{5}$ **b.** $7\frac{3}{10}$ **c.** 8   **d.** $7\frac{13}{21}$

____ 9. Divide: $\frac{14}{15} \div \frac{9}{10}$

    a. $1\frac{5}{27}$ **b.** $\frac{21}{25}$ **c.** $\frac{27}{28}$ **d.** $1\frac{1}{27}$

____ 10. Simplify using the order of operations: $2^3 - 4 \times 2 + 3^3 \div 9$

    a. 1   **b.** 3.89   **c.** 3   **d.** 11

____ **11.** Gasoline is sold at $1.67 per gallon. How much will 15.8 gallons cost?

     a. $26.39   **b.** $17.47   **c.** $9.46   **d.** $27.20

____ **12.** Simplify: $25.03 + 11.2 - 1.3$

     a. 34.93   **b.** 35.13   **c.** 12.93   **d.** 37.53

____ **13.** A race car driver traveled 273 miles in 3 hours. At this rate, how far could she travel in 8.5 hours?

     a. 1501.5 miles   **b.** 96.35 miles   **c.** 773.5 miles   **d.** 728 miles

____ **14.** Solve for n: $\dfrac{21}{25} = \dfrac{n}{325}$

     a. $n = 525$ **b.** $n = 126$ **c.** $n = 156$ **d.** $n = 6825$

____ **15.** My car traveled 774 miles on 36 gallons of gasoline. What is my car's mileage in miles per gallon?

     a. 4.65   **b.** 21.5   **c.** 464.4   **d.** 27,864

____ **16.** What is 19% of $640?

     a. $33.68   **b.** $121.60   **c.** $12.16   **d.** $3368.42

____ **17.** Write $\dfrac{17}{20}$ as a percent.

     a. 15%   **b.** 68%   **c.** 0.85%   **d.** 85%

____ **18.** Write $7\dfrac{2}{13}$ as a decimal. Round to 2 decimal places.

     a. 7.15   **b.** 7.65   **c.** 7.16   **d.** 7.26

____ **19.** Write 44% as a fraction.

     a. $\dfrac{11}{250}$ **b.** $\dfrac{.44}{100}$ **c.** $4\dfrac{2}{5}$ **d.** $\dfrac{11}{25}$

____ **20.** Gail borrowed $3800 at a 6.5 % simple rate of interest for two years. How much interest did she pay?

     a. $2470.00   **b.** $584.62   **c.** $24.70   **d.** $494.00

If you are familiar with the topics in this chapter, take this test now. If you can't answer a question, study the appropriate section of the chapter. If you are not familiar with the topics in this chapter, don't take this test now. Instead, study the examples, work the practice problems, and then take the test. This test will help you identify which concepts you have mastered, and which you need to study further. Use $\pi \approx 3.14$ in your calculations where necessary.

1. Find the complement of an angle that is 78°.

2. Find the supplement of an angle that is 123°.

3. Find the measure of an angle a, angle b, and angle c in the sketch below, which shows two intersecting straight lines.

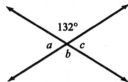

4. Find the perimeter of the rectangle with length 6.2 m and width 3.5 m.

5. Find the perimeter of a square where each side measures 4.2 m.

6. Find the area of a square where each side measures 5.6 cm.

7. Find the area of the rectangle with length 2.6 cm and width 0.7 cm.

8. Find the perimeter of a parallelogram with one side measuring 9.6 yd and another side measuring 3.2 yd.

9. Find the perimeter of a trapezoid with sides measuring 18 ft, 16 ft, 22 ft, and 23 ft.

10. Find the area of a parallelogram with base 28 inches and height 15 inches.

11. Find the area of a trapezoid with height 18 inches and bases that measure 14 inches and 21 inches.

12. Find the area of the figure below.

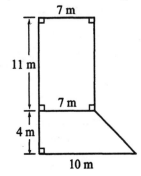

13. Find the third angle in the triangle if two of the angles are 41° and 116°.

14. Find the perimeter of a triangle whose sides measure 9.2 m, 4.1 m, and 7.8 m.

15. Find the area of a triangle with base 18 m and height 11m.

16. Evaluate exactly: $\sqrt{49}$

17. Evaluate exactly: $\sqrt{9} + \sqrt{81}$

18. Approximate $\sqrt{41}$. Round to the nearest thousandth.

19. Find the unknown side of the triangle below.

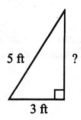

5 ft   ?

3 ft

20. Find the unknown side of the triangle below.

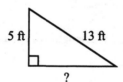

5 ft   13 ft

?

21. Find the diameter of a circle whose radius is 16 in.

22. Find the circumference of a circle whose diameter is 40 cm.

23. Find the area of the circle whose radius is 8 m.

24. Find the area of the shaded region below.

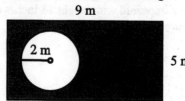

9 m

2 m

5 m

25. Find the volume of a rectangular solid with length 7 yd, width 8yd, and height 11 yd.

26. Find the volume of a sphere with radius 6 ft.

27. Find the volume of a cylinder with height 14 inches and radius 9 inches.

28. Find the volume of a pyramid with height 18 m and a square base measuring 23 m on a side.

29. Find the volume of a cone with height 27 m and radius 6 m.

30. Find n in this set of similar triangles below.

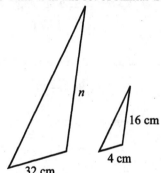

31. Find n in this set of similar triangles:

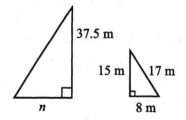

32. A track consists of two semicircles and a rectangle.

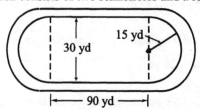

(a) Find the area of the field.

(b) It costs $0.22 per square yard to fertilize the field. What would it cost to complete this task?

If you <u>are</u> familiar with the topics in this chapter, take this test now. If you can't answer a question, study the appropriate section of the chapter. If you are <u>not</u> familiar with the topics in this chapter, don't take this test now. Instead, study the examples, work the practice problems, and then take the test. This test will help you identify which concepts you have mastered, and which you need to study further. Use $\pi \approx 3.14$ in your calculations where necessary.

_____ 1. Find the complement of an angle that is 76°.

     a. 94°   **b.** 14°   **c.** 74°   **d.** 104°

_____ 2. Find the supplement of an angle that is 119°.

     a. 29°   **b.** 71°   **c.** 61°   **d.** 241°

_____ 3. Find the measure of angle b and angle c in the sketch below, which shows two intersecting straight lines.

     a. $\angle b = 56°$ $\angle c = 56°$ **b.** $\angle b = 146°$ $\angle c = 56°$

     c. $\angle b = 34°$ $\angle c = 56°$ **d.** $\angle b = 146°$ $\angle c = 34°$

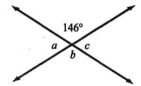

_____ 4. Find the perimeter of a rectangle with length 6.6 m, and width 4.5 m.

     a. 22.2 m   **b.** 17.7 m   **c.** 11.1 m   **d.** 10.1 m

_____ 5. Find the perimeter of a square where each side measures 4.7 m.

     a. 14.1 m   **b.** 22.09 m   **c.** 18.8 m   **d.** 9.4 m

_____ 6. Find the area of a square where each side measures 3.8 cm.

     a. 3.8 cm^2 **b.** 14.4 cm^2 **c.** 15.2 cm^2 **d.** 7.6 cm^2

_____ 7. Find the area of a rectangle with length 2.8 cm and width 1.2 cm.

     a. 11.29 cm^2 **b.** 4 cm^2 **c.** 8 cm^2 **d.** 3.4 cm^2

_____ 8. Find the perimeter of a parallelogram with one side measuring 9.4 yd and another side measuring 3.1 yd.

     a. 25 yd   **b.** 12.5 yd   **c.** 849.14 yd   **d.** 29.14 yd

_____ 9. Find the perimeter of a trapezoid with sides measuring 19 ft, 17 ft, 21 ft, and 24 ft.

     a. 79 ft   **b.** 81 ft   **c.** 83 ft   **d.** 78 ft

_____ 10. Find the area of a parallelogram with base 26 inches and height 14 inches.

     a. 3920 in^2 **b.** 80 in^2 **c.** 364 in^2 **d.** 40 in^2

_____ 11. Find the area of a trapezoid with height 12 inches and bases that measure 18 inches and 23 inches.

     a. 345 in^2 **b.** 216 in^2 **c.** 2484 in^2 **d.** 246 in^2

____ **12.** Find the area of the figure below.

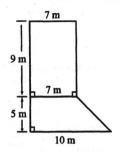

    a. 98 m²   **b.** 105.5 m²

    c. 119 m²   **d.** 113 m²

____ **13.** Find the third angle in a triangle if two of the angles are 43° and 114°.

    a. 203°   **b.** 23°   **c.** 47°   **d.** 157°

____ **14.** Find the perimeter of the triangle whose sides measure 9.4 m, 4.6 m, and 7.2 m.

    a. 21.2 m   **b.** 311.3 m   **c.** 14 m   **d.** 17.64 m

____ **15.** Find the area of a triangle with base 28 m and height 13 m.

    a. 121.3 m²   **b.** 242.7 m²   **c.** 364 m²   **d.** 182 m²

____ **16.** Evaluate $\sqrt{121}$ exactly.

    a. 17   **b.** 14,641   **c.** 12   **d.** 11

____ **17.** Evaluate $\sqrt{25} + \sqrt{49}$ exactly.

    a. 12   **b.** 13   **c.** 8.6   **d.** 74

____ **18.** Approximate $\sqrt{51}$. Round to the nearest thousandth.

    a. 7.1414   **b.** 7.14   **c.** 7.141   **d.** 7.1

____ **19.** Find the unknown side of the right triangle below.

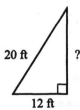

    a. 64 ft   **b.** 5.66 ft

    c. 16 ft   **d.** 23.32 ft

____ **20.** Find the unknown side of the right triangle below.

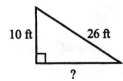

    a. 27.86 ft   **b.** 24 ft

    c. 18 ft   **d.** 36 ft

____ **21.** Find the diameter of a circle whose radius is 18 inches.

    a. 36 inches   **b.** 1017.9 inches   **c.** 113.1 inches   **d.** 9 inches

_____ **22.** Find the circumference of a circle whose diameter is 42 cm.

    a. 131.9 cm   **b.** 84 cm   **c.** 263.9 cm   **d.** 21 cm

_____ **23.** Find the area of a circle whose radius is 7 m.

    a. 49 m^2 **b.** 14 m^2 **c.** 44 m^2 **d.** 153.9 m^2

_____ **24.** Find the area of the shaded region in the figure below.

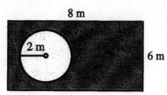

    a. 44 m^2 **b.** 12.57 m^2

    c. 35.4 m^2 **d.** 48 m^2

_____ **25.** Find the volume of a rectangular solid with length 10 yd, width 11 yd, and height 12 yd.

    a. 1210 yd^3 **b.** 142 yd^3 **c.** 1320 yd^3 **d.** 33 yd^3

_____ **26.** Find the volume of a sphere with radius 9 ft.

    a. 3052.1 ft^3 **b.** 254.46 ft^3 **c.** 729 ft^3 **d.** 113.1 ft^3

_____ **27.** Find the volume of a pyramid with a height 21 m and a square base measuring 14 m on a side.

    a. 1029 m^3 **b.** 4116 m^3 **c.** 2058 ^{3} **d.** 1372 m^3

_____ **28.** Find the volume of a cone with height 24 m and radius 5 m.

    a. 628 m^3 **b.** 3140 m^3 **c.** 942 m^3 **d.** 1884 m^3

_____ **29.** Find n in the similar triangles below.

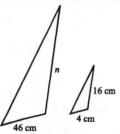

    a. 60 cm   **b.** 184 cm

    c. 11.5 cm   **d.** 64 cm

_____ **30.** Find n in the similar triangles below.

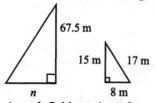

    a. 126.6 m   **b.** 36 m

    c. 76.5 m   **d.** 143.4 m

_____ **31.** A track field consists of two semicircles and a rectangle. Find the area of the field.

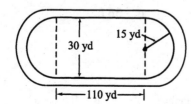

    a. 3653.25 yd^2 **b.** 3750 yd^2

    c. 3300 yd^2 **d.** 4006.5 yd^2

1. Find the perimeter of a rectangle with length 29.2 m and width 6.75 m.

2. Find the perimeter of a square where each side measures $13\frac{1}{4}$ in.

3. Find the perimeter of a triangle with sides that measure 9.2 cm, 11cm, and 8.9 cm.

4. Find the area of a parallelogram with height 8.2 m and a base that measures of 6.5 m.

5. Find the area of a triangle with height 18 inches and a base that measures 11 inches.

6. Find the area of a trapezoid with height 14 cm and bases that measure 9 cm and 19 cm.

7. Find the circumference of a circle with radius 4.4 inches. Round to the nearest tenth.

8. Find the area of the shaded region:

    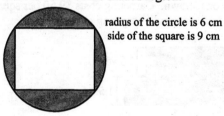

    radius of the circle is 6 cm
    side of the square is 9 cm

9. Find the area of the shaded region below.

    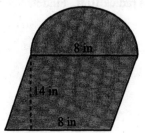

10. Find the volume of a cone with height 8 m and radius 6 m.

11. Find the volume of a rectangular solid with width 9mm, length 16mm, and height 9.5 mm.

12. Find the volume of a sphere with radius 8 yd.

13. In a triangle, two of the angles measure 42° and 56°. Find the measure of the third angle.

14. Find the area of the triangle below.

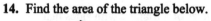
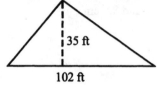

35 ft

102 ft

15. The figures below are similar. Find the value of n. Round to the nearest tenth if necessary.

10 cm

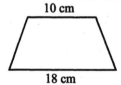

18 cm

n

13.5 cm

16. A cylindrical soup can has a height of 10 inches and a diameter of 6 inches. How many cubic inches of soup will it hold?

17. The Anderson's are carpeting a room with the dimensions shown. Carpeting costs $9.50 per square yard. How much will carpeting cost?

4 yd

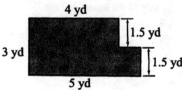
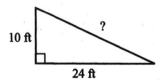

1.5 yd

3 yd

1.5 yd

5 yd

18. Approximate $\sqrt{116}$. Round to the nearest thousandth.

19. Find the length of the hypotenuse of the right triangle.

10 ft

?

24 ft

20. A farm silo in the shape of a cylinder is 32.5 ft high, and its circular base has radius 10 ft. Find its volume.

1. Find the perimeter of a parallelogram with one side that measures 13 cm and another that is 9.5 cm.

2. Find the perimeter of a square where each side measures $3\frac{7}{8}$ in.

3. Find the perimeter of a triangle with sides measuring 12.35 m, 8.05 m, and 25.1 m.

4. Find the area of a triangle with height 14 cm and base 19 cm.

5. Find the area of a parallelogram with height 10 cm and a base that measures of 6 cm.

6. Find the area of a trapezoid with height 14m and bases that measure 9m and 11 m.

7. Find the circumference of a circle with diameter 17.4 inches. Round to the nearest tenth.

8. Find the area of the shaded region in the figure below.

Inner radius is 5 cm
Outer radius is 8 cm

9. Find the area of the shaded region of this figure which is made up of a trapezoid and triangles.

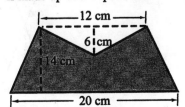

10. Find the volume of a pyramid with height 12 m and a square base with sides that each measure 8 m.

11. Find the volume of a hemisphere with radius 9 m.

12. Find the volume of a cylinder with height 5 inches and diameter 8 inches.

13. In a triangle, two of the angles measure 82° and 61°. Find the measure of the third angle.

14. Find the area of the following triangle. Round to the nearest hundredth.

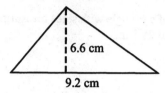

6.6 cm

9.2 cm

15. The figures below are similar. Find the value of the missing perimeter.

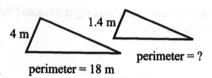

4 m

1.4 m

perimeter = 18 m

perimeter = ?

16. Ruth and Norman want to put down a 3-inch layer of loam on their front lawn, which measures 50 yd by 60 yd. How many cubic yards of loam do they need?

17. Joe is building a rectangular pen that measures 35 ft by 50 ft for his dog out of fencing material. Joe can by fencing for $3.25 per foot. How much will the dog pen cost?

18. Approximate $\sqrt{317}$. Round to the nearest thousandth.

19. Find the length of the hypotenuse of right triangle.

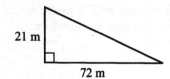

21 m

72 m

20. A Native American "teepee" is a cone with a circular base. If the radius is 10 ft and the height is 25 ft, what is the volume of the teepee? Round to the nearest hundredth.

25 ft

10 ft

1. Find the perimeter of a square where each side measures $4\frac{5}{8}$ inches.

2. Find the perimeter of a triangle with two sides that measure 6.85 cm each, and a third side that measures 8.2 cm.

3. Find the perimeter of a parallelogram with one side that measures $12\frac{1}{2}$ inches and another that is $8\frac{3}{4}$ inches.

4. Find the area of a trapezoid with bases 2.5 m and 1.75 m and height 6 m.

5. Find the area of a rectangle that has length 14 cm and width 18 cm.

6. Find the area of a triangle with base 15 m and height 22 m.

7. Find the circumference of a circle with radius 7.3 inches. Round to the nearest tenth.

8. Find the area of the shaded region. Round to the nearest tenth, if necessary.

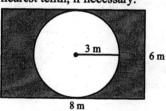

3 m
6 m
8 m

9. Find the area of the shaded region. Round to the nearest tenth, if necessary.

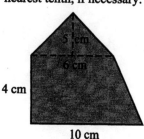

5 cm
6 cm
4 cm
10 cm

10. Find the volume of a sphere with radius 3.2 m.

11. Find the volume of a cone with height 6 m and radius 10 m.

12. Find the area of a box with width 2.8 ft, length 3.5 ft, and height 6.5 ft.

13. In a triangle, two of the angle measure 46° and 53°. Find the measure of the third angle.

14. Find the area of the triangle below. Round to the nearest hundredth.

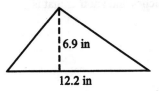

6.9 in

12.2 in

15. The triangles below are similar. Find the length of the missing side x.

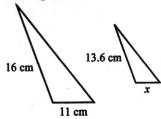

16 cm

13.6 cm

11 cm

x

16. An athletic field has the dimensions shown. What is the area of the field?

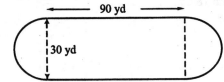

90 yd

30 yd

17. The Moore's are carpeting an area with the dimensions shown. Carpeting costs $12.00 per square yard. How much will the carpeting cost?

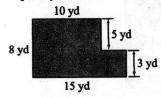

10 yd

5 yd

8 yd

3 yd

15 yd

18. Approximate $\sqrt{167}$. Round to the nearest thousandth.

19. Find the length of the hypotenuse of the right triangle.

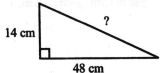

14 cm

?

48 cm

20. A pyramid has a square base measuring 50 ft on each side. Its height is 62 ft. Find the volume. Round to the nearest hundredth.

_____ 1. Find the perimeter of a trapezoid with sides that measure 11.6 inches, 9.29 inches, 5.3 inches, and 12 inches.

    a. 111 inches   **b.** 16.95 inches   **c.** 21.54 inches   **d.** 38.19 inches

_____ 2. Find the perimeter of a square with sides that measure 9.6 m.

    a. 92.16 m   **b.** 38.4 m   **c.** 19.2 m   **d.** 28.8 m

_____ 3. Find the perimeter of a parallelogram with one side that measures 15.3 cm and another that is 17 cm.

    a. 64.6 cm   **b.** 32.3 cm   **c.** 260.1 cm   **d.** 130.05 cm

_____ 4. Find the area of a square where each side measures 8.5 ft.

    a. 72.25 ft^2 **b.** 17 ft^2 **c.** 34 ft^2 **d.** 614.125 ft^2

_____ 5. Find the area of a triangle with base 4.5 m and height 6 m.

    a. 27 m^2 **b.** 13.5 m^2 **c.** 54 m^2 **d.** 10.5 m^2

_____ 6. Find the area of a trapezoid with bases that measure 9.2 cm and 7.7cm, and height 6.8 cm.

    a. 114.92 cm^2 **b.** 481.7 cm^2 **c.** 57.46 cm^2 **d.** 28.73 cm^2

_____ 7. Find the circumference of a circle with radius 8.3 ft. Round to the nearest tenth.

    a. 26.1 ft   **b.** 52.1 ft   **c.** 16.6 ft   **d.** 49.8 ft

_____ 8. Find the area of the shaded region.

Inner radius is 4 cm
Outer radius is 9 cm

    a. 78.5 cm^2 **b.** 31.4 cm^2

    c. 157 cm^2 **d.** 204.1 cm^2

_____ 9. Find the area of the shaded region.

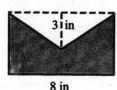

3 in
5 in
8 in

    a. 28 in^2 **b.** 16 in^2

    c. 35 in^2 **d.** 10 in^2

_____ 10. Find the volume of a cone with radius 6 m and height 12 m.

    a. 452.2 m^3 **b.** 904.3 m^3 **c.** 2713.0 m^3 **d.** 1356.5 m^3

_____ 11. Find the volume of a rectangular box having width 4.2 ft, length 5 ft, and height 2.4 ft.

    a. 25.2 ft^3 **b.** 44.2 ft^3 **c.** 50.4 ft^3 **d.** 62.2 ft^3

_____ 12. Find the volume of a sphere with radius 9 yd.

    a. 3829.7 yd^3 **b.** 3052.1 yd^3 **c.** 381.5 yd^3 **d.** 339.1 yd^3

_____ **13.** In a triangle, two of the angles measure 76° and 32°. Find the measure of the third angle.

     a. 82°   **b.** 108°   **c.** 72°   **d.** 76°

_____ **14.** Find the area of the triangle below. Round to the nearest hundredth.

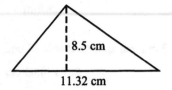

     a. 48 cm^2 **b.** 48.11 cm^2

     c. 96.22 cm^2 **d.** 32.07 cm^2

8.5 cm

11.32 cm

_____ **15.** The figures below are similar. Find the missing perimeter.

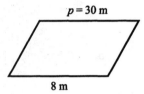

$p = 30$ m

$p = ?$

8 m

4.8 m

     a. $p = 23.6$ m   **b.** $p = 16$ m

     c. $p = 26.8$ m   **d.** $p = 18$ m

_____ **16.** A cylindrical gasoline tank is 50 ft high and has diameter 70 ft. How many gallons of gasoline will the tank hold if there are 7.5 gallons in 1 ft^3 ?

     a. 1,442,437.5 gal   **b.** 25,643.3 gal   **c.** 5,769,750 gal   **d.** 102,573.3 gal

_____ **17.** A rectangular picture frame measures 40 inches by 55 inches. To cover the picture inside the frame with glass cost $0.99 per square inch. What will be the cost of the glass to cover the picture?

     a. $6.60   **b.** $198.00   **c.** $198.66   **d.** $22.00

_____ **18.** Approximate $\sqrt{147}$. Round to the nearest thousandth.

     a. 121.24   **b.** 73.5   **c.** 12.124   **d.** 12.24

_____ **19.** Find the length of the hypotenuse in the right triangle below:

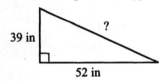

39 in

?

52 in

     a. 81 inches   **b.** 91 inches

     c. 89 inches   **d.** 65 inches

_____ **20.** Find the volume of this pyramid.

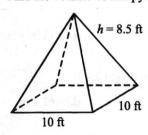

$h = 8.5$ ft

10 ft

10 ft

     a. 425 ft^3 **b.** 85 ft^3

     c. 850 ft^3 **d.** 283.33 ft^3

____ **1.** Find the perimeter of a rectangle that has length 23 cm and width 17 cm.

     a. 391 cm   **b.** 80 cm   **c.** 40 cm   **d.** 195.5 cm

____ **2.** Find the perimeter of a parallelogram with one side that measures 3.6m and another that is 4.2m.

     a. 15.6 m   **b.** 23.4 m   **c.** 15.12 m   **d.** 9.8 m

____ **3.** Find the perimeter of a triangle with sides that measure 14.3 inches, 4.39 inches, and 12.8 inches.

     a. 71.0 inches   **b.** 72.8 inches   **c.** 28.1 inches   **d.** 31.9 inches

____ **4.** Find the area of a circle with diameter 6 ft. Round to the nearest tenth.

     a. 36.0 ft^2 **b.** 18.8 ft^2 **c.** 28.3 ft^2 **d.** 113.0 ft^2

____ **5.** Find the area of a triangle with base 16 cm and height 13 cm.

     a. 104 cm^2 **b.** 208 cm^2 **c.** 58 cm^2 **d.** 29 cm^2

____ **6.** Find the area of a trapezoid with bases that measure 7 inches and 4 inches, and height 9 inches.

     a. 99 in^2 **b.** 49.5 in^2 **c.** 20 in^2 **d.** 252 in^2

____ **7.** Find the circumference of a circle with radius 6 ft. Round to the nearest tenth.

     a. 37.8 ft   **b.** 56.5 ft   **c.** 9.4 ft   **d.** 18.8 ft

____ **8.** Find the area of the shaded region.

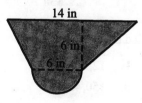

     a. 74.1 in^2 **b.** 88.3 in^2
     c. 148.3 in^2 **d.** 134.1 in^2

____ **9.** Find the area of the shaded region.

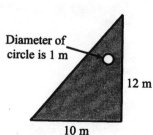

     a. 56.9 m^2 **b.** 119.2 m^2
     c. 59.2 m^2 **d.** 116.9 m^2

____ **10.** Find the volume of a sphere with radius 4 m.

     a. 50.2 m^3 **b.** 267.9 m^3 **c.** 150.7 m^3 **d.** 2641.8 m^3

____ **11.** Find the volume of a pyramid with height 18 m and whose rectangular base measures 6 m by 9 m.

     a. 162 m^3 **b.** 324 m^3 **c.** 648 m^3 **d.** 972 m^3

_____ **12.** Find the volume of a cylinder with height 10 ft and radius 8 ft.

     a. 2152 ft³   **b.** 251.2 ft³   **c.** 6310.1 ft³   **d.** 2009.6 ft³

_____ **13.** In a triangle, two of the angles measure 52° and 60°. Find the measure of the third angle.

     a. 68°   **b.** 78°   **c.** 60°   **d.** 64°

_____ **14.** Find the area of the triangle below. Round to the nearest hundredth.

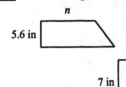

     a. 55.64 m²   **b.** 28.72 m²

     c. 15.9 m²   **d.** 27.82 m²

_____ **15.** The figures below are similar. Find the value of *n*. Round to the nearest tenth, if necessary.

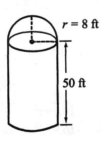

     a. $n = 14.4$ in   **b.** $n = 22.5$ in

     c. $n = 16.6$ in   **d.** $n = 15.8$ in

_____ **16.** Victor has a rectangular rose garden measuring 5 m by 8 m. Fertilizer costs $1.05 per square meter. How much will it cost Victor to fertilize the garden?

     a. $24.76   **b.** $27.30   **c.** $42   **d.** $38.10

_____ **17.** A silo (shown below) has a cylindrical shape with a hemispheric dome. Find the volume of the silo.

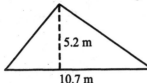

     a. 11,119.8 ft³   **b.** 12,191.6 ft³

     c. 11.655.7 ft³   **d.** 150,456.2 ft³

_____ **18.** Find $\sqrt{321}$ on a calculator. Round to the nearest thousandth.

     a. 17.91   **b.** 17.916   **c.** 117.231   **d.** 18

_____ **19.** Find the length of the hypotenuse in the right triangle below:

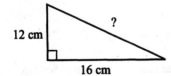

     a. 25 cm   **b.** 20 cm

     c. 28 cm   **d.** 41.76 cm

_____ **20.** Find the volume of a sphere with radius 6 in. Round to the nearest hundredth.

     a. 25.12 in³   **b.** 150.72 in³   **c.** 904.32 in³   **d.** 2712.96 in³

_____ **1.** Find the perimeter of a square where each side measures 7.2 cm.

     a. 28.8 cm   **b.** 51.84 cm   **c.** 14.4 cm   **d.** 25.92 cm

_____ **2.** Find the perimeter of a parallelogram with one side that measures 9.8 inches and another that is 13.7 inches.

     a. 94 inches   **b.** 23.5 inches   **c.** 134.26 inches   **d.** 47 inches

_____ **3.** Find the perimeter of a triangle with sides that measure 16.8 cm, 9.59 cm, and 14.4 cm.

     a. 12.71 cm   **b.** 127.1 cm   **c.** 40.79 cm   **d.** 32.39 cm

_____ **4.** Find the area of a rectangle that measures 17 yd by 19 yd.

     a. 72 yd^2 **b.** 323 yd^2 **c.** 36 yd^2 **d.** 161.5 yd^2

_____ **5.** Find the area of a trapezoid with height 8 m and bases that measure 5 m and 12 m.

     a. 25 m^2 **b.** 480 m^2 **c.** 68 m^2 **d.** 50 m^2

_____ **6.** Find the area of a triangle with base 14 inches and height 9 inches.

     a. 46 in^2 **b.** 126 in^2 **c.** 12.5 in^2 **d.** 63 in^2

_____ **7.** Find the circumference of a circle with radius 4 m. Round to the nearest tenth.

     a. 25.1 m   **b.** 50.2 m   **c.** 157.8 m   **d.** 12.6 m

_____ **8.** Find the area of the shaded region.

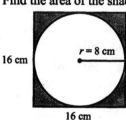

     a. 457.0 cm^2 **b.** 55.0 cm^2

     c. 13.8 cm^2 **d.** 62.3 cm^2

_____ **9.** Find the area of the shaded region.

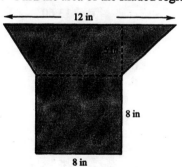

     a. 124 in^2 **b.** 114 in^2

     c. 94 in^2 **d.** 164 in^2

_____ **10.** Find the volume of a cylinder with height 3 m and radius 8 m.

     a. 226.1 m^3 **b.** 106.8 m^3 **c.** 602.9 m^3 **d.** 79.0 m^3

_____ **11.** Find the volume of a sphere with radius 5 ft.

     a. 1570 ft^3 **b.** 294.4 ft^3 **c.** 78.5 ft^3 **d.** 523.3 ft^3

_____ **12.** Find the volume of a cone with height 10 m and radius 6 m.

     a. 376.8 m^3 **b.** 1884 m^3 **c.** 628 m^3 **d.** 1130.4 m^3

____ **13.** In a triangle, two of the angles measure 44° and 57°. Find the measure of the third angle.

    a. 80°   **b.** 70°   **c.** 79°   **d.** 61°

____ **14.** Find the area of the triangle below. Round to the nearest hundredth.

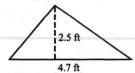

    a. 5.8 ft^2 **b.** 5.88 ft^2

    c. 11.75 ft^2 **d.** 23.5 ft^2

____ **15.** The figures below are similar. Find the missing side, *n*.

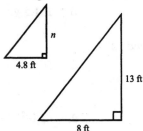

    a. $n = 9.8$ ft   **b.** $n \approx 21.7$ ft

    c. $n = 7.8$ ft   **d.** $n = 6.9$ ft

____ **16.** A cylindrical tank in a chemistry lab holds acid. The tank has a radius of 6 inches and a height of 18 inches. The acid weighs 16 g per cubic inch. What is the weight of the acid if the tank is full?

    a. 2034.7 g   **b.** 32,555.5 g   **c.** 127.2 g   **d.** 678.2 g

____ **17.** An athletic field has the dimensions shown below. What is the area of the field?

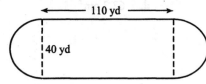

    a. 8344 yd^2 **b.** 5028 yd^2

    c. 1556 yd^2 **d.** 5656 yd^2

____ **18.** Approximate $\sqrt{185}$. Round to the nearest thousandth.

    a. 13.601   **b.** 13.602   **c.** 13.6   **d.** 13.60

____ **19.** Find the length of the hypotenuse in the right triangle below:

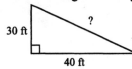

    a. 70 ft   **b.** 5 ft

    c. 55 ft   **d.** 50 ft

____ **20.** Find the volume of the cone below. Round to the nearest tenth.

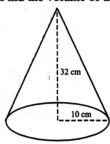

    a. 334.9 cm^3 **b.** 3340 cm^3

    c. 3349.3 cm^3 **d.** 3350 cm^3

If you <u>are</u> familiar with the topics in this chapter, take this test now. If you can't answer a question, study the appropriate section of the chapter. If you are <u>not</u> familiar with the topics in this chapter, don't take this test now. Instead, study the examples, work the practice problems, and then take the test. This test will help you identify which concepts you have mastered, and which you need to study further.

The ages of 600 students on a College campus were recorded. The following circle graph depicts the distribution of their ages.

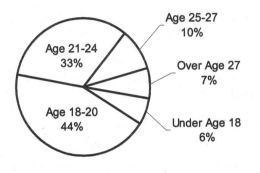

1. What age group comprises the largest percentage of the student body?

2. What percent of students are between the ages of 18 and 24?

3. What percent of students are under age 20?

4. If 600 students are at the College, how many students are 25-27 years old?

5. How many students are over age 25?

The following double bar graph indicates the number of new housing starts in Manchester during each quarter of 2003 and 2004.

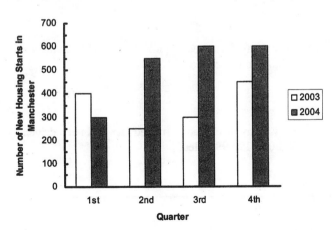

6. How many housing starts were there in Manchester in the third quarter of 2004?

7. How many housing starts were there in Manchester in the second quarter of 2003?

8. In what two quarters were the housing starts the same for 2004?

9. Which quarter(s) had the smallest number of housing starts?

10. How many more housing starts were there in the third quarter of 2004 compared to the third quarter of 2003?

11. How many more housing starts were there in the fourth quarter of 2003 compared to the second quarter of 2003?

The line graph below indicates the production and sales of color television sets by a major manufacturer during the specified months.

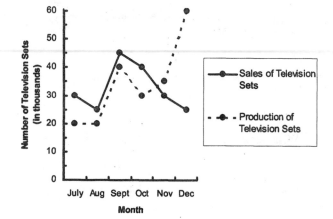

12. During what month was the production of television sets the highest?

13. During what month was the sales of television sets the lowest?

14. During what months were the sales of television sets greater than the production of television sets?

15. How many television sets were sold in September?

16. How many television sets were produced in December?

The histogram below tells us the number of miles a car was driven before the car was discarded or sold to a junk dealer.

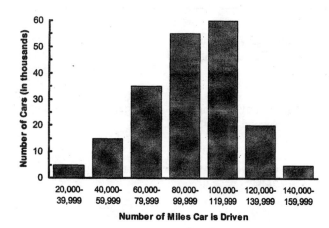

17. How many discarded or junked cars had been driven 60,000-79,999 miles?

18. How many discarded or junked cars had been driven 120,000-139,999 miles?

19. How many discarded or junked cars had been driven 100,000 miles or more?

20. How many discarded or junked cars had been driven 80,000-119,999 miles?

An administrative assistant produced the following number of pages on her computer.

Mon.	Tues.	Wed.	Thurs.	Fri.	Sat.
36	42	46	27	32	27

21. Find the mean number of pages produced per day.

22. Find the median number of pages produced per day.

23. Find the mode for the number of pages produced per day.

If you are familiar with the topics in this chapter, take this test now. If you can't answer a question, study the appropriate section of the chapter. If you are not familiar with the topics in this chapter, don't take this test now. Instead, study the examples, work the practice problems, and then take the test. This test will help you identify which concepts you have mastered, and which you need to study further.

The ages of 600 students on a College campus were recorded. The following circle graph depicts the distributions of ages.

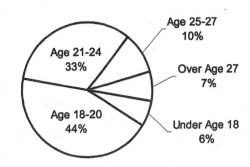

Age 25-27 10%

Age 21-24 33%

Over Age 27 7%

Age 18-20 44%

Under Age 18 6%

_____ 1. What age group comprises the smallest percent of the student body?

     a. Age 21-24   **b.** Under Age 18   **c.** Over Age 27   **d.** Age 25-27

_____ 2. What percent of the students are between the ages of 18 and 27?

     a. 94%   **b.** 87%   **c.** 93%   **d.** 77%

_____ 3. What percent of the students are age 21 or older?

     a. 43%   **b.** 33%   **c.** 50%   **d.** 56%

_____ 4. If 6000 students are at the College. How many students are 18-20 years old?

     a. 2640   **b.** 136   **c.** 264   **d.** 1980

_____ 5. How many students are under age 20?

     a. 3000   **b.** 300   **c.** 1980   **d.** 2640

An administrative assistant produced the following number of pages on her computer:

Mon.	Tues.	Wed.	Thurs.	Fri.	Sat.
36	42	44	28	32	28

_____ 6. Find the mean number of pages produced per day

     a. 35   **b.** 34   **c.** 36   **d.** 210

_____ 7. Find the median number of pages produced per day.

     a. 36   **b.** 34   **c.** 35   **d.** 210

_____ 8. Find the mode for the number of pages produced per day.

     a. 36   **b.** 32   **c.** 28   **d.** 42

This line graph indicates production and sales of color television sets by a major manufacturer during the specified months.

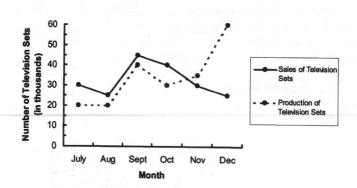

_____ 9. During what month was the sales of television sets the highest?

    a. December   **b.** September   **c.** July   **d.** November

_____ 10. During what months was the production of television sets the lowest?

    a. July & August   **b.** October & November

    c. August & December   **d.** November & December

_____ 11. During what months were the sales of television sets less than the production of television sets?

    a. July – August   **b.** July – November   **c.** July – October   **d.** Nov – Dec

_____ 12. How many television sets were sold in November?

    a. 35,000   **b.** 30,000   **c.** 40,000   **d.** 5000

_____ 13. How many television sets were produced in August?

    a. 30,000   **b.** 20,000   **c.** 5000   **d.** 25,000

This histogram tells us the number of miles a car was driven before the car was discarded or sold to a junk dealer.

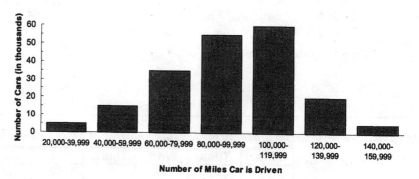

_____ 14. How many discarded or junked cars had been driven 40,000-79,999 miles?

    a. 90,000   **b.** 40,000   **c.** 50,000   **d.** 35,000

_____ 15. How many discarded or junked cars had been driven 80,000-139,999 miles?

    a. 120,000   **b.** 135,000   **c.** 55,000   **d.** 115,000

_____ 16. How many discarded or junked cars had been driven 120,000 miles or more?

    a. 20,000   **b.** 5,000   **c.** 30,000   **d.** 25,000

_____ 17. How many discarded or junked cars had been driven 60,000-119,999 miles?

    a. 150,000   **b.** 60,000   **c.** 115,000   **d.** 135,000

*The following double-bar graph
indicates the number of new housing
starts in Manchester during each
quarter of 2003 and 2004.*

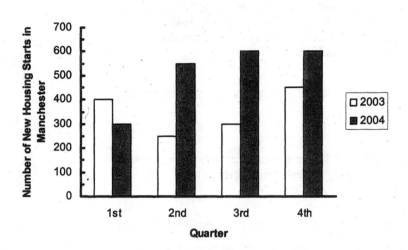

____ **18.** How many housing starts were there in Manchester in the second quarter of 2004?

     a. 550   **b.** 250   **c.** 500   **d.** 600

____ **19.** How many housing starts were there in Manchester in the first quarter of 2003?

     a. 400   **b.** 250   **c.** 300   **d.** 450

____ **20.** In what two quarters were the housing starts the same for different years?

     a. 2nd quarter and 4th quarter   **b.** 3rd quarter and 4th quarter

     c. 2nd quarter and 3rd quarter   **d.** 1st quarter and 3d quarter

____ **21.** When were the greatest number of housing starts?

     a. 4th quarter, 2004   **b.** 2nd quarter, 2004

     c. 3rd quarter and 4th quarter, 2004   **d.** 4th quarter, 2003

____ **22.** How many more housing starts were there in the fourth quarter of 2004 compared to the quarter of 2003?

     a. 300   **b.** 250   **c.** 350   **d.** 100

____ **23.** How many more housing starts were there in the fourth quarter of 2004 compared to the second quarter of 2003?

     a. 300   **b.** 250   **c.** 400   **d.** 350

A study at a major university concluded that many students are cheating. This pie graph depicts the percentage of students surveyed who have never cheated and those who have.

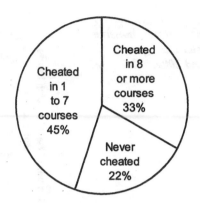

1. What percent of the students surveyed admitted to cheating?

2. If 330 of the surveyed students had never cheated, how many students were surveyed total?

The following double bar graph indicates the number of A's earned in college algebra at the state university during each semester (fall, spring, and summer) of 2003 and 2004.

3. How many A's were earned in college algebra during the fall and spring of 2003?

4. How many more A's were earned in the fall of 2004 compared to the summer of 2004?

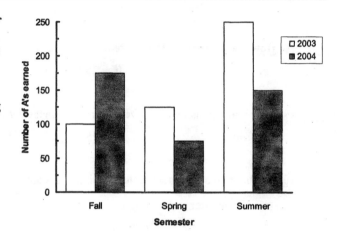

The line graph below indicates the rainfall in Ashbury for the first six month of two different years.

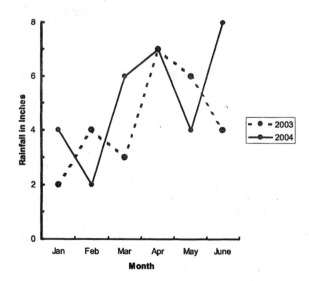

5. What was the total rainfall in February and March of 2003?

6. How much less did it rain in May of 2004 compared to June of 2004?

7. How much less did it rain in March of 2003 compared to May of 2003?

8. What was the total rainfall for the months of January through June of 2003?

The histogram below tells us how many sit-ups were accomplished by sixth grade students in a physical fitness test.

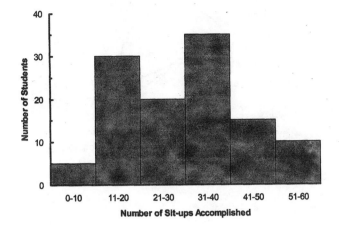

9. How many students accomplished between 21 and 50 sit-ups?

10. A student had to accomplish more than 30 sit-ups to meet minimum standards. How many students failed to meet minimum standards?

11. How many students accomplished 41-60 sit-ups?

12. How many students accomplished 50 sit-ups or less?

The Medway High School concession stand recorded the percentage of food orders they had all year from their customers. This circle graph shows the results.

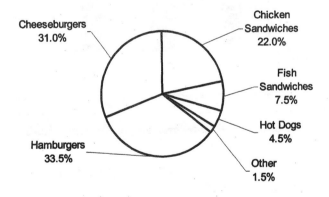

13. What percent of customers did not order hot dogs or cheeseburgers?

14. What percent of customers ordered cheeseburgers and fish?

15. If a total of 550 customers ordered chicken sandwiches, how many total customers did the concession stand have all year?

16. What percent of customers ordered hot dogs, hamburgers, and foods from the "other" category?

A history student has the following scores on eight quizzes: 21, 18, 15, 23, 16, 13, 14, 20

17. Find the mean quiz score.

18. Find the median quiz score.

Five houses were sold in Milford this week, at the following prices:
$169,000, $289,000, $349,000, $179,000, $250,000

19. Find the mean price.

20. Find the median price.

The pie graph shows the highest degree earned by persons aged 25 years and older living in a Midwestern town.

1. If the population of those 25 years old and older is 20,000, how many hold a Ph.D. degree?

2. What percent of the 25 and over population have no college degree?

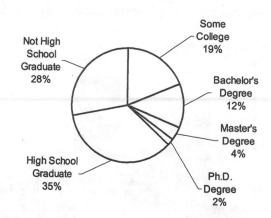

The following double bar graph indicates the number of people hired to help out with Christmas sales in one city in 2003 and 2004.

3. How many people were hired in November of 2004?

4. How many people were hired to help out with Christmas sales in 2004?

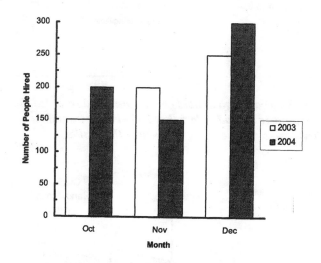

The line graph below indicates the items most frequently cited by the public as the chief problem facing local schools in the years 1981 to 1987.

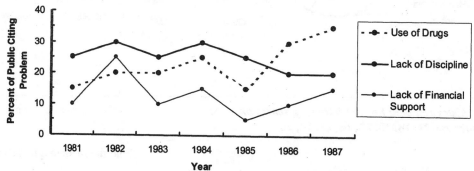

5. What item was cited as the chief problem by the largest percentage of the public in 1984?

6. In which years did the largest percent of the public cite use of drugs as the chief problem?

7. What item was cited as the chief problem by the smallest percentage of the public in 1986?

8. What percent of the public felt that use of drugs was the chief problem in 1983?

The following histogram gives us information about daily high temperatures in Pine Valley over a 135-day period.

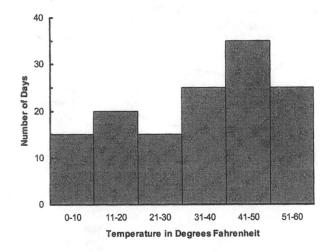

9. How many days had high temperatures greater than 30°F ?

10. How many days had high temperatures between 21°F and 50°F ?

11. How many days had high temperatures between 11°F and 30°F ?

12. How many days had high temperatures greater than 40°F ?

Professor Suarez surveyed her biology class and discovered the percentages depicted in the circle graph below.

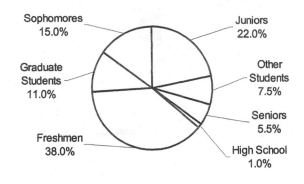

13. What percent of the class are undergraduates?

14. Only graduate students and undergraduates are taking the course for credit. Some gifted high school students, and students in the "other" category are auditing the course. What percent of the class are auditing the course?

15. What percent of the class is taking the course for credit?

16. If there are 88 juniors in the class, how many students are there total in the class?

The following temperature readings were obtained in a day from a sick child:
101.2°, 103.8°, 104°, 101.8°, 99.9°, 100.2°, 100.8°, 101°

17. What was the mean temperature? Round to the nearest tenth, if necessary.

18. What was the median temperature? Round to the nearest tenth, if necessary.

Seven homes were sold in Dover one week, at the following prices:
$389,000, $599,000, $299,000, $419,000, $1,219,000, $575,000, $205,000

19. Find the mean price.

20. Find the median price.

The pie graph shows the highest degree earned by persons aged 25 years and older living in a Midwestern town.

1. What percent of the 25 and over population hold a high school degree as their highest degree?

2. If the 25 and over population is 14,000, how many did not graduate from high school?

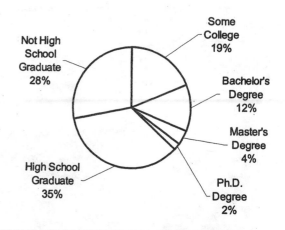

The following double bar graph indicates the number of people hired to help out with Christmas sales in one city in 2003 and 2004.

3. How many people were hired in December of 2003?

4. How many people were hired to help out with Christmas sales in 2003?

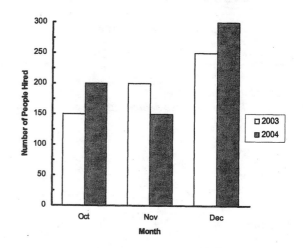

The line graph below indicates the items most frequently cited by the public as the chief problem facing local school in the years 1981 to 1987.

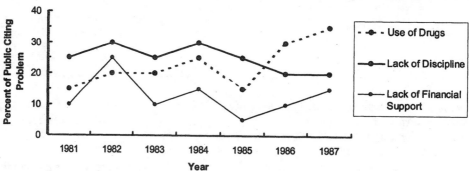

5. What item was cited as the chief problem by the smallest percentage of the public in 1983?

6. What percent of the public cited lack of discipline as the chief problem in 1982?

7. What item was cited as the chief problem by the largest percent of the public in 1986?

8. What percent of the public felt that use of drugs was the chief problem in 1985?

The following histogram gives us information about daily high temperatures in Pine Valley over a 135-day period.

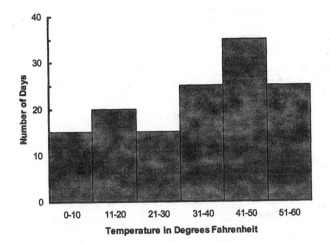

9. Which temperature range occurred most often?

10. How many days had high temperatures greater than 40°F?

11. How many days had high temperatures less than 21°F?

12. How many days had high temperatures less than 31°F?

In a survey of all students in a major northeastern university, the percentages depicted in the circle graph show the areas of the country that the students originated from.

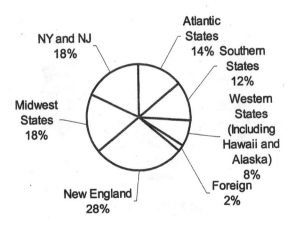

13. What percent of students come from the United States?

14. What percent come from Atlantic States, New York, or New Jersey?

15. What percent come from the Midwest or Western States (Including Hawaii and Alaska)?

16. What percent of students come from outside the Midwest?

A student had the following biology quiz scores:
28, 21, 19, 24, 26, 14, 12, 20

17. What was her mean score? Round to the nearest tenth, if necessary.

18. What was her median score? Round to the nearest tenth, if necessary.

Seven homes were sold in Cambridge this week, at the following prices:
$1,219,000, $539,000, $279,000, $259,000, $469,000, $379,000, $1,329,000

19. Find the mean price.

20. Find the median price.

A study at a major university concluded that many students are cheating. This graph depicts the percentages of students who have never cheated and those who have.

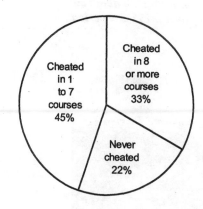

____ 1. What percent of students had cheated in at least one course?

    a. 45%   **b.** 78%   **c.** 55%   **d.** 33%

____ 2. If 675 of the surveyed students had cheated in one to seven courses, how many students were surveyed?

    a. 1150   **b.** 350   **c.** 630   **d.** 1500

This double bar graph indicates the number of A's earned in college algebra at the state university during each semester (fall, spring, summer) of 2003 and 2004.

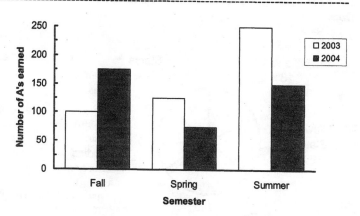

____ 3. How many A's were earned in college algebra during the fall semester of 2003?

    a. 75   **b.** 125   **c.** 100   **d.** 150

____ 4. How many more A's were earned in the summer of 2003 compared to the fall of 2004?

    a. 75   **b.** 125   **c.** 100   **d.** 150

The following graph indicates the rainfall levels in Ashbury for the first six months of two different years.

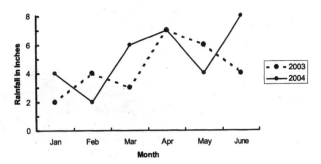

_____ 5. What was the total rainfall in January and May of 2004?

    a. 13 inches   **b.** 6 inches   **c.** 8 inches   **d.** 11 inches

_____ 6. How much more did it rain in June of 2004 compared to June of 2003?

    a. 3 inches   **b.** 12 inches   **c.** 8 inches   **d.** 4 inches

_____ 7. What was the total rainfall in March of 2004?

    a. 7 inches   **b.** 2 inches   **c.** 6 inches   **d.** 5 inches

_____ 8. What was the total rainfall in February and June of 2004?

    a. 10 inches   **b.** 13 inches   **c.** 14 inches   **d.** 12 inches

---

The following histogram shows how many sit-ups were accomplished by sixth grade students in a physical fitness test.

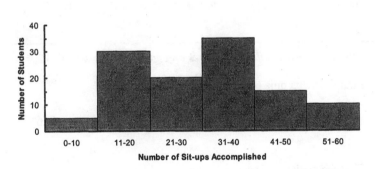

_____ 9. How many students accomplished at least thirty-one sit-ups?

    a. 60   **b.** 65   **c.** 40   **d.** 55

_____ 10. How many students accomplished thirty sit-ups or less?

    a. 40   **b.** 55   **c.** 45   **d.** 60

_____ 11. How many total students were tested?

    a. 120   **b.** 115   **c.** 110   **d.** 95

_____ 12. How many more students accomplished 31-40 sit-ups compared to 51-60 sit-ups?

    a. 25   **b.** 40   **c.** 20   **d.** 35

Answer questions 13-16 using this bar graph.

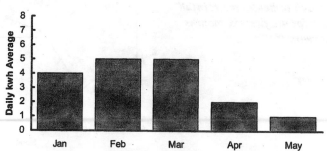

Electricity Usage: Average (per day) of kwh Used by Customer X, Jan-May 2001

_____ 13. What was Customer X's average daily kwh (kilowatt hours) usage in April?

     a. 3   b. 2   c. 4   d. 1

_____ 14. What was Customer X's average daily kwh usage in February?

     a. 6   b. 4   c. 5   d. 3

_____ 15. What was Customer Xs mean kwh usage for all 5 months?

     a. 4   b. 3   c. 4.3   d. 3.4

_____ 16. What was Customer X's median kwh usage for all 5 months?

     a. 4   b. 5   c. 3   d. 2

A geometry student has the following scores on eight quizzes: **20, 16, 17, 13, 10, 18, 14, 20**

_____ 17. Find the mean quiz score.

     a. 14   b. 16.5   c. 16   d. 18.25

_____ 18. Find the median quiz score.

     a. 16.5   b. 16   c. 14   d. 17

The final exam scores of a certain mathematics class were as follows: **90, 70, 63, 98, 95, 30, 54, 89, 84, 80, 68, 73, 77**

_____ 19. Find the mean score. Round to the nearest tenth.

     a. 74.7   b. 77.4   c. 75.4   d. 78.2

_____ 20. Find the median score.

     a. 75   b. 77   c. 80   d. 72

A study at a major university concluded that many students are cheating. This graph depicts the percentages of students who have never cheated and those who have.

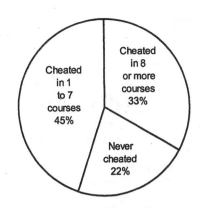

____ 1. If 675 of the surveyed students had never cheated, how many students were surveyed?

     a. 145.2   **b.** 682   **c.** 3000   **d.** 2400

____ 2. What percent of students had cheated?

     a. 78%   **b.** 45%   **c.** 22%   **d.** 33%

This double bar graph indicates the number of A's earned in college algebra at the state university during each semester (fall, spring, summer) of 2003 and 2004.

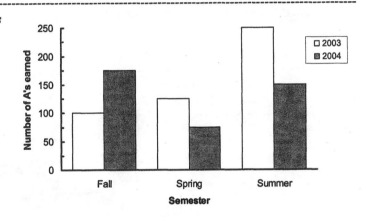

____ 3. How many A's were earned in college algebra in 2003?

     a. 425   **b.** 475   **c.** 875   **d.** 500

____ 4. How many more A's were earned in the spring of 2003 compared to the fall of 2004?

     a. 125   **b.** 25   **c.** 75   **d.** 50

The following graph indicates the rainfall levels in Ashbury for the first six months of two different years.

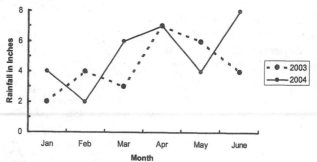

_____ 5. What was the total rainfall in the first six months of 2003?

     a. 31 inches   b. 26 inches   c. 21 inches   d. 18 inches

_____ 6. What was the difference in rainfall in March of 2003 compared to March of 2004?

     a. 4 inches   b. 6 inches   c. 3 inches   d. 2 inches

_____ 7. What was the total rainfall for February and March of 2004?

     a. 7 inches   b. 6 inches   c. 9 inches   d. 8 inches

_____ 8. What was the total rainfall for the first 3 months of 2003?

     a. 10 inches   b. 9 inches   c. 8 inches   d. 6 inches

The following histogram shows how many sit-ups were accomplished by sixth grade students in a physical fitness test.

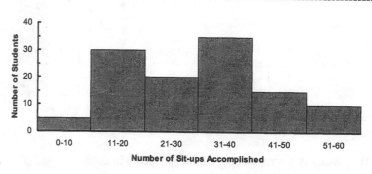

_____ 9. How many students accomplished less than 21 sit-ups?

     a. 40   b. 25   c. 30   d. 35

_____ 10. How many students accomplished more than 30 sit-ups?

     a. 60   b. 70   c. 80   d. 40

_____ 11. How many students accomplished 11 or more sit-ups?

     a. 115   b. 110   c. 105   d. 100

_____ 12. How many students accomplished 31-50 sit-ups?

     a. 30   b. 60   c. 50   d. 35

In a survey of all students in a major northeastern university, the percentages depicted in the circle graph show the areas that the students came from.

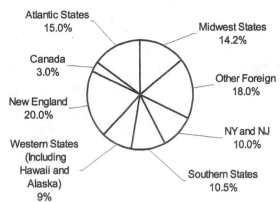

_____ **13.** What percent of students come from the United States?

     a. 97%   **b.** 79%   **c.** 100%   **d.** 98%

_____ **14.** What percent of students come from Canada, New York, or New Jersey.

     a. 13%   **b.** 30%   **c.** 33%   **d.** 18%

_____ **15.** What percent come from New England, or the Western States (including Alaska and Hawaii)?

     a. 9.3%   **b.** 26.3%   **c.** 34.2%   **d.** 29.3%

_____ **16.** What percent of students come from outside the Midwest?

     a. 14.2%   **b.** 85.2%   **c.** 85.8%   **d.** 80%

The children in a classroom have the following heights in inches: **35, 32, 28, 34, 22, 41, 38, 28**

_____ **17.** Find the mean height

     a. 32.25 inches   **b.** 33 inches   **c.** 28.4 inches   **d.** 29.5 inches

_____ **18.** Find the median height.

     a. 32.3 inches   **b.** 33 inches   **c.** 29.5 inches   **d.** 34 inches

---

Five homes were sold in Medway this week, with the following sales prices:
$165,000, $162,000, $189,000, $225,000, $202,000

_____ **19.** Find the mean price.

     a. $190,000   **b.** $188,600   **c.** $185,000   **d.** $189,000

_____ **20.** Find the median price.

     a. $189,000   **b.** $188,600   **c.** $205,000   **d.** $165,000

A study at a major university concluded that many students are cheating. This graph depicts the percentages of students who have never cheated and those who have.

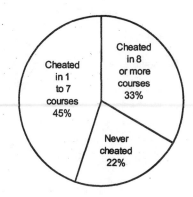

____ **1.** If 330 of the surveyed students had cheated in 8 or more courses, how many students were surveyed?

     a. 1000   **b.** 110   **c.** 330   **d.** 165

____ **2.** What percent of students had never cheated or had cheated in eight or more courses?

     a. 35%   **b.** 22%   **c.** 55%   **d.** 100%

This double bar graph indicates the number of A's earned in college algebra at the state university during each semester (fall, spring, summer) of 2003 and 2004.

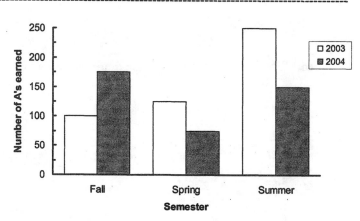

____ **3.** How many A's were earned in college algebra in 2003?

     a. 400   **b.** 875   **c.** 350   **d.** 475

____ **4.** During which semester were the most A's earned?

     a. Spring 2003   **b.** Summer 2003   **c.** Fall 2004   **d.** Summer 2004

The following graph indicates the rainfall levels in Ashbury for the first six months of two different years.

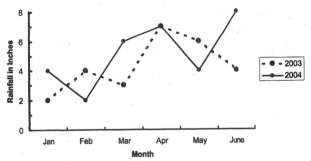

_____ **5.** What was the total rainfall for the first six month of 2004?

     a. 31 inches   **b.** 26 inches   **c.** 21 inches   **d.** 18 inches

_____ **6.** What was the difference in rainfall between March of 2004 and April of 2004?

     a. 3 inches   **b.** 1 inches   **c.** 0 inches   **d.** 2 inches

_____ **7.** What was the total rainfall for the first 3 months of 2003?

     a. 6 inches   **b.** 7 inches   **c.** 8 inches   **d.** 9 inches

_____ **8.** What was the total rainfall in June of 2004?

     a. 8 inches   **b.** 7 inches   **c.** 5 inches   **d.** 6 inches

---

The following histogram shows how many sit-ups were accomplished by sixth grade students in a physical fitness test.

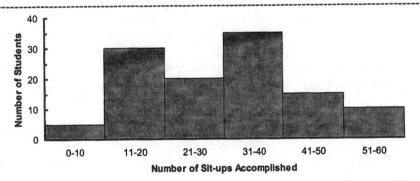

_____ **9.** How many students accomplished more than 40 sit-ups?

     a. 30   **b.** 55   **c.** 25   **d.** 20

_____ **10.** How many students accomplished less than 31 sit-ups?

     a. 45   **b.** 60   **c.** 70   **d.** 55

_____ **11.** How many total students were tested?

     a. 115   **b.** 100   **c.** 105   **d.** 110

_____ **12.** How many students accomplished 21 or more sit-ups?

     a. 70   **b.** 80   **c.** 75   **d.** 85

All freshmen at a large northeastern university were surveyed, asking their intended major. This circle graphs the percentages of their responses.

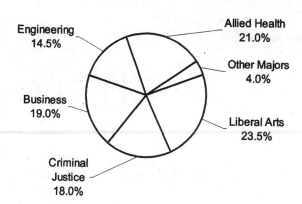

Engineering
14.5%

Allied Health
21.0%

Other Majors
4.0%

Business
19.0%

Liberal Arts
23.5%

Criminal
Justice
18.0%

_____ **13.** What percent of freshman are not business majors?

    a. 50%   **b.** 81%   **c.** 19%   **d.** 90%

_____ **14.** What percent of freshmen are in engineering, health, or "other" majors?

    a. 38.5%   **b.** 35.5%   **c.** 40.5%   **d.** 39.5%

_____ **15.** What percent of freshmen are not business or liberal arts majors?

    a. 57.5%   **b.** 65.5%   **c.** 56.5%   **d.** 63.5%

_____ **16.** If 665 freshmen said they were business majors, how many total freshmen were surveyed?

    a. 665   **b.** 3500   **c.** 2500   **d.** 1750

The high temperatures in degrees Fahrenheit for eight consecutive days last winter were as follow:
35°, 42°, 21°, 29°, 32°, 34°, 27°, 43°

_____ **17.** Find the mean high temperature. Round to the nearest tenth, if necessary.

    a. 33°   **b.** 31.8°   **c.** 30.5°   **d.** 32.9°

_____ **18.** Find the median high temperature. Round to the nearest tenth, if necessary.

    a. 30.5°   **b.** 31.8°   **c.** 33°   **d.** 32.9°

Five homes were sold in Medway this week, with the following sales prices:
$159,000, $136,000, $385,000, $178,000, $192,000

_____ **19.** Find the mean price.

    a. $200,000   **b.** $210,000   **c.** $178,000   **d.** $219,000

_____ **20.** Find the median price.

    a. $200,000   **b.** $210,000   **c.** $178,000   **d.** $219,000

1. Write "70 miles per 2.8 gallons" as a unit rate.

2. If Kelly drives 900 miles in 18 hours, how many hours of driving does she need to drive 1350 miles?

3. Multiply: $\dfrac{2}{3} \times \dfrac{7}{11}$

4. Subtract: $8\dfrac{1}{5} - 7\dfrac{2}{3}$

5. Simplify: $40 \div 2^2 + 3^5 - 5 + 10^2 \div 5 \times 8$

6. Divide: $0.02\overline{)254.084}$

7. Find 21% of $540.

8. Write 46.83% as a decimal.

9. Convert: $115 \text{ km} = \underline{\hspace{1cm}}$ miles

10. Convert: $389 \text{ m} = \underline{\hspace{1cm}}$ cm

11. Find the area of the triangle below.

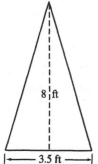

8 ft

|⟵ 3.5 ft ⟶|

12. Find the volume of the cone below. Round to the nearest hundredth.

10 cm

8 cm

Chapter 8: Cumulative Exam (FR) (cont.)   Name: _____

Page 2 of 2

The pie graph shows the highest degree earned by persons aged 25 years and older living in a Midwestern town.

13. What percent of the population holds the highest degree of Ph.D. or Master's?

14. If 6000 people of age 25 or older hold the Bachelor's degree as their highest degree, how many people of age 25 or older live in the town?

15. What percent have no degrees at all?

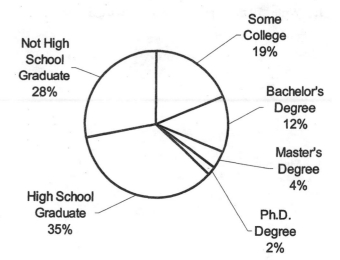

The following double bar graph indicates the number of people hired to help out with Christmas sales in one city in 2003 and 2004.

16. During which month and year were the most people hired?

17. How many people were hired in November and December of 2004?

18. How many people were hired in October, November, and December of 2003?

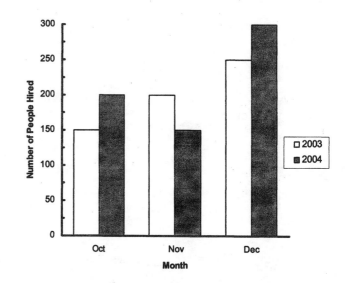

The daily low temperatures in degrees Fahrenheit for the first week of spring in Barrow, Alaska this year were:
10°, 5°, 6°, 13°, 4°, 11°, 22°

19. Find the mean low temperature for the week. Round to the nearest tenth.

20. Find the median low temperature for the week.

____ **1.** Write "528 feet per 6 seconds" as a unit rate.

     a. 3168 feet per second   **b.** 88 feet per second   **c.** 176 feet per second   **d.** 1.14 feet per second

____ **2.** If Clint drives 1500 miles in 31 hours of driving time, how many hours of driving at the same rate will it take to go 250 miles?

     a. 48 hours   **b.** 24 hours   **c.** 5 hours   **d.** 186 hours

____ **3.** Multiply: $\dfrac{7}{15} \times \dfrac{5}{8}$ **a.** $\dfrac{24}{7}$ **b.** $\dfrac{7}{24}$ **c.** $\dfrac{56}{75}$ **d.** $\dfrac{12}{23}$

____ **4.** Add: $10\dfrac{1}{5} + 2\dfrac{1}{10}$ **a.** $12\dfrac{2}{15}$ **b.** $12\dfrac{2}{10}$ **c.** $12\dfrac{3}{15}$ **d.** $12\dfrac{3}{10}$

____ **5.** Evaluate: $5^2 - 2 \times 6 + 4^3 - 16 \div 4$

     a. 73   **b.** 15.25   **c.** 29   **d.** 56

____ **6.** Multiply: 3.7×0.02

     a. 0.74   **b.** 7.4   **c.** 0.0074   **d.** 0.074

____ **7.** What is 38% of $580?

     a. $220.40   **b.** $15.26   **c.** $1526.32   **d.** $22.04

____ **8.** Write 68.91% as a decimal.

     a. 68.91   **b.** 0.6891   **c.** 6.891   **d.** 0.06891

____ **9.** Convert: 81 km = _____ miles

     a. 130.65 miles   **b.** 50.22 miles   **c.** 8.1 miles   **d.** 129.6 miles

____ **10.** Convert: 6.9 m = _____ cm

     a. 6.9 cm   **b.** 0.069 cm   **c.** 69 cm   **d.** 690 cm

____ **11.** Find the area of the trapezoid below.

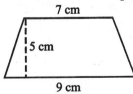

     a. 45 m²   **b.** 42 m²

     c. 40 m²   **d.** 35 m²

____ **12.** Find the volume of the pyramid below.

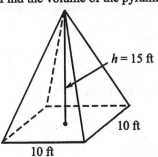

     a. 1500 ft³   **b.** 750 ft³

     c. 600 ft³   **d.** 500 ft³

Chapter 8: Cumulative Exam (MC) (cont.)   Name: _____

Page 2 of 2

This circle graph shows the highest degrees earned by persons aged 25 years and older living in a Midwestern town.

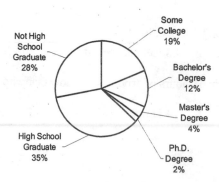

_____ **13.** If 2800 people of age 25 or over did not graduate from high school, what is the 25 and over population of the town?

     a. 10,000   **b.** 70,000   **c.** 784   **d.** 100,000

_____ **14.** What percent of the population age 25 or over have a high school diploma or a Bachelor's degree as their highest degree?

     a. 63%   **b.** 47%   **c.** 37%   **d.** 35%

_____ **15.** What percent only attended high school and never attended college?

     a. 37%   **b.** 35%   **c.** 63%   **d.** 47%

This double bar graph shows the number of people hired to help out with Christmas sales in one city in 2003 and 2004.

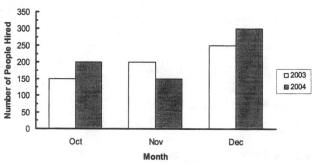

_____ **16.** During which month and year were the fewest people hired?

     a. October 2003, November 2004   **b.** December 2004

     c. October 2004, November 2004   **d.** October 2003

_____ **17.** How many people were hired in October and November of 2003?

     a. 600   **b.** 300   **c.** 400   **d.** 350

_____ **18.** How many people were hired in November and December of 2004?

     a. 550   **b.** 400   **c.** 450   **d.** 500

The daily low temperatures, in degrees Fahrenheit, for the first week of spring in Barrow, Alaska this year were:
4°, 3°, 5°, 15°, 12°, 23°, 9°

_____ **19.** Find the mean low temperature for the week. Round to the nearest tenth.

     a. 10.1° F   **b.** 11.8° F   **c.** 9° F   **d.** 71° F

_____ **20.** Find the median low temperature for the week. Round to the nearest tenth, if necessary

     a. 9° F   **b.** 71° F   **c.** 11.8° F   **d.** 10.1° F

If you <u>are</u> familiar with the topics in this chapter, take this test now. If you can't answer a question, study the appropriate section of the chapter. If you are <u>not</u> familiar with the topics in this chapter, don't take this test now. Instead, study the examples, work the practice problems, and then take the test. This test will help you identify which concepts you have mastered, and which you need to study further.

1. Add: $(-9)+(-13)$

2. Add: $-31+18$

3. Add: $9.4+(-6.1)$

4. Add: $7+(-6)+4+(-5)$

5. Add: $\dfrac{7}{12}+\left(-\dfrac{1}{4}\right)$

6. Add: $-\dfrac{2}{9}+\left(-\dfrac{1}{3}\right)$

7. Add: $-7.2+(-4.4)$

8. Add: $-8.1+5.6$

9. Subtract: $25-37$

10. Subtract: $-12-29$

11. Subtract: $\dfrac{5}{13}-\left(-\dfrac{3}{13}\right)$

12. Subtract: $-28-(-4)$

13. Subtract: $-3.7-(-6.2)$

14. Subtract: $3.4-6.8$

15. Subtract: $19-(-19)$

16. Subtract: $\dfrac{1}{4}-\left(-\dfrac{2}{5}\right)$

17. Multiply: $(-4)(-6)$

18. Divide: $-32\div(-12)$

19. Divide: $-72\div 8$

20. Multiply: $(4)(-3)(2)(-1)\left(-\dfrac{1}{4}\right)$

21. Divide: $\dfrac{98}{-7}$

22. Divide: $\dfrac{-\frac{3}{7}}{-\frac{7}{8}}$

23. Multiply: $(-9)(-2)(-3)$

24. Divide: $150 \div (-15)$

For problems 28-32, perform the operations in the proper order.

25. $26 \div (-2) + 14 \div (-7)$

26. $12 \div 3(5) + (-11) \div (-11)$

27. $5 + (-7) + 3(-4)$

28. $4(-7) \div (-10)$

29. $2 - (-8) + 25 \div (-5)$

30. $4(-6) + 3(-7) - (-12)$

31. $\dfrac{13 + 9 - 4}{4(-3)(4)}$

32. $\dfrac{42 \div (-6) - 2}{4(-9) + 3(-1)}$

33. Write in 70,000 scientific notation.

34. Write 0.0006 in scientific notation.

35. Write 359,000,000 in scientific notation.

36. Write 7.8×10^{-5} in standard notation.

37. Write 6.52×10^{5} in standard notation.

38. Write 1.5189×10^{-8}

If you __are__ familiar with the topics in this chapter, take this test now. If you can't answer a question, study the appropriate section of the chapter. If you are __not__ familiar with the topics in this chapter, don't take this test now. Instead, study the examples, work the practice problems, and then take the test. This test will help you identify which concepts you have mastered, and which you need to study further.

____ 1. Add: $(-7)+(-18)$ **a.** 11   **b.** 25   **c.** −25   **d.** −11

____ 2. Add: $-21+8$ **a.** 13   **b.** −13   **c.** −12   **d.** −29

____ 3. Add: $18.4+(-12.1)$ **a.** −30.5   **b.** 6.3   **c.** 30.5   **d.** −6.3

____ 4. Add: $9+(-8)+5+(-6)$ **a.** 0   **b.** −28   **c.** −2   **d.** 28

____ 5. Add: $\dfrac{5}{12}+\left(-\dfrac{1}{4}\right)$ **a.** $\dfrac{3}{8}$ **b.** $-\dfrac{5}{48}$ **c.** $\dfrac{1}{2}$ **d.** $\dfrac{1}{6}$

____ 6. Add: $-\dfrac{5}{9}+\left(-\dfrac{1}{3}\right)$ **a.** $\dfrac{1}{2}$ **b.** $-\dfrac{8}{9}$ **c.** $\dfrac{8}{9}$ **d.** $-\dfrac{1}{2}$

____ 7. Add: $-8.2+(-5.4)$ **a.** −2.8   **b.** 13.6   **c.** −13.6   **d.** 2.8

____ 8. Add: $-5.1+2.6$ **a.** 7.7   **b.** 2.5   **c.** −2.5   **d.** −7.7

____ 9. Subtract: $13-37$ **a.** −24   **b.** −26   **c.** −50   **d.** 24

____ 10. Subtract: $-15-24$ **a.** 39   **b.** −39   **c.** 9   **d.** −9

____ 11. Subtract: $\dfrac{8}{13}-\left(-\dfrac{3}{13}\right)$ **a.** $-\dfrac{5}{13}$ **b.** $\dfrac{5}{13}$ **c.** $-\dfrac{11}{13}$ **d.** $\dfrac{11}{13}$

____ 12. Subtract: $-23-(-5)$ **a.** 18   **b.** −28   **c.** 28   **d.** −18

____ 13. Subtract: $-2.7-(-9.2)$ **a.** 6.5   **b.** −11.5   **c.** 11.9   **d.** −6.5

____ 14. Subtract: $7.4-14.8$ **a.** 22.2   **b.** −7.4   **c.** 7.4   **d.** −22.2

____ 15. Subtract: $29-(-29)$ **a.** 0   **b.** −58   **c.** 68   **d.** 58

____ 16. Subtract: $\dfrac{3}{4} - \left(-\dfrac{1}{5}\right)$ a. $\dfrac{19}{20}$ b. $-\dfrac{4}{9}$ c. $\dfrac{4}{9}$ d. $-\dfrac{19}{20}$

____ 17. Multiply: $(-6)(-8)$ a. 14   b. 56   c. 48   d. -48

____ 18. Divide: $-35 \div (-14)$ a. 3   b. -2.5 c. 2.5   d. 490

____ 19. Divide: $-63 \div 7$ a. -8 b. -9 c. 441   d. 9

____ 20. Multiply: $(6)(-4)(2)(-1)\left(-\dfrac{1}{6}\right)$

   a. -8 b. -12 c. 12   d. 8

____ 21. Divide: $\dfrac{72}{-6}$

   a. 11   b. 12   c. -11 d. -12

____ 22. Divide: $\dfrac{-\frac{4}{7}}{-\frac{7}{11}}$

   a. $-1\dfrac{1}{14}$ b. $\dfrac{44}{49}$ c. $-\dfrac{28}{77}$ d. $-\dfrac{15}{49}$

____ 23. Multiply: $(-5)(-2)(-6)$

   a. -60 b. -42 c. 60   d. 42

____ 24. Divide: $160 \div (-16)$

   a. -10 b. -9 c. 9   d. 10

For problems 25 through 32, perform the operations in the proper order.

____ 25. $28 \div (-2) + 24 \div (-6)$

   a. 14   b. -18 c. 44   d. 18

____ 26. $12 \div 4(8) + (-13) \div (-13)$

   a. -25 b. 2.75   c. 25   d. 23

____ 27. $7 + (-9) + 3(-8)$

   a. 40   b. 26   c. 87   d. -26

____ **28.** $6(-3) \div (-10)$

    a. 1.8   **b.** −0.3   **c.** −1.8   **d.** 0.3

____ **29.** $3 - (-5) + 32 \div (-8)$

    a. −5   **b.** 5   **c.** −4   **d.** 4

____ **30.** $2(-9) + 4(-7) - (-13)$

    a. −23   **b.** −33   **c.** 52   **d.** 23

____ **31.** $\dfrac{21 + 2 - 8}{5(-3)(2)}$

    a. $1\frac{3}{4}$ **b.** $-\frac{1}{2}$ **c.** $-1\frac{3}{4}$ **d.** $1\frac{1}{30}$

____ **32.** $\dfrac{49 \div (-7) - 2}{2(-9) + 3(-2)}$

    a. $-\frac{3}{8}$ **b.** $\frac{5}{24}$ **c.** $-\frac{5}{24}$ **d.** $\frac{3}{8}$

____ **33.** Write 90,000 in scientific notation.

    a. 9×10^3 **b.** 9×10^5 **c.** 9×10^4 **d.** 9×10^{-4}

____ **34.** Write 0.0004 in scientific notation.

    a. 4×10^{-5} **b.** 4×10^{-4} **c.** 4×10^{-3} **d.** 4×10^4

____ **35.** Write 267,000,000 in scientific notation.

    a. 2.67×10^8 **b.** 2.67×10^7 **c.** 2.67×10^{-8} **d.** 2.67×10^{-9}

____ **36.** Write 3.4×10^{-5} in standard notation.

    a. 3,400,000   **b.** 3400   **c.** 0.00034   **d.** 0.000034

____ **37.** Write 9.18×10^5 in standard notation.

    a. 0.00918   **b.** 0.00000918   **c.** 918,000   **d.** 91,800,000

____ **38.** Write 1.6173×10^{-8} in standard notation.

    a. 1,617,300,000,000   **b.** 0.000000016173   **c.** 161,730,000   **d.** 1,617,300

1. Add: $-26+5$

2. Add: $-16.3+(-3)$

3. Add: $\dfrac{2}{9}+\left(-\dfrac{4}{7}\right)$

4. Subtract: $-14-(-19)$

5. Subtract: $-5-12$

6. Subtract: $\dfrac{4}{13}-\left(-\dfrac{1}{9}\right)$

7. Subtract: $-16.7-0.28$

8. Multiply: $(-6)(-4)(-2)$

9. Divide: $\dfrac{-\frac{3}{4}}{\frac{2}{3}}$

10. Divide: $(-28)\div\dfrac{1}{4}$

11. Multiply: $(-7)(9)(4)\left(-\dfrac{1}{7}\right)$

12. Simplify: $-21-3(-4)$

13. Simplify: $48\div8-(-5)(2)$

14. Simplify: $\dfrac{-8+12(3)}{8-(-6)}$

15. Simplify: $\dfrac{19-3(2)}{14-12\div2(3)}$

16. In 4 plays, or "downs", a football team lost 6 yards the first down, gained 9 yards the second down, lost 5 yards the third down, and then gained 12 yards the fourth down. What was their total yardage gained (or lost)?

17. Write 79,600,000 in scientific notation.

18. Write 0.0000341 in scientific notation.

19. Write 8.1×10^6 in standard notation.

20. Write 5.588×10^{-2} in standard notation.

1. Add: $-17+13$

2. Add: $-19.4+(-4.25)$

3. Add: $\dfrac{6}{7}+\left(-\dfrac{7}{8}\right)$

4. Subtract: $-8-(-16)$

5. Subtract: $-8-9$

6. Subtract: $\dfrac{2}{3}-(-3)$

7. Subtract: $-5.61-7$

8. Multiply: $(-4)(-7)(2)$

9. Divide: $\dfrac{-\frac{1}{9}}{\frac{9}{8}}$

10. Divide: $32\div\left(-\dfrac{1}{4}\right)$

11. Multiply: $(-11)(-2)(5)\left(\dfrac{1}{11}\right)$

12. Simplify: $-14-2(-6)$

13. Simplify: $56\div4(-2)-(-14)$

14. Simplify: $\dfrac{13-3(2)}{(9+5)\div(-2)}$

15. Simplify: $\dfrac{2(3)-(-7)(2)}{12-8(2)\div(-4)}$

16. Jose was on a diet. His chart of weekly gains (or losses) showed the following:

Week	Result	Week	Result
1st	lost 2 lb	4th	lost 3.5 lb
2nd	lost 3 lb	5th	gained 0.5 lb
3rd	gained 1.5 lb	6th	lost 1.25 lb

What was his total loss (or gain) for the 6-week period?

17. Write 2850 in scientific notation.

18. Write 0.0695 in scientific notation.

19. Write 1.08×10^5 in standard notation.

20. Write 7.09×10^{-4} in standard notation.

1. Add: $-18+(-13)$

2. Add: $7.3+(-0.94)$

3. Add: $-\dfrac{4}{5}+\dfrac{1}{3}$

4. Subtract: $-5-(-11)$

5. Subtract: $-9-21$

6. Subtract: $\dfrac{6}{7}-\left(-\dfrac{1}{6}\right)$

7. Subtract: $-38.9-2.65$

8. Multiply: $5(-9)(-2)$

9. Divide: $\dfrac{-\frac{2}{3}}{-\frac{4}{5}}$

10. Divide: $12\div\left(-\dfrac{1}{2}\right)$

11. Multiply: $(-4)(-5)(2)\left(-\dfrac{1}{5}\right)$

12. Simplify: $-26-2(-4)$

13. Simplify: $48\div8(3)(2)$

14. Simplify: $\dfrac{16-4(5)}{8\div2+2}$

15. Simplify: $\dfrac{6(7)-(-3)(-4)}{8-3(3)}$

16. A football team, in 4 plays, or "downs," did the following:

Down	Yards
1st	gained 7 yd
2nd	lost 15 yd
3rd	gained 10 yd
4th	gained 7 yd

What was their total yards gained (or lost) for the four downs?

17. Write 0.003829 in scientific notation.

18. Write 58,000,000,000 in scientific notation.

19. Write 7.6×10^{-5} in standard notation.

20. Write 5.333×10^{7} in standard notation.

_____ **1.** Add: $-13+9$

    a. -22 **b.** -4 **c.** 2 **d.** 22

_____ **2.** Add: $-3.4+(-2.2)$

    a. -5.6 **b.** -0.8 **c.** 0.8 **d.** 7.68

_____ **3.** Add: $-\dfrac{2}{9}+\dfrac{5}{7}$

    a. $\dfrac{1}{3}$ **b.** $-\dfrac{3}{2}$ **c.** $\dfrac{1}{21}$ **d.** $\dfrac{31}{63}$

_____ **4.** Subtract: $-29-7$

    a. 36 **b.** -22 **c.** -36 **d.** 22

_____ **5.** Subtract: $-17-(-3)$

    a. 20 **b.** -20 **c.** 14 **d.** -14

_____ **6.** Subtract: $\dfrac{3}{5}-\left(-\dfrac{3}{4}\right)$

    a. $\dfrac{27}{20}$ **b.** $\dfrac{3}{5}$ **c.** $-\dfrac{3}{20}$ **d.** $\dfrac{9}{20}$

_____ **7.** Subtract: $7.8-12.2$

    a. -5.6 **b.** -4.4 **c.** 5.6 **d.** 4.4

_____ **8.** Multiply: $(-7)(2)(-24)$

    a. 336 **b.** -336 **c.** -15 **d.** 15

_____ **9.** Divide: $\dfrac{-\frac{9}{10}}{-\frac{4}{5}}$

    a. $-\dfrac{18}{25}$ **b.** $\dfrac{18}{25}$ **c.** $\dfrac{9}{8}$ **d.** $\dfrac{8}{9}$

_____ **10.** Multiply: $(21)(-4)(3)\left(\dfrac{1}{5}\right)(5)$

    a. -253 **b.** 8 **c.** -87 **d.** 252

____ 11. Divide: $2 \div \left(-\dfrac{1}{4}\right)$

    a. −2   **b.** $-\dfrac{1}{8}$ **c.** −8   **d.** $-\dfrac{1}{2}$

____ 12. Simplify: $17 - 5(-3)$

    a. −28   **b.** 32   **c.** −8   **d.** −21

____ 13. Simplify: $23 + 7 \div (-7) + (-3)$

    a. 19   **b.** −9   **c.** −6   **d.** $\dfrac{81}{4}$

____ 14. Simplify: $\dfrac{-4 + 12 \div (-3)}{10 + 3(-2)}$

    a. −1   **b.** −2   **c.** −5   **d.** $-\dfrac{2}{5}$

____ 15. Simplify: $\dfrac{12 - (-12)}{12 - 6 \div 2}$

    a. $\dfrac{8}{3}$ **b.** 0   **c.** 8   **d.** $-\dfrac{12}{5}$

____ 16. In 1993, on the coldest day of the year in Barrow, the temperature was −57°F. The highest temperature recorded for the year was 72°F. What was the difference between these two extreme temperatures?

    a. 29°   **b.** 129°   **c.** −129°   **d.** 15°

____ 17. Write 94,100,000 in scientific notation.

    a. 9.41×10^8 **b.** 9.41×10^6 **c.** 9.41×10^5 **d.** 9.41×10^7

____ 18. Write 0.000528 in scientific notation.

    a. 5.28×10^4 **b.** 5.28×10^{-4} **c.** 5.28×10^{-3} **d.** 5.28×10^{-5}

____ 19. Write 5.8×10^3 in standard notation.

    a. 580   **b.** 5800   **c.** 58,000   **d.** 0.058

____ 20. Write 6.89×10^{-4} in standard notation.

    a. 68,900   **b.** 0.00689   **c.** 0.000689   **d.** 0.0689

Basic College Mathematics: Signed Numbers

____ **1.** Add: $-29 + 18$

     a. -27 **b.** -8 **c.** -11 **d.** 12

____ **2.** Add: $-3.9 + (-10.4)$

     a. 0.5 **b.** -14.3 **c.** -0.5 **d.** 14.3

____ **3.** Add: $-\dfrac{4}{9} + \dfrac{5}{8}$

     a. $\dfrac{13}{72}$ **b.** $-\dfrac{1}{8}$ **c.** -1 **d.** $\dfrac{77}{72}$

____ **4.** Subtract: $-9 - 4$

     a. -9 **b.** 9 **c.** 22 **d.** -13

____ **5.** Subtract: $-36 - (-27)$

     a. -9 **b.** -23 **c.** 9 **d.** -11

____ **6.** Subtract: $2.9 - 4.1$

     a. -13 **b.** -1.2 **c.** 1.2 **d.** 13

____ **7.** Subtract: $\dfrac{4}{3} - \left(-\dfrac{2}{5}\right)$

     a. $\dfrac{3}{4}$ **b.** $\dfrac{14}{15}$ **c.** $\dfrac{26}{15}$ **d.** $\dfrac{8}{15}$

____ **8.** Multiply: $3(-4)(-4)$

     a. -48 **b.** 0 **c.** 48 **d.** 288

____ **9.** Divide: $\dfrac{\frac{2}{9}}{-\frac{1}{4}}$

     a. $-\dfrac{1}{18}$ **b.** $\dfrac{1}{5}$ **c.** $-\dfrac{1}{36}$ **d.** $-\dfrac{8}{9}$

____ **10.** Divide: $-9 \div \left(\dfrac{1}{4}\right)$

     a. -36 **b.** -4 **c.** $-\dfrac{1}{4}$ **d.** 36

_____ **11.** Multiply: $(-8)(-2)(12)\left(-\dfrac{1}{6}\right)$

     a. 36   **b.** −32   **c.** 32   **d.** −36

_____ **12.** Simplify: $1-6(-3)$

     a. −19   **b.** −5   **c.** 19   **d.** 5

_____ **13.** Simplify: $25+9\div(-9)-4$

     a. −10   **b.** −4   **c.** 21   **d.** 20

_____ **14.** Simplify: $\dfrac{-11+15\div(-3)}{8+2(-3)}$

     a. −8   **b.** 8   **c.** −3   **d.** $-\dfrac{5}{2}$

_____ **15.** Simplify: $\dfrac{14-(-14)}{17-20\div 2}$

     a. $\dfrac{56}{3}$ **b.** $\dfrac{14}{5}$ **c.** 0   **d.** 4

_____ **16.** Alpine Computer Company had a loss in January of $60,000, a profit in February of $110,000, a profit in March of $95,000, and a loss in April of $35,000. What was their total profit (or loss) for these four months?

     a. Profit of $110,000   **b.** Loss of $110,000   **c.** Profit of $100,000   **d.** Profit of $90,000

_____ **17.** Write 279,000 in scientific notation.

     a. 2.79×10^2 **b.** 2.79×10^3 **c.** 2.79×10^5 **d.** 2.79×10^4

_____ **18.** Write 0.000387 scientific notation.

     a. 3.87×10^4 **b.** 3.87×10^{-3} **c.** 3.87×10^{-2} **d.** 3.87×10^{-4}

_____ **19.** Write 1.94×10^8 in standard notation.

     a. 194,000   **b.** 194,000,000   **c.** 1,940,000   **d.** 19,400

_____ **20.** Write 0.052834 in scientific notation.

     a. 5.2834×10^{-1} **b.** 5.2834×10^{-2} **c.** 5.2834×10^{-3} **d.** 5.2834×10^2

_____ **1.** Add: $-23+9$

    a. -14 **b.** -32 **c.** 14 **d.** -28

_____ **2.** Add: $-1.13+(-0.6)$

    a. -1.19 **b.** 1.73 **c.** -1.73 **d.** -0.53

_____ **3.** Add: $\dfrac{5}{9}+\left(-\dfrac{11}{12}\right)$

    a. -2 **b.** $-\dfrac{13}{36}$ **c.** $\dfrac{59}{36}$ **d.** $-\dfrac{1}{2}$

_____ **4.** Subtract: $-3.4-0.6$

    a. -2.8 **b.** -4 **c.** -2.8 **d.** 4

_____ **5.** Subtract: $-33-(-7)$

    a. -40 **b.** 40 **c.** -26 **d.** 26

_____ **6.** Subtract: $\dfrac{2}{11}-\left(-\dfrac{1}{2}\right)$

    a. $\dfrac{1}{11}$ **b.** $\dfrac{3}{13}$ **c.** $-\dfrac{1}{11}$ **d.** $\dfrac{15}{22}$

_____ **7.** Subtract: $-16-3$

    a. -19 **b.** 13 **c.** -13 **d.** 48

_____ **8.** Multiply: $(2)(-3)(-7)$

    a. -42 **b.** 42 **c.** -8 **d.** 8

_____ **9.** Divide: $\dfrac{-\frac{5}{7}}{-\frac{1}{2}}$

    a. $\dfrac{10}{7}$ **b.** $-\dfrac{10}{7}$ **c.** $\dfrac{5}{14}$ **d.** $-\dfrac{5}{14}$

_____ **10.** Divide: $8\div\left(-\dfrac{1}{8}\right)$

    a. 64 **b.** -1 **c.** -64 **d.** 1

____ **11.** Multiply: $(-4)(2)(15)\left(-\dfrac{1}{5}\right)$

    a. 4   **b.** $-42\dfrac{2}{3}$ **c.** -5 **d.** 24

____ **12.** Simplify: $-15-7(-3)$

    a. 6   **b.** 30   **c.** -22 **d.** -112

____ **13.** Simplify: $42 \div 7 - (-3)(-1)$

    a. -4 **b.** -9 **c.** 3   **d.** 4

____ **14.** Simplify: $\dfrac{-6+20(3)}{8-(-6)}$

    a. 3   **b.** $\dfrac{15}{2}$ **c.** $\dfrac{7}{8}$ **d.** $\dfrac{27}{7}$

____ **15.** Simplify: $\dfrac{6+9-4}{6(5)+(-9)(-2)-4}$

    a. $-\dfrac{1}{3}$ **b.** $\dfrac{1}{4}$ **c.** $\dfrac{11}{8}$ **d.** 0

____ **16.** An oxide ion has a negative electrical charge of -2. What is the total charge of 4 oxide ions?

    a. 8   **b.** -8 **c.** 4   **d.** 2

____ **17.** Write 28,700 in scientific notation.

    a. 2.87×10^3 **b.** 2.87×10^2 **c.** 2.87×10^4 **d.** 2.87×10^{-4}

____ **18.** Write 0.0079 in scientific notation.

    a. 7.9×10^{-2} **b.** 7.9×10^{-3} **c.** 7.9×10^{-4} **d.** 7.9×10^3

____ **19.** Write 2.44×10^3 in standard notation.

    a. 0.00244   **b.** 244,000   **c.** 2440   **d.** 24,400

____ **20.** Write 8.1×10^{-4} in scientific notation.

    a. 0.00081   **b.** 0.81   **c.** 0.0081   **d.** 0.000081

Name: _____

Basic College Mathematics: Introduction to Algebra

If you <u>are</u> familiar with the topics in this chapter, take this test now. If you can't answer a question, study the appropriate section of the chapter. If you are <u>not</u> familiar with the topics in this chapter, don't take this test now. Instead, study the examples, work the practice problems, and then take the test. This test will help you identify which concepts you have mastered, and which you need to study further.

For problems 1-6, combine like terms.

1. $26x - 50x$

2. $-6y + 12y - 3y$

3. $5a - 6b - 11a + 13b$

4. $7x - y + 9 - 19x - 4y + 5$

5. $4x - 13 + 4y + 7 - 9y + 16x$

6. $3a - 8b + 2c - 6b$

7. Simplify: $(4)(5x - 2y)$

8. Simplify: $(-5)(a + 9b - 6)$

9. Simplify: $(-3)(2.5a + 3b - 9c - 2)$

10. Simplify: $(6)(3x - y) - (4)(2x + y)$

11. Solve: $8 + x = 43$

12. Solve: $x + 3.5 = 6$

13. Solve: $x - \dfrac{7}{8} = \dfrac{1}{4}$

14. Solve: $8x = -72$

15. Solve: $3.6x = 18$

16. Solve: $\dfrac{2}{5}x = \dfrac{7}{10}$

17. Solve: $5x - 2 = 23$

18. Solve: $19 - 6x = 2x - 13$

19. Solve: $4(x+1) = 12 - 3(x-2)$

20. Solve: $2x + 5 = 3(10 - x)$

21. A truck weighs 2.5 tons more than a car. Translate the sentence into an equation using t to represent the weight of the truck and c to represent the weight of the car.

22. The length of a rectangle is 3 meters longer than double the width. Translate the sentence into an equation using l to represent the length and w to represent the width of the rectangle.

23. Mt. Parka is 1239 meters shorter than Mt. Aratat. Write an algebraic expression for the height of Mt. Parka using the variable a to describe the height of Mt. Aratat in meters.

24. A rectangular field has a perimeter of 126 meters. The length of the field is 9 meters less than double the width. Find the dimensions of the field. Solve using an equation.

25. A 23-foot board is cut into two pieces. One piece is 3.5 feet longer than the other. Find the length of each piece using an equation.

If you are familiar with the topics in this chapter, take this test now. If you can't answer a question, study the appropriate section of the chapter. If you are not familiar with the topics in this chapter, don't take this test now. Instead, study the examples, work the practice problems, and then take the test. This test will help you identify which concepts you have mastered, and which you need to study further.

____ **1.** Combine like terms: $38x - 50x$

    a. $88x$ **b.** $-12x$ **c.** $-88x$ **d.** $-12x$

____ **2.** Combine like terms: $-8y + 10y - 13y$

    a. $-15y$ **b.** $24y$ **c.** $-11y$ **d.** $5y$

____ **3.** Combine like terms: $4a - 7b - 12a + 17b$

    a. $-8a + 10b$ **b.** $-8a - 10b$ **c.** $8a - 10b$ **d.** $8a + 10b$

____ **4.** Combine like terms: $9x - y + 6 - 21x - 8y + 2$

    a. $-12x - 9y + 8$ **b.** $12x - 9y - 8$ **c.** $-12x$ **d.** $-12x - 9y - 8$

____ **5.** Combine like terms: $3x - 15 + 2y + 7 - 9y + 17x$

    a. $10x - 24y + 19$ **b.** $20x - 7y - 8$ **c.** $14x - 18y - 8$ **d.** $-6x + 2 + 9y$

____ **6.** Combine like terms: $7a - 6b + 2c - 4b$

    a. $9a - 10b$ **b.** $7a + 24b + 2c$ **c.** $9ac - 10b$ **d.** $7a - 10b + 2c$

____ **7.** Simplify: $(7)(5x - 2y)$

    a. $35x - 2y$ **b.** $12x - 2y$ **c.** $35x - 14y$ **d.** $12x - 9y$

____ **8.** Simplify: $(-2)(a + 7b - 12)$

    a. $-2a + 14b + 24$ **b.** $-2a - 14b + 24$ **c.** $-2a + 14b - 12$ **d.** $-2a + 7b - 12$

____ **9.** Simplify: $(-7)(1.5a + 3b - 4c - 5)$

    a. $-5.5a - 4b - 11c - 12$ **b.** $-10.5a + 3b - 4c - 5$ **c.** $-10.5a - 21b + 28c + 35$ **d.** $-10.5a - 21b - 4c - 5$

____ **10.** Simplify: $(5)(3x - y) - (3)(2x + y)$

    a. $9x$ **b.** $9x - 2y$ **c.** $9x + 2y$ **d.** $9x - 8y$

____ **11.** Solve: $11 + x = 53$

    a. 42 **b.** 64 **c.** $\dfrac{53}{11}$ **d.** No solution

____ **12.** Solve: $x + 2.5 = 8$

    a. 5.5 **b.** 10.5 **c.** 6.5 **d.** No solution

____ **13.** Solve: $x - \dfrac{2}{9} = \dfrac{1}{3}$

    a. $\dfrac{1}{9}$ **b.** $\dfrac{5}{9}$ **c.** $\dfrac{3}{2}$ **d.** $-\dfrac{3}{2}$

____ **14.** Solve: $8x = -120$

    a. -128 **b.** -112 **c.** -12 **d.** -5

____ **15.** Solve: $3.4x = 23.8$

    a. 20.4 **b.** 27.2 **c.** 80.92 **d.** 7

____ **16.** Solve: $\dfrac{3}{5}x = \dfrac{9}{10}$

    a. $\dfrac{3}{2}$ **b.** $\dfrac{9}{2}$ **c.** $\dfrac{3}{10}$ **d.** No Solution

____ **17.** Solve: $6x - 1 = 23$

    a. $\dfrac{11}{3}$ **b.** 4 **c.** 3 **d.** $\dfrac{23}{6}$

____ **18.** Solve: $19 - 3x = 4x - 23$

    a. 42 **b.** 6 **c.** -42 **d.** -4

____ **19.** Solve: $2(x - 8) = 25 - 7(x + 2)$

    a. $-\dfrac{5}{8}$ **b.** $-\dfrac{13}{4}$ **c.** 3 **d.** $\dfrac{35}{9}$

____ **20.** Solve: $2x + 15 = 3(20 - x)$

    a. 9 **b.** 15 **c.** -45 **d.** -15

____ **21.** A truck weighs 3.5 tons more than a car. Translate the sentence into an equation using t to represent the weight of the truck, and c to represent the weight of the car.

    a. $t = 3.5c$ **b.** $3.5t = c$ **c.** $t = 3.5 + c$ **d.** $3.5 + t = c$

____ **22.** The length of a rectangle is 9 meters longer than double the width. Translate the sentence into an equation using l to represent the length, and w to represent the width of the rectangle.

    a. $2l + 9 = w$ **b.** $l = 2w + 9$ **c.** $2(l + 9) = w$ **d.** $l = 2(w + 9)$

____ **23.** Mount Kimba is 2165 meters shorter than Mount Fulka. Let a be the height of Mount Fulka. Describe the height of Mount Kimba in terms of a.

    a. $a - 2165$ **b.** $a + 2165$ **c.** $\dfrac{a}{2165}$ **d.** $2165 - a$

____ **24.** A rectangular field has a perimeter of 130 meters. The length is 4 meters less than double the width. Find the dimensions of the field using an equation.

    a. $w = 21$ m $l = 38$ m
    b. $w = 23$ m $l = 42$ m
    c. $w = 20$ m $l = 36$ m
    d. $w = 26$ m $l = 48$ m

____ **25.** A 23-foot board is cut into two pieces. One piece is 7.5 feet longer that the other. Find the length of each piece using an equation.

    a. 8 ft and 15.5 ft   **b.** 8.5 ft and 14.5 ft   **c.** 9.25 ft and 16.75 ft   **d.** 7.75 ft and 15.25 ft

1. Combine like terms: $-15x + 21x - x$

2. Combine like terms: $14x - 9y + 2z - 3y - 12x + 5z$

3. Simplify: $-3(-x + 2y - 5x)$

4. Simplify: $0.8(x - 1.5y + 2.4z)$

5. Simplify: $-5(y - 6x - z) - (-3)(x - y + 2)$

6. Solve: $10 - 3x = -14$

7. Solve: $-y - 8 = y + 10$

8. Solve: $-5(x - 5) = 7(4 - 2x)$

9. Solve: $8 - 5(2 - x) = 5 + 3(x - 4)$

10. The temperature on Friday was 3° less than twice the temperature on Tuesday. Using F for Friday's temperature and T for Tuesday's temperature, translate the sentence into an equation.

11. The height of a triangle is 7 cm more that the length of its base. If b represents the length of the base, write an expression for the height of the triangle.

12. Frank is two years less than half as old as Thomas. If T represents Thomas' age, write an expression for Frank's age.

13. Angela's annual salary is $27,140. This is a 12% increase over last year's salary. What was last year's salary?

14. A triangle has three angles, A, B, and C. The measure of angle B is twice the measure of angle A, and the measure of angle C is $40°$ less than the measure of angle A. Find the measure of each angle.

15. The perimeter of a rectangle is 140 cm. Its width is one-third its length. Find the dimensions of the rectangle.

16. Solve: $2x + 3(x + 10) - 2 = 3x$

17. Solve: $2x + 12 + 7x = 3x + 9 + x$

18. A dress was on sale for 10% off the regular price. The sale price was $50.40. What was the regular price?

19. The area of a triangle is 300 ft². Its height is 10 feet. What is the measure of the base?

20. Professor Collins has 3 times as many students in her business math class as Professor Delorey. Professor Bench has twice the number of students in her business math class as Professor Delorey. The total number of students of all three professors is 192. How many students does Professor Delorey have?

1. Combine like terms: $-21a + 23a - a$

2. Combine like terms: $8c - 11d + 2c - 3d + 5 + d$

3. Simplify: $-6(a - 4d - 3c)$

4. Simplify: $0.6(x + 8y - 12)$

5. Simplify: $-2(y - x + 6z) - (-4)(x - y + z)$

6. Solve: $2 - 4x = -26$

7. Solve: $-y - 7 = y + 19$

8. Solve: $-9(x + 4) = 5(4 - x)$

9. Solve: $11 - 3(y - 4) = 8 + 2(1 - y)$

10. Mary is two inches more than half as tall as John. Translate the sentence into an equation using M to represent Mary's height, and J to represent John's height.

11. The second angle of a triangle is triple the first. The third angle is $23°$ more than the first. Use the letter x to describe each angle of the triangle.

12. The width of the rectangle is five less than half the length. Use the letter x to describe each dimension of the rectangle.

13. The number of acres in the McBride farm is 4.5 times the number of acres in the Smyth farm. Together the two farms have 550 acres. Using an equation, find the number acres that each farm has.

14. A rectangle has a perimeter of 48 m. The width is 2 m less than the length. Using an equation, find each dimension.

15. Virginia's salary is $35,100. This is an increase of 8% over last year's salary. Using an equation, find last year's salary

16. Solve: $2x + 3(x - 2) + 5 = 2(x + 2) + 1$

17. Solve: $4x + 5(x - 1) + 6x = 2(5x + 10)$

18. Grand bought a calculator for $67.50. This price was after a discount of 25%. Using an equation, find the price before the discount.

19. Three math professors had dinner and the bill came to $74. They want to leave the waitress a 20% tip. Using an equation, find how much each professor should pay if they each want to pay the same amount.

20. Jack is one year older than Steve. Steve is two years older than Dom. The sum of their ages is 101. Using an equation, find the age of each man.

1. Combine like terms: $22y - 23y + 15$

2. Combine like terms: $7x - 13y + 9 - 2x + 4y - 12$

3. Simplify: $-7(-a - 2b + 3c)$

4. Simplify: $1.6(2x - 5y - 8z)$

5. Simplify: $5(y - 6x - 5z) - 3(x - 2y + z)$

6. Solve: $17 - 2x = -19$

7. Solve: $12 - y = y + 6$

8. Solve: $-4(3 - 5x) = 2(4 - x)$

9. Solve: $10 - 4(3 - y) = -6 - 2(y - 2)$

10. Jeff is three years less than twice as old as Natalie. Translate the sentence into an equation using J to represent Jeff's age, and N to represent Natalie's.

11. The length of the first side of a triangle is half the length of the second side. The length of the third side is 5 cm more than triple the length of the second. Use the letter x and find expressions to represent the length of each side.

12. The Butler family vacation cost $780 more than the Tomlinson family vacation. The Perry family vacation cost $142 less than the Tomlinson vacation. Use the letter v to represent the cost of the Tomlinson family vacation and find expressions to represent the cost of the other two vacations.

13. The measure of the second angle of a triangle is twice the measure of the first, and the measure of the third angle is 5 more than twice the measure of the second. Use an equation to find the measure of each angle of the triangle.

14. A 130-ft length of pipe is divided into two pieces. One piece is 12.5 ft longer than the other. Using an equation, find the length of each piece.

15. The perimeter of a rectangle is 180 m. The length is 5 m more than double the width. Using an equation, find the dimensions of the rectangle.

16. Solve: $5 + 2(x - 10) + 1 = x + 5$

17. Solve: $4(x - 3) + 10 = 12$

18. Patricia's bill for one year of college is $24,500. The tuition charge costs $4000 more than the "room and board" costs. The bill also includes $500 for fees and other charges. Using an equation, find the amount of the yearly tuition charge.

19. A rented car costs $20 per day plus a flat fee of $35, no matter how many days the car is rented. Maria rented a car for a total cost of $175. Using an equation, find the number of days she had the car.

20. Gina needs $4500 to pay for a vacation to the Swiss Alps. She already has $1500 saved. Using an equation, find how much should she save every month in order to have enough money in 10 months.

____ **1.** Combine like terms: $-15y + 19y - 2y$

     a. $2y$ **b.** 3 **c.** $19 - 16y$ **d.** $-36y$

____ **2.** Combine like terms: $19x - y - 2z + x + 5y + 2z$

     a. $20x + 4$ **b.** $19x + 4y - 4z$ **c.** $20x + 4y - 4z$ **d.** $20x + 4y$

____ **3.** Simplify: $-7(x - y - 2z)$

     a. $-7z - 7y - 14z$ **b.** $-7x + 7y - 14z$ **c.** $-7x + 7y + 14z$ **d.** $7x - 7y - 14z$

____ **4.** Simplify: $(2.4)(a - 0.2b + 3.5c)$

     a. $2.4a + 2.2b + 5.9c$ **b.** $2.4a - 4.8b + 8.4c$ **c.** $2.4a - 4.8b + 84c$ **d.** $2.4a - 0.48b + 8.4c$

____ **5.** Simplify: $-4(7x - 3y - z) - (-6)(9x - z + 2)$

     a. $-82x + 12y - 10z + 12$ **b.** $26x + 12y - 2z + 12$

     c. $26x + 12y + 2z + 12$ **d.** $26x + 12y - 2z - 12$

____ **6.** Solve: $9 - 3x = 27$

     a. 12 **b.** $\dfrac{9}{2}$ **c.** -6 **d.** 12

____ **7.** Solve: $2(7 - x) = 3(x + 3)$

     a. -1 **b.** 1 **c.** $\dfrac{23}{5}$ **d.** 5

____ **8.** Solve: $-x - 7 = -2x - 11$

     a. -4 **b.** 4 **c.** 14 **d.** -14

____ **9.** $7 - 5(2 - x) = -(x - 8)$

     a. $\dfrac{5}{4}$ **b.** $\dfrac{7}{2}$ **c.** -4 **d.** $\dfrac{11}{16}$

____ **10.** Solve: $5(x + 9) - 23 = 42$

     a. 4 **b.** 5 **c.** -4 **d.** 16

____ **11.** Solve: $3x + 31 = x - 25$

     a. 28 **b.** -28 **c.** 13 **d.** 16

____ 12. The length of the second side of a triangle is 15 cm longer than twice the length of the first side. Using f for the first side and s for the second side, translate the sentence into an equation.

    a. $s = 2f + 15$ **b.** $s = 2f - 15$ **c.** $2s + 15 = f$ **d.** $2s + 15 = \frac{1}{2}f$

____ 13. The length of a rectangle is 7 m less than triple the width. If w represents the width, write an expression for the length, 1.

    a. $1 = \frac{1}{3}w - 7$ **b.** $1 = 3w - 7$ **c.** $1 = \frac{1}{3}w + 7$ **d.** $1 = 3w + 7$

____ 14. The temperature on Wednesday was $8°$ more than a third of Tuesday's temperature. If T represents Tuesday's temperature, write an expression for Wednesday's temperature, W.

    a. $W = 3T + 8$ **b.** $W = 3T - 8$ **c.** $W = \frac{1}{3}T + 8$ **d.** $W = \frac{1}{3}T - 8$

____ 15. A salesman has a base salary of $1400. He receives an additional 3.5% commission on his total sales. Last month his total salary was $2800. Which equation could be solved to find the amount of his total sales?

    a. $1400 + x + 0.035x = 2800$ **b.** $3.5x = 1400$

    c. $x + 0.035x = 2800$ **d.** $1400 + 0.035x = 2800$

____ 16. The population of Glendale this year is 3200 more than half of last year's population. The population this year is 26,300. Which equation could be solved to find last year's population?

    a. $\frac{1}{2}x + 3200 = 26,300$ **b.** $2x - 3200 = 26,300$

    c. $\frac{1}{2}x - 3200 = 26,300$ **d.** $x + \frac{1}{2}x + 3200 = 26,300$

____ 17. The perimeter of a rectangle is 90 cm. Its width is half its length. Which equation could be solved to find the dimensions of the rectangle?

    a. $L + \frac{1}{2}L = 90$ **b.** $2L + 2\left(\frac{1}{2}L\right) = 90$

    c. $2L + 2(L - 2) = 90$ **d.** $2L + 2(L + 2) = 90$

____ 18. A man's suit was on sale for 15% off the regular price. The sale price was $216.75. What was the regular price?

    a. $249.26   **b.** $250   **c.** $225   **d.** $255

____ 19. The area of a triangle is 45 cm^2. The base of the triangle is 6 cm. What is the height of the triangle?

    a. 12 cm   **b.** 15 cm   **c.** 7.5 cm   **d.** 30 cm

____ 20. Five times a number plus four times the same number is equal to 360. What is the number?

    a. 4   **b.** 80   **c.** 200   **d.** 40

____ 1. Combine like terms: $-13c + 16c - 2c$

    a. 2   **b.** $-c$ **c.** $14 - 12c$ **d.** c

____ 2. Combine like terms: $17x - y - z + 5z - x + 2$

    a. $-y + 20$ **b.** $16x + 3z + 2$ **c.** $16x - y + 4z + 2$ **d.** $17x - 3xyz + 5z + 2$

____ 3. Simplify: $-4(3a - 2b - 5)$

    a. $-12a + 8b + 20$ **b.** $-12a + 6b - 20$ **c.** $-12b - 8b - 20$ **d.** $-a - 6b - 18$

____ 4. Simplify: $(3.7)(x + 2y - 0.3z - 5)$

    a. $3.7x + 5.7y + 3.4z - 1.3$ **b.** $3.7x + 7.4y - 1.11z - 18.5$

    c. $3.7x + 7.4y - 11.1z + 18.5$ **d.** $3.7x + 7.4y - 11.1z - 18.5$

____ 5. Simplify: $-3(7x - 5y) - (-2)(9 - y)$

    a. $-21x + 17y - 18$ **b.** $-21x + 17y + 18$ **c.** $-21x + 13y + 18$ **d.** $-21x - 17y - 18$

____ 6. Solve: $6(2 - x) = 4 - 3(x + 4)$

    a. $\dfrac{20}{3}$ **b.** $\dfrac{8}{7}$ **c.** $-\dfrac{4}{3}$ **d.** 7

____ 7. Solve: $-x - 13 = 11 - 5x$

    a. 0   **b.** 4   **c.** -4 **d.** 6

____ 8. Solve: $23 - 4x = 19$

    a. -1 **b.** 6   **c.** 1   **d.** -6

____ 9. Solve: $4 + 3(x - 4) = 8 - 2(x - 2)$

    a. 4   **b.** 0   **c.** -20 **d.** 20

____ 10. Solve: $3(x - 5) + 2x = 10$

    a. -5 **b.** 4   **c.** 5   **d.** 1

____ 11. Solve: $3(x + 2) + 9 = 14$

    a. $-\dfrac{1}{3}$ **b.** -3 **c.** 1   **d.** $\dfrac{8}{3}$

_____ 12. The temperature on Monday was 16° colder than the temperature on Saturday. Using M for Monday's temperature and S for Saturday's temperature, translate the sentence into an equation.

     a. $S = M - 16$ **b.** $M = S - 16$ **c.** $M = -16S$ **d.** $S = -16M$

_____ 13. The width of a rectangle is 5 cm less than one-half the length of the rectangle. If L represents the length of the rectangle, write an expression for the width, w.

     a. $w = \dfrac{1}{2}L - 5$ **b.** $w = \dfrac{1}{2}L + 5$ **c.** $w = 2L + 5$ **d.** $w = 2L - 5$

_____ 14. The measure of the third angle of a triangle is 9° more than twice the measure of the first angle of the triangle. If x represents the measure of the first angle, write an expression for the measure of the third angle, y.

     a. $y = \dfrac{1}{2}x + 9$ **b.** $y = 2x - 9$ **c.** $y = \dfrac{1}{2}x - 9$ **d.** $y = 2x + 9$

_____ 15. A saleswoman has a base monthly salary of $1400. In addition, she receives a 2.5% commission on her total sales. Last month her total salary was $2400. Which equation could be used to find the amount of her total sales?

     a. $x + 0.025x = 2400$ **b.** $1500 + x + 0.025x = 2400$

     c. $1500 + 0.025x = 2400$ **d.** $1500 + 2.5x = 2400$

_____ 16. A triangle has three angles, A, B, and C. The measure of angle B is one-half the measure of angle A. The measure of angle C is 26° larger than the measure of angle A. Which equation could be used to find the measure of each angle?

     a. $x + 2x + (x - 26) = 180$ **b.** $x + \dfrac{1}{2}x + (x + 26) = 180$

     c. $x + 2x + (3x + 26) = 180$ **d.** $2x + x + (x + 26) = 180$

_____ 17. The population of Hastings this year is 46,400. This is a 3.2% increase from last year's population. Which equation could be used to find last year's population?

     a. $x + 3.2x = 46,440$ **b.** $0.032x(46,440 - x) = x$

     c. $x - 0.032x = 46,440$ **d.** $x + 0.032x = 46,440$

_____ 18. A car mechanic charged $162 for parts and $25 per hour for labor to install a new muffler. If the total cost was $237, how many hours did it take the mechanic to do the installation?

     a. $2\dfrac{1}{2}$ **b.** 3   **c.** $3\dfrac{1}{2}$ **d.** 1

_____ 19. A car salesman's base monthly salary is $2500. He also receives a 3% commission on his total monthly sales. One month he earned a total of $3850. What were his total sales that month?

     a. $45,000   **b.** $50,000   **c.** $1350   **d.** $35,000

_____ 20. A car is purchased with a $500 down payment, and 36 equal monthly payments. If the total amount to be paid is $4460, how much is each monthly payment?

     a. $120   **b.** $95   **c.** $100   **d.** $110

Basic College Mathematics: Introduction to Algebra

____ **1.** Combine like terms: $8a + 6a - 13a$

     a. $3a$ **b.** a **c.** 1 **d.** $15a$

____ **2.** Combine like terms: $9x - 5y + z + 7 - 8x$

     a. $x - 5y + z + 7$ **b.** $x + z$ **c.** $-4xy + z + 7$ **d.** $-4xyz + 7$

____ **3.** Simplify: $5(4x - 5y + 1)$

     a. $20x - 25y + 1$ **b.** $20x + 25y + 5$ **c.** $-5xy + 5$ **d.** $20x - 25y + 5$

____ **4.** Simplify: $(-6.7)(x - 2.5y - z + 1)$

     a. $-6.7x - 16.75y - 6.7z + 1$ **b.** $-6.7x + 9.2y + 7.7z - 6.7$

     c. $-6.7x + 16.75y + 6.7z - 6.7$ **d.** $10.05x + 6.7z - 6.7$

____ **5.** Simplify: $(-2)(6a - 5b) - (-6)(b - 3a)$

     a. $-9a - 16b$ **b.** $12a - 16b$ **c.** $30a - 6b$ **d.** $-30a + 16b$

____ **6.** Solve: $5(3 - x) = -5(4 - 2x)$

     a. -7 **b.** $\dfrac{7}{3}$ **c.** 1 **d.** $-\dfrac{7}{3}$

____ **7.** Solve: $3 - 5x = 19$

     a. 4 **b.** -4 **c.** $-\dfrac{16}{5}$ **d.** $-\dfrac{5}{16}$

____ **8.** Solve: $6 - 4(x - 2) = x + 3(4 - x)$

     a. -7 **b.** 1 **c.** $-\dfrac{7}{4}$ **d.** -2

____ **9.** Solve: $10 + 7(-x + 4) = 5 - 3x + 4$

     a. $-\dfrac{43}{10}$ **b.** 7 **c.** $\dfrac{29}{4}$ **d.** $\dfrac{28}{3}$

____ **10.** Solve: $2x + 3(x + 4) = 7$

     a. -1 **b.** 1 **c.** 2 **d.** $\dfrac{3}{5}$

____ **11.** Solve: $4(x-5)+3=3$

    a. 0   **b.** $\dfrac{5}{4}$ **c.** 5   **d.** –5

____ **12.** The temperature on Monday was 19° warmer than the temperature on Saturday. Using M for Monday's temperature and S for Saturday's, translate sentence into an equation.

    a. $M=19-S$ **b.** $M=S-19$ **c.** $M=19S$ **d.** $M=S+19$

____ **13.** The length of a rectangle is 7 inches more than triple the width. If w represents width, write an expression for the length, l.

    a. $l=3w-7$ **b.** $l=7w+3$ **c.** $l=3w+7$ **d.** $l=7-3w$

____ **14.** The measure of the second angle of a triangle is three more than half the measure of the first angle. If x represents the measure of the first angle, write an expression for the measure of the second angle, y.

    a. $y=2x+3$ **b.** $y=\dfrac{1}{2}x+3$ **c.** $y=2x-3$ **d.** $y=\dfrac{1}{2}x-3$

____ **15.** Marty received twice as many votes as Larry. There were 850 votes cast total. Which equation could be used to find how many votes each candidate received?

    a. $2x+x=850$ **b.** $2(2x)=850$ **c.** $x+x+2=850$ **d.** $x+850=2x$

____ **16.** The width of a rectangle is five less than the length. The perimeter of the rectangle is 48 cm. Which of the equations could be used to find the dimensions of the rectangle?

    a. $L+(L+5)=48$ **b.** $L(L-5)=48$ **c.** $2L+2L-5=48$ **d.** $2L+2(L-5)=48$

____ **17.** The population of Marion this year is 27,900. This is a 6% decrease from last year's population. Which of the equations could be used to find last year's population?

    a. $x-0.06x=27,900$ **b.** $x-0.6x=27,900$

    c. $x+0.06x=27,900$ **d.** $0.06x(27,900-x)=x$

____ **18.** A rectangular field has a perimeter of 210 feet. The length is 25 feet longer than the width. Find the dimensions of the field.

    a. $l=130,\ w=80$ **b.** $l=65,\ w=40$ **c.** $l=55,\ w=30$ **d.** $l=60,\ w=45$

____ **19.** Pedro's car is worth 1/3 of what he paid for it 6 years ago. Its current value is $2300. What did Pedro pay for the car originally?

    a. $7000   **b.** $6600   **c.** $4600   **d.** $6900

____ **20.** Mukul earns $3400 more per year than his wife Theresa. Their combined income is $87,400. How much does Mukul earn?

    a. $42,000   **b.** $84,000   **c.** $45,400   **d.** $44,500

1. Add: $8\frac{1}{2} + 7\frac{1}{3}$

2. Multiply: 6.13×11.24

3. Divide: $3\frac{1}{2} \div \frac{3}{8}$

4. Find 32% of $5000.

5. Find n: $\frac{n}{3} = \frac{105}{4.5}$

6. Convert: 26 lb = _____ kg.
   Round to the nearest hundredth.

7. Convert: 193 cm = _____ m.
   Round to the nearest hundredth.

8. Find the area of a triangle with height 26 inches and base 8 inches.

9. Find the hypotenuse of the right triangle below.

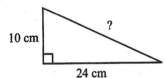

10. Find the mean of these grades:
    69, 77, 68, 75, 55, 82, 96
    Round to the nearest hundredth.

11. The histogram to the right shows the number of customers that brought their cars in for an oil change at Mary Lou's car dealership during one week. How many more customers came in on Tuesday compared to Wednesday?

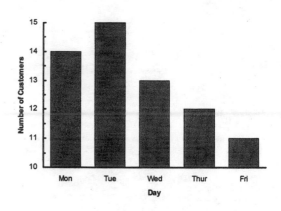

12. Add: $-7 + (-15) + 26$

13. Multiply: $\left(-\dfrac{5}{2}\right)\left(-\dfrac{7}{10}\right)$

14. Solve: $23 - 4x = 7$

15. Solve: $2(x+10) + 3(x-2) = 2(x+10)$

16. Combine like terms: $-5y + 2x + 10y - x + 8y - 15x$

17. Claire is one year older than her sister Nancy. Nancy is three years older than her sister Sheila. Sheila is one year older than her brother David. David is five years older than his brother Mike. The sum of the five siblings' ages is 120 years. Find the age of each.

18. An 85-ft length of pipe is divided into two pieces. One piece is four times as long as the other. Find the length of each piece.

19. The width of a rectangle is 8 cm less than its length. The perimeter is 44 cm. Find the dimensions of the rectangle.

20. A salesperson has a base monthly salary of $2500, plus a 3% commission on total sales. Last month her total salary was $3040. What was the amount of her total sales?

____ 1. Add: $6\frac{1}{3}+2\frac{1}{2}+4\frac{1}{5}$

     a. $13\frac{1}{30}$ b. $13\frac{1}{10}$ c. $12\frac{3}{10}$ d. $12\frac{3}{5}$

____ 2. Multiply: 3.04×5.6

     a. 17.024   b. 15.3824   c. 19.04   d. 16.8224

____ 3. Divide: $10\frac{1}{4}\div\frac{5}{8}$

     a. $6\frac{13}{32}$ b. $10\frac{1}{5}$ c. $14\frac{2}{5}$ d. $16\frac{2}{5}$

____ 4. Find 30% of $540.

     a. $18   b. $1800   c. $162   d. $16.20

____ 5. Find n: $\frac{n}{2}=\frac{45}{3}$

     a. $n=9$ b. $n=30$ c. $n=35$ d. $n=270$

____ 6. Convert: 63 lb = _____ kg

     a. 28 kg   b. 630 kg   c. 28.602 kg   d. 138.6 kg

____ 7. Convert: 372 m = _____ km

     a. 0.372 km   b. 37.2 km   c. 3.72 km   d. 0.0372 km

____ 8. Find the volume of a sphere whose radius is 15 cm.

     a. 14,130 cm³   b. 942 cm³   c. 235.5 cm³   d. 5298.75 cm³

____ 9. Find the length of the missing leg in the triangle below:

     a. 36 cm   b. 14 cm
     c. 69.31 cm   d. 9 cm

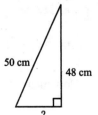

50 cm   48 cm   ?

____ 10. Find the mean of these grades: 71, 72, 87, 96, 82, 76. Round to the nearest hundredth, if necessary.

     a. 69.14   b. 79   c. 96.8   d. 80.67

_____ 11. The histogram below shows the number of students that used the audiovisual center in the college library this week. How many total students used the center all this week?

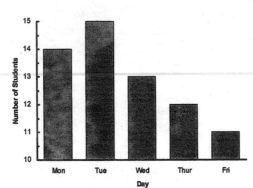

    a. 63 students   **b.** 65 students

    c. 64 students   **d.** 62 students

_____ 12. Add: $-7+(23)+(-11)+19$

    a. -153 **b.** 38 **c.** 24 **d.** 8

_____ 13. Multiply: $\left(-1\frac{1}{2}\right)(-20)$

    a. -30 **b.** 25 **c.** 30 **d.** -25

_____ 14. Solve for z: $23-3z=-4$

    a. $z=9$ **b.** $z=\frac{1}{5}$ **c.** $z=-24$ **d.** $z=81$

_____ 15. Solve for x: $3(x-2)+5(x+4)=5(x+4)$

    a. $11\frac{1}{3}$ **b.** $\frac{6}{13}$ **c.** 18 **d.** 2

_____ 16. Combine like terms: $-3y+2x-10y-5x+2y$

    a. $-11y-3x$ **b.** $-15y+3x$ **c.** $-15y-3x$ **d.** $-11y+7x$

_____ 17. The measure of the second angle of a triangle is twice the measure of the first angle. The measure of the third angle is $10°$ less than the measure of the first angle. Find the measure of the second angle.

    a. $47.5°$ **b.** $80°$ **c.** $37.5°$ **d.** $95°$

_____ 18. Phyllis paid $408 for new wall-to-wall carpeting in her living room. The carpeting was $12 per square yard, plus a $120 installation charge. How many square yards did she buy?

    a. 26 sq yd   **b.** 34 sq yd   **c.** 44 sq yd   **d.** 24 sq yd

_____ 19. Medway High School has 504 students this year. This is 12% more than last year. How many students were there last year?

    a. 492   **b.** 450   **c.** 494   **d.** 564

_____ 20. Rick is a salesman whose base monthly salary is $2200. He earns 5% commission on total sales. Last month his total earnings were $2525. What was his total sales amount last month?

    a. $6500   **b.** $2651.25   **c.** $1050   **d.** $2305

1. Add: $5268 + 284 + 105$

2. Simplify: $10 + 3^3 + 5^2 \div 5 - 6$

3. Divide: $3\dfrac{2}{3} \div \dfrac{1}{2}$

4. Subtract: $\dfrac{19}{24} - \dfrac{5}{16}$

5. Multiply: $\begin{array}{r} 3.85 \\ \times\, 0.22 \\ \hline \end{array}$

6. Subtract: $-\dfrac{3}{5} - \left(-\dfrac{8}{11}\right)$

7. Simplify: $\dfrac{-6 + 15 \div (-3)}{6 - 2(4)}$

8. Change $\dfrac{19}{57}$ to a percent.
   Round to the nearest hundredth.

9. What percent of 200 is 8?

10. 23.4 is 130% of what number?

11. Find 15% of $156.

12. Change $\dfrac{3}{8}$ to a decimal.

13. What is $1\dfrac{2}{5}$ as a percent?

14. Write 85% as a fraction in lowest terms.

15. Write 0.52 as a fraction in lowest terms.

16. In the primary election in Medway, 8040 voters were registered, but only 6834 people voted. What percent of the registered voters voted in the primary?

17. Dave rode 25 miles on his bike in $2\frac{1}{2}$ hours. At his rate, how long would it take him to ride 35 miles?

18. Solve for n. Round to the nearest tenth.
$$\frac{63 \text{ gallons}}{10 \text{ hours}} = \frac{n \text{ gallons}}{16 \text{ hours}}$$

19. Convert: 629 cm = _____ m

20. Convert: 15.29 km = _____ miles
Round to the nearest hundredth.

21. A pump is running at 90 gallons per hour. How many quarts per minute is this?

22. Write 8,702,000,000 in scientific notation.

23. Find the volume of the circular cylinder below.

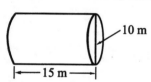
10 m

15 m

24. Grant has the following chemistry quiz scores:
77, 23, 96, 25, 71, and 98
Find his mean score.

25. Write 2.54×10^7 in standard notation.

26. How many inches is 354 cm? Round to the nearest hundredth.

27. An infant weighed 2.8 kilograms. How much did it weigh in pounds?

28. Joe and Eileen drove 350 kilometers in one day. How many miles is this?

29. Find the perimeter of a parallelogram with sides measuring 10.5 ft and 3.8 ft.

30. Find the area of the shaded region in the figure below.

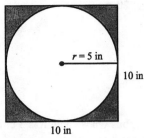

$r = 5$ in

10 in

10 in

31. The circle graph indicates the results of a survey of 400 car and truck owners. How many do not own a foreign-made vehicle?

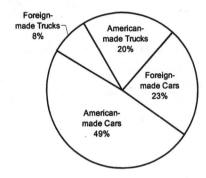

Foreign-made Trucks 8%

American-made Trucks 20%

Foreign-made Cars 23%

American-made Cars 49%

32. Emma designed a triangular flowerbed with a base of 20 ft and a height of 15 ft. Fertilizer costs $0.85 per square foot. How much will it cost Emma to fertilize the flowerbed?

33. A boat travels 15 miles south and then 11 miles east. How far is the boat from its starting point? Round to the nearest tenth, if necessary.

34. Evaluate exactly: $\sqrt{121} - \sqrt{36}$

35. Write "682 miles in 4 days" as a unit rate.

36. Solve for n. Round to the nearest tenth.
$$\frac{9.2}{12} = \frac{16.1}{n}$$

37. If 2 centimeters on a map represents 75 miles, what distance does 3.2 centimeters represent?

38. Find the circumference of a circle whose diameter is 22 cm. Round to the nearest hundredth.

39. Find the length of the hypotenuse of a right triangle whose legs are 15 cm and 20 cm.

40. Evaluate: $\sqrt{289}$

41. What is the area of a rhombus whose height is 5 cm and whose parallel sides are 8 cm and 12 cm?

42. Five homes sold for the following prices: $179,000, $189,000, $208,000, $389,000, and $119,000. What was the median price?

43. Simplify: $(5)(-2)(-3)$

44. Simplify: $(-11)-(-3)$

45. Simplify: $\dfrac{-15+(-2)}{(-2)\div(-1)}$

46. Solve for x: $5+2(x-3)=10-3(x-5)$

47. Simplify: $-5(d-3c)-8(5c-11d)$

48. Solve for x: $7-5(3-x)=-3-(2x+4)$

49. The length of a rectangle is five less than twice the width. The perimeter is 50 cm. Using an equation, find the dimensions of the rectangle.

50. There are 696 students at Medway High School this year. This is a 4% drop in enrollment from last year. Using an equation, determine how many students were enrolled last year.

Final Examination (MC)
Basic College Mathematics

Name: _____

____ **1.** Simplify: $5002+182-105$

    a. 5079   **b.** 4925   **c.** 5289   **d.** 4715

____ **2.** Simplify: $2^4 \div 4 + 5 \times 2^2 + 15 \div 3$

    a. 27   **b.** 41   **c.** 29   **d.** 5.67

____ **3.** Divide: $6\frac{5}{8} \div \frac{1}{3}$

    a. $2\frac{5}{24}$ **b.** $19\frac{7}{8}$ **c.** $7\frac{1}{8}$ **d.** $\frac{8}{159}$

____ **4.** Add: $\frac{17}{36} + \frac{15}{24}$

    a. $\frac{8}{15}$ **b.** $\frac{4}{9}$ **c.** $6\frac{2}{5}$ **d.** $1\frac{7}{72}$

____ **5.** Multiply: $\begin{array}{r} 5.95 \\ \times\, 0.099 \\ \hline \end{array}$

    a. 0.58905   **b.** 0.58805   **c.** 0.49665   **d.** 5.8905

____ **6.** Subtract: $-\frac{7}{9} - \left(-\frac{3}{8}\right)$

    a. $-\frac{29}{72}$ **b.** $-\frac{4}{72}$ **c.** $-\frac{10}{17}$ **d.** $-\frac{10}{72}$

____ **7.** Simplify: $\dfrac{-8+18\div(-2)}{5+4(-3)}$

    a. $-\frac{5}{6}$ **b.** $\frac{1}{7}$ **c.** $2\frac{3}{7}$ **d.** $1\frac{1}{6}$

____ **8.** Change $\frac{9}{17}$ to a percent. Round to the nearest hundredth.

    a. 5.29%   **b.** 52.941%   **c.** 53%   **d.** 0.529%

____ **9.** What percent of 145 is 29?

    a. 500%   **b.** 2%   **c.** 20%   **d.** 5%

____ **10.** 17.9 is 40% of what number?

    a. 44.75   **b.** 29.83   **c.** 7.16   **d.** 0.4475

____ **11.** Find 32% of 5280.

    a. 16,500   **b.** 168.96   **c.** 3590.4   **d.** 1689.6

____ **12.** Change $\frac{5}{8}$ to a decimal.

    a. 0.0625   **b.** 6.25   **c.** 0.00625   **d.** 0.625

_____ 13. What is $1\frac{4}{5}$ as a percent?

     a. 1.8%   b. 200%   c. 180%   d. 0.18%

_____ 14. Write 60% as a fraction in lowest terms.

     a. $\frac{3}{5}$ b. $\frac{2}{5}$ c. $\frac{6}{10}$ d. $\frac{0.60}{100}$

_____ 15. Write 0.64 as a fraction in lowest terms.

     a. $\frac{32}{50}$ b. $\frac{16}{25}$ c. $\frac{3}{4}$ d. $\frac{64}{100}$

_____ 16. In the general election, there were 10,900 people registered to vote, but only 5777 voted. What percent of the registered voters is this?

     a. 189%   b. 5.3%   c. 47%   d. 53%

_____ 17. Ralph rode 35 miles on his bike in $3\frac{1}{2}$ hours. At this rate, how long would it take him to ride 47.5 miles?

     a. 4.75 hours   b. 45 hours   c. 4.5 hours   d. 475 hours

_____ 18. Solve for n: $\dfrac{85 \text{ liters}}{10 \text{ hours}} = \dfrac{n \text{ liters}}{15 \text{ hours}}$

     a. $n = 127.5$ b. $n = 12.75$ c. $n = 56.67$ d. $n = 255$

_____ 19. Convert: 1.9 km = _____ cm

     a. 1,900,000   b. 19,000   c. 19   d. 190,000

_____ 20. Convert: 62.5 m = _____ yards

     a. 57.34   b. 62.5   c. 68.125   d. 573.4

_____ 21. A pump is running at 9.2 quarts per hour. How many gallons per hour is this?

     a. 92 gal / hr   b. 2.3 gal / hr   c. 36.8 gal / hr   d. 4.6 gal / hr

_____ 22. Write 2,560,000 in scientific notation.

     a. 2.56×10^{-6} b. 2.56×10^{6} c. 25.6×10^{6} d. 2.56×10^{-5}

_____ 23. Find the volume of a pyramid with height 20 m and with a rectangular base that measures 25 m by 36 m.

     a. 18,000 m^3 b. 4500 m^3 c. 6000 m^3 d. 9000 m^3

_____ 24. Clay is building a pen for his dog. He plans to make it rectangular in shape and measuring 40 ft by 50 ft. He can buy fencing for $3.75 per ft. How much will the fencing for his dog pen cost?

     a. $675   b. $337.50   c. $142.22   d. $48

_____ 25. Write 3.55×10^{-3} in standard notation.

     a. 35,550   b. 0.0355   c. 0.355   d. 0.00355

_____ 26. How many feet is 406 cm? Round to the nearest hundredth.

     a. 0.406 ft   b. 1219.2 ft   c. 13.32 ft   d. 12,378 ft

____ **27.** An infant weighs 4.2 kilograms. What is this weight in pounds?

    a. 6.4 lb   **b.** 1.91 lb   **c.** 9.24 lb   **d.** 1.89 lb

____ **28.** My car used 18.4 liters of gas on a long trip. How many gallons is this? Round to the nearest hundredth.

    a. 4.86 gal   **b.** 184 gal   **c.** 69.70 gal   **d.** 1.91 gal

____ **29.** Find the perimeter of a parallelogram with sides measuring 13.2 cm and 5.2 cm.

    a. 18.4 cm   **b.** 68.64 cm   **c.** 32.6 cm   **d.** 36.8 cm

____ **30.** Find the area of the shaded region in the figure below.

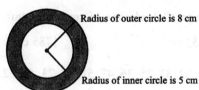

Radius of outer circle is 8 cm

Radius of inner circle is 5 cm

    a. 200.96 cm^2 **b.** 122.46 cm^2

    c. 78.5 cm^2 **d.** 279.46 cm^2

____ **31.** The circle graph indicates the results of asking 400 people which of these four football teams they like best this year. How many people do not like Stanford?

    a. 56   **b.** 344

    c. 14   **d.** 86

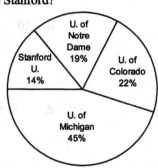

____ **32.** Sabrina has the following math quiz scores: 19, 24, 25, 17, 13, and 18. Find her mean score, to the nearest tenth, if necessary.

    a. 18   **b.** 19   **c.** 18.5   **d.** 19.3

____ **33.** A boat travels 12 miles west and then 8 miles north. How far is the boat from its starting point? Round to the nearest tenth, if necessary.

    a. 14.4 miles   **b.** 20 miles   **c.** 4 miles   **d.** 104 miles

____ **34.** Evaluate exactly: $\sqrt{100} - \sqrt{64}$

    a. 1   **b.** 2   **c.** 3   **d.** 4

____ **35.** Write "432 gallons in 48 hours" as a unit rate.

    a. 216 gal / 24 hr   **b.** 108 gal / 12 hr   **c.** 54 gal / 6 hr   **d.** 9 gal / hr

____ **36.** Solve for n: $\dfrac{6.4}{n} = \dfrac{7.5}{10.2}$ Round to the nearest tenth.

    a. $n = 4.7$ **b.** $n = 12.0$ **c.** $n = 11.9$ **d.** $n = 8.7$

____ **37.** If 3 centimeters on a map represents 150 miles, what distance does 5 centimeters represent?

    a. 90 miles   **b.** 2250 miles   **c.** 250 miles   **d.** 50 miles

____ **38.** Find the circumference of a circle whose diameter is 54 cm. Round to the nearest hundredth.

    a. 339.12 cm   **b.** 2289.06 cm   **c.** 169.56 cm   **d.** 114.53 cm

____ **39.** Find the length of the hypotenuse of a right triangle whose legs measure 45 cm and 60 cm.

    a. 75 cm   **b.** 10.25 cm   **c.** 39.69 cm   **d.** 105 cm

____ **40.** Evaluate: $\sqrt{324}$

    a. 18   **b.** 19   **c.** 17   **d.** 16

____ **41.** What is the area of a rhombus whose height is 7 cm and whose parallel sides are 15 cm and 17 cm?

    a. 892.5 cm^2 **b.** 112 cm^2 **c.** 153 cm^2 **d.** 1785 cm^2

____ **42.** Eleven applicants for a certain position had the following ages: 32, 33, 25, 36, 48, 51, 28, 23, 54, 52, 45. What was the median age?

    a. 38.82   **b.** 33   **c.** 36   **d.** 38.5

____ **43.** Simplify: $(10)(-3)(-5)$

    a. 2   **b.** 150   **c.** −150   **d.** 18

____ **44.** Simplify: $-13-(-2)$

    a. −26   **b.** −11   **c.** 15   **d.** 26

____ **45.** Simplify: $\dfrac{-20+(-3)}{(-3)\div(-1)}$

    a. $\dfrac{17}{3}$ **b.** $-\dfrac{17}{3}$ **c.** $-\dfrac{23}{3}$ **d.** −30.5

____ **46.** Solve for x: $10+3(x-5)=20-2(x-1)$

    a. $x=2\dfrac{3}{5}$ **b.** $x=13$ **c.** $x=4\dfrac{3}{5}$ **d.** $x=5\dfrac{2}{5}$

____ **47.** Simplify: $-2(x-4y)-3(6y-5x)$

    a. $13x-10y$ **b.** $-7x-22y$ **c.** $-17x-26y$ **d.** $13x+26y$

____ **48.** Solve for x: $6-3(x-5)=-2-(x+1)$

    a. $x=-4$ **b.** $x=-4.5$ **c.** $x=4$ **d.** $x=12$

____ **49.** The length of a rectangle is three less than twice the width. The perimeter is 84 cm. Using an equation, find the dimensions of the rectangle.

    a. *width* = 39 cm *length* = 21 cm   **b.** *width* = 15 cm *length* = 27 cm   **c.** *width* = 27 cm *length* = 15 cm   **d.** *width* = 21 cm *length* = 39 cm

____ **50.** There are 4368 residents in Morrisville this year. This is a 4% drop in population from last year. Using an equation, determine how many people lived in Morrisville last year.

    a. 4550   **b.** 175   **c.** 4543   **d.** 4193

Chapter 1: Pretest (FR)

1. Three hundred fifty-two thousand four hundred sixteen
2. $40,000 + 3000 + 200 + 80 + 9$
3. 8,074,625
4. 2273
5. 2583
6. 164
7. 58,947
8. 14,762
9. 2141
10. 177,551
11. 43,964,444
12. 96
13. 24,234
14. 5292
15. 394,273
16. 0
17. 4582 R2
18. 186
19. 5^6
20. 64
21. 12
22. 32
23. 15
24. 583,000
25. 83,400
26. 20,000,000
27. 1300
28. 30,000,000,000
29. 974 miles
30. $15
31. $264
32. 350,417

Chapter 1: Pretest (MC)

1. a
2. d
3. b
4. b
5. a
6. c
7. c
8. a
9. b
10. d
11. b
12. a
13. b
14. a
15. d
16. d
17. c
18. b
19. b
20. a
21. d
22. b
23. c
24. a
25. d
26. a
27. a
28. c
29. b
30. d
31. b
32. c

Chapter 1: Form A

1. 4,305,605
2. 631
3. 662
4. 216,827
5. 528
6. 1566
7. 4837
8. 617
9. 7^4
10. 37,600
11. 25
12. 32
13. 15,000
14. $12.20
15. $27

Chapter 1: Form B

1. 8,844,103
2. 1316
3. 2198
4. 5315
5. 700
6. 1512
7. 3696
8. 901 R2
9. 3^6
10. 2,550,000
11. 61
12. 78
13. 5600
14. $5152
15. 25 miles per gallon

Chapter 1: Form C

1. 95,634,783
2. 919
3. 52,135
4. 2261
5. 0
6. 39,200
7. 243,460
8. 542
9. 8^4
10. 653,000
11. 49
12. 62
13. 1600
14. 5916
15. 307

Chapter 1: Form E

1. c
2. d
3. b
4. c
5. c
6. a
7. b
8. c
9. b
10. a
11. c
12. d
13. d
14. a
15. a

Chapter 1: Form D

1. b
2. c
3. a
4. d
5. a
6. a
7. c
8. b
9. c
10. c
11. b
12. b
13. b
14. d
15. a

Chapter 1: Form F

1. c
2. a
3. b
4. d
5. d
6. c
7. a
8. b
9. d
10. a
11. d
12. b
13. a
14. b
15. b

Chapter 2: Pretest (FR)

1. $\dfrac{4}{8}$

2.

3. $\dfrac{6}{47}$

4. $\dfrac{1}{6}$

5. $\dfrac{1}{3}$

6. $\dfrac{1}{7}$

7. $\dfrac{5}{8}$

8. $\dfrac{5}{11}$

9. $\dfrac{13}{3}$

10. $\dfrac{65}{9}$

11. $19\dfrac{3}{4}$

12. $7\dfrac{2}{5}$

13. $2\dfrac{7}{17}$

14. $\dfrac{3}{56}$

15. $\dfrac{3}{7}$

16. $54\dfrac{1}{6}$

17. 1

18. 2

19. $1\dfrac{7}{11}$

20. $10\dfrac{1}{2}$

21. 12

22. 45

23. 77

24. 75

25. $\dfrac{29}{60}$

26. $\dfrac{35}{36}$

27. $6\dfrac{2}{3}$

28. $5\dfrac{37}{42}$

29. $\dfrac{2}{15}$

30. $8\dfrac{1}{6}$

31. $9\dfrac{11}{36}$

32. 18

Chapter 2: Pretest (MC)

1. a
2. a
3. b
4. d
5. a
6. b
7. b
8. d
9. d
10. a
11. c
12. d
13. c
14. a
15. a
16. b
17. a
18. d
19. a
20. b
21. b
22. c
23. c
24. b
25. b
26. d
27. a
28. b
29. c
30. a
31. d
32. b

Chapter 2: Form A

1. $2\times3\times5\times5$

2. No; 5×19

3. $\dfrac{3}{13}$

4. $\dfrac{2}{3}$

5. $\dfrac{32}{5}$

6. $2\dfrac{5}{33}$

7. $2\dfrac{11}{30}$

8. $\dfrac{44}{105}$

9. $\dfrac{3}{8}$

10. 144

11. $\dfrac{65}{120}$

12. $16\dfrac{1}{6}$

13. $5\dfrac{1}{4}$

14. $\frac{7}{8}$

15. 21

16. $\frac{17}{30}$

17. $\frac{5}{24}$

18. $40\frac{3}{5}$

19. $\frac{1}{8}$

20. $\frac{7}{8}$

14. $5\frac{3}{8}$

15. $\frac{5}{7}$

16. 1

17. $40\frac{3}{8}$ sq.ft.

18. 118 packets

19. $\frac{5}{8}$ cord

20. $\frac{15}{16}$ cup

15. $15\frac{23}{40}$

16. $\frac{27}{40}$

17. $137\frac{11}{20}$ sq. ft.

18. 180 packages

19. $\frac{7}{24}$ crate

20. $2\frac{9}{16}$ inches

Chapter 2: Form B

1. $2\times2\times2\times7$

2. No; 5×13

3. $\frac{3}{10}$

4. $\frac{7}{30}$

5. $\frac{23}{7}$

6. $4\frac{5}{13}$

7. $3\frac{4}{25}$

8. $\frac{35}{48}$

9. $\frac{1}{7}$

10. 408

11. $\frac{60}{125}$

12. $10\frac{13}{20}$

13. $1\frac{11}{45}$

Chapter 2: Form C

1. 2×31

2. No; $2\times5\times10$

3. $\frac{5}{16}$

4. $\frac{11}{28}$

5. $\frac{35}{8}$

6. $4\frac{9}{17}$

7. $6\frac{3}{10}$

8. $\frac{5}{143}$

9. $\frac{3}{38}$

10. 420

11. $\frac{72}{315}$

12. $5\frac{1}{2}$

13. $\frac{33}{40}$

14. $5\frac{1}{2}$

Chapter 2: Form D

1. c

2. d

3. b

4. d

5. c

6. a

7. b

8. a

9. d

10. b

11. d

12. b

13. a

14. c

15. c

16. b

17. d

18. a

19. c

20. d

Chapter 2: Form E

1. c
2. b
3. b
4. d
5. a
6. c
7. d
8. d
9. b
10. c
11. a
12. a
13. c
14. c
15. b
16. d
17. b
18. c
19. a
20. b

Chapter 2: Form F

1. c
2. b
3. b
4. a
5. d
6. b
7. a
8. a
9. b
10. d
11. c
12. b
13. d
14. d
15. d

16. a
17. d
18. d
19. b
20. c

Chapter 2: Cumulative Exam (FR)

1. 3801
2. 46,549
3. 960
4. 1568
5. 7^5
6. 25,700
7. 36
8. 37.5 miles per gallon
9. $15.40
10. $\dfrac{17}{25}$
11. $\dfrac{1}{35}$
12. $\dfrac{19}{30}$
13. $8\dfrac{5}{9}$
14. $3\dfrac{23}{40}$
15. $\dfrac{20}{77}$
16. 42
17. $536\dfrac{5}{8}$ sq. ft.
18. 125 packages
19. $\dfrac{2}{15}$ bag
20. $19\dfrac{1}{2}''$ by $13\dfrac{1}{2}''$

Chapter 2: Cumulative Exam (MC)

1. b
2. a
3. d
4. b
5. c
6. c
7. b
8. a
9. d
10. d
11. b
12. c
13. a
14. a
15. b
16. c
17. c
18. a
19. d
20. b

Chapter 3: Pretest (FR)

1. Thirty-two and nine hundred twenty-five thousandths
2. 0.0391
3. $8\dfrac{13}{100}$
4. $\dfrac{5}{8}$
5. 3.49, 3.5, 3.501, 3.51
6. 689.6
7. 3.062
8. 28.65
9. 37.256
10. 26.48
11. 65.583
12. 0.08852
13. 5870.3
14. 49.81
15. 1.389
16. 0.368
17. 0.8125
18. $0.3\overline{18}$
19. 1.03
20. $31.70
21. 30.4
22. $9.52

Chapter 3: Pretest (MC)

1. b
2. a
3. c
4. a
5. d
6. b
7. c
8. c
9. a
10. b

11. b
12. d
13. a
14. c
15. d
16. d
17. b
18. a
19. b
20. a
21. c
22. c

Chapter 3: Form A

1. Three and two hundred seventy-nine thousandths
2. $\dfrac{41}{250}$
3. 9.09, 9.9, 9.903, 9.91
4. 6547.284
5. <
6. 7.75
7. 19.438
8. 10.9095
9. 27.184
10. 3.98164
11. 1.14
12. $1.41\overline{6}$
13. 0.079
14. $43.05
15. 0.0515
16. 0.786
17. 22.3 miles per gallon
18. $128.86
19. Jesse ($200.45)
20. $16.43

Chapter 3: Form B

1. Nine hundred forty-three ten thousandths
2. $\dfrac{21}{200}$
3. 8.08, 8.8, 8.801, 8.81
4. 0.70
5. <
6. 26.65
7. 21.817
8. 14.9089
9. 16.1588
10. 2.44494
11. 17.8
12. 0.375
13. 0.256
14. $45.37
15. 62.644
16. 0.385
17. 24.5 miles per gallon
18. 1.7 inch
19. $9.95
20. $31.20

Chapter 3: Form C

1. Eight and twenty-five ten thousandths
2. $\dfrac{101}{200}$
3. 6.199, 6.9919, 6.995, 6.9991
4. 793.004
5. >
6. 11.78
7. 23.436
8. 11.7129
9. 6.185
10. 1.61868
11. 14

12. $0.4\overline{6}$

13. 0.815

14. 100 days

15. 0.0945

16. 0.158

17. $539.32

18. $10,535.00

19. 14.69 miles

20. $133.88

Chapter 3: Form D

1. c
2. b
3. d
4. c
5. a
6. a
7. d
8. a
9. a
10. c
11. d
12. a
13. b
14. c
15. a
16. b
17. d
18. a
19. b
20. c

Chapter 3: Form E

1. b
2. c
3. a
4. b

5. c
6. a
7. c
8. c
9. d
10. d
11. b
12. c
13. d
14. d
15. d
16. a
17. c
18. b
19. b
20. a

Chapter 3: Form F

1. a
2. a
3. b
4. d
5. b
6. a
7. a
8. d
9. b
10. b
11. a
12. d
13. c
14. b
15. d
16. d
17. a
18. c
19. a
20. b

Chapter 4: Pretest (FR)

1. $\dfrac{15}{29}$

2. $\dfrac{3}{10}$

3. $\dfrac{7}{2}$

4. $\dfrac{7}{12}$

5. $\dfrac{8}{23}$

6. $\dfrac{3 \text{ aspirin}}{50 \text{ athletes}}$

7. $\dfrac{3 \text{ pounds}}{20 \text{ square feet}}$

8. 36.5 miles / hour

9. $27 per CD player

10. $\dfrac{23}{49} = \dfrac{37}{101}$

11. $\dfrac{126}{48} = \dfrac{52}{88}$

12. Yes

13. No

14. 19

15. 16

16. 26

17. 6

18. 800

19. 6

20. 2.75 cups

21. 324 miles

22. 511 miles

23. 72 defective bulbs

24. 2.6 runs

25. 10,680 people

Chapter 4: Pretest (MC)

1. b
2. b
3. a
4. d
5. b
6. c
7. c
8. a
9. b
10. d
11. c
12. a
13. a
14. b
15. a
16. c
17. b
18. b
19. c
20. d
21. d
22. b
23. a
24. a
25. c

Chapter 4: Test Form A

1. $\dfrac{9}{26}$

2. $\dfrac{98 \text{ miles}}{5 \text{ gallons}}$

3. 1.79 pounds / week

4. $75.28 / share

5. 52 grams of fat

6. 11 hitters

7. d

8. d

Chapter 4

9. 55
10. 1.3
11. 5.25 (or 5.3) tablespoons
12. 8.1 ounces
13. 52.8 words
14. 120 miles
15. $508.06
16. 98 polar bears
17. 99 teachers
18. 135 to 13
19. 355 customers
20. 120,575 votes

Chapter 4: Test Form B

1. $\dfrac{4}{5}$

2. $\dfrac{291 \text{ miles}}{10 \text{ gallons}}$

3. 114 words per minute

4. $16.63 per share

5. 28 cents per ounce

6. 67 baskets

7. False

8. True

9. $n = 3$

10. $n \approx 11.7$

11. $n = 50$ cups

12. $n \approx 7.8$ ounces

13. 600 miles

14. 230.4 miles

15. 100 defective

16. 440 trout

17. 17 days

18. 2 to 5

19. 100 students

20. 40.45 feet

Chapter 4: Test Form C

1. $\dfrac{2}{9}$

2. $\dfrac{121 \text{ words}}{2 \text{ minutes}}$

3. 35.5 miles per gallon

4. $122.75 per share

5. $1.40

6. 18 gallons

7. True

8. False

9. $n = 7$

10. $n = 10$

11. $n \approx 1.2$ min

12. $n \approx 5.0$ cakes

13. 1920 miles

14. 12 cm

15. 75 defective

16. 120 ft tall

17. 47 weeks

18. 14 ft by $21\frac{1}{2}$ ft

19. 8000 boxes

20. 950 students

Chapter 4: Test Form D

1. c
2. b
3. a
4. d
5. c
6. b
7. a
8. b
9. d
10. c
11. c
12. b

13. a
14. d
15. b
16. d
17. a
18. b
19. c
20. c

Chapter 4: Test Form E

1. a
2. d
3. b
4. c
5. b
6. c
7. c
8. c
9. a
10. b
11. d
12. a
13. c
14. b
15. a
16. c
17. d
18. b
19. b
20. c

Chapter 4: Test Form F

1. b
2. a
3. c

Chapter 4

4. b
5. c
6. d
7. b
8. a
9. c
10. d
11. a
12. d
13. b
14. c
15. c
16. a
17. a
18. b
19. c
20. d

Chapter 4: Cumulative Exam (FR)

1. 46 cents per oz
2. 19.2 miles per gallon
3. True
4. $n = 16.5$
5. $n = 32.5$
6. $n \approx 20.3$ lb
7. $n = 437.4$ gal
8. 777.78 miles
9. 1.14 sticks
10. 1.82 in
11. $\dfrac{27}{32}$
12. $9\dfrac{5}{8}$
13. $20\dfrac{9}{16}$
14. $810
15. 16.692

16. 5286
17. 185.37
18. 32 pieces
19. $265.95
20. 1.0609

Chapter 4:
Cumulative Exam (MC)

1. c
2. a
3. a
4. b
5. b
6. d
7. c
8. b
9. c
10. c
11. a
12. b
13. d
14. d
15. c
16. b
17. a
18. d
19. b
20. a

Chapter 5: Pretest (FR)

1. 23%
2. 39.1%
3. 659%
4. 157%
5. 0.3%
6. 0.9%
7. 19%
8. 31%
9. 24.9%
10. 29.1%
11. $7\frac{1}{2}\%$
12. $2\frac{3}{8}\%$
13. 70%
14. 7.5%
15. 310%
16. 118.75%
17. 57.14%
18. 14.29%
19. 91.30%
20. 89.47%
21. 840%
22. 225%
23. 0.17%
24. 0.75%
25. $\frac{8}{25}$
26. $\frac{59}{100}$
27. $1\frac{1}{5}$
28. $1\frac{4}{5}$
29. $\frac{11}{150}$
30. $\frac{17}{300}$
31. $\frac{49}{80}$
32. $\frac{167}{400}$
33. 72.8
34. 30.08
35. 89.47%
36. 73.81%
37. 3000
38. 682
39. 57.14%
40. $18.00
41. 37.5%
42. $7172
43. $504

Chapter 5: Pretest (MC)

1. b
2. a
3. d
4. a
5. b
6. c
7. c
8. b
9. c
10. a
11. d
12. d
13. c
14. a
15. a
16. d
17. b
18. a
19. a
20. d
21. d
22. c
23. c
24. a
25. b
26. b
27. a
28. d
29. d
30. b
31. c
32. a
33. b
34. a
35. c
36. b
37. d
38. a
39. d

Chapter 5: Test Form A

1. 5.29%
2. 261%
3. 79%
4. 0.81%
5. 33.75%
6. 662.5%
7. 326.14%
8. 73/800
9. 0.96
10. 300%
11. 140
12. 14.07
13. 24%
14. 80%
15. $42.46
16. 8%
17. 5%
18. $744
19. 86.62%
20. $74,115.50

Chapter 5: Test Form B

1. 1.3%
2. 59%
3. 629%
4. $7\frac{1}{2}\%$
5. 42.5%
6. 312.5%
7. 189.23%
8. $\frac{19}{300}$
9. 3.9
10. 37.5%
11. 6300
12. 4800
13. $510
14. 40%
15. 2625
16. $4896
17. 5 lb
18. 7742
19. 25.45%
20. 13%

Chapter 5: Test Form C

1. 86.1%
2. 1.69%
3. 1364%
4. 0.07%
5. 38.75%
6. 925%
7. 1.98%
8. $\frac{11}{160}$
9. 75
10. 37.5%
11. 420
12. 6.48
13. $78

14. 30%
15. $46,000
16. 76.39%
17. 227,476
18. $22.31
19. 63%
20. 5.5%

Chapter 5: Test Form D

1. b
2. a
3. c
4. d
5. c
6. a
7. b
8. d
9. a
10. b
11. c
12. c
13. b
14. a
15. d
16. a
17. b
18. c
19. c
20. a

Chapter 5: Test Form E

1. d
2. c
3. a
4. b
5. b
6. c
7. d
8. a

9. c
10. d
11. a
12. b
13. a
14. a
15. b
16. c
17. b
18. d
19. a
20. c

Chapter 5: Test Form F

1. c
2. b
3. d
4. a
5. d
6. b
7. a
8. c
9. d
10. c
11. b
12. a
13. c
14. d
15. d
16. c
17. c
18. a
19. d
20. b

Chapter 6: Pretest (FR)

1. 204
2. 72
3. 7040
4. 3200
5. 2880
6. 52
7. 7360
8. 6810
9. 82.3
10. 0.023
11. 695.1
12. 0.597
13. 2797 m
14. 86.444m
15. 6290
16. 1.939
17. 0.0418
18. 5700
19. 0.832
20. 12,500
21. 6.30
22. 2.07
23. 50.84
24. 1076.36
25. 96.39
26. 136.4
27. $58\frac{4}{5}$ feet
28. (a) 86° (b) No
29. 24.6 miles
30. 67.5 gal / hr

Chapter 6: Pretest (MC)

1. b
2. c
3. b
4. d
5. c
6. a
7. b
8. a
9. a
10. d
11. c
12. a
13. b
14. d
15. d
16. c
17. a
18. a
19. b
20. c
21. c
22. a
23. d
24. c
25. b
26. b
27. d
28. d
29. c
30. a

Chapter 6: Test Form A

1. 24,288
2. 2
3. 168
4. 0.2923
5. 613
6. 213,000
7. 51,200
8. 0.000123
9. 53.17
10. 9.41
11. 21.82 miles
12. 70.95 liters
13. 112.5 gal / hr
14. 90 yd
15. 34.44°C
16. 25,420
17. 14.12 lb
18. 49.25 inches
19. 8lb, 4 oz
20. −56.2°F

Chapter 6: Test Form B

1. 13
2. 9504
3. 12.5
4. 170,000
5. 0.0359
6. 0.0124
7. 0.006951
8. 45,200
9. 0.000319
10. 7.39
11. 12.67 gal
12. 86.8 miles
13. 303.3 cm
14. 1.33 qt / min
15. 71.6°F
16. 5 rolls
17. 71.73 kg
18. 31.94 yards
19. 8 lb, 11 oz
20. −90.4°F

Chapter 6: Test Form C

1. 2.25
2. 5760
3. 6336
4. 0.00913
5. 652,000
6. 12.324
7. 0.712
8. 68,900
9. 2.945
10. 38.64
11. 23.32 quarts
12. 1384.6 km
13. 67.5 gal / hr
14. 5°C
15. 54 yards
16. 27.78°C
17. 6 rolls
18. 8 1b, 2 oz
19. 55 mph
21. 2.7 inches

Chapter 6: Test Form D

1. a
2. c
3. d
4. d
5. b
6. a
7. c
8. a
9. d
10. b
11. d
12. b
13. c
14. c
15. b

16. d
17. a
18. b
19. c
20. a

Chapter 6: Test Form E

1. b
2. d
3. a
4. a
5. c
6. b
7. b
8. d
9. a
10. c
11. b
12. c
13. d
14. a
15. a
16. d
17. b
18. b
19. c
20. a

Chapter 6: Test Form F

1. d
2. a
3. b
4. c
5. d
6. c
7. a
8. c

Chapter 6

9. b
10. d
11. c
12. b
13. a
14. b
15. c
16. c
17. a
18. d
19. b
20. d

Chapter 6: Cumulative Exam (FR)

1. 13.2 ft / sec
2. 68°C
3. 1.9 m
4. 19.25 lb
5. 9.5 gallons
6. 126.08 in
7. 6100 cm
8. $21\frac{5}{8}$
9. $1\frac{5}{6}$
10. 37
11. $38.54
12. 14.83
13. 773.5 miles
14. 112
15. 39 mpg
16. $101.40
17. 12.5%
18. 4.13
19. $\frac{13}{20}$
21. $212.50

Chapter 6:
Cumulative Exam (MC)

1. b
2. c
3. a
4. d
5. a
6. b
7. a
8. d
9. d
10. c
11. a
12. a
13. c
14. c
15. b
16. b
17. d
18. a
19. d
20. d

Chapter 7 Pretest (FR)

1. 12°
2. 57°
3. $\angle b = 132°$
   $\angle a = \angle c = 48°$
4. 19.4 m
5. 16.8 m
6. 32.4 cm²
7. 1.8 cm²
8. 25.6 yd
9. 79 ft
10. 420 in²
11. 315 in²
12. 111 m²
13. 23°
14. 21.1 m
15. 99 m²
16. 7
17. 12
18. 6.403
19. 4 ft
20. 12 ft
21. 32 inches
22. 125.6 cm
23. 201.0 m²
24. 32.4 m²
25. 616 yd³
26. 904.3 ft³
27. 3560.8 in³
28. 3174 m³
29. 1017.4 m³
30. 128 cm
31. 20 m
32. (a) 3406.5 yd²
    (b) $749.43

Chapter 7 Pretest (MC)

1. b
2. c
3. d
4. a
5. c
6. b
7. d
8. a
9. b
10. c
11. d
12. b
13. b
14. a
15. d
16. d
17. a
18. c
19. c
20. b
21. a
22. a
23. d
24. c
25. c
26. a
27. d
28. a
29. b
30. b
31. d

Chapter 7 Test Form A

1. 71.9 m
2. 53 inches
3. 29.1 cm
4. 53.3 m²
5. 99 in²
6. 196 cm²
7. 27.6 inches
8. 32.0 cm²
9. 137.1 in²
10. 301.4 m³
11. 1368 mm³
12. 2143.6 yd³
13. 82°
14. 1785 ft²
15. 7.5 cm
16. 282.6 in³
17. $128.25
18. 10.770
19. 26 ft
20. 10,205 ft³

Chapter 7 Test Form B

1. 45 cm
2. $15\frac{1}{2}$ inches
3. 45.5 m
4. $133 \, cm^2$
5. $60 \, m^2$
6. $140 \, cm^2$
7. 54.6 inches
8. $122.5 \, cm^2$
9. $188 \, cm^2$
10. $256 \, m^3$
11. $1526.0 \, m^3$
12. $251.2 \, in^3$
13. $37°$
14. $30.36 \, cm^2$
15. 6.3 m
16. $250 \, yd^3$
17. $552.50
18. 17.804
19. 75 m
20. $2616.67 \, ft^3$

Chapter 7 Test Form C

1. $18\frac{1}{2}$ inches
2. 21.9 cm
3. $42\frac{1}{2}$ inches
4. $12.75 \, m^2$
5. $252 \, cm^2$
6. $165 \, m^2$
7. 45.8 inches
8. $19.7 \, m^2$
9. $47 \, cm^2$

10. $137.2 \, m^3$
11. $628 \, m^3$
12. $63.7 \, ft^3$
13. $81°$
14. $42.09 \, in^2$
15. 9.35 cm
16. $3406.5 \, yd^2$
17. $1140
18. 12.923
19. 50 cm
20. $51,666.67 \, ft^3$

Chapter 7 Test Form D

1. d
2. b
3. a
4. a
5. b
6. c
7. b
8. d
9. a
10. a
11. c
12. b
13. c
14. b
15. d
16. a
17. b
18. c
19. d
20. d

Chapter 7 Test Form E

1. b
2. a
3. d

4. c
5. a
6. b
7. d
8. a
9. c
10. b
11. b
12. d
13. a
14. d
15. a
16. c
17. a
18. b
19. b
20. c

Chapter 7 Test Form F

1. a
2. d
3. c
4. b
5. c
6. d
7. a
8. b
9. b
10. c
11. d
12. a
13. c
14. b
15. c
16. b
17. d
18. a
19. d
20. c

Chapter 8 Pretest (FR)

1. Age 18-20
2. 77%
3. 50%
4. 600
5. 1020
6. 600
7. 250
8. 3rd quarter and 4th quarter
9. 2nd quarter, 2003
10. 300
11. 200
12. September
13. July and August
14. November and December
15. 40,000
16. 25,000
17. 35,000
18. 20,000
19. 85,000
20. 115,000
21. 35
22. 34
23. 27

Chapter 8 Pretest (MC)

1. b
2. b
3. c
4. a
5. a
6. a
7. b
8. c
9. a
10. c
11. c
12. a
13. d
14. c
15. b
16. d
17. a
18. d
19. a
20. b
21. c
22. a
23. d

Chapter 8 Test Form A

1. 78
2. 1500
3. 225
4. 25
5. 7
6. 4
7. 3
8. 26
9. 70
10. 55
11. 25
12. 105
13. 64.5%
14. 38.5%
15. 2500
16. 39.5%
17. 17.5
18. 17
19. $238,200
20. $205,000

Chapter 8 Test Form B

1. 400
2. 63%
3. 150
4. 650

Chapter 8

5. Lack of discipline
6. 1986 and 1987
7. Lack of financial support
8. 20%
9. 85 days
10. 75 days
11. 35 days
12. 60 days
13. 80.5%
14. 8.5%
15. 91.5%
16. 400
17. 101.6°
18. 101.1°
19. $555,000
20. $419,000

Chapter 8 Test Form C

1. 54%
2. 3920
3. 250
4. 600
5. Lack of financial support
6. 30%
7. Use of drugs
8. 15%
9. $41° - 50°$
10. 60 days
11. 35 days
12. 50 days
13. 96%
14. 31.5%
15. 25.5%
16. 82.5%
17. 20.5
18. 20.5
19. $639,000
20. $469,000

Chapter 8 Test Form D

1. b
2. d
3. c
4. a
5. c
6. d
7. c
8. a
9. a
10. b
11. b
12. a
13. b
14. c
15. d
16. a
17. c
18. a
19. a
20. b

Chapter 8 Test Form E

1. c
2. a
3. b
4. d
5. b
6. c
7. d
8. b
9. d
10. a
11. b
12. c
13. b
14. a
15. d
16. c

17. a
18. b
19. b
20. a

Chapter 8 Test Form F

1. a
2. c
3. d
4. b
5. a
6. b
7. d
8. a
9. c
10. d
11. a
12. b
13. b
14. d
15. a
16. b
17. d
18. c
19. b
20. c

Chapter 8 Cumulative Exam (FR)

1. 25 miles per gallon
2. 27 hours
3. $\dfrac{14}{33}$
4. $\dfrac{8}{15}$
5. 192
6. 12,704.2
7. 113.4
8. 0.4683

9. 71.3 miles
10. 38,900 cm
11. 14 ft^2
12. 167.47 cm^3
13. 6%
14. 50,000
15. 28%
16. December 2001
17. 450
18. 600
19. 10.1°F
20. 10°F

Chapter 8 Cumulative Exam (MC)

1. b
2. c
3. b
4. d
5. a
6. d
7. a
8. b
9. b
10. d
11. c
12. d
13. a
14. b
15. c
16. a
17. d
18. c
19. a
20. a

Chapter 9 Pretest (FR)

1. −22
2. −13
3. 3.3
4. 0
5. $\dfrac{1}{3}$
6. $-\dfrac{5}{9}$
7. −11.6
8. −2.5
9. −12
10. −41
11. $\dfrac{8}{13}$
12. −24
13. 2.5
14. −3.4
15. 38
16. $\dfrac{13}{20}$
17. 24
18. $2\frac{2}{3}$
19. −9
20. −6
21. −14
22. $\dfrac{24}{49}$
23. −54
24. −10
25. −15
26. 21
27. −14
28. 2.8
29. 5
30. −33

31. $-\dfrac{3}{8}$
32. $\dfrac{3}{13}$
33. 7×10^{4}
34. 6×10^{-4}
35. 3.59×10^{8}
36. 0.000078
37. 652,000
38. 0.000000015189

Chapter 9 Pretest (MC)

1. c
2. b
3. b
4. a
5. d
6. b
7. c
8. c
9. a
10. b
11. d
12. d
13. a
14. b
15. d
16. a
17. c
18. c
19. b
20. a
21. d
22. b
23. a
24. a
25. b
26. c

27. d
28. a
29. d
30. b
31. b
32. d
33. c
34. b
35. a
36. d
37. c
38. b

Chapter 9 Test Form A

1. −21
2. −19.3
3. $-\dfrac{22}{63}$
4. 5
5. −17
6. $\dfrac{49}{117}$
7. −16.98
8. −48
9. $-\dfrac{9}{8}$
10. −112
11. 36
12. −9
13. 16
14. 2
15. $-\dfrac{13}{4}$
16. Gained 10 yards
17. 7.96×10^{7}
18. 3.41×10^{-5}
19. 8,100,000
20. 0.05588

Chapter 9 Test Form B

1. −4
2. −23.65
3. $-\dfrac{1}{56}$
4. 8
5. −17
6. $3\frac{2}{3}$
7. −12.61
8. 56
9. $-\dfrac{8}{81}$
10. −128
11. 10
12. −2
13. −14
14. −1
15. $\dfrac{5}{4}$
16. Lost $7\frac{3}{4}$ pounds
17. 2.85×10^3
18. 6.95×10^{-2}
19. 108,000
20. 0.000709

Chapter 9 Test Form C

1. −31
2. 6.36
3. $-\dfrac{7}{15}$
4. 6
5. −30
6. $\dfrac{43}{42}$
7. −41.55
8. 90
9. $\dfrac{5}{6}$

10. −24
11. −8
12. −18
13. 36
14. $-\dfrac{2}{3}$
15. −30
16. Gained 9 yards
17. 3.829×10^{-3}
18. 5.8×10^{10}
19. 0.000076
20. 53,330,000

Chapter 9 Test Form D

1. b
2. a
3. d
4. c
5. d
6. a
7. b
8. a
9. c
10. d
11. c
12. b
13. a
14. b
15. a
16. b
17. d
18. b
19. b
20. c

Chapter 9 Test Form E

1. c
2. b
3. a

4. d
5. a
6. b
7. c
8. c
9. d
10. a
11. b
12. c
13. d
14. a
15. d
16. a
17. c
18. d
19. b
20. b

Chapter 9 Test Form F

1. a
2. c
3. b
4. b
5. c
6. d
7. a
8. b
9. a
10. c
11. d
12. a
13. c
14. d
15. b
16. b
17. c
18. b
19. c
20. a

Basic College Mathematics: Answers to Chapter Tests

Chapter 10

Chapter 10 Pretest (FR)

1. $-24x$
2. $3y$
3. $-6a+7b$
4. $-12x-5y+14$
5. $20x-5y-6$
6. $3a-14b+2c$
7. $20x-8y$
8. $-5a-45b+30$
9. $-7.5a-9b+27c+6$
10. $10x-10y$
11. 35
12. 2.5
13. $1\frac{1}{8}$
14. -9
15. 5
16. $1\frac{3}{4}$
17. 5
18. 4
19. 2
20. 5
21. $t=2.5+c$
22. $1=2w+3$
23. $a-1239$
24. width = 24 meters
    length = 39 meters
25. shorter piece = 9.75 ft
    longer piece = 13.25 ft

Chapter 10 Pretest (MC)

1. d
2. c
3. a
4. a
5. b
6. d

7. c
8. b
9. c
10. d
11. a
12. a
13. b
14. d
15. d
16. a
17. b
18. b
19. c
20. a
21. c
22. b
23. a
24. b
25. d

Chapter 10 Test Form A

1. $5x$
2. $2x-12y+7z$
3. $3x-6y+15z$
4. $0.8x-1.2y+1.92z$
5. $33x-8y+5z+6$
6. 8
7. -9
8. $\frac{1}{3}$
9. $-\frac{5}{2}$
10. $F=2T-3$
11. Height $=b+7$
12. Frank $=\frac{1}{2}T-2$
13. $x+0.12x=27,140$
14. $x+2x+x-40=180$

15. $2L+2\left(\frac{1}{3}L\right)=140$
16. -14
17. $-\frac{3}{5}$
18. $56
19. 60 feet
20. 32

Chapter 10 Test Form B

1. a
2. $10c-13d+5$
3. $-6a+24d+18c$
4. $0.6x+4.8y-7.2$
5. $6x-6y-8z$
6. 7
7. -13
8. -14
9. 13
10. $M=\frac{1}{2}J+2$
11. $x=$ 1st angle
       $3x=$ 2nd angle
    $x+23=$ 3rd angle
12. $x=$ length
    $\frac{1}{2}x-5=$ width
13. Smyth = 100 acres
    McBride = 450 acres
14. Length = 13, width = 11
15. $32,500
16. 2
17. 5
18. $90
19. $29.60
20. Dom is 32, Steve is 34, Jack is 35

Chapter 10 Test Form C

1. $-y+15$

T-208

2. $5x - 9y - 3$

3. $7a + 14b - 21c$

4. $3.2x - 8y - 12.8z$

5. $-33x + 11y - 28z$

6. 18

7. 3

8. $\dfrac{10}{11}$

9. 0

10. $J = 2N - 3$

11. $x =$ Length of 2nd side
   $\dfrac{1}{2}x =$ Length of 1st side
   $3x + 5 =$ Length of 3rd side

12. $v =$ Tomlinson cost
   $v + 780 =$ Butler cost
   $v - 142 =$ Perry cost

13.   1st angle $= 25°$
   2nd angle $= 50°$
   3rd angle $= 105°$

14. 58.75 ft, 71.25 ft

15. $w = 28\dfrac{1}{3}$ m; $1 = 61\dfrac{2}{3}$ m

16. 19

17. $\dfrac{7}{2}$

18. $14,000

19. 7 days

20. $300

Chapter 10 Test Form D

1. a
2. d
3. c
4. d
5. b
6. c

---

7. b
8. a
9. d
10. a
11. b
12. a
13. b
14. c
15. d
16. a
17. b
18. d
19. b
20. d

Chapter 10 Test Form E

1. d
2. c
3. a
4. b
5. c
6. a
7. d
8. c
9. a
10. c
11. a
12. b
13. a
14. d
15. c
16. b
17. d
18. b
19. a
20. d

Chapter 10 Test Form F

1. b

---

2. a
3. d
4. c
5. d
6. b
7. c
8. b
9. c
10. a
11. c
12. d
13. c
14. b
15. a
16. d
17. a
18. b
19. d
20. c

Chapter 10
Cumulative Exam (FR)

1. $15\dfrac{5}{6}$

2. 68.9012

3. $9\dfrac{1}{3}$

4. $1600

5. 70

6. 11.804 kg

7. 1.93

8. 104 in^2

9. 26 cm

10. 74.57

11. 2

12. 4

13. $\dfrac{7}{4}$

14. 4

15. 2

16. $-14x + 13y$

17. $C = 28$; $N = 27$;
    $S = 24$; $D = 23$;
    and Mike = 18

18. 17 ft and 68 ft

19. 7 cm = width;
    15 cm = length

20. $18,000

Chapter 10
Cumulative Exam (MC)

1. a

2. a

3. d

4. c

5. b

6. c

7. a

8. a

9. b

10. d

11. b

12. c

13. c

14. a

15. d

16. a

17. d

18. d

19. b

20. a

Final Examination (FR)

1. 5657

2. 36

3. $7\frac{1}{3}$

4. $\frac{23}{48}$

5. 0.847

6. $\frac{7}{55}$

7. $5\frac{1}{2}$

8. 33.33%

9. 4%

10. 18

11. $23.40

12. 0.375

13. 140%

14. $\frac{17}{20}$

15. $\frac{13}{25}$

16. 85%

17. $3\frac{1}{2}$ hr

18. $n = 100.8$

19. 6.29 m

20. 9.48 mi

21. 6 qt per min

22. 8.702×10^9

23. 1177.5 m^3

24. 65

25. 25,400,000

26. 139.48 inches

27. 6.16 lb

28. 217 mi

29. 28.6 ft

30. 21.5 in^2

31. 276

32. $127.50

33. 18.6 mi

34. 5

35. 170.5 miles per day

36. 21

37. 120 mi

38. 69.08 cm

39. 25 cm

40. 17

41. 50 cm^2

42. $189,000

43. 30

44. −8

45. $-\frac{17}{2}$

46. $5\frac{1}{5}$

47. $-25c + 83d$

48. $x = \frac{1}{7}$

49. Width = 10 cm
    length = 15 cm

50. 725

Final Examination (MC)

1. a

2. c

3. b

4. d

5. a

6. a

7. c

8. b

9. c

10. a

11. d

12. d

13. c

14. a

15. b

16. d

17. a

18. a

19. d

20. c

21. b

22. b

23. c

24. a

25. d

26. c

27. c

28. a

29. d

30. b

31. b

32. d

33. a

34. b

35. d

36. d

37. c

38. c

39. a

40. a

41. b

42. c

43. b

44. b

45. c

46. d

47. a

48. d

49. b

50. a